RUSSIANS

Also by Gregory Feifer

The Great Gamble
Spy Handler (with Victor Cherkashin)

RUSSIANS

The People behind the Power

by GREGORY FEIFER

TWELVE

NEW YORK BOSTON

Twelve

Hachette Book Group

237 Park Avenue

New York, NY 10017

www.HachetteBookGroup.com

Printed in the United States of America

RRD-C

First Edition: February 2014

10 9 8 7 6 5 4 3 2 1

Twelve is an imprint of Grand Central Publishing.
The Twelve name and logo are trademarks of Hachette Book Group, Inc.

The Hachette Speakers Bureau provides a wide range of authors for speaking events. To find out more, go to www.hachettespeakersbureau.com or call (866) 376-6591.

The publisher is not responsible for websites (or their content) that are not owned by the publisher.

Library of Congress Cataloging-in-Publication Data

Feifer, Gregory, author.
  Russians : the people behind the power / by Gregory Feifer.
    pages ; cm
  Includes bibliographical references and index.
  ISBN 978-1-4555-0964-5 (hardcover) — ISBN 978-1-4555-0965-2 (ebook) — 978-1-4555-7345-5 (international edition) 1. Russia (Federation)— Social life and customs. 2. Social values—Russia (Federation) 3. National characteristics, Russian. 4. Political culture—Russia (Federation) I. Title.
  DK510.762.F45 2013
  947.086—dc23

2013021656

For Mama

CONTENTS

RUSSIANS

Outside the Kremlin, August 19, 1991. (*Igor Tabakov*)

When I returned to Moscow the following year—here at the Kievskaya train station—during the first heady days of post-communism, the government was staving off economic collapse. (*Adam Goodheart*)

1

The Hidden Russia

One of the characteristic operative features of [Muscovite political culture] is, whether one is dealing with the sixteenth century or with the twentieth, the rule *"Iz izby soru ne vynesi"* (literally, "Do not carry rubbish out of the hut") remains in operation: i.e., one does not reveal to non-participants authentic information concerning politics, political groupings, or points of discord.

—Edward Keenan, "Muscovite Political Folkways"[1]

Nothing suggested the day would be different from other Mondays in Vilnius, the capital of what was then the Soviet republic of Lithuania. That meant no breakfast for more than two hours after our train arrived because no cafés we found while wandering the baroque city's entrancing but empty streets would open until 9:00 a.m. If, however, what gave their staffs the right to show up for work when office employees did was supposedly egalitarian communism, Lithuanians had so little liking for it that they were busy fomenting opposition to Soviet rule, having declared independence from Moscow the previous year.

Soviet troops had killed more than a dozen people in January when they suppressed a protest supporting Lithuania's nationalist government. But there had been no violence since then, and on the tranquil morning of August 19, 1991, it would have been hard to imagine that the Soviet republic would soon be not only independent but also a member of the European Union. Three days later, however, that would be very imaginable.

I was nineteen that summer of my first—and, it would turn out, last—visit to the dying USSR. After capping my freshman year in college with three months in Moscow, I was on a weeklong lark through the Baltic republics with a young, irrepressibly good-natured correspondent for the Soviet Union's most daring new television station. Hunting for *something* to eat, Kolya and I encountered only a lone driver cursing his broken-down truck and several dog walkers amid architecture that would have looked more at home on the Mediterranean than anywhere near the usual sprawl of prefabricated Soviet housing. We trudged along cobblestoned streets lined by decaying buildings with pretty courtyards that appeared to have remained unchanged for a century until we found another café. Luckily Kolya, short for Nikolai, was a skilled charmer as well as an up-and-coming reporter and close friend. Banging on the glass door, he convinced the stern waitress within to supply us with coffee and rolls, testimony to another fact of Soviet life: sufficient inventiveness or persistence often got what you wanted. Kolya even induced the pretty young woman to smile and disclose her phone number before she asked whether we'd heard the news that day.

"We're just off the train," Kolya replied. "We're lucky enough to have seen you on this lovely morning."

"Well, you might want to know there's been a coup in Moscow," she said deadpan.

Since Kolya's own little coup of securing our breakfast had involved overcoming the typical Lithuanian reluctance to speak Russian, the language of the oppressors, we guessed she was trying to joke with us. Still, we returned to the train station to inquire about tickets back to Moscow just in case they might be needed.

There were no tickets to Moscow. Or to Leningrad, as St. Petersburg was then called. No tickets to anywhere in the vast Soviet Union, not even for a hefty bribe, which usually produced seats when none were supposedly available. Struggling to contain a touch of panic, we rushed to the platforms. Since my Soviet visa wasn't valid for Vilnius, my presence there was illegal. But wanting to stay out of trouble and to rescue the suitcases I'd left in Moscow were secondary to not wanting to miss anything historic that might be taking place there. A real crisis still seemed unlikely, especially because we saw nothing out of the ordinary—at least no crowds storming trains. Taking no chances, however, we found a young conductor on a train heading to Leningrad—the closest we could get to Moscow—and bribed our way into a sleeping compartment.

Far from being sold out, the train was virtually empty. When it jolted out of the station, the only others in our car were the conductor and a friend of his, who were sharing a bottle of vodka: more testimony to the lack of Soviet interest in supply and demand, we hoped, than an indication that a coup had truly taken place. As the train rattled northeastward, we still didn't know whether the waitress had been joking or that we'd lucked onto one of the last trains out of Vilnius before rail traffic was halted.

Several hours later, the loudspeaker in our compartment crackled to life. During a news conference taking place in Moscow, which was barely audible, a group of old-guard Politburo bosses announced that they'd formed an emergency committee to take temporary control of the Soviet Union because General Secretary Mikhail Gorbachev was ill.

Kolya's dark complexion turned pale. "Then it *is* true," he whispered. "And it's the end!"

That wasn't overdramatization on his part. Kolya had started at Channel 2 earlier that year while he was still a third-year college student, after the station's launch by Boris Yeltsin, then the increasingly powerful president of the Soviet Union's Russian Republic, by far the largest of the fifteen Soviet republics. The station, one of Yeltsin's efforts to burnish his credentials as a reformer, attracted some of the brightest stars of television journalism, who were given the freedom to broadcast their own scripts from a cramped studio inside Moscow's sprawling television complex. Kolya's work for the country's most aggressive news channel—not to mention a temporary job at CNN's Moscow bureau, where we'd met earlier in the summer—would surely put him in serious trouble during the recriminations that would no doubt follow.

Fishing out a bottle from his backpack, he poured a large shot of vodka into a stained tea glass. Down the corridor, the conductor was hosting a loud, drunken card game. His acrid tobacco smoke billowed into the corridor as the train rattled past green fields and forests under looming gray clouds.

"They won't send you to Siberia," I said, unable to think of anything more reassuring.

"Oh yes they will. Our whole station will go. We'll be first."

"You'll think of a way out. Pour another shot."

He poured. The train trundled on. I thought I already knew enough about Russia to appreciate how resigned and brave Kolya was.

———

Getting to the moon would have been easier than finding a hotel room in Leningrad. We spent the night in the very cramped apartment of a friend of a friend of mine on the outskirts of town, where flipping between television channels produced only *Swan Lake* on his small screen: a sure sign of trouble. The following morning, our host—an enterprising young waiter obsessed by his large collection of previously banned Western rock albums—got us overnight train tickets to Moscow by calling in a favor. A favorite oxford shirt of mine was added to the cost.

Before leaving, we joined a mass of protesters who had taken over Nevsky Prospekt, the city's main thoroughfare. The sun shone brightly. Until very recently, the red, white and blue flags of imperial Russia that some were waving would have been a display of shocking insubordination to the communist regime. We now knew that Gorbachev, who had initiated the policies of *perestroika* (attempted economic restructuring) and *glasnost* (considerable loosening of controls on free speech), had been put under house arrest while he was vacationing in Crimea. It was up to the people to take a stand against the coup, and they were doing it. After seventy years of communist repression, the unbelievable appeared to be unfolding before our eyes.

We went to sleep on the train that evening, uncertain whether we'd make it to Moscow because a curfew had been imposed. Dark clouds hanging over the capital in the morning made the weather cold as well as rainy, and the news that Soviet armored personnel carriers had killed three young protesters near the US embassy during the night further darkened the mood.

Kolya went to the television studios to find out what was happening, and I made my way to the so-called White House, an architectural eyesore built in the 1980s on the Moscow River to house the Russian Republic's parliament, now the center of protest against the coup plotters who were holed up in the Kremlin, not far away. Yeltsin was inside with a group of other self-styled "democrats." As thousands milled around outside, the streets were littered with gutted buses, iron rods and a seemingly random collection of objects that had been hauled there to construct "barricades" of symbolic importance that wouldn't have done more to stop an attack than the protesters' umbrellas. However, a division of unarmed tanks that had been persuaded to back Yeltsin had maneuvered to stand with their turrets pointing away from the building, demonstrating solidarity. Many were adorned with flowers.

That more people who were presumably hunkering down in their apartments didn't join the relatively thin crowds in a city of some ten million heightened a general feeling of foreboding that the coup might succeed. The protesters formed a human chain around the White House, where dozens of so-called *meetingi* sprang up: circles of citizens who argued about the merits of the protest and its chance of success. Others huddled around the few people who had radios, grasping at any scrap of news about what was happening in the White House and the Kremlin. More crowds gathered in front of soldiers who had blocked off access to the Kremlin and Red Square. Agitated protesters tried to persuade the soldiers to join them. "Listen to the people!" one middle-aged woman screamed, but it was impossible to determine the effect.

By late afternoon, I was back near the White House when a man announced that the standoff had ended. The radio he was carrying had broadcast a report that the coup plotters had dispersed, some to make a desperate effort to meet with Gorbachev in Crimea. A plane carrying Yeltsin allies was in hot pursuit.

As if on cue, the summer clouds dispersed and a bright sun shone on what felt like a liberated city. Could it really be over? Certainly the atmosphere quickly changed. Happy clusters of Muscovites stood around laughing and exchanging war stories about the tense hours that had just ended as if they were long past. As the sun set, municipal workers set up a stage in front of the White House. Rock bands materialized, their music adding to the celebration of deliverance by the exhilarated crowds that walked about, discharging nervous energy. Despite the great flow of beer and vodka, however, it was supremely difficult to believe the plotters had been faced down, their last attempt to save communism foiled. Soviets had waited for this day for decades. An impossible dream had come true: Russia was free!

Soon, it seemed, the USSR would be a part of the international community, enjoying the West's previously unimaginable freedom and prosperity. That was the common expectation. The reality was a precipitous economic collapse that had actually begun well before Yeltsin signed an accord in December of 1991 formally disbanding the Soviet Union. In the decade that followed, hyperinflation wiped out Russians' savings while crooked privatization deals enabled a handful of Kremlin-connected insiders to snatch many of the state's richest assets. The helplessness of the former superpower the world had respected and feared made many people feel deeply humiliated. Large numbers began resenting the West for not doing more to help—and, many thought, for gloating.

Eight years and many visits after the 1991 attempted coup, I returned to Moscow to live. My arrival coincided with another watershed: an explosion of protest against NATO's bombing of Serbia. Powerless to stop it, Russians released a decade of bottled-up anger, most visibly in the form of eggs, paint and other projectiles hurled by rowdy crowds at the American embassy's thick yellow walls. Passing by during the height of the demonstrations, a gleeful taxi driver pointed at the ooze-covered building. "The Americans think they can do anything they want," he said. "But we won't let them!" Widespread public opinion was even more hostile.

A well-dressed young man who overheard me talking to a visiting British friend on a crowded street warned us to stop speaking in English "or I'll kill you." Politicians took their cue from the people, fashioning foreign conflict into a test of loyalty to the Motherland for the first time since the Soviet collapse, helping plunge debate about the issue to the level of chest beating. Strident cries in support of "our Slav brother" Serbs widened the sense of antagonism between Russia and the West. For us mistreated Russians, the operative word was *nashi,* "ours."

The outcry was prompted partly by Yeltsin's political paralysis during an economic meltdown in 1998, when the government defaulted on its debts and inflation soared. A collective war whoop sounded throughout the country with its collapsed economy and scandal-ridden political system. Marat Guelman, a gallery owner and stalwart of the Moscow art world, leaped on the irony. "When globalization's the thing and the whole world's trying to become integrated," he said at the time, "the Russian idea is to exist alone, apart from the rest."

Although anti-Americanism hasn't since returned to that high point despite regular denunciations under a new leader who has compared the United States to Nazi Germany, it remains strong among many Russians.

Vladimir Putin shot out of obscurity in 1999 by exploiting growing nostalgia for the USSR, fueled by the disappointment, uncertainty and crisis that brought Yeltsin's reform era to a shuddering halt.

Once in power the following year, Putin set about building an authoritarian regime whose control would expand for more than a decade, until soaring corruption on top of another economic downturn—a much smaller one, triggered by the global financial crisis of 2008—prompted another backlash. A new middle-class urban population nurtured during a decade-long oil boom launched the first serious protest against Putin's rule in December of 2011, when tens of thousands of newly disillusioned Russians demonstrated against rigged parliamentary elections. Although Putin was easily reelected to a new six-year term the following year, whereupon he renewed his assault on democratic practices, the unhappiness over his return to office for a tenure that could last another dozen years, until 2024, raised new questions about the country's future.

Will Russia forever be separated from the West? Why do so many of its people continue admiring their authoritarian leaders? Have they learned nothing from their painful past? Western observers tend to look for signs of inevitable progress toward liberal democracy in Russians' growing Internet use, together with their huge appetite for imported consumer goods and in the opinions of a small group of opposition leaders who, not surprisingly, predict Putin's imminent demise. I think they tend to ignore the country's historical record, its culture and the opinions of the vast majority of a people whose behavior and values have been patterned differently from ours. My explanation of the gap between those analyses and the country I've spent so much time in lies largely in a hidden Russia, a way of thinking and acting that is elusive to foreigners because it's intentionally kept obscure.

I believe official institutions, the kind the West depends on for governing, have functioned so inefficiently in Russia because their real role is largely to hide the workings of a collection of crony arrangements informed by a traditional political culture that has shaped the country's history for centuries. Putin resurrected it after a decade of Westernizing reform under Yeltsin. The current president's "clients" in Russian officialdom—the bureaucrats and businessmen loyal to him—make up the actual governing structure, even though their official titles don't necessarily indicate that. The difficulty in seeing things as they are lies in the beneficiaries' suppression of the transparency and legality they perceive as threatening them, misleading observers about the true nature of the country's governance.

Is Russia fated to develop along its own path? Do its people possess a special Russian soul or intrinsic qualities that keep them from embracing Western values? I think the going political scheme has survived not for those reasons but for very practical ones: it has enabled society to remain more or less stable despite the sweeping upheavals that have transformed life since the Soviet collapse. Whether that will remain true as the public confronts new change can't be predicted, especially because the coercive nature of Putin's administration makes it inherently unstable. But the discomfiting fact is that a vast number of Russians are active participants in a system whose main work is to protect itself, partly through a state bureaucracy that has doubled in size in recent years.

"To get anything done—register a new company for example—you have to pay bribes, so people don't draw up official documents," Roman Shleinov, an editor of the crusading newspaper *Novaya Gazeta* and an astute observer of Russian corruption, told me. "Instead, they've become used to making agreements face-to-face." The result is a country of informal ties, "from the gypsy cabs on every street to the biggest companies, which need the Kremlin's secret approval for their deals."

The pages that follow cite examples of such dealings in schools, shops, offices, factories and the corridors of power. My chief purpose in offering them is to describe the behavior and attitudes that sustain the system as well as its sources, including the country's difficult climate and geography and a correspondingly difficult history, often dressed up in comforting historical myths. I'll also explore some of the paradoxes central to the Russian psyche, including the generally weak work ethic in a country that has produced some of the world's greatest artistic and scientific advances and the importance of family ties and friendship in a place where hardship, often worsened by cruelty, is legendary.

I aim to identify and describe what foreigners rarely see about the Russian people's motives and goals by explaining the informal system's role in many aspects of life. Heeding the Russian admonition to *smotri v koren'*, "look at the roots," I'll explore its influence before, during and after communism partly by tapping another rich, perceptive source of wisdom about the fundamental Russian character: the descriptions and reflections of Dostoevsky, Chekhov, Gogol and other writers and intellectuals. Starting with descriptions of the visible aspects of social attitudes and behavior, I'll go on to explore how they inform—and are shaped by—the concealed political culture. While my overarching purpose is to make Putin's actions understandable—and help readers measure just how far Moscow may be willing to go in its geostrategic challenge to the West—*Russians* will also attempt a definitive explanation of what makes Russia Russian—not merely today or yesterday in the Soviet period and before—but for as long as national characters retain their identity.

During my eight years in Russia as a journalist, I interviewed hundreds of people, from kindergarten children to *babushki*—the archetypal grandmothers—to powerful political and cultural figures, factory directors, workers and farmers. I've traveled from Russia's western borders across the country's nine time zones to its remote far east and from the subtropical Black Sea to the permanently frozen far north. However, much of my knowledge comes not from interviews, during which Russians are rarely at their most candid, but from participating in daily life and from long, leisurely conversations that offered insight into popular attitudes toward sex, vodka, religion and the West.

———

My first interest in Russia was entirely personal. My glamorous, very self-confident Russian mother represented another world from London and Connecticut, where I grew up. I gathered from her that Russia was a different kind of place where conduct often seemed more shaped by instinct and emotion than convention of any kind. Her behavior seemed to say that Russians value love and camaraderie above professional success and social standing. How to square that perception of them with the national ethos mystified me because I pictured the USSR much as my friends did: a miserable place where people waited hours in line for toilet paper, many fearing imprisonment or shooting. My mother's descriptions of her childhood helped form an image of a vast, gray wasteland where children were lucky to eat an orange on New Year's, the most expansive Soviet holiday. How lucky she was to have escaped!

Greatly prizing beauty and creativity, she often displayed her disdain of things Soviet in her criticism of their bad taste on top of their shoddiness, an aspect of communist control that seemed to go with its severity. Whatever one's views about current Russian tastes, it's not accidental that many see themselves as aesthetes, a reaction to decades of life under enforced mediocrity.

My mother's faith in innate Russian talent also represents the kind of paradox in which the country is rich. Few would argue Russians have made glorious contributions to art, literature and dance, but she goes further. Even if Russians didn't invent cars or airplanes, she sometimes says only half in jest, their huge gifts would have enabled them to do a better job of it if they had.

Like many who lived under Stalin, she was lucky to have survived, having been born to a single mother whose husband, an airplane designer, was arrested in 1937 during Stalin's Great Terror. I knew virtually nothing about that or other aspects of my grandmother's struggles when I was growing up in rural Connecticut, where she also lived. I viewed her as a very kind but somewhat clueless-seeming fish out of water. She was born in the Volga River city of Kazan, where her grandfather, the family patriarch, was a savvy grain merchant who survived the civil war that followed the 1917 Revolution by giving the Bolsheviks desperately needed flour. Legend has it that my great-great-grandfather could discern what region grain came from by its smell.

My mother met my American father in 1959, when he was a guide at the first American National Exhibition in Moscow, the venue for the celebrated Nixon-Khrushchev kitchen debate. A dashing, outgoing twenty-six-year-old, he'd studied French history at Harvard but learned Russian in the navy because the burgeoning Cold War made the Soviet Union fascinating to him. Lured to Moscow by the promise of adventure exploring America's reviled enemy, he was captivated by the surprising warmth and informal nature of the relations between the people he met, whose friendships he often found deeper and less focused on superficialities than those among his friends in the West, partly because hardship made warmth necessary. A graduate student at Columbia University at the time, he soon returned for an exchange year at Moscow State University, when he spent months attending court trials for his first book, *Justice in Moscow*, which helped launch his sparkling career as a journalist. He later made many return trips.

The ease of communication he found went for relations between men and women, too. While his romance with my mother was still unlikely, I think most of her story, from her first days in a freezing Siberian cabin to her coming of age with bohemian friends in Moscow, helps illustrate some fundamental values that underlie Russia's various political and economic systems. As for me, having first traveled to Russia for the excitement it promised, I kept returning because I thought I recognized similarities between the people's current attitudes and behavior and what I'd read of Russian history in college and graduate school: a window into the human condition.

Of course I'm not suggesting that some things haven't radically changed, including the ambitions of my old friend Kolya, with whom I traveled to Vilnius in 1991. The eager young reporter who was helping his country transform itself has lost much of his idealism. No longer able to do honest reporting of any depth, he switched to working for foreign television companies and joined the millions of his compatriots whose chief interests are cars, dachas and designer clothes. Although a strong supporter of his country's opposition leaders, he now feels, like many others, that his main priority is to protect his private life from a corrupt state whose main concerns are its own.

Despite that trend, however, efforts are still under way to build a civil society—the groups outside government and business that help shape public life—that would enable the population to defend its interests these two decades after communism's collapse. In the face of tremendous obstacles erected by an increasingly repressive regime, those attempts may someday help lay the groundwork for fundamental changes. So what's on the minds of the millions who push into Moscow's subway cars and squirm in its immense traffic jams? What are the thoughts and concerns of the far greater numbers of country dwellers whom foreigners rarely see, let alone talk to? What do they think about themselves and about life in general?

Generalizations must be suspect. It's no easier to sum up the huge country with people who are disparate in so many ways than to categorize America, where Tea Party supporters differ so greatly from New York liberals. Still, I believe certain qualities are recognizably Russian and that Americans and other Westerners would do well to ponder some of them. Like it or not, Russia, for all its manifest and concealed shortcomings, remains a great power with formidable material and cultural strengths and an inclination and capacity to challenge us—which is highly unlikely to change soon. For centuries, the country was a giant force, even when its economy was more stunted and its government even more malign than now. Surely it will continue to confound us with ideas and designs very different from our own for as long as anyone can reasonably foresee.

Roustam Tariko, the billionaire owner of Russian Standard vodka, at a Moscow charity ball. (*Justin Jin / justinjin.com*)

2

Extravagance

Money is like down—one puff and it's gone.
                                        —Old Russian saying

You see them in front of downtown Moscow's five-star hotels and fancy restaurants: rows of luxury cars jammed on sidewalks, forcing pedestrians into the traffic-choked streets. Matrix points of a privileged city within a city, they come with bodyguards, tough men who help maintain the distinction between their employers and the vast bulk of lesser Russians by directing wilting stares of suspicion at passersby. Maybe that's why I was the only one who appeared to notice a line of especially costly automobiles inching down Bolshaya Dmitrovka, a narrow street of pre-Revolutionary brick buildings around the corner from the Kremlin, on a bitter April evening in 2009. Bone-chilling wind lashed the huddled pedestrians shuffling across ice-covered sidewalks past the Mercedes, Bentleys and Hummers, mostly black with impenetrably tinted windows.

I'd almost broken my neck by slipping on the treacherous ice, surprised once again, as foreigners in Moscow often are, by the women in perilously high stilettos who click by with apparent ease. Surprised, too, that the administration of a city blanketed in snow and ice for half the year allows shops to pave the sidewalks in front of their doors with slippery tiles. However, those weren't the concerns of the passengers in the luxurious cars, which stopped at velvet ropes cordoning off a red carpet. It led to a five-story building that was sparkling under banks of brilliant lights. Photographers snapped as glitterati emerged from the backseats: leggy women in alluring dresses, men in suits and shirts with collars opened wide. Bodyguards in dark jackets and two-way radio receivers buttoned in their ears kept nervous watch.

The evening's affair was devoted to the opening of yet another exclusive Moscow restaurant. While the Soviet Union excelled in broadcasting prescriptions for reforming the world, until the dying days of the USSR, not a single Japanese restaurant—or a French, Italian or American one—broke the numbing uniformity of dour state establishments that served the same cuts of overcooked meats and soggy vegetables to those lucky enough to get in. By the end of the 1990s, however, chain outlets offered sushi on virtually every third corner. Now the addition of Nobu, the latest outpost of the upscale international chain, would provide another little playground for the city's rich and powerful.

My invitation to its launch reflected Russia's often paradoxical shifts in ideology and interests since 1991: it came from the former head of the CIA's Soviet division, who knew Nobu's co-owner Robert De Niro. The former intelligence officer had enlisted my help in inviting some of his ex-KGB adversaries. Now that the Cold War was over, they were potential collaborators in a future Hollywood film that carried a promise of big bucks. But my main interest in attending was to gauge what effect, if any, the global financial crisis that had just bashed Russia was having on the city's legendary social life.

Inside, the main room was dramatically dark. The white-haired former KGB officers dropped their steely guard to gawk as politicians mingled with businessmen amid an army of models sporting enough eye shadow to make up for decades of Soviet rule, when cosmetics were often unavailable. Their kind of loud chic can seem in bad taste in Paris: too outrageous for a predominantly bourgeois society. In fad-crazy New York, it often appears unnatural because it's poorly copied. But something about Moscow enables its women to carry off risqué designer wear better than almost anywhere else. Maybe the secret lies in the essential lawlessness of the city's gritty streets, which carry more than a whiff of danger. Or the jarring contrast between extravagance and the heart-wrenching shabbiness of the great unwashed. In Russia, anything goes.

As dance music pounded, waiters with fixed smiles distributed flutes of Champagne and sushi canapés. More photographers circled celebrities and "minigarchs": the second-tier millionaires and billionaires who aspire to join the oligarchs. Unlike the journalists, hangers-on and people providing party services, those who counted were very much at home amid the restaurant's international panache of wood, brushed steel and mosaic-tile. The evening's crowd could have been visitors from another land with no connection to the vast mass of "ordinary" Russians.

The conversation centered on purchases and play. No mention was made of the financial crisis that was spinning the economy into a deep abyss. The price of oil, which accounts for almost a third of Russia's GDP, had dropped from $130 per barrel in July 2008 to forty dollars, with devastating consequences. The economy, which had grown by 8 percent in 2008, shrank by the same amount the following year. By January, millions of Russians had lost their jobs, the stock market had shed more than three-quarters of its value compared to the previous year, and no prediction of improvement was taken seriously. But I overheard another of Nobu's partners, an ethnic Azeri billionaire named Aras Agalarov, whose son was married to the daughter of Azerbaijani President Ilham Aliyev, curtly shrugging off the implications. Agalarov's development empire includes a Moscow luxury shopping mall and the city's most exclusive suburban housing complex. Most houses still under construction had already been sold, the cheapest for ten million dollars.

Although many of Moscow's wealthiest lost billions of dollars during the crisis, especially those who had built their business empires with the help of hugely leveraged spending sprees, they would soon benefit from generous government spending. Two hundred billion dollars would help bail out banks and some of the largest companies owned by the wealthiest oligarchs. When the economy picked up the following year, depleted fortunes would promptly resume their prodigious expansion.

Elsewhere in the room, talk continued of favorite restaurants, holiday destinations and De Niro's expected appearance. A would-be starlet in a little black dress grew impatient with the complaints of two foreign businessmen about Russian bureaucracy. "But Moscow has everything, isn't that why you're here?" she interrupted. "Why would you be anywhere else?" Like others who assert that everything Russian is bigger, better and grander, she spoke as if the poverty, potholes and streets deep in muddy slush were of no concern to anyone who mattered.

When I first arrived in Moscow, armed with dislike for the communist elite, I was surprised by how diverting it was to visit the few hard-currency restaurants open to foreigners and select bribe-paying Soviets with connections. Although hardly opulent, places like the musty Spanish Bar in the old Moscow Hotel next to the Kremlin provided a cherished sense of exclusivity. Its dishes bore but slight resemblance to real tapas, but watching lucky patrons swagger into the little oasis as if they were royalty was instructive. Although the explosion of new restaurants and bars since then helped erase that particular inequity of the communist system, a growing demand for exclusivity created a profusion of ever-more-expensive restaurants that have turned the city into a diners' paradise for those who can afford them. And while present-day Russia can't be compared to the Soviet Union in terms of freedom and opportunity, its displays of extravagance can be as appalling as communist deprivation was grim. Or so it seems to me.

Stories about various forms of excess are legion. An American businessman who examined the books of a Moscow telecommunications company to help prepare it for floating on the stock exchange told me he was surprised to find the firm owned a shooting range in central Moscow, where the managers unwound by firing rounds from Kalashnikov automatic rifles. "When I asked about it in his office, the chief operating officer proudly produced a machine gun fitted with a laser sight," the American said. "He proceeded to point it at me in alarming jest."

The excessiveness comes from startling changes that have made Moscow home to the world's largest collection of young millionaires, many in their twenties. The capital reportedly also boasts seventy-eight billionaires, more than any other city in the world.[1] The first Bentley sold there several years ago is said to have been bought by a twenty-four-year-old. Now they're a common sight, inching ahead in monumental traffic jams on streets that used to be scarcely lit and nearly empty. Their owners often also love luxury at sea. One of the leading oligarchs owns four of the world's most expensive yachts, including a new one—to replace another he gave as a gift—that cost five hundred million dollars.

Not that you need to visit Russia to know something about the country's superrich. A strappingly tall forty-eight-year-old who is considered Moscow's most eligible bachelor—who bought the New Jersey (now Brooklyn) Nets basketball team before running for president, then launching a political party—is among the most infamous. Shortly before Mikhail Prokhorov temporarily became Russia's richest man, he was arrested in the fancy French ski resort of Courchevel on suspicion of participation in a prostitution ring. Since it's well known that the country's wealthy men export young women to entertain their entourages on holiday, most Russians were amused by the charge. Quickly released, Prokhorov soon launched *Snob*, a magazine that costs twenty dollars an issue. His arrest drew international attention not only because of his wealth and status but also because it provided a glimpse into the closed society of the Russian elite. In January, when the best skis in Courchevel sell for twenty thousand dollars and the "in" nightclub charges thousands of dollars for its top tables, local wags call it Courchevelski. That's because Russia's richest arrive for two weeks of very extravagant partying.

The spending sprees are affecting the international market for art as well as prime European real estate. In Sotheby's Moscow office, housed in a swank office building near the Kremlin, director Mikhail Kamensky told me wealthy Russians who have been buying expensive cars and houses for years are increasingly adding paintings and sculpture to their holdings. "It's coming back as a new fad for buying luxury, but not in buildings or hardware," he said. "It's creating a trend to invest a lot, not just in art but also in a lifestyle of collecting."

Oligarch Roman Abramovich, the owner of Britain's Chelsea Football Club, lost billions of dollars in 2008, but not before buying a Lucian Freud painting for $33 million and a series of three paintings by Francis Bacon for $86 million. The driving force behind his affection for art was his new girlfriend, thirty-two-year-old socialite Daria Zhukova, a former model and the daughter of another billionaire, Alexander Zhukov, an economist who was also a deputy prime minister. Zhukova launched Moscow's newest contemporary art gallery, called Garage, which is housed in a massive avant-garde bus depot built in the 1920s.

Marat Guelman, who is sometimes called the entrepreneurial leader of Russian avant-garde art, says the publicity surrounding the opening of Garage helped sire a new appreciation for contemporary art. Not long ago, Guelman, who wears a scrappy beard and publishes a literary magazine called *Pushkin*, was using his selling skills as a public relations consultant to Vladimir Putin's Kremlin. Guelman's bohemian-chic, exposed-brick-wall apartment in an upscale pre-Revolutionary Moscow neighborhood serves as an informal gathering place for artists who, carrying on an enduring Russian tradition, often drop by unannounced for coffee or vodka. Sitting there, near a life-size female mannequin encrusted in a glass mosaic like a giant disco ball, he told me that seventy years of socialism left many bare walls that would-be oligarchs are now eager to adorn. Although a handful of top collectors know more about art than he does, most are unsure of themselves. "French collectors are delighted to discover new artists and buy their work cheaply. Russians tend to buy expensive pictures by names they learned in grade school."

How truly different are Russia's rich from others in the world? An old joke about a man who's just bought a Christian Dior tie still applies. Spotting another Russian wearing the very same tie, he approaches to ask how much he paid for it. "A hundred dollars" is the proud reply.

"Ha! *I* paid *two* hundred."

As Guelman says, extravagance is partly a reaction to the decades of Soviet austerity, when wallets and purses were immediately emptied whenever their owners spied something worth buying in the knowledge that another chance would be unlikely to materialize. But over-the-top spending is more than that in a country whose tsars built some of the world's most lavish palaces—as well as the world's largest cannon and bell, both of which were too big to function. Aliona Doletskaya sees it as a reflection of national character. When I visited the former longtime editor of Russian *Vogue*, who is called Russia's Anna Wintour, in the magazine's offices in a nineteenth-century building several blocks from Nobu, we sat on clear plastic Philippe Starck chairs. The admirably composed fiftysomething blonde with shoulder-length hair spoke in flawless British English that edged toward whispers, as if she were confiding great secrets.

"For years, I remember hearing 'New Russian, New Russian, New Russian,'" she said of the disparaging term for the country's nouveau-riche. "Suddenly I realized that's what *I* am, a New Russian."

The doyenne of fashionable Muscovites and one of their chief arbiters of taste said the thick gold chains and cheap red sport jackets favored by capitalist thugs during the years following the Soviet collapse are long gone. Now the very wealthy spend for "pure entertainment."

"Russians love spending money. The generosity of sharing fun is in our blood. Being able to spend without thinking is a gift. You invite as many people as possible to your house and throw everything you've got on the table." Spending with abandon is called *gussarskoe*, meaning "like a hussar"—the dashing, fast-living, hard-drinking imperial cavalry officer. Status symbols are all-important for satisfying that impulse. "Very expensive, very unique cars, houses in Sardinia, in England...Russians invest a lot in houses. And in yachts for cruising the Mediterranean, they love them," Doletskaya said.

The main preserve of such lifestyles is Rublyovka, a suburban region where Moscow's wealthiest have built sprawling mansions behind high metal gates. Once a zone for dachas of the Soviet elite, the area is now home to the compounds of oligarchs and ministers—as well as Putin, who travels there along the Rublyovo-Uspenskoye Road, for which it's named. Closed to most cars under communist rule, the narrow way winds through a dense fir forest fronted by an endless stretch of billboards advertising French real estate and Philippine maid services. In the formerly rustic settlement of Zhukovka, a Gucci shop neighbors a Lamborghini dealership. When I interviewed the billionaire vodka and banking magnate Roustam Tariko nearby, it was on a bench on his front lawn, within spitting distance of one of his cars, a million-dollar Bugatti Veyron. His apparent disregard for it as it stood baking under a hot summer sun seemed typically cavalier.

"Those bastards," complained Gera Kiva, an elderly cousin of my mother's who worked for forty years as an engineer and teacher of automation technology before hyperinflation in the 1990s wiped out his life savings. Although he welcomed the collapse of communism, he joined the great majority of Russians who became vocal supporters of Putin, under whose rule the oil boom created most of Moscow's countless millionaires and billionaires. He also took to dismissing Western criticism of the president, including mine, as the reflection of a desire to see Russia back on its knees. Now he's unhappy, although not yet to the point of dissent. So are the very many Russians who openly rail against the corruption that chokes daily life and its beneficiaries in the Kremlin, whose behavior they call *bezpredel*, "without limits." It's virtually impossible to ride in a Moscow taxi without hearing the kind of complaints that used to be whispered only in the privacy of Soviet kitchens.

"Those greedy bastards," Gera repeated with not so much as a fleeting thought that he or anyone like him can do the slightest thing to counter them. "They stole my country." Still, Gera's lucky because he and his wife,

Lucia, are supported by their two sons, who work for private companies and live in large suburban houses they recently built for their families. Many others often speak, as they've been doing since the collapse of communism, about a new revolution waiting just around the corner.

———

The Bolshevik Revolution was supposed to have eliminated class conflict. Having condemned egalitarianism as "petit bourgeois," Stalin characterized Soviet society by 1936 as "two friendly classes and a layer": workers, peasants and the intelligentsia. He failed to mention its most privileged members, the communist elite, which he cultivated by abolishing limits on Party members' salaries and instituting a graduated pay scale, along with perks that would help keep subordinates loyal. Although some later argued that the *nomenklatura*, as the officials who ran the USSR came to be called—the term literally means a list of posts—could not be considered a social class because the Party drew its members from all groups, historian Michael Voslensky nevertheless called it a "concealed class." Describing the various Party bosses and managers who lived in sprawling apartments and relaxed in large dachas behind high walls to which they sped in specially reserved highway lanes, he estimated their numbers at around three million, roughly 1.5 percent of the population, and illustrated the great lengths to which the coddled elite hid its private use of supposedly public property.[2]

> It is just as improper for a *nomenklatura* official to own his own dacha as it is to own his own car. Infringement of this unwritten law would expose the offender to being suspected of being a free-thinker or being not very sure of his future in the *nomenklatura*. Consequently a head of desk who buys a dacha will do so in the name of his parents; if he buys a car, it will be in the name of one of his grown-up children or his brother. This is his way of avoiding any suspicion of having petit-bourgeois leanings, while enlarging his share of the collective property of the *nomenklatura*.[3]

Voslensky mentions a telling joke. One day the mother of a Central Committee official who lives on a collective farm visits her son in Moscow. After staying in his luxurious apartment, enjoying his opulent dacha and eating excellent meals prepared from food bought in special stores, she nevertheless wants to return home as quickly as possible.

"What's the matter, Mother?" her son asks. "It's lovely here; don't you want to stay?"

"It *is* lovely," she replies, "but very dangerous. What if the Reds come?"

If Russia's current one percent aren't like you and me, to paraphrase F. Scott Fitzgerald's celebrated statement, they're also unlike the rich of other countries. Despite the desire to show off by spending in a very big way, the instinct for self-preservation still compels most of them to hide the full extent of their wealth. Extravagant acquisitions made in the names of spouses and children remain common. And although the surge in art sales helped buoy the local art scene for more than a decade, purchases began dropping off around 2010 because most collectors—including more than 80 percent of Guelman's onetime clients—now live abroad.[4] Those who make up an ever-larger share of the rich back home—officials and others whose fortunes depend on their connections to the state—tend not to collect art because they're more interested in hiding their no doubt ill-gotten gains instead of displaying them on their walls. In 2012, soon after Guelman moved his gallery to Vinzavod, or "wine factory," a sprawling nineteenth-century industrial space that's become a center of the city's art world, he announced he was closing it. Others followed suit.

Fighting the urge to display wealth is an increasingly good idea for everyone in Russia. With the Soviet authorities, under whom hiding became its own kind of art, swept away, the danger today often comes from the tax police. Masked officers sometimes raid the offices of political critics, possible rivals and lesser threats to Kremlin favorites. Almost always, the offending parties' real dereliction is to have shown themselves to be insufficiently loyal to the Kremlin or allowed themselves to be perceived as such. The danger of arbitrary punishment from the authorities remains a key aspect of life for Russia's tycoons. In a country that runs on crime, where law enforcers are believed to be among the most corrupt officials, fear may be the only effective way of putting limits on lawlessness.

Fear has also been used to carry out a redistribution of wealth—which is to say back under the control of the state, where Putin is chief among a collection of officials whose roles more closely resemble those of Mafia dons than public servants. An American investment banker in Moscow characterizes the newest rich as "thugs" who demand kickbacks of up to 70 percent in all their deals. "We now consider 40 percent average," he told me under the condition I wouldn't name him. "Everything's being sucked out of the economy because they think only about what they can deposit into their offshore bank accounts before they lose their jobs, or worse." When the government quietly ordered managers of Russia's state energy companies to declare their unofficial incomes and assets along with those of their subordinates several months before Putin's reelection in 2012—an indication of how bad the situation has become—many panicked but proceeded to reveal as little as possible. Putin later launched a drive to "nationalize Russia's elite"—a common description of his purpose for enacting regulations passed in 2013 that bar officials from owning foreign bank accounts and other assets. The new rules put even the outwardly obedient under threat.

Estimates for the amount illegally spirited abroad from Russia each year reach above $70 billion. One especially well-placed source put the 2012 figure at $49 billion, or 2.5 percent of the GDP. Shortly before stepping down after eleven years, the usually taciturn Central Bank governor revealed his calculations of so-called capital flight, saying more than half was accomplished by one unnamed "well-organized group of individuals."[5]

His description of "shady operations conducted by firms directly or indirectly linked to each other by payments" appeared to back widespread circumstantial evidence that officials are routinely involved in massive underhanded schemes, such as the $230 million tax fraud uncovered by the now well-known lawyer Sergei Magnitsky in 2009. He said thieves used corporate seals and tax documents that police had confiscated during a raid on a foreign investment fund in 2007 to hijack several companies it controlled. Impersonating company employees, they pleaded guilty to crimes for which the company was subsequently fined in order to make it appear unprofitable. The three companies then proceeded to apply for the largest tax refund in Russian history, which was granted the same day. Arrested by the same police investigators whom he had exposed, Magnitsky died in jail in a pool of his own urine after being tortured and denied medical care for failing to recant his accusations. Tracking some of the money, the independent newspaper *Novaya Gazeta*—protected partly by its high profile and influential supporters—later linked officials from a tax office Magnitsky had accused of taking part in the fraud to the purchase of luxury apartments in Dubai and the United States.

The tension between the need or desire to display wealth and power and the wish to remain safe by obscuring it pervades Lukoil, a company that operates gasoline stations in many foreign countries, including the United States, where the opening of the first station in 2003 sanctioned an appearance by Putin. Founded by Vagit Alekperov, Russia's third-richest man at the time I spoke to him—although estimates of oligarchs' fortunes cannot be fully trusted—Lukoil has its headquarters on an old, tree-lined boulevard in Moscow's center. Amid the street's neoclassical architecture, Lukoil's concrete-and-glass building, constructed during the final Soviet years and later given to the company, is something of an eyesore.

Although it may look odd in a city where glamour seems to be everything, Lukoil's workaday image has been a vital factor in its success. The Kremlin's drive to control the country's energy industry, by far its largest source of wealth and power, has led to dispossessing and even imprisoning once high-riding tycoons. Nevertheless, Alekperov's Lukoil—Russia's largest private oil firm and number two overall, after state-controlled Rosneft—remains hale, if not entirely unscathed.

The company headquarters differ in other ways from typical office buildings. The security measures require visitors to spend half an hour passing through numerous checkpoints manned by a private army of guards. I was divested of my camera, cell phone and even my passport before a spokesman escorted me to the president's executive suite, where more men wearing berets and earpieces that gave them the look of special-forces troops waited. My final destination was a large anteroom staffed by a single saccharine receptionist. Behind it, a small, wood-paneled room offered sofas, armchairs and a wall decorated with photos of Alekperov with Putin, Prime Minister Dmitri Medvedev and the late Orthodox Church Patriarch Alexiy II.

The rise of Russia's leading oligarchs to pinnacles of wealth and influence—at levels barely imaginable to most people during the lawless, literally murderous free-for-all 1990s—has made them legendary. Together with the envy and dislike the captains of industry prompt in their fellow

Russians, they also earn grudging respect for their often relaxed, if haughty, personas—reminders that they were once like everyone else. They are Russia's biggest superstars, and the expectation of meeting one made me nervous as well as excited.

An automatic door opened and in walked the CEO. Ruggedly handsome, with close-cropped gray hair that matched the color of his suit, Alekperov had the brusque manner of a self-made man. Unlike most other oligarchs, who knew little about industry before acquiring their assets in the mid-1990s, he started by dirtying his hands as an oil-field worker.

Born in the Azerbaijani capital, Baku—the world's first oil boomtown before the Revolution of 1917—eighteen-year-old Alekperov followed in his father's footsteps by finding work in the Soviet republic's Caspian Sea oil fields. In the 1970s, he moved to the forbiddingly rough territory of western Siberia, where major new oil fields were being tapped in endless expanses of steppe and virgin forest. By 1990, he'd worked his way up to first deputy oil minister. His job overseeing all Soviet oil production provided an ideal position for putting together what would become the country's top oil company from formerly state-owned fields and refineries. Visits to the American company Chevron, Italian Eni and other foreign oil giants opened his eyes to possibilities back home, where, he said with characteristic understatement, he saw the Soviet industry's "problems."

Alekperov persuaded Yeltsin, then still head of the Russian Republic, to give him control of three of its biggest oil fields. Lukoil took its name from the three—located near the Siberian towns of Langepas, Urai and Kogalym—which Alekperov and two others built into a vertically integrated company that Alekperov privatized after the Soviet collapse the following year.

"I see the oligarchs positively," he told me. "They spend most of their lives working, and they're very responsible to their shareholders and workers. They make unique investments in Russian industry and in the United States, Europe and Asia." However, Alekperov draws a distinction between Lukoil and other major companies run by more visible oligarchs who borrowed huge amounts during the great oil boom in the first decade of the twenty-first century. "Our heads weren't spinning from high oil prices," he insisted of his company's conservative investment strategy. As a result, Lukoil suffered significantly less during the financial crisis of 2008.

Far more threatening is the arbitrary power Putin returned to the hands of the state officials whom fleets of black Audis and Mercedes ferry around town. Although entrepreneurs continue earning immense fortunes, it's now at the pleasure of those ruling bureaucrats, who tend to see private business as an extension of the state, an attitude nowhere more evident than in the rise of massive state industries run by Putin's former KGB cronies. Sergei Chemezov, who served with him in the East German city of Dresden in the 1980s, is now chairman of state-run Russian Technologies, a massive defense-industry umbrella company that includes the country's arms export firm Rosoboronexport; Avtovaz, maker of the Lada automobile; and Black Sea resorts. Another former KGB officer named Igor Sechin is CEO of state-owned Rosneft, the country's leading oil company. Widely believed to be the boss of bosses, Sechin, Putin's former deputy chief of staff, heads a powerful clan of *siloviki*, "strongmen" who run the country's security services. Many saw him as the country's second-most-powerful man after Putin. Although Sechin left the government after Putin returned to the presidency in 2012, he retains great influence because in addition to heading Rosneft, he is a board member of the main state energy holding company, Rosneftegaz.

Some of the *siloviki*, who are among Russia's newest rich, helped the Kremlin reestablish its control of the economy by taking over private companies. Sechin himself was responsible for orchestrating the downfall of the largest loser in that process, who was once the country's wealthiest oligarch. Mikhail Khodorkovsky rapidly assembled a massive empire in the 1990s by intimidating his rivals and sometimes diluting the shares of major stakeholders to take control of his many businesses. But although he was known as one of the most ruthless oligarchs by the time he put together the Yukos oil company, his reputation improved after he'd cemented his control of the firm. Khodorkovsky was among the first to hire European accountants to bring the company's practices up to Western standards. Investing in infrastructure and equipment to improve production was also rare in an environment where capitalism often meant seizing or stealing as much profit as quickly as possible—perhaps a somewhat understandable perception, given the generations who grew up on propaganda portraying that as the free market's basic operating principle.

After a decade of decline brought on by the Soviet collapse, oil production began to recover thanks in no small part to new techniques imported by a handful of Texas oilmen who brought new fracking and other extraction methods to Russia. As the Georgetown University scholar Thane Gustafson has made clear, no company was more receptive than Yukos, whose pioneering work soon made it number one.[6] The new culture of maximizing productivity clashed with the old Soviet way of doing things, however. Khodorkovsky deployed legions of young, laptop-wielding executives to ensure Yukos's wells were pumping out as much as they were supposed to by cutting out waste and rooting out double bookkeeping. Slowed by massive bureaucracy that virtually ruled out innovation, the old establishment saw him as a serious threat.

Already disliked by his business peers, the upstart broke more rules by criticizing Putin, who planned to reestablish state control over the all-important oil industry after he became president in 2000. The multibillionaire seriously angered the Kremlin by lobbying parliament to privatize Russia's network of pipelines, at the time, the government's last remaining means of exercising control.

In April 2003, Khodorkovsky announced that Yukos would merge with another top oil company, Sibneft, to create a firm whose reserves would rival the biggest multinationals'. He was also huddling with ExxonMobil and ChevronTexaco, which were interested in buying stakes in the new enterprise. Khodorkovsky, who openly bankrolled liberal opposition parties and set up a prominent charitable foundation, was seen as a menace more than a mere nuisance. In October, masked special forces officers stormed his plane on a Siberian runway and arrested him.

Tried and sentenced for fraud and tax evasion, the once haughty tycoon came to be seen by many Russians as a symbol of the ruin faced by those who opposed or resisted Putin. After he was sent to serve an eight-year term in Chita, a desolate Siberian city four thousand miles east of Moscow, Yukos was dismantled and most of its assets sold to a scarcely known company with a temporary address in another provincial city. That company, the single bidder in a highly suspect auction, soon resold the properties to Sechin's Rosneft, the state oil firm Putin was transforming into the country's largest and most powerful. Although the Kremlin hadn't outright seized Yukos, its flimsy legal cover fooled few. The message was unmistakable: private businesses, no matter how big and powerful, would remain private only if the state approved.

In the spring of 2009, Khodorkovsky was returned to Moscow for another trial on a new charge that even some of his critics considered absurd: that the owner of Yukos had stolen twenty-five billion dollars, nearly the company's entire income, over a period of six years. The second trial was held in a shabby courthouse on a quiet downtown street next to a park. Its panoramic view includes the Moscow River and the White House, the seat of government where Putin—who, then between his second and third presidential terms, was serving as prime minister—had his offices. Although the public had long lost interest in Khodorkovsky, his supporters, who included prominent dissidents and a few celebrities, stood in line to observe the charade of justice in the second-floor courtroom. I joined them on a day so beautiful it seemed to buoy even the spirits of Khodorkovsky's elderly parents, who attended most days.

At the top of the stairs, a platoon of tough-looking men with shaved heads and black flak jackets guarded the room with Kalashnikovs while Khodorkovsky sat in a cage of thick bulletproof glass. Dressed in a brown cotton jacket and Soviet-looking jeans, he looked fit but grayer than at his first trial, as would be expected after his years in Siberia. Looking up from talks with his lawyers, who included some of the country's most prominent human rights defenders, he occasionally smiled.

Grim-faced prosecutors in ill-fitting military-style uniforms opened the proceedings by reading the charges in barely audible monotones that put even one of the accusers to sleep. Taking notes and studying documents through his rimless eyeglasses, Khodorkovsky seemed almost irrelevant, a curiosity in his cage who surely knew that one of the show trial's chief purposes was to further humiliate him. But although his expression sometimes seemed to hint of mocking the proceedings, he also played along, as if in mad hope the court could somehow be influenced. Hours of prosecutorial droning, including reading every word of many Yukos contracts, pushed the mood in the cramped room toward despondency. By the time the prosecutors moved on to reciting minutes of shareholders' meetings, I was fidgeting less from the pain of sitting on one of the unforgiving plastic benches than the discomfort of witnessing the banal machinery of authoritarianism plodding toward an inevitable outcome. The judge announced a recess only after a guard had begun snoring.

"You don't know a thing about the system until you've found yourself in its claws," Khodorkovsky wrote during his trial, describing it as "a single enterprise, whose business is legalized violence."[7] Found guilty of course, he was sentenced to an additional six years in prison. They probably won't be his last. In 2013, state-controlled NTV television aired a documentary alleging that Khodorkovsky took part in the murder of a Siberian mayor in the 1990s. Many believe the film was groundwork for a third criminal case against him.

Although he stands out as a symbol of injustice, Khodorkovsky is hardly an isolated case: in the space of a decade, one of every six businessmen in Russia faced some form of prosecution.[8] Around the time of his second trial, I met billionaire Victor Makushin, the founder of a scrap-metal empire who confirmed that upper bureaucrats' success in taking back the better part of Russia's oil industry emboldened them to appropriate a larger slice of all pies by demanding ever-bigger kickbacks and bribes. That, Makushin stated, made the overseers of Putin's regime the country's predominant criminal group. "Officials have amassed huge powers," he said in his modest office on the grounds of a Moscow factory. "They represent the greatest threat to business, and you can't turn to the courts for relief because judges are afraid of ruling against the authorities. It's a huge drag on the economy."

Soon after I spoke to him, Makushin was charged with criminal activities and fled abroad. If any doubt about the motives existed, he was blocked by officials from seeking bankruptcy, which would have protected his company after it was forced to stop production. He could only look on as Sberbank, the state savings bank, which happened to have loaned his once booming enterprise $63 million months before the surprise charges were filed, took it over. At the time, the governor of the southern Stavropol region bragged to Putin that he had prohibited Makushin from closing one of his plants there, which again prevented him from filing for bankruptcy.[9] His case demonstrates that the *siloviki* and others in the Kremlin are less interested in the economy than in their tap on it. Just as Soviet leaders cared more about their control of the socialist system than addressing its massive inefficiencies, the current ones are more intent on preserving their cut of Russia's form of capitalism than improving it. The results of a 2012 poll that revealed more than half of respondents believed they could not protect their property from possible takeover were no surprise.[10]

Alekperov talked about the government and its problems in a kind of code. As the country's biggest private oilman at a time when the state was continuing to acquire oil assets in one strong-arm way or another, his position uncomfortably resembled Khodorkovsky's before he was imprisoned. Lukoil had even developed plans to emulate Yukos's aggressive business model before Khodorkovsky's arrest prompted Alekperov to drop them. Although the former Soviet oilman doubtless shares the industry's overwhelming distaste for Khodorkovsky, Lukoil's CEO said he would make no judgments. "I'm sure our legal practices are transparent enough and I hope the right decisions will be made...But I knew Mikhail personally, respect and sympathize with him. From the very beginning, I said of course he should be punished if he's guilty. But the court determines what the punishment should be, not I."

———

Alekperov had reason to be concerned. Soon after state-owned Rosneft had swallowed most of Yukos, it began targeting lucrative Lukoil oil fields in the country's Arctic far north. Those assets, like many in Russia, lie beneath some of the world's least hospitable terrain, in that case the remote Nenets Autonomous region.

Alexei Barinov, an oil executive turned politician, was the last regional governor to take office in Russia before Putin abolished gubernatorial elections in favor of Kremlin appointments in 2005. The following year, he was charged with fraud and embezzlement in connection with a previous job he had held. That happened after the region's local legislators, in a rare show of defiance, butted heads with the Kremlin by unanimously refusing to approve Putin's decision to sack the region's representative to Russia's upper house of parliament.

Declaring that the interference in Nenets came from people whose interests "don't correspond to the interests of the region or its government," Barinov declined to keep the legislators in line. Arrested the following day, he was quickly fired. However, some locals were convinced his apparent political defiance was just an excuse to throttle him over the real reason for his ouster: he was protecting Lukoil's local subsidiary, which he'd headed in his previous job. Nenets residents—many of whom praised Barinov for financing schools and libraries—said their former governor's transgression lay in opposing Rosneft's moves to assume control of Lukoil fields in the region. His tactic was delaying deals between the two companies while insisting Rosneft pay nine hundred million rubles ($33 million) it owed in back taxes.

Some Nenets residents compared Barinov's arrest to Khodorkovsky's. Most appeared resigned to their region's fate. An earnest regional legislator named Nikolai Fomin explained that Barinov's arrest was part of a carefully planned Kremlin scheme to dismantle the local government and take control of the region's oil and gas reserves. "Our example sent a signal to all governors," Fomin said in his cramped office in what passes for Naryan-Mar's town center. "The signal was that if you don't play by the rules they invented, the same's in store for you." In that case, Fomin continued, the Kremlin counted on the isolation of Nenets to execute its corporate takeover. "We're located at the end of the earth. So a few people go out and yell on the tundra, will anyone hear us?"

Back in Moscow, Alekperov rolled with the punches. No one at Lukoil said anything publicly about the loss of its northern oil fields, nor was anything done to shore up Barinov. Deferential as before, Alekperov professed to feel no pressure from the government. Competition for oil licenses might be more open and more understandable, he said, with more companies competing. However, "Lukoil gets its licenses for developing its fields from the state, which has the right to determine how its property is exploited; to enact whatever regulations it sees fit." The state's belief that a number of oil fields should be considered strategic was "understandable," since it will make them available to future generations. "Their availability will wait until more oil is needed or there's more money to develop them."

Alekperov's doormat tactic has paid off. Apparently on good terms with the Kremlin, he's often seen with Putin. The one possible development Alekperov admitted to fearing is the "undoing" of the competition in Russia's oil industry, which began in the 1990s. After I spoke with him, domination by a single company, as in the gas industry, became reality when Rosneft announced it would buy BP's joint venture with a Russian oil firm called TNK, which would boost the Kremlin's share of the world's largest oil industry from 40 percent to more than 50 percent and cement Putin's drive to put the energy industry back in state hands.

That development—and the Kremlin's influence over businessmen it wants to do its bidding in general—has implications abroad, where Moscow uses its vast natural resources as an instrument of foreign policy. A

"transnational oil company," as it describes itself, Lukoil is already the largest source of direct Russian investment abroad and predicts that half its
business will soon be conducted outside the country.

More than simply to consolidate power at home, Putin has used control
over the energy sector to pursue his goal of restoring Russia to the ranks
of the great powers, along the lines he outlined in his doctoral thesis in
1997. His logic is simple: the more countries depend on Russia for their
energy needs, the more leverage Moscow has over them. The Kremlin
hopes Europe's current reliance on Russia for a third of its natural gas will
inevitably grow as demand inexorably increases. For now, beyond simply
exporting energy, Russia is using companies such as Lukoil and its state
natural gas monopoly Gazprom to buy control of pipelines, utilities and
other infrastructure that delivers Russian energy directly to European
consumers.

Those worried by the inroads Russian companies have made in Europe
warn that, unlike Western firms, which lobby largely in their own interests,
Russian companies, both state-controlled and private, play an important
role in Kremlin strategizing. Increasing control over foreign energy industries not only generates larger profits for Moscow but also helps cultivate
political influence in target countries—more, according to Harvard University's Marshall Goldman, than the Red Army did during the Cold War.
"The Russians have that weapon," he told me at the height of Gazprom's
wealth in 2008, "and there's nothing you can do to counter it."

Former Czech president Vaclav Havel raised the same alarm about
the drive to reestablish influence in former Soviet Bloc countries. Before
his death in 2011, Havel told me that "Russian companies are undoubtedly influencing the behavior of various Czech political parties and politicians. I've seen several cases where the influence started quietly, then slowly
began projecting onto our foreign policy. I can only advise serious discretion and great caution." In 2009, Havel led a group of prominent Central
and Eastern European politicians who published an open letter directing
that message to President Obama. The West, they wrote, should abandon
its mistaken belief that the end of the Cold War and the expansion of the
EU and NATO into the former Soviet Bloc guarantees their countries are
"safe."

Moscow's success has been dramatic during the past several years. Goldman said the threat from its control over the European energy market was

made clear when Moscow shut off gas to Ukraine during a price dispute in 2006, which disrupted supplies to Western Europe. "It intimidates, and in a sense, it neutralizes the country," he said. "If you look at Germany's policies after that incident, they become much more timid in challenging some of the things countries might do that would upset the Russians."

The 2008 campaign of the administration of George W. Bush to put Ukraine and Georgia on a path to NATO membership provoked fury in Moscow. Despite international outrage over Russia's summer invasion of Georgia months earlier, German chancellor Angela Merkel—whose country gets more than 40 percent of its natural gas from Russia—led the opposition to Washington's plan, which was defeated. At the same time, Germany blocked proposed European Union regulations that would have restricted foreign companies from buying European energy utilities, a policy that could have slowed Gazprom's advance into Western Europe.

That kind of acquiescence appeared to begin changing in 2012, when the European Commission launched a major investigation into Gazprom's anticompetitive practices in eight European countries. At the time of this writing, the case promised to force Gazprom to lower its prices, which would be especially threatening for Moscow at a time when supplies from new and diverse sources, such as American shale gas, and the development of liquefied natural gas are significantly depressing prices. Backed by new EU regulations and resolve, Eastern European countries have begun taking back control of their pipelines by breaking up their energy utilities—a major threat to Gazprom, which is responsible for providing up to 20 percent of the government's revenues and a major source of Putin's influence in the world. Since 2008, Gazprom's market capitalization of more than $360 billion—which fueled confident predictions the company would become the world's largest by that measure—has declined to below $80 billion. Despite the looming clouds for Gazprom, however, Russia has stuck to its old strategy of pouring billions of dollars into the construction of pipelines to Europe and other tactics it hopes will lock in European customers. Far from integrating into Western institutions, as many hoped in the 1990s, Moscow is continuing to wage a new kind of Cold War with new kinds of maneuvering. Although it's nowhere as threatening as it used to be, the Western disinclination to publicly acknowledge the conflict has helped undermine attempts to develop a common European policy toward Russia, another factor in Moscow's successes.

———

Growing up in London during the real Cold War, I corresponded with my Muscovite second cousins, whose innocuous letters were written with Soviet censors in mind. When I finally met them during my first trip to Moscow in 1991, it was in their parents' cramped gray concrete-block apartment in a mind-numbing stretch of residential buildings. We sat at their living room table knocking back vodka and eating heavy meat dishes with pickled vegetables. Between stories about the deprivations of Soviet life and my parents' courtship, my relatives told me they believed my fiercely independent mother had been destined to escape the Soviet Union.

Although the great majority of Soviets may have been hugely materialistic because consumer goods had long been scarce, what you wore or in rare cases drove mattered little in one sense because almost everything was poor in quality and style. The change came almost instantly after the collapse of communism. A year later, the novelty of meeting a foreigner was gone and my relatives had many more questions about how much things cost in America. I also noticed a hint of disappointment. What kind of relative was I, the personification of the West for them, not to be driving a BMW or Mercedes, or even hope to acquire one soon? What did I think a degree in history and literature would do for my future? I was headed nowhere near luxury and they could sense it. Within the decade, my cousins, who worked for new private companies, had built themselves swank suburban houses, were vacationing abroad every summer and had lost almost all interest in me. Not that they had time anyway: the sink-or-swim atmosphere of the 1990s required those who wanted to win in professional life to work incredibly hard, especially if they weren't among the lucky few positioned to profit from a disintegrating economic system—or criminals. The successful had little concern, let alone respect, for the huge mass who couldn't graduate from the bankrupt Soviet way of doing things.

The return of capitalism, relentlessly denounced as the chief source of evil under Soviet rule, says more about the Russian people than about their economy, the current tooth-and-claw version of which shares underlying aspects of the Soviet and even tsarist versions. Among early critics of the social order was a minor nobleman named Alexander Radishchev, who made big waves in 1790 by publishing a polemic called *A Journey from St. Petersburg to Moscow.* Radishchev was among the first members of Russia's intelligentsia, and many credit his book with marking the start of the country's intellectual history. Stopping in villages along the road between Russia's two major cities, its traveler protagonist depicts the misery of Russia's serfs, who made up 95 percent of the population and were bought and sold as though they were property, with no say in their fates. Describing the estate of a landowner who flourished because he overworked his serfs, Radishchev wrote, "Do we think our citizens are happy because our granaries are full and their stomachs empty? Or because one man blesses the government, rather than thousands? The wealth of that bloodsucker does not belong to him," he concludes. "It has been acquired by robbery and deserves severe punishment according to law."[11]

Although Radishchev didn't call for revolution—he blamed the nobles, not the tsar—his screed helped initiate a storied revolutionary tradition among critics of a regime whose aristocracy was subservient to its rulers in ways rarely seen in the West. In Europe, feudalism developed over centuries to include a tradition of obligation to peasants. By contrast, the concept of nobility was imported to Russia from a distinctly different world and installed by decree. One of the most important steps, by Empress Catherine the Great, instituted a charter of the nobility, a ranking system for the monarchy's manipulation.

Not unlike the communists, who promised to right tsarism's inequities, Putin—who has done more than anyone to reshape present-day Russia to his whim—said he'd establish a "dictatorship of the law" to level the playing field for all Russians. Like the Bolsheviks' dictatorship of the proletariat, Putin's system turned out to be all about dictatorship and very little about the law. The manner in which he took power had much to do with that. Plucked from obscurity in 1999 to become Boris Yeltsin's chosen successor, Putin was a last resort when Yeltsin's inner circle was panicking about being unseated by a rival political group. (That was when some political competition was still allowed.) More than anyone else, it was a single businessman—one who exemplified the term "oligarch" and even helped coin it—who was responsible for Putin's appearance on the scene. There would have been no Putin as we know him without Boris Berezovsky, who was once called the godfather of the Kremlin—although "consigliere" would have been more accurate because the power broker's influence was far from all-powerful.

Berezovsky's balding crown and clipped, machine-gun speech was part of a brand most Russians associate with the perceived evils of the Yeltsin regime. In the 1990s, the fifty-three-year-old former mathematics professor owned a private car dealership, Russia's first, with an exclusive license to sell Mercedes. After buying rich oil fields for a song in a questionable closed auction, he parlayed them into the Sibneft oil empire—which was to have merged with Khodorkovsky's Yukos—working his way into Yeltsin's entourage along the way. He also bought control of Russia's flagship Aeroflot airline and put together a media industry.

In 1996, Berezovsky led a group of the country's biggest tycoons in backing Yeltsin's long-shot reelection campaign. Soon after, he bragged to the *Financial Times* that he and six other financiers—who he said controlled half the Russian economy—got the president reelected. It was those seven men the Russian media dubbed the "oligarchs." "Now we have the right to occupy government posts and enjoy the fruits of our victory," Berezovsky said.[12]

Several insiders have told the Berezovsky-Putin story, but none as well as Sergei Dorenko, a former news anchor at Channel 1, Russia's top station when Berezovsky controlled it in the 1990s. I spoke to the handsome journalist, whose deadpan baritone is unmistakable to Russians, in Rublyovka, the suburb housing Moscow's wealthiest. Dorenko asked that we meet at his club for SUV owners, nestled next to a helicopter dealership.

Berezovsky had hired him in 1999 to anchor a series of Sunday evening news analysis programs that would assault the opposition, which was battling for control of the Kremlin ahead of a presidential election the following year. It was then, when Yeltsin's deeply unpopular presidency was coming to an end with no plausible successor, that Berezovsky assumed a central role in concocting the unlikely choice of the scarcely known Vladimir Putin. Having recently climbed coattails to become the head of the Federal Security Service, the FSB—formerly part of the KGB—Putin was appointed prime minister that August in a move that shocked the establishment. No one predicted he would last long—except for Berezovsky. Dorenko remembered the businessman-cum-covert-strategist as the only member of "the Family," as the Kremlin kitchen cabinet was dubbed, who believed in victory in the election that loomed the following June. "You take care of the masses," Dorenko said Berezovsky told him. "And I'll take care of the elite."

A popular former prime minister named Yevgeny Primakov and

Moscow's then-powerful Mayor Yuri Luzhkov headed the opposition to the Kremlin. As the election approached, Dorenko used his program to pour libelous vitriol on them. He told me Berezovsky was also vital to the Kremlin's forthcoming victory because "he forced other people to believe in it. Everyone else in Yeltsin's circle was thinking of where to flee to save themselves—but Berezovsky went around yelling, 'We'll defeat them all, *defeat them all!*' and kept it up even after falling ill with pneumonia. While he was lying on a hospital bed with an intravenous needle in him, I kept saying, 'Stop yelling, Borya, lie still.'"

When he was well enough, Berezovsky flew across the country in his private jet persuading influential governors to defect from the Luzhkov-Primakov alliance. "Explaining things like a chess master," he almost single-handedly cobbled together a pro-Kremlin political party called Unity. On New Year's Eve, Yeltsin dramatically resigned, appointing Putin acting president. The new heir had already captured public support by launching a popular second war in Chechnya that—after the decade of humiliating deferral to the West—fed a growing nationalism and eagerness for confrontation. With Putin's approval ratings skyrocketing, his ascension virtually assured him victory in the election three months later.

But the alliance between Berezovsky and his new cronies in government soon began crumbling. In June, the prickly tycoon, now a member of parliament, wrote an open letter criticizing new legislation aimed at boosting Putin's powers largely by reining in the country's regional governors. Then he said he'd be obliged to vote against the bill, which represented a "threat to Russia's territorial integrity and democracy." Berezovsky's open break with the president brought threats of prosecution for fraud in connection with his holdings in Aeroflot, among other large companies. Before the end of the year, he'd fled to London, where he remained in exile, fiercely criticizing the Kremlin and bankrolling opposition groups until his suicide in 2013.

Some of the lurid details of Berezovsky's fall emerged in a London courtroom two years before his death, when he sued Roman Abramovich, his former protégé, for $6.8 billion, saying that Abramovich had bilked him of his share of Sibneft, ORT television (now Channel 1) and other businesses by bullying him into selling his stakes before handing the companies to the government. The case was fascinating for its details not only of how some of the oligarchs acquired their Soviet spoils, but also how Putin later snatched some of them back. Abramovich, whose fortune under Putin soared to an estimated seventeen billion dollars, claimed he owed Berezovsky nothing after having paid him billions for his political influence. He explained that the two had met on a private yacht in 1994 to agree that Berezovsky would use his Kremlin connections to persuade the government to privatize oil fields Abramovich would buy in a closed auction. In return for Berezovsky's political protection—in Russian, *krysha*, literally "roof"—Abramovich said he financed the older man's luxurious lifestyle by chartering planes, booking five-star Riviera hotels and buying resort houses costing many hundreds of millions of dollars.

Losing the case deeply humiliated Berezovsky, who was ordered to pay Abramovich more than fifty million dollars for his legal fees. His fortune now believed to be seriously depleted—he sold an Andy Warhol painting and was rumored to have borrowed five thousand dollars to pay for a plane ticket—he withdrew from public life. In April 2013, he hanged himself in a locked bathroom of a mansion outside London. In an interview with the Russian edition of *Forbes* magazine days earlier, he'd said he wanted nothing more than to return to Russia. "Khodorkovsky saved himself," he reflected. "That doesn't mean I have lost myself. But I've lived through a lot more of my own reevaluations and disappointments than Khodorkovsky. I lost the meaning."[13] Unloved as he was back home, his death nevertheless came as a shock, marking the end of an era as well as another gratifying victory for the president whom Berezovsky, more than anyone else, had helped create. As if to confirm that interpretation, Putin's spokesman said Berezovsky had recently written the Russian leader to beg forgiveness for his "many mistakes."

According to Dorenko, what had really finished the magnate in Russia were his political aspirations: winning the presidency for Putin had been only part of his ambition. Eager to become more than a backroom Kremlin power broker, the oligarch had approached the president with the idea of creating two new political parties, modeled on the American system, one of which would be headed by Berezovsky himself. "So he went to Putin," Dorenko explained, "but he failed to understand that he was sitting opposite someone who was already president.

" 'Borya,' I told him, 'to you he's no longer Volodya [a diminutive of the name Vladimir]. Look above his head and you'll see the seal of an imperial eagle. From the moment he took the president's seat, you became just one of his subjects. Not a citizen but a subject.'"

That observation says much more about the nature of Russian rule than about Putin himself. When the Marquis de Custine visited Russia in 1839, the French aristocrat was struck by the servility of even the highborn. Custine, who would write *Empire of the Czar: A Journey through Eternal Russia* shortly after returning to France, noted the Russian court's instant switch from its ordinarily relaxed behavior to groveling whenever the emperor appeared. Without suggesting that obsequiousness was or is universal in Russia, I think bowing to the highest authority, even by the rich, was typical. That's largely because the image of the sovereign-autocrat's power, regardless of his real strength, is crucial for keeping the system from collapsing from infighting. Berezovsky became the exception that proved the rule—the rich will almost always stay rich only if they show fealty.

After becoming president in the all-or-nothing battle against the Kremlin's opposition, Putin may well have felt he had to destroy all potential opponents—including Berezovsky and many others who helped install him in office—because he lacked his own power base. He built authority not by enacting a dictatorship of the law, which seemed to be an excuse for using law enforcement agencies to destroy his rivals, but by relying on the support of a traditional oligarchy empowered by the Kremlin's coercive authority. He did it methodically. After curtailing governors' powers, then threatening some of the country's leading businesses with tax fraud investigations, he went on to oversee the state takeover of the pro-Luzhkov media—among Russia's best—all the while gauging public and political reaction before taking the next step. Neither stood in his way. Clearing his path for himself, he created a far more corrupt and inequitable system than anything seen under Yeltsin.

Like most regimes not based on genuine popular support in an era of open access to information, Putin's is inherently unstable and requires vigilant maintenance of the leader's strong image, however antiquated that may now appear to foreigners. He regularly tells private businessmen what they should be doing with their money and assets. One of his tirades, at the height of Russia's oil boom in 2008, helped push the entire economy off a precipice. It came during a visit to the Volga River city of Nizhny Novgorod, where he demanded to know why the CEO of a company named Mechel was absent from a meeting with metals executives. "Illness is illness," he said after learning the billionaire was at home sick. "But I think he should get well as soon as possible. Otherwise we'll have to send him a doctor and clean up all the problems."

After he accused the company of price fixing and tax fraud, it lost six billion dollars overnight, depressing the entire Russian stock market by 5 percent, the start of a downward spiral soon made far worse by the global financial crisis. Those consequences were evidently far less important to Putin than demonstrating that he remained in charge.

———

Myths about the extent of the chaos and criminality that characterized Yeltsin's 1990s form an important part of Putin's image. The Kremlin's story is that he saved Russia, or at least restored it to working order, by ending wanton crime, taming the oligarchs and putting the country's riches back to work for the people. That he allowed them to continue to work, but for his own benefit and that of his cronies, is closer to the truth.

Former First Deputy Prime Minister Boris Nemtsov, who was among Yeltsin's "young reformers" and once his chosen successor, knows many of the oligarchs well. Shortly after Putin became president in 2000, Nemtsov organized a meeting between him and the country's most powerful Yeltsin-era businessmen. The purpose was to arrange a truce: if the oligarchs promised to stay out of politics, the president would call off the tax police and prosecutors who had begun investigating top companies.

Nemtsov, a tall, swarthy bachelor with a sharp tongue, appears on glossy magazine covers, sometimes bare-chested, but more often in blue blazer with an open-collar white shirt. During one of my interviews with him in his spacious, high-ceilinged apartment in one of Moscow's seven neo-Gothic Stalin-era skyscrapers, he challenged Putin's argument that the Yeltsin years in the 1990s were rampant with mass theft. At the same time, he acknowledged that most Russians associated that grim period with democracy.

"We know what happened then. Unemployment. Other huge problems in the economy. Many people impoverished, children wandering homeless. So people still connect freedom with economic hardship."

Indeed, the hardship was so overwhelming that privatization and other reforms were often aimed not at an equitable distribution of former Soviet property but at jump-starting an economy ruined by decades of consummate inefficiency and woeful mismanagement. With factories idle, oil wells drying up and a huge part of the national workforce unemployed—as if the country were in a fatal depression—the first priority of the young reformers under President Yeltsin was to get assets and enterprises as quickly as possible into the hands of people who might get them working, never mind how.

One of those reformers was Maxim Boycko, a chief architect of privatization. In 1992, he shared a cramped Moscow office with a thirty-two-year-old Harvard law school student who helped him act as a liaison between the government and advisers working under Harvard professor Jeffrey Sachs. Boycko, still a very youthful-looking executive of a top advertising agency when I interviewed him years later, told me the old Soviet managers didn't want to give up control of their state-owned enterprises because they sucked out money for themselves while running their companies into the ground. Among the privatizers' main goals was to somehow rip the companies from their control. "You shouldn't assume ours was an orderly country with a national consensus," Boycko said in flawless English. "Now that socialism is behind us, we can sit down quietly and start building capitalism and democracy with due order under due process. That was absolutely not true then."

During the country's mass privatization, each Russian was issued a voucher that could be sold or used to buy shares in a wave of auctions of the old enterprises. But contrary to conventional wisdom that the voucher system was aimed at a fair distribution of state assets, it was little more than an openly acknowledged bribe to get Russians to accept privatization. As for the later privatization schemes—in which the country's oil industry went to Berezovsky, Khodorkovsky and a few other Kremlin insiders for next to nothing in rigged auctions—Boycko said, "The top consideration was finding people with the ability to invest in oil and other enterprises whose production was in very serious decline, or to attract investment."

A partner of the New York law firm White and Case, John Erickson was newly arrived in Moscow in 1992 when the World Bank approached him with a request to advise Boycko's agency, the State Committee for State Property Management, or GKI (for the Russian name Goskomimushchestvo). Erickson said opposition from competing state agencies controlled by old-guard managers created tremendous pressure to move quickly. He told me he'd get a call at four o'clock in the afternoon, "and they'd say, 'We need a draft investment company regulation on Yeltsin's desk by nine o'clock tomorrow morning.' In a sense it was a race. The over-riding concern, over and above doing it perfectly properly, was speed. Get it done, get the genie out of the bottle before somebody could turn it back." Although there was "a lot of chaos" in the 1990s, Erickson believes the enactment of new, Western-style laws meant the country was Westernizing.

In the murky free-for-all that followed communism's collapse, most successful businessmen exploited loopholes or resorted to outright crime to compile their huge fortunes. At one point, Berezovsky relied on a criminal gang of Chechens to do his dirty work. But although the economic chaos was real and disturbing enough, it was only part of the picture then. Yelt-sin guaranteed individual rights and freedom of speech. He also installed the young technocrats in government who drafted the country's Western-izing, democratizing reforms. Rampant as they were, crime and corruption took place on a smaller scale than now. According to the government's own anticorruption committee, the average Russian company paid a whopping $135,000 in bribes each year after the first four years of Putin's presidency—up from $23,000 when he took office.

In short, Putin didn't clean up crime. He only made it look that way by institutionalizing crime after making certain the Kremlin was the domi-nant player. "Whatever the apparent gains of Russia under Putin," observed Stanford professor and future U.S. ambassador to Russia Michael McFaul about the myth that Putin had rescued the country from the bankrupt, law-less 1990s, "the gains would have been greater if democracy had survived."[14]

As for his promise to leave the oligarchs alone if they stayed out of poli-tics, Putin failed to keep his end of the bargain. The oligarchs who do the Kremlin's bidding continue reaping huge fortunes. Those who don't have been prime targets in the president's attack on anyone who stands in his way or even hints at the possibility.

Putin threatens and destroys even some who give no indication of opposing him, only of getting too big for their breeches. Like the seventeenth-century French nobleman Nicolas Fouquet, who hosted a party so lavish it gave Louis XIV an excuse to arrest him, Azeri business-man Telman Ismailov found himself in trouble in 2009 after throwing an opening party for his new billion-dollar Turkish hotel, which has ten res-taurants and a beach with nine thousand tons of artificial sand.[15] Ismailov paid Sharon Stone, Richard Gere, Mariah Carey, Paris Hilton and Tom

Jones to attend. At one point, he was reported to have danced as hundred-dollar bills rained from the ceiling. Many believe the images angered Putin, who is especially sensitive about oligarchs' conspicuous spending abroad. A close ally of former Moscow Mayor Yuri Luzhkov—who, after his failed challenge to the Kremlin, maintained an uneasy relationship with Putin despite showing all the outward attributes of loyalty—Ismailov also owned a sprawling outdoor market in the capital where Chinese and other traders sold hundreds of millions of dollars' worth of contraband goods. It was soon shut down before Ismailov temporarily fled to Turkey.

The conventional wisdom in the West is that hard work tends to be rewarded. In Russia, many who build wealth still often see it confiscated in one way or another. If the relationship between Russia's wealthy and its leaders resembles its iterations in previous eras, however, Moscow's new money is changing the city's old face. Like another transplant from the West, a new development of corporate glass skyscrapers called Moscow City looms over everything built before it. One of the antiseptic new buildings, the billion-dollar Mercury City Tower, was Europe's tallest upon its completion—until the showcase of angular, pink mirrored glass was overtaken by its neighbor the Federation Tower.

The latest installments of Moscow's grand architectural projects, together with many smaller complexes of office and residential buildings, are cropping up like the proverbial mushrooms. Although most of the new construction is unimaginative—one friend complained that "rich Russia is even less attractive than impoverished Russia"—that's hardly unique to Moscow. The splurging by the superrich has helped make the city one of the world's most expensive, but that, too—like its filthy and often slushy streets—apparently must be lived with. What often seems intolerable, even for the superrich—"often" being daily or twice daily—is the city's horrendous traffic, which leaves millions stuck in cars for hours, breathing terribly polluted air. A 2013 survey by the satellite navigation company TomTom rated Moscow traffic as the world's worst.

Igor Shein, editor of the Russian edition of the *Robb Report*, a consumer magazine for the very wealthy, said it will be difficult to do something about that. "Russians are behaving better abroad," he told me—a claim visitors from other countries to Europe's luxurious resorts may challenge. "But back home, they still behave very immodestly. They drive like crazy and do what they want in all sorts of other ways."

A century and a half ago, the Marquis de Custine feared an explosion in the country he saw as "a cauldron of boiling water, tightly closed and placed on a fire that is becoming hotter and hotter." With the lack of concern on the part of today's superrich for the people as a whole rivaling that of earlier eras, the anger is again never far from the surface. The wealthy also know in their bones that their power is fragile, as do the rulers about their own.

My grandmother
Serafima (left) in a
Moscow park with an
unidentified friend.

The Khuzikhanov family
in Kazan. My grandfather
Mutakhar is on the top
right next to his brother,
Lukman. His parents
are in the second row,
along with Mutakhar's
unidentified girlfriend.
Shamil, the third brother,
is on the bottom right next
to his sister.

Serafima's husband Zhora
with his mother and
daughter Natasha, who is
ill with meningitis.

3
Poverty

Poverty is no vice.

—Old Russian saying

V isiting Russia for the first time seemed like a homecoming long delayed by the Soviet refusal to grant any of my family a visa. What struck me most on arriving in Moscow on a hot June day in 1991 was how shoddily constructed the prefabricated housing was. Eager to learn about the land whose language I spoke but about which I otherwise knew very little, I found myself trying to disguise my revulsion at the way its people were forced to live.

I would spend the summer in a residential area of the city's northwest, where acres and acres of nearly identical apartment complexes looked like slums built with carelessness and disregard for architectural integrity, not to mention aesthetic sensibility, even when brand-new. The concrete blocks hulked along a stretch of overgrown weeds that passed for a park and included several abandoned building sites—locals had stolen the bricks for use at their dachas, I was informed, because none were available for sale— and a padlocked "palace of culture" with an empty theater and library. Networks of dirt paths through uncut grass connected the buildings to pockmarked asphalt sidewalks.

Like many Moscow buildings, the one that would be my temporary resi- dence had a facade of unattractively colored panels glued together with a white substance that had dripped down from the joints, an assault to the senses that seemed to signify contempt for its occupants. Inside, the bare concrete entryway was filthy and the shuddering little elevator smelled of body odor and the dried, tobacco-soaked spit that dotted the floor. Although I'd been prepared to see widespread deprivation, I was astonished to learn I'd arrived at a desired address in an elite neighborhood to which lucky residents had flocked from the polluted center.

The shock didn't last long. Regardless of the size of their bank accounts, almost everyone in the Soviet Union lived in conditions that people in developed countries would consider impoverished. The apartment I occupied was small but cozy. The minuscule bathroom had only one faucet for the sink and bathtub—the tap swung from one to the other—and there would be no hot water for the month of August, supposedly for annual maintenance. But the apartment's interior, like many I saw that summer, had been decorated with care, albeit with garish velour furniture. The building's residents, mostly middle-class and middle-aged, spent much of their time grumbling about queues: store shelves were often empty. On my first trip to a local supermarket, I saw people waiting in line for as long as four hours for slices of beef that appeared blackened from rot. Thanks to a severe shortage of tobacco in addition to almost everything else, vendors at outdoor food markets sold glass jars filled with nearly spent cigarette butts.

It seemed logical to think that a little free trade would transform life for people whose days seemed to revolve around scrounging for food and goods that I'd always taken for granted. However, Western optimism that Russia would quickly rebound when restrictions were lifted after the collapse of communism sounded naive even then. Now, in the second decade of the twenty-first century, there are no such lines at supermarket chains where everything is available—if you can afford it. Some of Moscow's huge new stores are in shopping centers near suburban apartment complexes that knock up against old villages that had lain beyond the capital's sprawl until very recently. The new buildings have something in common with the plans for share-everything communities drawn by idealists during the early Soviet years. The fancy stores, gyms, kindergartens and other amenities and services of the new, capitalist versions make them islands of security where residents enjoy at least partial insulation from the dangers and uncertainties of inner Moscow.

Drive beyond the capital's expansive limits, however, and you encounter a very different country, only slightly changed from the Soviet Union I saw in 1991. A smattering of officials, businesspeople and Mafia members ensure that rural Russia has some of Moscow's trappings: garish brick mansions, Toyota Land Cruisers with dark tinted windows and new restaurants. But poverty is endemic, beginning abruptly where Moscow ends, although the boundary keeps changing as the city's outskirts push ever outward, riding roughshod over old wooden settlements. Beyond them, decent roads give way to uneven asphalt riddled with gaping potholes that often degenerates to barely passable dirt roads in impoverished villages. Even some sections of the highway to St. Petersburg, the main road linking the country's two largest cities, still have only two lanes, which sometimes pass rows of traditional rural cottages. Tourists admiring the ornate latticework of those little structures, ubiquitous from the Baltic Sea thousands of miles east into Siberia, may be visited by fairy-tale images of princes, peasants and firebirds. The reality is less magical. Many houses have no indoor plumbing and most toilets are in outhouses.

Taking account of the pervasiveness of poverty is important for understanding Russia because its specter hangs over even those not directly affected. Today's dilapidation is evidence of the latest stage in Russia's long history of widespread, often overwhelming destitution in the countryside, where many peasants—who made up 80 percent of the population as recently as the early twentieth century—have barely been able to eke out a living from the fields for as long as anyone can remember. Under the tsars, much of the land was owned by rich absentees who cared little about their peasants, most of whom remained serfs until 1861. Soviet industrialization, launched in the 1930s with the aim of making the USSR into a great military power, further hindered the development of agriculture. All investment for new factories was squeezed from miserably oppressed farmers already suffering the crippling effects of forced collectivization. It may therefore seem surprising that contemporary rural Russia is sometimes even more depressed than it was under the last decades of Soviet rule, and that many people are poorer than they'd been as collective farmers.

The village of Priamukhino, a scattering of houses half lost in forests and fields some ninety minutes northwest of Moscow, is no exception. The settlement would easily go unnoticed except for its church. Standing at the top of a rise reached by a narrow road, the stately yellow neoclassical structure, like many of the country's rural churches, completes a picture that is as sad as it is beautiful, as if it has survived from a nineteenth-century novel. The melancholy—partly prompted by the church's peeling paint, grounds full of weeds and the short-lived foliage of willowy, white birches—seems to have something to do with the resignation that summer's respite is short, nature is powerful and life is hard.

Not all is well in Priamukhino, if it ever has been. The church was saved from collapse in the 1990s by an energetic young priest named Andrei Nikolaev, a relative newcomer who became a local fixture. One freezing night in 2006, local firefighters called to Father Andrei's house arrived to find it enveloped in flames. Inside they found the remains of five people. The priest had burned to death together with his wife and three young daughters in an apparent act of arson that shocked nearby residents. "Notwithstanding Christian forgiveness," said the regional governor upon taking personal charge of the investigation, "such crimes are never forgiven."

In contemporary Russia, however, such crimes are also rarely solved. And because Father Andrei's killing, if that's what it was, followed several suspected murders of other rural clergy members, it appeared to reflect a growing malaise in the Russian countryside. I wanted to find out the extent to which that was true.

Father Andrei's suspected murder echoed history. In the mid-nineteenth century, a wave of arson swept through Russia at a time when radical anarchist and revolutionary movements sought to undermine the tsars' rule. Priamukhino happened to play a role in those movements as the ancestral family seat of Mikhail Bakunin, a nineteenth-century aristocrat who became a founder of anarchism, which critics blamed for spreading terrorism. Nevertheless, Lev Tolstoy, Ivan Turgenev and the influential critic Vissarion Belinsky were among the literary celebrities who visited Bakunin's sprawling estate, which surrendered to serious decay under Soviet rule. After 1991, would-be scholars and hippie types joined the self-described anarchists who camped on the estate grounds to sing, debate, or simply hang out.

When I visited Father Andrei's house several weeks after the catastrophe, children's toys and bits of furniture were visible among the charred remains. The house had stood on the side of a muddy lane along with some twenty similarly weather-beaten wooden structures. It was an eerie sight: most of the houses were abandoned. At the moment, the only sign of life, apart from barking dogs, cawing crows and the occasional distant rumbling of lone cars, was the sound of a rake. It belonged to Nikolai Gavrilov, who was clearing slush from the tiny front yard of a house several plots down from Father Andrei's, one of only three still inhabited on the street.

Although it was unclear where the scrappy grass of Gavrilov's property ended and the communal road of muck began, he was doing a meticulous job. Wearing surplus military trousers tucked into high felt boots, the sixty-four-year-old appeared prematurely aged. His skin was battered, his eyes squinty and his large nose crooked. European visitors to nineteenth-century Russia sometimes observed that peasants often expressed an innate hospitality, even sweetness, to visitors, despite being very hard-pressed. That's rarely true now. Looking up from his work as if his dearest wish were to avoid the trouble outsiders often brought, Gavrilov initially refused to answer questions about his age or anything else, including his neighbor Father Andrei.

"Everything's fine here!" he barked in apparent defiance of his surroundings. "Just like everywhere else."

Had life changed during the past decade?

"No!"

Had a lot of people left? Most of the houses seemed empty.

"People come and go as they please; is there anything wrong with that?"

Some time later, Gavrilov admitted feeling sorry for Father Andrei's dead children but said he'd never spoken to the priest himself. The other neighbors I saw among the few who remained also refused to speculate about the cause of the fire. But some complained that the national media had seized on a theory that village drunks killed Father Andrei in anger at his refusal to give them money for drink. A domestic dispute was far more likely, they said.

Nazira Babaeva discounted that theory. She lived a short drive from the village church in a Soviet brick apartment house made more forlorn than usual because it stands alone amid open fields. Mounting a filthy concrete stairway to Babaeva's floor, I entered her clean but shabby apartment with its worn, brown-colored furniture. A handsome woman who worked in the local post office, she told me that Father Andrei's death broke her heart. Tears formed in her eyes when she said, *"Batyushka"*—an archaic word for "father," commonly used for priests—"did great things here." Chief among them, she said, was providing villagers with counsel and help and advising them about the power of prayer. Before he came in the 1990s, she continued, "I didn't know who I was, even whether I was christened."

Babaeva raced to Father Andrei's house when she heard about the fire on the freezing night in December of 2006. "It smelled of burning flesh, but I hoped the family had gotten out and the smell was of their cats." Her voice dropped to a whisper. "It's very bad for us now." Remembering Father Andrei, she mentioned an operation her young daughter was scheduled to have on a day she wasn't permitted to leave work. "He was the only one I could ask for help, and he took her, he didn't abandon us."

"They all got on well," she said of the priest and his wife. "Mother and father loved their children, and I never heard a sharp word from anyone." She also discounted the theory that drunks wanted to steal the church's icons. "They're drunk, but kind. Everyone loved Father Andrei. I think it was..." She broke off, choked with tears, then resumed in a clear voice. "Only God almighty knows what happened."

Priamukhino lies in the region of Tver, whose capital is the medieval city of the same name on the upper Volga River. More important than Moscow in early Russian history, it was called Kalinin under Soviet rule. Tver's residents like to cite Nikolai Gogol's famous quip about Russia's two great misfortunes: fools and bad roads. In the 1990s, one of the region's representatives in parliament tried to reverse Tver's disintegration by rebuilding the roads. Sergei Yushenkov was a well-liked former Red Army officer who had taught Marxism-Leninism at a Moscow military academy before giving key support to Boris Yeltsin during the coup attempt in 1991. He became a liberal icon, crusading against corruption and in favor of individual rights, often on television. But the lawmaker died when a gunman shot him outside his Moscow apartment in 2003 in one of Russia's many unsolved high-profile murders, and his region's roads remain in terrible shape.

As for fools, residents say people smart enough to leave did so long ago, after the region's main employers, obsolete Soviet-era factories, had closed along with its collective farms, part of a dramatic series of changes that transformed Russian society. Elena Orlova, the head of the surrounding Kuvshinovo district, said its population dropped from twenty thousand to sixteen thousand in a few years. "Nothing is being produced here," the earnest, middle-aged administrator lamented. "People have lost their connection to the land, and it's frightening. There's nothing to keep the young here anymore."

Kuvshinovo is named after Yulia Kuvshinovo, who founded a local paper factory that employed three thousand workers at the turn of the twentieth century. Under Soviet rule, the factory doubled as a social welfare system, building schools, a theater, a hospital and a sports complex. Now its seven hundred employees work and live amid a rotting infrastructure it no longer supports. Orlova warned me not to try to equate life in provincial towns with the big city because the two are "completely different." Kuvshinovo's transformation mirrored changes throughout Russia, where the GDP fell 34 percent between 1991 and 1995—a larger contraction than in the United States during the Great Depression—while wages plummeted along with employment. Crime, including murders, doubled.[1]

Some of the direst conditions can be found in a number of Russia's four hundred so-called monocities, whose residents largely depend on single industries. Their plight exploded on national television soon after the global financial crisis of 2008 during mass protests in a small town near St. Petersburg called Pikalevo, where the closing of a factory belonging to one of the richest oligarchs, metals magnate Oleg Deripaska, disrupted the lives of nearly everyone. After the local utility cut hot water and heating, residents blocked a highway, demanding that Putin intervene. He swooped in by helicopter to be filmed calling the plant owners "cockroaches" and forcing a chastened Deripaska to restart the factory. Elsewhere, protesters braved the blows of riot police at small, isolated rallies in the far-eastern city of Vladivostok, the exclave of Kaliningrad, on the Baltic Sea, and other regions to less effect. Although the government said it would help more than three hundred monocities diversify their economies, there's very little evidence of anything having been done there.

The poverty and despair are contributing to a national population crisis that a tiny increase in birthrates in 2009—thanks partly to financial bonuses for baby-producing parents—hasn't resolved. Reluctance to conceive children whose lives would be difficult and possibly short is a major cause. Another is the high mortality rate sustained by poor diet, persistent smoking, rampant alcoholism and crippling disease. After seven decades of enormous Soviet sacrifices in pursuit of a better life, three times more Russians now die of heart-related illnesses than do Americans or Europeans. The life expectancy of the average Russian male in 2012—when the population declined for the twentieth year in a row—was sixty-four years, up from fifty-nine a few years earlier but still fully a dozen fewer than for an American. In that respect, the country ranks 166th in the world, one peg above Gambia.

While the Kremlin says it considers the country's shrinking population one of its most serious problems, officials have done almost nothing to tackle poverty, one of its main causes. According to the government's own reports, seventeen million people, more than 12 percent of the population, live below the poverty line, which it sets at monthly earnings of less than $220. But critics say those numbers are misleading in the way Kremlin figures usually are, and not only because the minimum assortment of consumer goods the government deems necessary for survival would leave people ravenous if they tried to hold down a job paying that amount. Although incomes rose several times during last decade's oil boom, inflation grew as fast or faster, especially the price of staple goods. That erased the gains in many people's incomes, while average monthly pensions rose to only roughly $300 and the gap between rich and poor yawned ever wider. One recent study showed that while the richest Russians doubled their wealth in the last two decades, two-thirds of the population are no better off than they were in 1991, and the poor only half as well off than they were then.[2] All in all, the World Bank has calculated that roughly a quarter of the population is "highly vulnerable to poverty," with more hovering just above the poverty line.[3]

Standing off a deeply potholed road, the maternity clinic nearest Priamukhino looked little different than it did a century ago. Charmingly quaint as its two-story wooden facade may appear, the floorboards and peeling paint inside inspired little confidence even before I noticed the ancient look of the medical instruments. But the director proudly announced that her clinic continues to host several births a year despite the fall of the national birthrate to a third of its level in the 1980s, the last decade of Soviet rule. The numbers remain worryingly low, partly because infant mortality is very high.

A short drive away, the minuscule village of Lopatino, its slumping cottages lining another muddy dirt road through wooded hills, had sunk to being almost moribund, even tinged with apocalypse. All but two of the houses were empty during my visit. Tree branches had broken through the windows of some of the abandoned structures, several of which had gaping holes in their roofs. Tatyana Yevseeva lived alone in one of the occupied houses. Small but hardy-looking in her old housecoat and black shawl, the elderly woman's sparkling eyes and warmth of spirit belied her struggle to survive. Like her few neighbors who remained in the region, she lived mostly on what she grew, preserved and raised, including potatoes and pigs. To help plant and harvest the vegetables, her five children visited periodically from Estonia and Ukraine as well as elsewhere in Russia.

Yevseeva insisted I stay for tea she could hardly have afforded to share. Unlike many of the region's elderly, she was neither dejected nor angry. On the contrary, she displayed a cheeky wit in the singsong lilt she gave to a dialect that had survived nearly a century of communist conformism. "We live not badly; I can't complain, dear." *Ne khudo*, her archaic term for "not badly," sounded almost poetic. But when she stopped chuckling and turned serious, it was to say, "It's just that everyone has left, there's nowhere to go for a chat and of course it gets very lonely. But what can you do?"

Yevseeva's heartbreaking poverty and isolation was stark proof that life for many used to be at least materially richer under the USSR. She was born and lived her entire life in Lopatino, where the local administration employed her as a "work brigade" leader. Now eighty years old and plagued by eye problems, she had to walk half a day, mostly uphill, to a neighboring village to buy medicine. The town authorities helped by supplying wood for cooking and heating to supplement the logs she bought from local woodcutters. "The biggest problem is that young people steal my wood," she said with a sigh.

Several incongruous magazine photographs of teenage pop stars were pinned to the stained orange wallpaper of her tiny house. Although an outhouse served as her toilet, Yevseeva was fortunate to have running water in her kitchen. That might boost the price of her house to several hundred dollars if she succeeded in selling it, but she said she'd be left with nothing if she did. "There's no money to fix anything but how could I leave my home? I built and built it, mostly with my own hands. And when my time comes I'll die here, lying on the stove"—the tiled source of heat and comfort. "What's wrong with that?" she said with a smile.

Despite its crisis, the Tver region could have been thriving. Its land is arable and its climate temperate, at least relative to most of Russia. More important, it's close to Moscow, the nexus of a highly centralized economy that's the source of up to 80 percent of the GDP, according to some estimates. Tver would almost certainly prosper in other circumstances, under a different kind of government with different priorities.

Dramatic upheaval almost decimated the tsarist economy's agrarian foundation in the early twentieth century, when communist policies forced the rapid industrialization and urbanization that transformed Soviet society. My great-grandmother Polina Stepanova was among the uprooted, driven partly by famine from a two-story house in her native Volga River city of Kazan during the tumultuous early 1920s, when poverty was nearly universal. The former seat of a powerful khanate of Turkic Tatars—one of the successors to the Mongol Empire that ruled over what became European Russia from the thirteenth to fourteenth centuries—Kazan was racked by the civil war that followed the 1917 Revolution. It wiped out the landed gentry and battered the small bourgeoisie to which my ancestors belonged, having pulled themselves out of serfdom barely two generations earlier.

Leaving behind her husband—a school inspector whose grain-merchant father was the family patriarch—Polina took her two daughters, my grandmother Serafima and her sister Kaleria, to the fertile southern Krasnodar region. There they eventually moved into a large room in a communal apartment with Polina's second husband, an accountant like her. A meek, intelligent child, Serafima was nine when the Revolution took place. Never taking to her new home or her alcoholic, bullying stepfather, she was lucky to be enrolled in medical school. On graduating, she was assigned to a tuberculosis ward in a former palace thirty miles outside Moscow, where rural villages would soon become suburbs. Serafima began specializing in radiology.

Her broad face gave her a distinguished if not quite beautiful appearance. Generous and forgiving by all accounts, she was a saintly figure whose turbulent childhood reinforced her highly cautious nature and susceptibility to bouts of despair. Working under the socialized healthcare system suited her, and she soon earned a reputation for being expert at reading very poor-quality X-rays to determine whether patients had contracted tuberculosis. Soon after arriving, Serafima fell in love with a student at an aviation research center, an institution of great Soviet pride, in the neighboring town of Zhukovsky.

A gifted draftsman, Georgy Leimer—nicknamed Zhora—was handsome, with thick, fair hair, a pointed nose and a furrowed brow that added to his serious demeanor. His German surname came from his grandfather, a Bavarian beer brewer who had settled in Russia in 1855, one of the so-called Volga Germans recruited under Alexander II to help modernize the country. Although Georgy's surname was the only thing about him that was remotely German, it was a liability during those murderous years. In the early 1930s, Stalin launched the first expulsions of Communist Party members, known as purges, and the authorities began filling the Gulag in earnest. The randomness of victims' selection and guilt by association helped spread fear. And the worst was still ahead.

Still, Serafima adopted Zhora's name when they married. After he joined the nearby Central Aerohydrodynamic Institute as an aircraft designer working under the legendary flight pioneer Andrei Tupolev—whose group would create the famous planes bearing his name—the young couple moved into a two-room apartment in a simple clapboard house, along with Zhora's mother and, soon after, a baby daughter.

Disaster struck in 1936, when little Natasha died of meningitis at the age of four. Although she had no proof, Serafima blamed herself for infecting her beloved daughter with bacteria from her tuberculosis dispensary. Stricken with guilt, she was unable to sleep until Zhora prevailed upon her to travel to the Crimean Black Sea shore, where she was treated at a sanatorium—treatment she could afford, thanks to her medical union. Zhora's letters to her included tender admonishments to stop crying, intimate little jokes and insistence that the past couldn't be changed.

A year later, on a freezing night in November 1937 at the height of Stalin's Great Terror, a knock sounded at their door. The NKVD secret police, predecessor to the KGB, had accused Tupolev of plotting to organize a Russian Fascist party, an obviously, even ridiculously, fabricated charge. His protégés and subordinates were also being targeted, including Zhora, who was arrested that night. Like countless other wives and mothers of the millions who disappeared, Serafima joined long lines of desperate women who were queuing in vain at prisons and NKVD buildings for information about their loved ones. After more than a year waiting outside the Leningrad prison where her son Lev Gumilev was held, Anna Akhmatova described their despair in her poem "Requiem."

> *I learned how faces fall,*
> *How fear looks out from lowered eyes,*
> *How suffering inscribes cruel pages*
> *Of marks like cuneiforms on cheeks,*

How curls of dark and ash-blond hair
Suddenly turn silver,
The smile fades on submissive lips,
And fear trembles inside a hollow laugh.
I pray not for myself alone
But all who stood there with me
In bitter cold and July heat
Under a blind red wall.[4]

Pregnant with her second child, Serafima suffered a miscarriage.

After the Nazi invasion of the Soviet Union in 1941, she and the rest of her clinic's staff were relocated to the Siberian city of Irkutsk, where some of the worst of the war's wounded were being evacuated for treatment. Provided accommodation in a tiny wooden shack barely kept warm by a small cast-iron stove during a bitterly cold winter, she worked long hours in a military hospital. Having lost hope of ever seeing Zhora again, she caught the eye of a dashing surgeon, a Tatar from a distinguished family of doctors and intellectuals who happened to be from Serafima's home city of Kazan. The Revolution had scattered Mutakhar Khuzikhanov's family, and he, the eldest—a highly skilled doctor who published in Soviet medical journals—had settled in the North Caucasus city of Nalchik, where he married an ethnic Russian woman and started a family.

Desperate for another child despite her straitened circumstances, Serafima gave birth in February 1943 to a daughter after a romance with Mutakhar. Keeping little Tatyana alive was another struggle. To warm the baby on the coldest nights, Serafima stayed up so she could keep turning her to face the stove. No doubt stress was responsible for Serafima's failure to be able to nurse her. With no baby formula available, she was lucky to find a temporary wet nurse. Often poorly nourished and sick, Tatyana cried constantly, but she survived.

As war made already dire living conditions worse, Stalin reversed the few gains society can be said to have achieved under Soviet rule. Despite the turmoil of its early years, communism did help to level previously vast inequalities. Country estates were taken over by peasants, housing in cities was allocated to the poor and salaries were made more equitable. Under Stalin, however, inequality rose, and housing remained especially scarce.[5]

After the war, Serafima returned to Moscow, where she had no job and nowhere to live. Mother and daughter were forced to stay with various friends and relatives in a succession of communal apartments already crammed to capacity. They spent six months sleeping on the floor of a room belonging to a cousin of Serafima's named Olga Kiva. Two-year-old Tatyana cried and shouted for days, keeping everyone up many nights "as if in anger," Olga told me. Serafima and Tatyana later moved into a tiny basement room with the wife of Zhora's only brother, Anatoly, who had also been arrested, and the couple's daughter.

Serafima eventually found work at a tuberculosis dispensary in an old neighborhood of central Moscow. Given a room measuring all of eighty-six square feet, she felt very lucky. A former nursery in a once elegant apartment building with thick walls and large windows, the room was cozy and sunlit, and it overlooked the street. It was the first home Tatyana now remembers. My mother's first real memory of herself is of screaming there at the top of her lungs and not knowing why.

In his 1897 short story "Peasants," Chekhov—whose first career was as a doctor who often treated patients too poor to afford medical care—introduces a character who describes the effects of widespread destitution. Conditions were most deplorable in the countryside, where people lived "worse than cattle . . . they were coarse, dishonest, dirty, and drunken; they did not live at peace with one another but quarreled continually, because they feared, suspected, and despised each other."[6]

A century later, for many people, outright poverty was just a short jump from communist deprivation after the Soviet collapse in 1991 removed what little remained of a social safety net. Among the many millions left to fend for themselves was the family of my second cousin Ulugbek Khojaev. His grandfather, the brother of my mother's surgeon father Mutakhar, settled in Uzbekistan after their family fled Kazan. Although he soon disappeared without a trace after marrying an Uzbek woman, his enterprising son Taufik rose from construction worker to become the Soviet republic's transportation minister. "I was no dissident," the gregarious, down-to-earth former bigwig told me in the late 1990s at his house in the Uzbek capital, Tashkent, where he owned an electronics factory and cargo planes that hauled goods from Dubai. "But I could have risen to the very top if I'd kept my mouth shut."

I first met Taufik's son Ulugbek at a party in a cramped Moscow apartment in 1991, when he was in his thirties. Tall, handsome and smiling, he greeted me with the effusive generosity typical in Central Asia, asking about every one of my family members in an easy manner that made it seem as if he'd known me from childhood. Ulugbek's warmth—more than the usual importance that people from his part of the world impart to relations that wouldn't be considered particularly close in the West—reflected his extraordinary self-assuredness. An A student in Tashkent, he had moved in Moscow in 1979 to study engineering at the Bauman Moscow State Technical University, considered Russia's best.

He married an outgoing young woman named Natalia soon after graduating and by the time their first son, Sasha, was born in 1990, he was well on his way to a respectable academic career, teaching mechanical engineering while writing a doctoral dissertation on stress analysis in metals. Meanwhile, it was clear to them the Soviet economy was imploding. Natalia's job with the Communist Party youth organization, the Komsomol, granted her weekly visits to a special store that sold products unavailable elsewhere: caviar, cheese, even olive oil. But children's supplies were almost unobtainable anywhere. After lunch during the week, she would take time off work to scour the neighborhood shops for lines worth joining. Since diapers didn't exist, Natalia used the largest women's menstrual pads she could find. The most pressing problem, however, was baby formula, which was especially scarce because it was in great demand even by otherwise uninterested shoppers who snapped it up to barter for other products.

No Soviet-made baby formula was available, and imports were strictly rationed. But Ulugbek's volunteering to help unload trucks of it when they arrived at a local store at night earned him a double ration of four cans, which would last a day and a half. Because of the constant struggle, Natasha began supplementing the baby's diet with food and juice.

When Sasha's first birthday arrived, Natalia and Ulugbek could spare only a single American dollar to spend on a present. They took it to an Irish hard-currency supermarket, one of Moscow's first Western shops, where they bought an exotic fruit: bananas. Matters would only get worse. Prices were liberalized the following year—released from Soviet controls that had kept them very low—and inflation skyrocketed. "You could get by before because prices were low even if there was nothing to buy, and maybe you got lucky or you had friends or ties and could buy things on the black market," Ulugbek later recalled. "Now salaries suddenly became worthless." His amounted to six dollars a month. Unable to feed his family, he left academia, relying on his father's connections to help find a job in business.

Ulugbek's postcommunist transition was successful: he eventually went on to work for General Electric and other Western companies. Nevertheless, he sent Sasha to live and study in Germany (he and his younger brother Timur speak fluent English and German) because Russia is far from the kind of place he envisioned it would become when he could afford to buy only two apples a week. "Back then it was hard, but we didn't feel ruined," he says. "We weren't starving because we were doing all sorts of things to get by. We were never completely broke, and in many ways it was a happy time."

Thanks to his dark, non-Slavic complexion, xenophobic police often make a point of stopping Ulugbek on the street to demand his passport, sometimes even ordering him or his driver to head to a local police station for a formal check. Before Putin came to power in 2000, he says, "no one believed Russia would return to authoritarianism. Absolutely no one could have envisioned there would be a quiet counterrevolution, that tough limits on newspapers and television would return, that corruption would become far worse." In these times, he adds, the old optimism is gone.

More than that, although many ordinary people no longer struggle just to survive, much of Russia's outward prosperity is deceptive. "Half my friends eat porridge in order to be seen driving into town in their Volkswagens or BMWs," Natalia says. "That's the Russian mentality. People want to show off so much that several generations will live crammed into one or two rooms or refuse to see a doctor when they're sick in order to flash the newest iPhones." For the many more who still struggle to survive, the ongoing spread of poverty today is very much part and parcel of the new oil-rich Russia, kept in place despite the authorities' populist promises by the exploitative nature of the country's rule.

———

The most obvious cause of current Russian poverty is the breakdown of Soviet-era infrastructure. Starting in the 1920s, labor camp prisoners hacked out settlements across the inhospitable expanses of Siberia and the country's far north to exploit the oil, metals and other natural resources found there. The expansion built on the tsarist campaign to conquer the vast territory, which had taken place with great speed because very few indigenous people lived there to stand in the way. Over the next half century, economic planners encouraged hundreds of thousands more to relocate there, and the government lavished huge sums on inefficient schemes to transplant people to regions where no "normal" economy would have beckoned them. Without Communist political control, the physical difficulties have made many Siberian communities unsustainable today. If the region of Tver would be thriving in other circumstances, that can't be said of the vast, far-flung stretches of territory that constitute most of Russia: land barely fit, or totally unfit, for human habitation.

That was more than clear to me during my visit to the Arctic city of Novoi Urengoi, in the western Siberian region of Yamal Nenets, where I'd flown to see the area that holds some of the world's largest reserves of natural gas. The city's concrete-slab buildings—painted in garishly bright colors in an attempt to offset the psychological burden of months of darkness, isolation and subzero temperatures—rise from endless stretches of drab tundra covering the gas fields. It's a company town where the state gas monopoly, Gazprom, is king and gloves are a good idea even when I visited in relatively balmy August.

While other Siberian settlements are shrinking toward expiration as their residents move south, the local Gazprom subsidiary was busy constructing new buildings and roads to its far-flung gas deposits and production units. Relatively high wages, good benefits and long vacations draw workers willing to brave nine-month winters, when temperatures often hover around minus forty degrees Fahrenheit. But those not employed by the gas company are less lucky. After years of subsidies carried over from the Soviet era, when company and state were virtually indistinguishable, Gazprom's Urengoigazprom subsidiary recently carried out a "restructuring," its euphemism for transferring the city's power utility and housing services to municipal authorities. City officials claimed the transfer was barely noticeable to residents, but those I talked to said that hundreds of workers were laid off and a large percentage of the city's population is barely able to afford the price increases.

A grizzled-looking welder named Pavel Gavrilyuk interrupted a stroll with his grandson in the city's barren main square to speak to me. Barely surviving by doing piecework after being laid off, he was an illustration of the true human cost of Russia's gas bonanza. "Pensions are less than two hundred dollars a month—what can you buy with that?" he said. "Anyway, what's the point of living in the north? But who needs you back home where you came from so long ago?"

One would be forgiven for being a little surprised to hear such pessimism in a city founded a mere thirty years ago to tap newly discovered energy reserves. Many arrived on temporary assignments that paid more than they earned back home, then stayed and raised families. Now a large number have been left to fend for themselves in precarious living conditions after the state lost interest in supporting them. Their presence constitutes one of the Soviet Union's largest economic legacies. Clifford Gaddy of the Brookings Institution, an expert in Russian economic inefficiencies, believes twelve to fifteen million people live in Siberia and Russia's far-eastern regions who probably wouldn't be there if not for government inducements. "You can restructure a factory," he told me from Washington. "You can bring in new management, retrain people and produce new products that are hopefully better designed for the market. But historically and everywhere, it's extremely difficult to downsize large cities."

Gaddy reckons that as much as 2 percent of the country's gross domestic product goes to supporting residents of extreme, isolated areas, to which food and other consumer products must be delivered by plane because roads and railways don't exist or are too dangerous to use in winter. But Novoi Urengoi's officials, wary of saying anything that might be interpreted as critical of the government, assured me there's nothing wrong with the way things are now handled. In the new glass-fronted building that houses Gazprom's local subsidiary, deputy director Valery Marinin praised his company for taking the first steps toward revamping the old Soviet economic model. "Gazprom used to be involved in everything from gas production to farming. But companies must narrow their focus to what they're supposed to be doing in order to be profitable. We produce gas, and the city should see to its own municipal services."

However, there's been no indication so far that the kind of restructuring Gazprom has undertaken is making municipal operations more efficient. If the city is in charge of building the roads and maintaining housing with tax revenues, Gaddy said, there will be "pots of money at the disposal of local politicians" who "of course" will want to use it to line their own pockets.

Locals complained that state-controlled Gazprom does what it wants by claiming to be a private company. Svetlana Kozlova, a retired worker who was selling gloves and woven goods in a small stall in the center of town, was embittered by the company's practice of barring most residents from using the new roads it built from Novoi Urengoi to its gas fields' production facilities because they're supposedly private property. Some of the new asphalt was laid on old roads that are the only means of reaching faraway towns and settlements. "You're nobody if you don't work for Gazprom," she said. While the company is making officials rich as it helps make Russia an energy superpower, average citizens must bear the burden of the Soviet past. "Housing is scarce, rents are high and many of us are barely scraping by," Kozlova added. "People lived their whole lives in the north, built this place up, endured hardship, developed illnesses and are left with nothing."

———

Russian poverty is hardly unique to far-flung locations or even outside the capital. Although Moscow is by far the country's wealthiest area, with plenty of funds to maintain gas pipelines, electricity plants and roads, a visit to most parts of the city will reveal poor living conditions everywhere. Amid newly renovated apartments with their gleaming double-glazed windows are many that haven't seen a lick of paint since Soviet days. They are likely to be inhabited by the elderly, some of whom can be seen on streets and in underpasses—hunched over, sometimes kneeling, holding out their hands and keeping eyes peeled for police. Most cross themselves profusely when a passerby deposits some coins.

Among them is Evgenia Pavlova, a seventy-six-year-old pensioner I found sitting in a corner on a row of crowded steps one chilly October morning. The former schoolteacher, who earned a pension roughly equivalent to thirty dollars a month, said scraping together enough money for food and medicine was tough. She pinned whatever hopes she had on Putin. "It's difficult for him alone to cope," she said. "We need ten Putins. He's trying to do something, but I don't know if he'll succeed."

Her words reflect popular opinion in the regions, evidence that despite the wave of protest against him from the urban middle class, Putin has been largely successful in painting himself as a protector of common people whose main platform in the 2012 election was a promise to boost social spending. Although most increases went to the military, Putin pledged to spend tens of billions of dollars on hiking wages for health-care professionals, schoolteachers and university professors in addition to increasing child support, student stipends and buying more housing for war veterans during the course of his six-year term. Economists warned that the spending would seriously strain the government's budget, while other promises, such as curbing alcoholism, were too general to even approximate their cost.

When demonstrators in Moscow briefly set up a tent camp following Putin's May 2012 inauguration to call for fair elections and an end to authoritarian repression, some observers compared their effort to America's Occupy Wall Street movement. As a perceptive sociologist named Boris Kagarlitsky observed, however, Occupy was nationwide in scope, operating under clear slogans everyone understood and many Americans supported. By contrast, "the Moscow protests have taken place against a backdrop of largely silent regions," he said.

That wasn't because most Russians like official policy or are afraid of speaking out. "Their silence has more to do with the fact that the protesters in Moscow do not reflect their particular interests and needs."[7] Putin understood that decades of Soviet cradle-to-grave care have conditioned Russians to expect the state to provide pensions, education and subsidized utilities, while Russia's constitution still guarantees free medical care for everyone. No matter that the state's support is often little more than theoretical. According to the World Health Organization, the quality of Russian health care ranks 130th in the world—down from twenty-second in the 1970s.

Russians aren't oblivious to the situation. Almost 60 percent of respondents to a recent survey by the independent Levada Center polling agency were dissatisfied with their medical care. People I've asked about it say the country is divided into two groups: a lucky few who can afford good care in private clinics and the vast majority, who have been left with almost no safety net and sometimes have no choice but to bribe doctors. But the Levada Center's Marina Krassilnikova told me that despite overwhelming unhappiness with the situation, most remain wedded to the idea of socialized medicine. That includes wealthy Russians who prefer to have the option of paying more for services if they want to. "People just aren't ready to give up the right to free medical care under any circumstances," Krassilnikova explained, "even though they know they can't exercise it."

The situation is even worse in St. Petersburg than Moscow. Although the glorious architecture of Russia's "second city" is one of the wonders of the world, much of it is in terrible condition, even steps from the central thoroughfare, Nevsky Prospekt. Few foreign tourists ogling the restored facades suspect that many people live in crumbling apartments behind them, where dank interiors are also dark because burned-out lightbulbs are often not replaced.

The devastation of World War II, when up to a million residents trapped by the Nazi blockade during the siege of Leningrad died of cold and hunger, is partly responsible for the housing shortage. Sixty-five years later, great baroque buildings remain cut up into warrens of communal apartments—shared quarters with dingy, dirty corridors and other "public spaces" where families' use of the same bathrooms and kitchens can make life miserable. Such living conditions echo those depicted by Fyodor Dostoevsky almost a century and a half ago, when his gambling helped keep him in or near poverty. In his novel *Poor Folk*, a lowly clerk describes squeezing into alcoves behind curtains where the smell of rotting garbage soon appears to pass "because you take on the same bad smell yourself, and so do your clothes and hands and everything else…" Birds die in the air filled with smoke from cooking, and "there's always old washing hanging on strings in the kitchen."[8]

Families that shared all that—and sometimes their bedrooms—with several other families also involuntarily shared intimate details of their lives, unless they whispered and moved on tiptoe. That's next to impossible when people are rushing to get to work in the morning and irritation at having to stand in line to use common bathrooms easily explodes into anger. Such scenes made much of domestic life tense during the Soviet years, and while there are far fewer communal apartments today, they still number more than a hundred thousand in St. Petersburg. The mayor recently complained that a project to phase them out might take another century to complete at its current rate.[9]

Aside from the specific character of Soviet-style communal living, the widespread nature of Russian poverty may not appear much different than in other countries where large swaths of the population are poor. But another difference—and another explanation for the great nostalgia for the communist past—is that until the Soviet collapse, many Russians were relatively well educated and presumably able, if not necessarily willing, to openly object to the massive inequities.

Why put up with unfair inequality in society? Because in spite of being downtrodden, many Russians believe, if largely unconsciously, that they have a stake in the current system. The corruption that ensnares almost everyone gives a critical mass of people reason to believe that they also benefit.

If the disintegration of Soviet-era infrastructure partly accounts for the rapid economic collapse of many regions, corruption helps explain why it continues getting worse. Perhaps nowhere is its role in deepening poverty starker than on Kamchatka, which is fascinating not only for its unique natural beauty but also for the corruption that has ensnared the poverty-stricken local population in a more visible way than in most other regions. One of the last great spawning grounds of Pacific wild salmon, the far-eastern peninsula is a place where hunger and fraud are feeding a culture of poaching that's endangering the region's entire ecosystem as well as some salmon species.

Deeply isolated in Soviet days, when it was a closed military zone with a strategic submarine port, Kamchatka can still be reached from the mainland only by a single highway or ferry. Petropavlovsk-Kamchatsky, its decrepit capital, is a poster city for "forgotten by time." Gray, water-stained buildings of crumbling concrete line lush hills that descend toward the Pacific Ocean. Besides the twenty-odd fishing trawlers that had been impounded for poaching when I visited and were moored a slight distance from shore, the once bustling port is crammed with rusting ships and scrap metal. The isolation and lack of infrastructure mean that apart from fishing, there's almost no other way to earn a living.

Kamchatka's human poverty seems heightened by its exquisite landscape. I'd traveled there to research a story about the potential for tourism in the region. The spectacularly verdant land of untamed rivers has twenty-nine active volcanoes, hot, spurting geysers, rare Steller's sea eagles and the world's densest concentration of brown bears. But any tourism that could help sustain at least some of the peninsula's residents seems a very long way off in a region so poor I couldn't help feeling depressed much of the time. Driving for several hours beneath snow-peaked mountains with two other journalists, I crossed the narrow peninsula from its eastern, Pacific coast toward the Sea of Okhotsk in the west. We encountered almost no one until we reached a crumbling village called Ust-Bolsheretsk, where fishermen in rusty trailers parked on the banks of the Bolshaya ("Big") River were eating pieces of salted salmon on dark rye bread, washed down with vodka and tea.

Every year, millions of salmon fight their way up the Bolshaya and its sister rivers. When poachers deplete one species, they move on to another. One deeply weathered man in his fifties who wouldn't give his last name said that everyone on Kamchatka poaches. "There's no work here, only fish. Everyone feeds his family however he can, and that's by catching fish. You go hungry if you don't."

The Sea of Okhotsk lies several miles south of Ust-Bolsheretsk, along a section of flat tundra that stinks of rotting fish. As murky waves lapped the volcanic sand on a barren beach on the day we were there, warmly dressed fishermen in rubber boats cast nets into the water. Officially they were catching halibut, but under their piles of fish, we glimpsed another species they'd hidden: wild sockeye salmon, out of season and illegal to catch.

Back in Petropavlovsk-Kamchatsky, regional officials assured me that only 10 percent of the fish caught in and around Kamchatka is poached—and fishing department chief Alexander Krenge said the administration was dealing with the problem. But most Kamchatkans dispute the government's figures, including businessman Valery Vorobiev, the frustrated head of Akros, one of the peninsula's largest fishing companies. Standing on the bridge of one of his Norwegian-built fishing trawlers at dock, he said criminal gangs poach at least half the fish sold from Kamchatka. "That's ruinous for salmon," he said. "In Kamchatka alone, more than one hundred thousand tons are poached each year, and most only for their caviar. After the fish are slashed open, they're thrown away."

Vorobiev estimated some salmon species have declined by half in recent years. Inland, locals say criminal groups organize brigades of fifteen to twenty men who are flown upriver by helicopter. Their poaching deprives Kamchatka's bears of their natural prey, forcing them to raid human settlements for food.

Kamchatka's leading environmental activist, Andrei Abikh, told me the peninsula's industrial-scale poaching is possible only because officials charged with protecting fish are thoroughly corrupt. "The racket goes all the way to the top," he said. "Everyone wants a cut. It's gotten to the point where police, secret service and even judges are participating in poaching from our rivers."

A fish vendor named Vadim Chernov went further. Standing behind a line of tables laden with whole fish and fish heads at a busy outdoor market in the town of Elizovo, near the capital, the young man with a kindly demeanor and tidy clothes was the only seller who risked speaking to me. He said 90 percent of salmon sold there is poached. "The industry could easily be cleaned up, but that would cut into the authorities' profits from bribes and fines. Most of the local catch goes abroad, so locals are forced to poach, and we have no choice but to buy their catch from them, although it's just not right."

Environmentalists say plundering the region's unique natural resources could cause the collapse not only of Kamchatka's ecosystem but also the Pacific's entire wild salmon population. Every Kamchatkan knows the danger but also understands that their region has descended too deep into crime for there to be any hope for change in the foreseeable future.

The poor are pawns in a political-economic system contrived to keep those in power powerful and rich. Although the stake most people have in the going scheme is tiny, it's been enough to help isolate the majority of Russians from one another and keep them from acting in their common interests by joining forces against the country's top-down corruption. Payoffs also undermine the police, judiciary and other institutions civil society must rely on to enforce the law. Unlike many corrupt countries where the strongest critics can still struggle to act honestly and call at least some officials to account, in Kamchatka as in most parts of Russia, there's nowhere to turn.

———

Russian poverty is too pervasive to measure except by approximation. Even many Muscovites have only a sketchy impression of how bad things are in many rural communities. Ethnic minorities—of which there are hundreds in Russia, comprising some 20 percent of the population—often have it even worse. In the Nenets Autonomous region in Russia's far north, a land above the Arctic Circle where the sandy soil is locked in permafrost, the indigenous Nenets people are under serious threat. When I visited the tiny settlement of Krasnoe, where hunting and fishing are the main economic activities, young people were leaving for towns and alcoholism was crippling many of those who remain.

Many Nenets men spend most of the year herding reindeer, their chief source of food, on the tundra. Piotr Vylka, who had retired two years earlier, passed his time building sleighs in the small wooden house where he lived. An avuncular type who complained of having too much time on his hands, Vylka sang a traditional song for me, the kind men sing for entertainment during the long months of lonely herding. The mournful guttural verses about a confrontation between a young girl and an old man who wants her jewelry end with her pushing him onto a bonfire.

Vylka said he'd helped herd up to six thousand reindeer in the north of the region, which, at the height of its nine-month winter, sees no daylight at all. Average temperatures hover around minus thirteen degrees Fahrenheit. During the brief summer, mosquito swarms can be savage enough to kill adult reindeer—or so said Vylka, adding that he nevertheless enjoyed life on the tundra and was bored at home.

Nenets people now comprise only about a tenth of the population of the Nenets Autonomous region. More than half its residents are Russian, most of whom work in the region's oil industry and live in the nearby capital of Naryan-Mar, an old lumber port whose buildings are of wood, blackening Soviet concrete or corrugated metal. Beginning in the 1930s, the Soviet authorities forced many nomadic Nenets to settle in villages as a way of asserting political control and introducing modernization. Some Nenets continued to herd reindeer for collective farms while their children lived in state-run boarding schools. A local historian named Yuri Kanev, a former director of one of those schools, described how seriously the programs disrupt the traditional Nenets way of life. "Children from the age of seven to about sixteen are cut off from their families to live in school for most of the year under the direction of strangers. Little good can come of that."

The forced change helped drive many to idleness and alcoholism. Victor Yanzinov, a psychologist who treats alcohol and drug abuse in Naryan-Mar's ramshackle hospital, said 5 percent of the region's population is now reportedly under treatment for serious alcoholism—a fraction of those who need it, he added—and the situation for local Nenets is far worse. "Conditions are very bad in Nenets villages. Residents have gone crazy for drink and it's putting the very existence of the Nenets under threat. Maybe the most frightening thing is that people don't know the real situation. The statistics don't begin to reflect the facts."

The collapse of the USSR worsened the situation by ending Soviet subsidies. Young people began their migration to cities, where, as a young physician named Rais Ibragimov explained, unemployment and drugs awaited. "Not knowing how to function in an urban, industrial environment," he said, "they just don't mesh with the rhythm of city life and they're oppressed by its social structure." Both Ibragimov and Yanzinov bitterly criticized the authorities for doing virtually nothing to address the problems.

Back in the village of Krasnoe, Maria Vylka, the herder's wife, insisted that life under the Soviet Union had been better and happier. "Things are worse now. Young people have started acting like bandits, even killing people; there was a murder right *here!* People were nicer before."

Psychologist Yanzinov said that despite the prevalence of alcoholism and drug abuse, the government provides almost no funds for its treatment or research. His clinic had no computer, so he couldn't maintain a database of medical conditions, for example—let alone connect to the Internet. Still, there's little doubt about the relationship between poverty and Russia's widespread epidemics, including tuberculosis, the frequency of which—in a country with one of the world's highest number of billionaires—has more than doubled since 1991. In Russia's gruesome prisons, the disease kills some five thousand people a year, and many of the hundred thousand prisoners released annually are infected. In the general population, tuberculosis kills more than twenty thousand people a year, compared to around five hundred in the United States, which has a population more than twice as large. World health experts have warned about a time bomb waiting to go off that could greatly damage many more countries than Russia alone.

The epidemic of HIV and AIDS, the largest in Eastern Europe and Eurasia, is even more worrisome. Registered cases in 2012 numbered more than seven hundred thousand, up from fewer than half a million as recently as 2008, but no such figure can be trusted in a country that blamed the Pentagon for AIDS during the Cold War. Experts say the real rate is at least double the official number—and growing, thanks largely to the use of heroin, which is also rapidly spreading.

Although AIDS is the third leading cause of premature death—compared to the twenty-third in the United States—Moscow no longer accepts funding from the United Nations UNAIDS program or other international organizations because it sees itself as a donor country, not a recipient of help. However, the government doesn't finance programs that had been until recently supported by foreign agencies.[10] Insufficient funding for known cases of AIDS virtually guarantees that patients receive generally inferior treatment, and poor people get by far the worst from the badly fraying social services and healthcare system. The United Nations places Russia seventy-first in the world in human development, after Albania and just above Macedonia. (Norway is first; the United States thirteenth.)

Still, despite the turmoil wreaked in Krasnoe by sickness and substance abuse, life is relatively good compared to other tundra villages, many of which are barely self-sufficient. That's largely because it is the only settlement connected to the region's capital by a dirt road. And, a villager assured me, the fact that it sits on its own supply of natural gas, which residents use to heat their houses, makes it "almost paradise."

Faced with obvious disintegration of the social fabric, the authorities in Moscow have issued appeals for radical change. In 2009, then-President Medvedev published a manifesto specifying the urgent need for everything from overhauling the country's flagrantly corrupt legal system to reducing the number of its time zones from eleven to nine in order to make life more efficient in the sparsely populated far east. However, Kremlin policies supposedly designed to tackle some of the problems are actually making them worse. Tinkering with the time zones and scrapping daylight saving time in 2010 did the country far less harm than Putin's decision five years earlier to abolish elections for the country's regional governors in favor of Kremlin appointments. Although he partly restored direct voting in 2012, the inclusion of new restrictions made the concession virtually meaningless. With little oversight from the federal government and no need to answer to voters, local administrations have become mired in corruption and infighting and pay even less attention to their people's well-being.

When I traveled through the country's far east, it seemed clear to me that the massive distance from Moscow heightened people's sense of abandonment by their government. Anton Chekhov encountered some of the same sentiments when he visited the region in 1890. The distance from Moscow, he said, meant people "are not afraid to talk aloud here."

There's no one to arrest them and nowhere to exile them to, so you can be as liberal as you like. The people for the most part are independent, self-reliant, and logical...An escaped convict can travel freely on the steamer to the ocean, without any fear of the captain giving him up. This is partly due to the absolute indifference to everything that is done in Russia. Everybody says: "What is it to do with me?"[11]

Today, many Russians in the far-flung region have left to seek work elsewhere, and those who remain increasingly look to China for their survival.

Isolated from the rest of the country by the taiga—endless tracts of unsettled land covered by scrubby evergreens—the city of Blagoveshchensk offers insight into Russia's relationship with China, its flourishing southern neighbor. It stands on the Amur River, which divides the two countries along a line the supposedly congenial Soviet Union and People's Republic of China contested during bloody skirmishes in the 1960s. When relations began thawing twenty years later, consumer-starved Chinese flocked across the border to buy Soviet cars, farm machinery, pots and pans and anything else they could lay their hands on. Now the trade moves in the opposite direction. From Blagoveshchensk's barren, litter-strewn riverbank, the Chinese city of Heihe, on the other side, is clearly visible in the form of skyscrapers and giant cranes that are helping construct ever more buildings. As the Chinese city grows, stagnation continues to depress Blagoveshchensk across the river, where the Chinese are helping sustain life.

In winter, trucks and buses cross the ice in both directions. In spring, when the ice begins melting, passengers board small, battered hovercraft that skim over the river and up the sandy banks, kicking up large dust clouds. I watched as people bent over plastic bags bulging with clothing and other goods crammed themselves onto the ferries, which left every few minutes from the Chinese side. Most of the passengers were Russians whom Chinese vendors pay to carry goods to Blagoveshchensk, where—as in other cities of Russia's far east—they sell the goods at a bustling outdoor market.

In stark contrast to largely apathetic Russians, the Chinese who work in Blagoveshchensk do more than sell merchandise. Next to a market stall, a lanky cobbler named Yo Xiaoching, who was nailing new soles onto a pair of shoes, said it was far easier to find work in Blagoveshchensk than in China. The numbers explain why. While fewer than a million people occupy Russia's vast Amur region, the Chinese region of Heilongjiang, across the river, is bursting at the seams with almost forty million people. And despite strict new Russian laws limiting the number of Chinese permitted to work in Blagoveshchensk, Yo said it was still attractive to go there because "there's no work at all on the Chinese side."

With racist hate crimes endemic in Russia and nationalists spreading fear of a swelling menace on Russia's border, most Chinese in Blagoveshchensk keep to themselves, maintaining a determinedly low profile. Nevertheless, Blagoveshchensk residents tend to be less suspicious of them than they were during the years immediately following the Soviet collapse. A smartly dressed middle-aged clothes designer named Tatyana Sorokina said she actually felt more reliant on China than Moscow, thousands of miles west. "It's just a fact of life," she explained. "We depend on the Chinese for so many things; any development they accomplish here is also good for us."

Dependence on China isn't new. Residents told me they wouldn't have weathered Russia's steep economic decline in the 1990s without affordable Chinese products. Eighty-year-old Nikolai Alexandrovich said he survived mainly on Chinese potatoes during the worst years of Stalinism in the 1930s. "If it weren't for the Chinese, we'd be walking around naked and hungry today because our authorities have only helped Russia's far east decline. All they care about is battling each other for control and lining their pockets."

In addition to clothes and electronics, most food sold in Blagoveshchensk comes from China. And in a city principally consisting of decaying log houses and prefabricated Soviet concrete hulks, the most prominent sign of the Chinese presence is new construction. The city's only world-class accommodations are at the Asia Hotel. With its towering glass facade, the building is Blagoveshchensk's tallest by far. He Wenyan, the CEO of the Chinese company that built it, drives a Bentley coupe said to be the only such car in the Amur region. In the hotel's massive revolving restaurant on the top floor, He, a proud but soft-spoken man, argued that Blagoveshchensk would be far worse off without the Chinese. "We're good for the Russians. We help sustain their market economy," he said. But while locals tend to agree, political experts say that the Kremlin is in denial about the long-term threat to Russia's far east.

Russia took Blagoveshchensk from the Chinese relatively recently, in

1856, as a voluble sociologist named German Zheliabovsky reminded me in his cramped first-floor office, predicting that China may again control the city sooner rather than later. Beijing has been buying Russian arms for a major military buildup, and Moscow, he said, doesn't realize that Russia will eventually have to share some land with China to avoid conflict. "Our military alone won't be able to hold the far east. Russian people will have to live here." For that to happen, he added, after apologizing for stating the obvious, there will need to be jobs.

———

Back in the village of Priamukhino, my inquiries into what may have caused the deaths of Father Andrei and his family produced little more than vague theories. But they did help expose a dying way of life in towns and villages across the country, where residents can ordinarily rely only on themselves for basic necessities. A census in 2010 revealed that more than a third of Russia's 153,000 villages—and nearly two-thirds in some regions—house fewer than ten residents.[12] The continuing mystery surrounding Father Andrei's death reflected not so much a penchant for conspiracies in the countryside or evidence of the anarchy Russians have feared for centuries but the desperation of people struggling to subsist in a town where other considerations are secondary. Village head Alexander Volkov, who had no explanation for how the deaths happened, said tales of a population gone mad compounded the pain from the loss of an entire family. In the dilapidated wooden building that houses his office, he talked about the television crews that "swooped in here, filmed vodka bottles they themselves had brought, then broadcast that everyone here is a drunk and a vandal. Of course that hurt us."

"The rich have the gold, the poor have the fun," goes an old Russian saying much favored by Soviet propagandists. I saw the opposite in Tver. As its residents' hopes for a better life steadily decline, one change stands out amid the caved-in roofs and broken windows: new summer dachas belonging to affluent residents of Moscow and St. Petersburg, roughly three hours northwest by car, are going up here and there. Elderly survivors in the villages say they themselves will be gone within a decade or two, leaving their land to the moneyed newcomers.

(Igor Tabakov)

4
Drinking

The passion for drinking is innate in Russia.
                                    —Nikolai Leskov (1831–95)

I don't like drunkards, but I don't trust those who don't
drink.
                                    —Maxim Gorky (1868–1936)

However much vodka you buy, you'll still have to run back
for more.
                                    —Russian saying

As if the beleaguered residents of Novoi Urengoi needed another
reminder of the elements' crushing domination even at the height
of summer, endless dark clouds hung over the concrete-slab apartment
blocks that stand amid the town's gritty industrial sprawl on my second visit
there. I'd returned to the Arctic Yamal Nenets region of western Siberia to
observe the alarming effects of climate change on the surrounding landscape and had spent the day driving through a vast expanse of sandy tundra
that stretches beyond the town limits, where scrubby brush and stunted
trees growing above the permafrost struggle to complete their foliation
cycles during the three months when the winter relaxes its choke hold there.
    The tundra eventually gives way to the world's biggest frozen peat bog,
an area larger than Texas, much of it dotted with puddles and ponds, some

as big as lakes. Most are expanding because Siberia is melting. Enormous tracts of tundra frozen for tens of thousands of years are thawing so fast you can see the water level rising from year to year. The melting is releasing carbon dioxide and methane, greenhouse gases that have been trapped in the permafrost for more than ten thousand years. Now they bubble up so violently in some of the lakes that it prevents them from freezing even in the depths of winter. Siberia is among the best places to observe such effects of climate change because no warm jet stream or other weather pattern moderates its harsh continental climate. Thus it reflects even the smallest changes in global conditions sooner than elsewhere.

My guide was a botanist from the Siberian city of Tomsk, hundreds of miles to the south, who had been sounding a lonely alarm about the transforming landscape. Fair-haired and handsome, Sergei Kirpotin, who was in his late forties, had an appropriately weathered face and the unhurried, easygoing manner of someone who spends a lot of time in the wilderness. We were accompanied by two more environmental scientists from other parts of Siberia and a couple of Kirpotin's students who were taking advantage of the small sum I'd agreed to pay him for expenses to conduct climate-change research. After parking the rattling van we'd driven along remote, broken roads, we waded into the bogs.

The going was even tougher than expected, at least by me. With every step, our feet sank deep below the spongy lichen and moss that obscured the boundary between the semisolid ground and marsh water that stretched to the horizon. I couldn't help thinking what a great setting it would make for a chase scene in a horror film in which the victim can move no faster than a snail. Even worse were the mosquitoes, gnats and other flying insects that mounted ferocious sorties whenever we strayed too close to their territory near elevated bumps along the flat ground that had been thrown up by the heaving permafrost. Why no one lived in that harsh and utterly barren landscape was no mystery.

But it was also stunningly beautiful. The never-ending expanse was splashed with patches of red, green, blue and other colors of the tundra's fast-blooming flora. Fields of cranberries, blueberries and currants stretched as far as the eye could see. The berries were tiny but surprisingly sweet and delicious. Picking handfuls, I imagined I was the first human to have touched the bushes growing in this or that spot.

Kirpotin described how the expanding ponds and lakes were eating into land normally covered by acres and acres of spongy white lichen, which reflected the sun's rays back into space. As the lichen disappeared, the earth absorbed more warmth, reinforcing a snowballing cycle of rising temperatures. As further evidence, telephone poles near the town that had been sunk deep into the permafrost thirty years ago now tilted in all directions, forcing the authorities to replace them with new ones bolted to concrete ties resting on top of the wet ground.

While Kirpotin pointed out dead brush surrounding the ponds and other evidence of the fast-rising water level, a young female student collected plant samples in plastic bags. I thought it odd that the other two scientists, men in their late middle age, weren't collecting samples, measuring lichen coverage or, apparently, doing anything besides loafing around. Taciturn but otherwise perfectly friendly, they dismissed my attempts to interview them by issuing single-sentence generalities, as if afraid of being censured for even implying that anything, nature included, could be wrong with Mother Russia.

After several hours of sloshing around, we piled back into the van for the bumpy ride back to our hotel, another concrete-slab affair. Like all our arrangements, the reservations had been organized through the local administration and required special permission from the Federal Security Service that took weeks to obtain. It was a given that the authorities were keeping an eye on me, even though there was apparently nothing sensitive about my presence in the region.

As we separated to rest before dinner, one of the scientists, a leading environmental expert from the neighboring region of Khanty-Mansiisk, invited me to his room to taste some smoked fish. His expressions of pride in it were the first time I'd heard any enthusiasm from him about anything, and I accepted, postponing my note-jotting about the day to be friendly. Fifteen minutes later, I found the entire group inside his room huddled around an ancient coffee table laden with several filets of cured fish and cluttered with greasy glasses and plastic cups. The beer I'd brought was dismissed as superfluous. The tiny room's straining refrigerator was crammed with the botanists' pooled resources, mostly cheap vodka with names like Siberia and Old Omsk. Struggling to hide my apprehension at being unable to leave any time soon, I pulled up a rickety wooden chair, apologizing that I could stay only a few minutes.

The others were sitting on a brownish Soviet-era couch and easy chair, both pocked by many cigarette burns. A window was open, but not enough to cut the cigarette smoke and heavy smell of fish. Although the exceedingly polite scientists cleared a greasy plastic plate for me, my arrival had clearly put a damper on their fun. Victor, the gaunt, red-faced, balding man who had invited me, was sharing the room with Kirpotin and his other colleague, Alexander. He lost no time trying to revive the mood by pouring vodka from a half-empty bottle into the cups and glasses. Much as I'd have preferred lousy beer to lousy vodka, especially on my empty stomach, I knew better than to cause offense by protesting.

Everyone held up an overfull glass. *"Za znakomstvo!"* boomed Kirpotin in the obligatory first toast in honor of a stranger: "To our acquaintance!" We all clinked our glasses while looking each other in the eye, according to custom, before downing our shots. The warm, acrid liquid burned going down, but to leave anything in a glass unless the drinking is already well under way is bad form for Russian men, and I was all too practiced in suppressing grimaces. Mastering the technique for getting vodka down had been tough at first, especially the harsh, poor-quality stuff often served and swilled in the regions. I found something distasteful about the method most of my Russian friends used: a demonstrative exhale before the raising of glasses. But it often worked, so I emptied my lungs silently.

Afterward, everyone reached for a *zakuska*, a bite of food to chase down the alcohol, for which pickles or other marinated tidbits are considered best. Delicious dark Russian rye bread also serves the purpose very well, so well that just taking a smell—a technique said to have originated when bread was in short supply under communism—can also work. Russia's preeminent historian of vodka, Alexander Nikishin—whose staunch defense of Russian greatness matched his expansive collection of antique bottles, posters and accoutrements that make up most of the displays at the vodka museum attached to Moscow's Kristall factory (which produces Stolichnaya and some of Russia's other famous brands, including Limonnaya and Moskovskaya)—rails against the proliferation of new, sweeter-tasting "ultra-premium" vodkas. "Vodka has to be like it's always been," Nikishin told me. "Unpleasant-tasting and smelling, but it gives a certain satisfaction when you drink it with the right *zakuski*." I wasn't really looking forward to the dry-looking white fish that had sat out for God knows how long, but it turned out to be delicious—delicate, with a slight smoky taste, not at all salty. "It's wonderful," I said.

I'd felt the mood in the room change even as the vodka ran down my throat. The reserved scholars suddenly perked up. Smiling, Victor named the fish, which I'd never heard of, a local species of carp. "I'm the only one who knows where to get the really good stuff here," he boasted.

"He may be a botanist, but he's expert in fish," Alexander informed, his voice thick with sarcasm as he poured more vodka.

"*Anekdot!*" Victor announced: the Russian word for "joke," this one for my benefit. "Putin and Bush are fishing in Siberia. Putin sits grimly while Bush, frantically slapping at mosquitoes on his arms and neck, looks over at the motionless Russian president.

"'Vladeemeer, what the hey?' he asks naively. 'Why aren't they biting you?'

"'It's forbidden!' Putin answers sternly."

Raising his glass, Victor concluded with "Well, *davaite* [let's go]!" We clinked again and downed another round.

Not missing a beat, Alexander—a short man with dark hair and a mustache who specializes in photographing the tundra—added his contribution. "You know the difference between Russians and Americans?" His look at me started me mumbling something about attitudes toward the rule of law until he cut me off.

"Americans love their country and hate everyone who disagrees with them." He paused to pour more shots. "Russians dislike their country and hate everyone who agrees with them."

More jokes followed in quick succession, as if in a lighthearted game of one-upmanship. The Russian joke is told as much to relieve some of the pressure caused by life's everyday absurdities as to elicit laughter. Famously developed under communism, the *anekdot* still thrives today, its barbed irony directed chiefly at the newest oppressor class: the corrupt bureaucrats who are edging out rich New Russians. As more shots were poured and consumed, I gave up all hope of returning to my room and, in the vodka's warm glow, began basking in the company of my new acquaintances. We may have been sitting in a smelly Soviet-era room in the middle of barren nowhere, but now somehow that seemed cozy, even cool. Perhaps that's because vodka seems to have an effect that's especially suited to places like Russia. You feel soppier, more sentimental than under the influence of other forms of liquor, often until you're jolted back to reality with an expression of the racism or sexism that are openly accepted in everyday life.

"It's not true that Russia has the most beautiful women," Victor said at one point, despite the presence of Kirpotin's shy young protégée. "It's just that we drink more vodka."

By then it was getting late and with a full day of work ahead, starting with an early morning, I suggested dinner. There was little reaction. Fifteen minutes later, I tried again. "I suppose we do have to eat," Victor replied reluctantly. "But really, I'd rather stay here." I felt lucky that all the fish and bread had been consumed. "Of course we have to eat," Kirpotin said sometime later, rousing everyone to his feet.

When we finally stepped outside, the warmth I felt toward my companions began extending toward dilapidated Novoi Urengoi itself. Whether or not feelings of brotherly or sisterly love for one's drinking companions are universal, I found myself revising my attitude toward Russia as we plodded, heavily soused, along dirt paths through vacant lots surrounding the hotel. Where else would you have such an experience? "It's not such a bad place," you find yourself thinking. The cold, the crudeness and other unpleasantness, including the stares from local thugs driving battered BMWs and Mercedes toward one of the town's few bars, make you feel even closer to your companions because everyone's in the mess together. Emerging slowly but volubly onto a dusty main street, which was deserted except for occasional police casting suspicious glances, we were the greatest of friends. I suspect such feelings fuel the love a certain number of foreigners feel, or believe they feel, for Russia. The alcohol-fueled, come-what-may attitudes that often take hold of you provide a rush of excitement: the promise of hedonistic pleasure and abandon, heightened by a sense of real or perceived danger and great distance from more sober sensibilities back home.

————

The restaurant was decorated with cheesy mirrored panels and a revolving disco ball. Eyeing us as we stumbled in, a table of what appeared to be prostitutes had to shout to be heard above the synthesized drumbeat of the blaring pop music. More vodka helped wash down dinner, and the new toasts included paeans to Victor's Khanty-Mansiisk and Kirpotin's Tomsk, cities I solemnly vowed to visit as soon as I could. Although I was beyond recalling how much we drank, I remember Kirpotin remaining levelheaded throughout and looking out for us weaker-minded revelers. When Victor, who'd done most of the pouring in the hotel, suddenly passed out at the table in the middle of dinner, everyone else continued as if nothing had happened. Later, we carried him back to the hotel.

Imagine my surprise when I looked into his room early the next morning to find him gnawing on a cheap salami and pouring from a freshly opened bottle of vodka. "Come in, have a shot!" he offered cheerfully. Head pounding, I made my excuses with difficulty. He let me know that I was letting him down when I left to conduct interviews. Most were with independent businessmen who were being hounded by the authorities, the closest I could find to political opposition in a town dominated by Gazprom.

Returning late in the afternoon, I found the men again sitting around the coffee table, now together with the young graduate student, and working on beer. I'd soon learn that they'd spent the entire day there. When I joined them, they were recalling their previous trips to various parts of Siberia. Only then did it dawn on me why they seemed to have done no work when we'd driven into the tundra the previous day: there *was* no work to be done. They were on a *kommandirovka*.

Literally, *kommandirovka* means nothing more than "business trip." Actually, it's often an excuse to drink oneself silly while away from wives, girlfriends, parents and other mundane realities. Given the opportunity to travel, ostensibly for work, Victor and Alexander jumped at it as they'd obviously often done in the past. Sitting in their tiny, stuffy room drinking all day seemed like misery to me, but that's why they'd come to Novoi Urengoi. This time I couldn't even persuade them to leave for dinner.

Journalists everywhere may be notorious for heavy drinking on their frequent *kommandirovki*, but I've rarely seen Westerners put away as much as some of my Russian colleagues can. Arriving at a Moscow airport at eight o'clock one morning in 2005 for a trip to cover parliamentary elections in Chechnya, when that region was still ruined by war and extremely dangerous, I was perhaps foolishly surprised to find a table of journalists knocking back bottle after bottle of beer. On the rickety Soviet-era plane to the neighboring Stavropol region, some continued drinking in the Russian tradition, which favors cognac during air travel. One Russian photographer in particular, who worked for an international news agency, excelled in upholding the tradition. Pressing his bottle of cheap Armenian brandy on random passersby, he appeared to take refusals from those bold enough to decline as personal insults. Those who agreed were also loudly chastised for taking swigs he invariably judged to be too small.

My trip had been arranged by the government to show off its claims that Chechnya's new pro-Kremlin authorities were stabilizing the region, which the Russian army had bombed into the Stone Age. No one then knew it would be the start of a remarkable drive that would rebuild the capital Grozny from a pile of rubble in a few short years. Meanwhile, in Stavropol, we boarded several small buses for the two-hour drive into Chechnya in a convoy escorted by special-forces troops riding in Soviet-era jeeps. The drunk photographer continued drinking. Polishing off the last of his cognac, he pleaded with others for beer before falling asleep, his head resting on the shoulder of a BBC correspondent who, despite nervously practicing lines for an upcoming live report, was too polite to ask the slumbering man to move. Jolted awake on the potholed road, the photographer tried convincing the driver to stop for more alcohol despite the potential danger from snipers and lack of any place to buy it. When we arrived at our first polling station in an elementary school, a tiny trickle of locals dressed in their Sunday best was also arriving to cast ballots while commandos toting massive automatic rifles set up a perimeter around the area to protect us. Wary of the watchful eyes of government officials and informers in a village where everyone knew everyone else, residents recited admiration for the pro-Moscow administration, repeating government pronouncements almost verbatim.

The photographer roused himself as we were leaving the bus. Laboriously gathering his camera bag and supplies, he tripped and fell down the bus steps, flinging his gear everywhere. His stumble had a welcome effect: embarrassed for the first time by everyone's laughter, he ended his bullying. Somehow he managed to pick up his camera and bags and take the photos he needed.

The rest of the trip continued in the same fashion, the toleration of his behavior being even more significant than his prodigious drinking in a place where alcohol abuse is the norm for many.

Countless cultures revel in drinking and many countries, especially northern ones such as Finland, face serious alcoholism problems. Britain's per capita alcohol consumption, especially in Northern Ireland, isn't far behind Russia's and neither is Portugal's. Is drinking in Russia really any different? If so, does it say anything about its society?

According to official statistics, Russians drink eighteen liters, or almost five gallons, of pure alcohol a year per person. Although the World Health Organization, which tends to adopt conservative estimates, puts the number slightly lower, at around sixteen liters, that's twice the internationally recommended limit. The WHO places three other countries higher in per capita consumption: Moldova, the Czech Republic and Hungary. In Russia, however, adult males are responsible for around 90 percent of it, meaning they drink a staggering thirty-five-plus liters, according to a 2011 WHO report that estimated every fifth male death is attributable to the effects of alcohol.[1]

The *Primary Chronicle*, a history of Kievan Rus'—the state that preceded Moscow and other northern principalities and that formed the foundation of modern Russia—explained the Kievan princes' rejection of Islam by citing the religion's prohibition of alcohol.[2] *"Rusi est vesele piti, ne mozhet bez nego byti,"* Prince Vladimir supposedly told the Muslim delegates who had come to convert him: "People of Rus' are merrier when they drink, living without it, they can't think." While the account is almost certainly untrue, it illustrates popular conceptions about the importance of drink in Russian life and thought.

If language is among the main determinants of culture, Russia's drinking has made a rich contribution. The words and phrases Russians use for their participation in the essential activity include *screw, pour, warm up, lick, hit the liver, rub in, fill up, pour in the eyes, suck, look through a prism, go deaf, enter nirvana, splash, get younger, read a label, organize a festival, grab a bear* and many, many more—up to 350 such euphemisms, one expert has counted. There are almost as many rules and superstitions. Here are a few:

Vodka must be poured into glasses standing on a table, not raised in one's hand.

When pouring, one arm should not cross another.

Toasting the memory of the dead should be done only with vodka, and
with no clinking of glasses.

Drinking from someone else's glass will make you a drunkard.

Once opened, bottles should always be emptied. (I saw not a single vio-
lation of that rule during all my years in Russia.)

Empty bottles should not be left on a table; at best, they should be
placed on the floor.

Violating any of these rules will bring certain bad luck.

Middle-class dinner parties typically involve long hours around tables
where many consider eating something to pass the time between countless toasts. During the communist era, when going to a restaurant was a
rare treat and "going out" usually meant dinner at someone else's home,
most Soviets laid on their feasts in living rooms, cramming together tables
in front of the couch and pulling up all available chairs. Family snapshots
of birthday, anniversary and most other celebrations from the late Soviet
period invariably depict relatives and friends squashed together around
tables laden with caviar, pickled vegetables, cold cuts of meat and a multi-
tude of bottles. Even today, tables are usually set with *zakuski* when guests
arrive—main dishes come out hours later. Once seated, guests are expected
to remain there for the foreseeable future, imbibing shot after shot, with
breaks only for the bathroom and to smoke, often outside or in stairwells.
Toasts invariably include "To women!" Females are allowed to sip from
their shot glasses, reinforcing the common perception of them as members
of the weaker sex. When the time comes for guests to leave, there are special toasts for that, too. Among the variations, *"Na pososhok"*—"A glass for
the journey home"—is the most common.

That's when people leave on good terms. My mother described many
parties in Soviet days that began in celebratory moods around the table
with the usual toasts and speeches, laughter and jokes, but ended with
guests, mostly men, lying drunk on the floor. Some would have to be carried out. Others would begin arguments that would sometimes spill out
onto the streets. "It was a disgusting spectacle," she said, "but considered very normal." That's because vodka was regarded as a panacea for
everything—"woe, bad fortune, sickness, all life's evils," my mother added.
"True happiness could only be perceived under the influence of vodka.
Vodka was God."

What I find most difficult about drinking in Russia today is the offense refusal causes. A very close friend who sometimes drinks heavily has rebuked me angrily for declining to quaff more than the too many we'd already had. According to him, I'm committing the unpardonable offense of forcing him to drink alone. That attitude can be a serious problem when I'm working. On the one hand, even a sip of liquor can affect my thinking. On the other, waving off a proffered drink in someone's office can set a bad tone, especially for an interview. So in the interest of getting decent answers and weaving them into a story in time for a deadline, I have, like so many other foreigners in Russia, often tried to limit my intake while concentrating on maintaining a level head.

Visitors to Moscow and St. Petersburg tend to take more notice of the effects of drinking than the residents, who are inured to its consequences. As in most other countries, parks and other public spaces invariably contain homeless drunks. Their numbers are often joined by groups of beer-drinking young people, no matter what the time of day. Unlike the United States, Russia has no laws against carrying open bottles of beer or liquor outdoors, and you see a lot of it, but even that's common elsewhere. What most distinguishes Russian drinking and makes it far more dangerous is a form of bingeing called *zapoi*—drinking sprees that can last from a day or two to a couple of weeks, during which Russians essentially shut themselves off to drink themselves into repeated stupors. "A real Russian man can find his way out of any *zapoi*," goes an old saying. But those benders—indulged in by rich and poor alike—seriously increase the incidence of sudden heart failure. They are further evidence of the country's deep passion for drinking with abandon, as opposed to just having one or two with dinner. Contrast France, for example, which takes wine seriously, but where many limit their intake to one or two glasses.

I believe Russia's attitudes to drinking reflect something deeper in the country's culture: a sense of pessimism about the ability to better oneself. Russian fatalism helps explain why there are nearly two million officially recognized alcoholics in the country—surely a serious understatement— and more than ten million *alkashy*, people who drink at the first opportunity.

———

Beyond a justification for drinking to the point of stupefaction, vodka's allure is enhanced by the widespread belief that it was first conceived in

Russia. Although a number of non-Russian scholars contend it probably arrived from Poland, Moscow's traditional bitter rival, Russians tend
to defend the claim jealously. In support or not, they often say that the
word *vodka* is derived from *voda*, Russian for water. Is it? Historian Edward
Keenan questions the common belief, saying the real Russian diminu-
tives for water, *voditsa* and *vodichka*, bear stresses on the second syllable
("vod-EE-tsa" and "vod-EE-chka"),[3] whereas *vodka* retains what he
believes is the original Polish stress on the first syllable ("VOD-ka"). The
Russian diminutive for vodka, *vodochka* (pronounced "VOD-ochka"), also
stresses the first syllable, which may indicate that it derived from the Polish
wódka.

Keenan thinks vodka dates to the sixteenth century, when distillation was first developed in Eastern Europe. Other Western scholars claim
that knowledge about distilling spirits from wine—the key development
for making vodka—spread across Europe from France earlier, reaching
Poland between the twelfth and fourteenth centuries.[4] Still others believe
the Slavs learned to distill from the Tatars.

Whatever the truth, Russia's national drink is little more than pure alcoholic spirits diluted with water. For centuries, vodka distilled from rye was
considered the best, and many Russians still hold to that conviction.[5] Other
varieties are produced chiefly from wheat or potatoes, although today's
Russians dismiss Polish potato vodka as a bastardization. Since early distillation techniques resulted in many poisonous impurities, flavorings such
as honey were often added to improve taste. Techniques improved significantly in the eighteenth century, when it was discovered that filtering vodka
through charcoal removed many of the impurities, and it became an integral part of the process.[6]

But the liquor now known as vodka wasn't called that until relatively
recently. Before the mid-1700s, it was known as *vino*, wine, because it was
considered essentially to be "grain wine."[7] *Vodka* initially developed as an
unofficial term. High-quality aromatic vodkas—as opposed to the poorer
stuff drunk mostly by peasants—were called *nastoiki* (infusions). The range
of flavors expanded in the first half of the nineteenth century, when dis-
tillers began adding fruit essences—including anise, cherry and black
currant—for their taste instead of to mask impurities.

The very best vodkas were produced by landowning gentry, who were granted distilling rights by the tsar and could afford to produce the purest spirits—sometimes making just two liters of vodka for every hundred liters of raw materials—because they received grain free from their serfs and logged wood for charcoal from their own forests. Distillation was usually a pastime, but fierce competition to produce the best was partly responsible for the international acclaim that Russian vodka first won in the eighteenth century.[8] However, the explosion of factory production for profit in the 1800s resulted in a serious decline in quality.

Many of the top private distilleries, including two of the biggest, Smirnov and Shustov, were founded around midcentury. In the 1860s, an average distillery produced six thousand *vedr*, or buckets—an old Russian measurement of liquid volume equal to 12.3 liters—annually. By 1900, 2,200 distilleries were producing seventy-eight million *vedr*, making Russia the main European producer and distributor of spirits, surpassing runners-up Germany and Austria-Hungary.[9]

The generally low quality of privately distilled vodkas in the nineteenth century prompted the development of new standards by the renowned chemist Dmitri Mendeleev, who is much better known for having conceived the periodic table of the elements. Mendeleev helped define what's perceived to be the ideal for Russian vodka today: spirits distilled from grain and diluted with water to a concentration of 40 percent.[10] The tsarist government later adopted his formulation as the standard for state-produced vodka, and well-known current brands such as Stolichnaya and Russkii Standart still claim to use his method.

———

For the poorest Russians, even the cheapest varieties of vodka are a luxury. Instead, many drink the Russian version of moonshine: *samogon*, literally "self-distilled." The tradition of producing and drinking *samogon* is only slightly less storied than that of vodka as a whole, but its effects have proved far deadlier.

Although Moldova, the Czech Republic and Hungary have higher per-capita alcohol consumption than Russia, as noted, their territories are tiny in comparison. The Russian damage from drinking is staggering. Alcohol poisoning kills some forty thousand people a year—compared to about three hundred in the United States—and plays a role in more than half of all premature deaths. According to the government, 38 percent of Russians between the ages of twenty and thirty-nine suffer from alcoholism. The number jumps to 55 percent for those between the ages of forty and fifty-nine. Prime Minister Medvedev has called those numbers a "natural disaster."

What took place in Pskov in 2006 was shocking even by those standards. About 370 miles northwest of Moscow and a stone's throw from the Estonian border, Pskov is the site of a crucial eleventh-century victory by a Russian prince against an order of Teutonic knights, dramatized by the legendary Soviet filmmaker Sergei Eisenstein in his film *Alexander Nevsky*. The city later became the seat of a thriving principality that was a member of a powerful Baltic trading alliance called the Hanseatic League, but its celebrated past has been eclipsed by economic depression, despite the construction of food-processing plants and machine-building factories that provide locals with mostly humble manufacturing jobs. Like their counterparts throughout the country, doctors, teachers and other professionals left the rural region en masse after the Soviet collapse, leaving behind mainly low-paid blue-collar workers together with the elderly and unemployed.[11]

So when local hospitals began filling up with people whose skin and eyes had turned a ghastly shade of yellow in the summer of 2006, the news initially attracted little attention beyond the region. The patients were suffering from the unmistakable signs of poisoning: toxic hepatitis had destroyed their livers, causing poisons to build up in their bodies. With the early onset of an unusually harsh winter, many more showed up at the hospitals during the following months. Up to a thousand people were hospitalized and when more than a hundred died painfully slow deaths, alarms finally sounded in Moscow.

Despite the severity of its epidemic, Pskov was but one of several regions distressed by poisonings that year. The spike turned out to have been indirectly caused by a government campaign against the illegal production of alcohol. Driving prices higher, the crackdown prompted more people to buy booze on the black market, where it's often laced with cheap industrial solvents that contain twice the concentration of alcohol as regular spirits. Even tiny amounts can be deadly.

Pskov's profusion of manufacturing plants includes factories producing cleaning solutions, antifreeze and many other solvents. No doubt workers or bosses sold industrial alcohol to middlemen who supplied it to individuals and gangs that mixed moonshine from the cheapest possible ingredients, often masking the flavor with additives before pouring it into used bottles of legitimate liquor that were sold in local grocery shops and kiosks.[12] Most of the victims were homeless. Some were poisoned by a medical disinfectant that was especially cheap because it was exempt from taxes.[13]

Pskov's high rate of poisonings could have happened anywhere in Russia, where roughly half of alcohol sales are illegal. Thus many people die not just because they drink but because they do it dangerously, consuming not only moonshine but also anything containing alcohol, including cologne, cleaning fluid and even jet fuel. Hundreds more pass out and freeze to death overnight every winter, boosting alcoholism's contribution to Russia's looming demographic crisis and helping drive men's life expectancy down to sixty-four years, as I've mentioned, compared to seventy-four for women. That has helped skew the sex ratio to its most imbalanced point since 1979, with women now outnumbering men by more than ten million as the population continues to shrink.[14]

Massive drinking continues despite ever-present reminders of the risks—along with smoking, which is heavier, per capita, than anywhere else in the world—partly because Russians tend to overestimate how healthy they are. According to a recent study, 95 percent think they're in good or fair health, despite their poor diets and infrequent exercise.[15] The same study found that although most Russians understand the links between activities such as drinking and smoking and chronic disease, they tend to accept the risks as inevitable consequences of their lifestyles.

That attitude says something about a national character formed and sustained under difficult living conditions, and it's getting worse. Although vodka drinking has remained relatively stable since the Soviet collapse, heavy marketing of drinks lower in alcohol, such as beer—which many Russians don't consider a "real" alcoholic drink—have contributed to skyrocketing sales, especially among the young. Hard as it may be to believe, Russia's already legendary alcohol consumption has tripled since the collapse of communism, when drinking was among the few means of escaping the bleak realities of Soviet life.

In 1961, my father, George, spent an academic year as a graduate exchange student at Moscow State University. Founded in the late eighteenth century by the renowned physicist Mikhail Lomonosov—a legendary polymath who discovered an atmosphere on Venus and helped shape the modern Russian language—MGU, as it was known, had recently moved to the largest of Stalin's seven iconic neo-Gothic skyscrapers that loomed over the city from Sparrow Hills, then called Lenin Hills.

Much had changed since Stalin's death eight years earlier. Nikita Khrushchev's thaw had loosened restrictions on life and work, although it would be only three years until a group of old-guard conspirators would remove him from power. Their coup d'état would end his campaign of de-Stalinization and replace him with Leonid Brezhnev, who was backed by countless cadres of Soviet officials who'd been threatened by Khrushchev's boat-rocking reforms. Meanwhile, the year 1961, when the Soviets sent Yuri Gagarin into orbit around the earth to make him the first man in space, was still deep in the Cold War era.

When I was a teenager, my dad confidently assured me that sickness from drinking to excess is so unpleasant that I'd never want to do it more than a few times in my life. Although I'm still struggling with that lesson, my father apparently learned it for good from his experiences in Moscow. At work on a Columbia University dissertation about the Soviet legal system, he spent some of his days visiting courtrooms. He bunked with a humorless roommate in a single room of a dormitory that formed one of the sprawling university building's wings. It went without saying that the roommate had been selected for his political loyalty, but other students my father befriended in the dormitory were far livelier and more interesting. Nevertheless, he made certain to be out on the evening of the day they got their monthly stipends, and took pains to remain away at late as possible. That was to avoid being given a water glass full of vodka to drink, an inevitability if he arrived before his friends finished their evening in the usual way, passed out on their beds or the floor, often stacked like cordwood and stinking of vomit.

Although the stipends were small, just over a ruble a day, the de rigueur party that followed featured sausage and cheese in addition to bottles of vodka. The revelry set the students back nearly half their stipends, forcing them to exist largely on free bread from the cafeteria for the last ten days of the month. They washed their meals down with "white nights" tea—hot water—part of a diet so grim that when they got their next stipends, there was no question they would need to celebrate again by drinking themselves into oblivion. So it went, in the traditional Russian pattern that had startled Western visitors to Russia in the sixteenth century: famine broken by loud, drunken feasts.

Brezhnev's ascent ended any hope that the creaking Soviet economy, which had slightly improved under Khrushchev, would be further reformed. Instead, spending on the military ballooned, and the only way the Kremlin could alleviate the consequences of that and even more crippling effects of the central planning system was to permit more goods and services to reach the vast majority of Soviets by closing its eyes to at least some of the growing corruption. Pilfering from state stores enabled shopkeepers to exchange cigarettes and food for, say, medical checkups or car tires. Proliferation of that kind of arrangement, which had previously only permeated the top levels of the state bureaucracy, enabled Brezhnev's regime to plod on more or less unchanged until his death in 1982. However, it also reinforced the indolence and cynicism that had become widespread.

After Khrushchev freed millions of political prisoners from the Gulag labor-camp system following Stalin's death in 1953, there was no going back to the tyrant's terror. Instead, the bleak Brezhnev era became mired in self-absorption. During the *zastoi*—the stagnation, as the period became known—Soviets showed outward loyalty to the Party but were largely free to criticize it among family and friends in the relative safety of their very cramped kitchens. Alcohol dulled the monotony of life.

People used a sign language to discuss drinking on the street. Two fingers held at the neck meant someone was looking for someone else to split a bottle and its cost; three fingers meant three people. The state retail market being what it was, alcohol also became a hot commodity on the booming black market. A journalist named Vitaly Korotich—who would become the editor of the groundbreaking magazine *Ogonyok*, the Soviet equivalent of *Life* magazine, which began crusading for reform under Mikhail Gorbachev's *perestroika* years later—recently described the central role vodka played during those drab years:

As a means of smoothing relations, as a bribe, an aperitif, a sou-
venir, medicine and, well, whatever else, vodka fulfilled many life
goals. It ceased being just an alcoholic drink and became one of
the most important aspects of Soviet life…The phrase, "You won't
get anywhere without a half-liter," entered the professional lexicon.
That's how we lived.[16]

Switching off became the easiest form of protest under a regime that
still crushed dissent. Although his work became widely known only after
his death in 1990, writer Venedikt Erofeev has since become one of the
intellectual figures most closely associated with the drunks of the *zastoi*.
Expelled from Moscow State University during his second year in the
1950s, Erofeev drifted around the Soviet Union, working a series of odd
jobs that included laying telephone cables near Moscow. His prose poem
Moskva-Petushki, which was completed in 1970 and first distributed as
samizdat—self-published literature passed around in secret—describes an
alcohol-soaked, hallucinatory day in the life of a character named Venichka
Erofeev (after the diminutive form of Venedikt). Ostensibly the account of
his train trip from Moscow to the suburban town of Petushki, eighty miles
to the northwest, the short work is loaded with literary allusions and celebrated in Russia today for its brilliantly comic depiction of the Brezhnev
era, which was so perversely stultified that severe alcoholism appeared to
be the norm. Erofeev opens with his protagonist trying to remember the
previous day, indistinguishable from most others.

I mean, as soon as I came out onto Savyelov Station, I had a glass of
Zubrovka [vodka] for starters, since I know from experience that as
an early-morning tipple, nobody's dreamed up anything better so far.
Anyway, a glass of Zubrovka. Then after that—on Kalayev
Street—another glass, only not Zubrovka this time, but coriander
vodka. A friend of mine used to say coriander had a dehumanizing effect on a person, i.e., it refreshed your parts but weakened
your spirit. For some reason or other it had the opposite effect on
me, i.e., my spirit was refreshed, while my parts went all to hell.
But I do agree it's dehumanizing, so that's why I topped it up with
two glasses of Zhiguli beer, plus some *Albe-de-dessert* [port] straight
from the bottle, in the middle of Kalayev Street.

Of course, you're saying: come on, Venya, get on with it—what did you have next? And I couldn't say for sure. I remember—I remember quite distinctly in fact—I had two glasses of Hunter's vodka, on Chekhov Street. But I couldn't have made it across the Sadovy ring road with nothing to drink, I really couldn't. So I must've had something else.[17]

Venichka has been fired from his job as a cable fitter after accidentally having sent out graphs charting his co-workers' productivity relative to the amount of alcohol they'd consumed.

Before my time, our production schedule looked like this: in the morning we would sit and play three-card brag for money (you know how to play brag?). Okay. After that we'd get up, unroll a drum of cable and lay it underground. Then, obviously, we'd sit back down and kill some time, each in his own way. I mean, everyone has a different temperament, different aspirations; one would be drinking vermouth; another, slightly more basic, *Fraîcheur* eau-de-cologne; and the ones with a bit of class would be on the cognac [from] Sheremetyevo airport. Then we'd go to sleep.

And the next morning, well, first we'd sit down and have a drink of vermouth. Then we'd whip yesterday's cable back up out of the ground and chuck it away, because it'd got soaked through, naturally.[18]

Venichka's innovation is to do away with the charade of laying any cable at all. Now a celebrated literary hero, his recipes for alcoholic drinks are the stuff of urban legend. ("Tears of a Komsomol [Communist Party youth group] Girl: lavender water, 15g; Verbena herbal lotion, 15g; mouthwash, Forest Water eau-de-Cologne, 30g; nail varnish, 2g; mouthwash, 150g; lemonade, 150g.")

Literature aside, vodka production increased eightfold between 1940 and 1980.[19] The stagnation period, *zastoinyi*, came to be jokingly referred to as *zastolnyi*, or "at the table," where most people consume their vodka. The authorities began cracking down on production in earnest only after the death of Brezhnev, a serious drinker, in 1982. He was replaced by former KGB chief Yuri Andropov, who is believed to have initiated his own reforms, including those involving alcohol, because he had unique knowledge about the Soviet Union's deep-seated problems, many of which were hidden from the people. Soon sales of liquor, as well as cologne and other liquids containing alcohol, were forbidden before 11:00 a.m.[20]

But it wasn't until the ascension of Mikhail Gorbachev in 1985 that the Kremlin began waging serious war against alcoholism. Believed to have been encouraged by hard-liners in his regime, Gorbachev launched a major antialcohol campaign in May of that year, when the government enacted a series of resolutions called Measures to Overcome Drunkenness and Alcoholism. Alcohol was banned at official functions, Party members and officials who visibly abused it were dismissed and liquor production was drastically curtailed. Millions of people were persuaded to join a temperance group called the All-Union Voluntary Society for the Struggle for Sobriety. Alcohol prices were increased and its sale was banned before 2:00 p.m.[21] Even today, former Soviets shake with anger when they recall the closure of distilleries and the destruction of some of the USSR's best vineyards in Ukraine and Moldova. Although alcohol consumption declined that year, the policy soon proved to be an utter disaster.

As supplies dwindled, mass fights broke out in the huge queues that grew ever longer outside the increasingly fewer stores that sold alcohol. People began producing moonshine at home, mostly from sugar and yeast, which led to widespread shortages and rationing of those commodities. Many who weren't already doing so turned to anything containing alcohol, including window-cleaning solvents and de-icing solution for airplanes, to quench their thirst.[22]

Historian Sergei Roy writes that drug addiction grew along with the huge spike in alcohol poisonings. "I mean lethal ones, for who would bother to count the near-lethal writhing of wretches who felt sorry they'd survived? The number of lethal alcoholic poisonings grew fourfold immediately after the 1985 order, as desperate citizens started drinking anything remotely believed to contain alcohol: eau de cologne, lotions, toothpaste, glue, shoeshine, furniture varnish, nail varnish."[23]

Jokes multiplied along with hatred for Gorbachev: "Do you have this cologne?" a man at a barbershop asks, then exhales toward his barber. Shaking his head, the barber breathes back on his client. "No, only this kind."

Another man who has been waiting for hours in a queue for vodka decides to go to the Kremlin to give Gorbachev a thrashing instead. When he returns an hour later, a comrade still waiting in line asks how it went. The man shakes his head. "That line was even longer."

Gorbachev's antialcoholism campaign was far from the first failure of its kind. Previous attempts ran into a central dilemma: although successive governments wanted to reduce alcohol production, they depended on liquor taxes for revenue, a paradox dating back four centuries, when such levies were first introduced as a way to reduce drinking. Gorbachev restricted vodka sales so that Russian workers would help shore up communism by returning to the assembly line, but his policy actually hastened the Soviet Union's demise because it also caused a substantial drop in government revenues. Vodka taxes had at one point provided a quarter of the entire Soviet budget when prices for Moscow's other main cash cow, oil for foreign export, began hitting all-time lows. By printing more money to make up some of the difference, the Kremlin did even more to worsen the inflation that accelerated the communist downfall.[24]

The drive to increase revenues has undermined the goal of decreasing alcohol consumption since Ivan III established the first state alcohol monopoly in 1475. Ivan the Terrible introduced the first state *kabak*, or tavern, in the 1530s, and they were soon producing and selling spirits in major towns throughout the principality of Muscovy.[25] Since profits went directly to the state treasury, officials were inclined to promote drinking.[26] The English ambassador Giles Fletcher observed in 1591 that the tsar encouraged his subjects to drink in state-owned taverns, where "none may call them forth whatsoever cause there be, because he hindereth the emperor's revenue."[27] Peter the Great later took the opposite approach, attempting to increase taxation by abolishing a state monopoly on alcohol production and encouraging private distillation. By time Catherine the Great assumed the throne in 1762, alcohol taxes accounted for a third of the state budget.

And so on, through the reigns of Alexander I, Nicholas I and others. By 1862, the state was getting half its revenue from alcohol taxes.[28] At the time, Nikolai Chernyshevsky, considered the father of Russia's revolutionary movement, denounced his colleagues for supporting the vodka tax and thereby sacrificing their duty to "promote national honor, the moral welfare of the nation, justice and fairness…The only reason for its existence is monetary. Its sole purpose and concern is money, money, money."[29]

The issue prompted another great moralist, Chernyshevsky's contemporary Fyodor Dostoevsky, to plan a novel he wanted to call *The Drunkards*. He later folded its characters into *Crime and Punishment*, whose Semyon Marmeladov remains one of Russia's best-known alcoholic archetypes. The drunks of Russian literature such as Marmeladov and Venichka Erofeev tend to be viewed sympathetically, as people whose spirits are crushed by the social inequities of an oppressive state. They are variants of the "little man" in Russian literature, among them an impoverished and derided clerk at the center of Nikolai Gogol's story "The Overcoat." Having scrimped and saved to buy a cherished new coat only to have it stolen, he dies from illness soon after a high-ranking official he approaches for help dresses him down for wasting his time.

Dostoevsky's Marmeladov, another low-ranking clerk, speaks in a ludicrously high-flown manner: his sole, pathetic gesture of dignity. The protagonist, Raskolnikov, first meets him in a tavern, where he observes that Marmeladov's hands are dirty, his nails black and his filthy coat has one remaining button.

> His face was bloated from continual drinking and his complexion was yellow, even greenish. From between his swollen eyelids his little reddish slits of eyes glittered with animation. But there was something very strange about him; his eyes had an almost rapturous shine, they seemed to hold both intelligence and good sense, but gleams of something like madness showed in them as well.[30]

Having squandered his destitute family's money on drink and pawned his uniform, Marmeladov is afraid to return home, a tiny room he occupies with his wife and three small children. He confesses that he has just begged thirty more kopeks from a beloved older daughter, who has been sold into prostitution to raise money:

> "And surely she needs them for herself, now, eh? What do you think, my dear sir? Now she must take care to be always neat

and clean. And that neatness, that special cleanness, costs money, you understand... Well sir, and I, her own father, took those thirty kopeks of hers for drink! And I am drinking it, sir! I have already drunk it all!... Now who could be sorry for a wretch like me, eh?"[31]

No one, he concludes, rationalizing his behavior by claiming a thirst for suffering, the Russian crucible for spiritual purity. Like other alcoholics in Russian literature, Marmeladov's character is comic, but his fate is more tragic than pathetic, his alcoholism a grotesque example of the humiliation to which characters are driven by the highly bureaucratic nature of St. Petersburg life. If Raskolnikov revolts against poverty by committing the novel's central crime, his parallel Marmeladov accepts his fate, suffers and dies.

———

Alcoholism continued spreading and the quality of vodka declining until the introduction of yet another state vodka monopoly in 1894 under the reforming Finance Minister Sergei Witte. During the so-called fourth liquor monopoly, hundreds of state distilleries, which maintained higher standards than even the top private producers, were built. With the outbreak of World War I in 1914, the government banned sales of all privately produced alcoholic drinks under a dry law meant to combat drunkenness among soldiers. Vodka continued to be sold widely nevertheless, chiefly in expensive restaurants, since the measure was largely seen as a ban aimed at the lower classes.[32]

After the Revolution, the Bolsheviks put all private producers out of business by appropriating their assets. Some were transferred to Moscow State Wine Warehouse no. 1, which later formed the basis of the famed Kristall distillery.

Although Lenin reduced alcohol production, Stalin lifted all restrictions by 1925, and deaths from drinking soon surpassed their prewar level.[33] The dictator's decision was explicitly meant to raise revenues that would enable the communist regime to refuse foreign investment. "What's better, the yoke of foreign capitalism or the sale of vodka?" Stalin is said to have asked. "Naturally, we will opt for vodka."[34] His policy came to be known as *pyanyi budzhet* ("drunken budget").

Half a century later, historian Sergei Roy wrote, the Soviet Union's "alcoholic nightmare" could be explained by the role that liquor, along with oil, played as the "backbone of the nation's budget."

Virtually all types of consumer goods were in short supply in the shops, but there was hardly ever a shortage of vodka, and people bought it not only because they were thirsty (although the nation's innate thirst should by no means be underrated) but because there was little else to buy. Where supplies of vodka ran dry, all economic life came to a halt: The budget had no money to pay the workers' wages with.

Some economists pointed out that the Marxian "commodity-money-commodity" formula had degenerated into the "vodka-money-vodka" form especially adapted to the Soviet way of life. I'd go a step further and insist that vodka was money, or *zhidkaya valyuta*, "liquid currency," as it was commonly called. Especially in the rural areas ordinary money would not buy you anything, while vodka—anything you might wish. On our trips through Siberia we regularly carried a goodish supply of *spirt*, or pure alcohol—practically the only means of obtaining transportation. With enough *spirt*, you could travel by helicopter even—always provided you could find a pilot sober enough to fly it, that is. Or take a *babushka* in a village who had to have her small plot of land plowed for planting potatoes, her principal subsistence crop. She just had to save a bottle of *samogon* hooch (vodka would be regarded as luxury) to pay the tractor driver, or her plot would go unplowed.[35]

Despite the widespread public drunkenness, it was all but impossible to buy vodka in Moscow shops when I first visited in 1991, more than three years after Gorbachev's antialcoholism campaign had ended. The scarcity reflected the economy's mortally crippled condition. Except for the little Beriozki stores that sold selected products to foreigners and privileged Soviets for foreign currency, which was illegal for most to possess, many shelves remained almost completely empty of everything that summer.

(Outdoor markets, called *rynki*, were different. Part of a loosely regulated gray market run with the help of criminal groups, they sold fresh produce for higher prices.) The few shops that did stock at least some products were so foul-smelling from (I presumed) mold and rot that I barely managed the arduous task of actually buying something when I tried. It required jostling through weary crowds crammed around display cases to glimpse what happened to be on sale. Next you determined how much you wanted and multiplied the number or weight by the price shown. God forbid you would have to ask an invariably dour salesperson, who would shake her head before reluctantly scribbling the figure on a scrap of paper. Then you stood in line elsewhere in the store for a cashier using an ancient register to ring up a receipt that you would bring back to the original display. After more pushing and more waiting, a salesperson would eventually reluctantly cut the very inferior cheese or sausage you'd chosen.

Gorbachev's relaxation of the administrative coercion that had kept the Soviet economic system running, however wastefully, for seven decades was based on hope that freedom from the quotas and orders imposed by the state planning agency Gosplan—which left not even the production of toothpicks up to supply and demand—would encourage factory managers and other lower-ranking officials who oversaw production lines to run their own industries more efficiently. After all, the logic went, they knew what needed to be done better than their superiors. But reducing central control actually helped bring the system down. The government set artificially low prices; when available, products were very cheap. The result was that enterprises had little incentive to produce goods and stores had little more to sell them. However, there was huge incentive to steal—that is, to steal from the state.

Much of Muscovites' time went into trying to guess where to get what they wanted or needed. For vodka, it was often restaurants because they still received supplies. I did best at the Rossiya Hotel, a huge, ghastly 1970s cube neighboring the Kremlin. Approaching the kitchen's back entrance, which faced the Moscow River and where one or more waiters were invariably loitering, dragging on cigarettes, you'd ask how much they would be willing to sell, then haggle over the price. A bottle cost roughly the equivalent of a dollar in rubles, several times more expensive than the official price. *Pshenichnaia*, or wheat vodka, was among the smoothest to be had, and you could often get several bottles. If a restaurant failed, you'd try another or a store's back entrance.

Foreigners had the option of frequenting one of a handful of seedy hard-currency bars, most of which were in hotels from which ordinary Soviets were barred. Burly KGB bouncers stood at the doors, stopping any locals bold enough to attempt to enter. Russians told me they could differentiate by looking at people's eyes: those of foreigners weren't dulled by weariness and resignation. Among the most popular haunts was the smoky bar in the basement of the 1970s Intourist Hotel near the Kremlin, now the site of the Ritz-Carlton. There, Western would-be entrepreneurs seeking business deals mingled with shady criminal types, prostitutes and foreign students. It wasn't a place where you'd want to spend much time, but you could buy as many big cans of Löwenbräu beer as you wanted if you could pay for them in dollars. And some foreign embassies gave weekly parties. One of the most popular was held at the German embassy, where most foreign passports got you in and beers cost two dollars.

Arriving in Moscow had transformed me from an impoverished college student into royalty. In addition to the relative wealth my few dollars conferred on me, stories of my life in the land of freedom and plenty made me interesting to Russians no matter how boring I actually was. Utterly cynical about their government and society and no longer afraid of punishment by the authorities, the young people I met were keen to snap up any bit of knowledge I could offer about the West. The collapse of the Soviet system's mores and strictures, which took place far more quickly than most people realized at the time, gave them a great sense of personal liberty. Free time was spent foraging for food and drink to serve at parties, which were usually held in the apartments of parents summering at their dachas. Their crumbling world made life a great adventure.

Outside Moscow, alcohol was even harder to come by. Visiting nearby Zagorsk, the site of one of Russia's four most important monasteries, I spent a day exploring the beautiful town before spotting a state restaurant that was miraculously open. I was with my friend Kolya—the young television correspondent with whom I'd soon travel to Vilnius—who persuaded a dark-haired waitress to seat us, which she did grudgingly, although we were the only patrons. Then she disappeared, leaving us to pore over a menu filled with a long list of the usual dishes: beef entrecôte, *pilmeni* (dumplings), *bliny*, *borsch*. Having made our choices, we waited ravenously for the waitress—in vain. After some time, it emerged that she and the rest of the staff were busy carting crates of beer from the kitchen to a van outside. Finally persuaded to approach our table, she patiently listened to our orders before sternly informing us that all the menu's dishes were unavailable. What about starters? we asked hopefully. Those too. Okay, what about two beers? Now irritation blazed from her eyes. There was no beer.

Pointing to a waiter who was wheeling another load of crates out the door, Kolya adopted his sweetest tone, free of his usual irony in such cases. "Darling, can't we just have a couple of bottles? We've traveled here all the way from Moscow; surely you wouldn't want us to leave with a bad impression of your town." His charm produced a compromise: two bowls of thin *borsch* grudgingly brought to our table.

The following year, 1992, when price controls were lifted and inflation skyrocketed, a dollar went from being worth twenty-seven rubles to two hundred, and the value would continue rising into the thousands. But now you could buy bottles of Pshenichnaia vodka from any number of Muscovites, many of them elderly, who desperately crowded around the entrances to train stations, metro stations and pedestrian underpasses by the hundreds, hawking food, drink, used clothes, toothbrushes, anything they could sell to make a few kopeks.

———

If alcoholism was a Soviet nightmare, it approaches the level of Armageddon today. Like computer-chip capacities, Russians' alcohol intake has almost doubled every decade since the 1970s. After years of talk about imposing a new state monopoly on spirits (which private manufacturers would be obliged to use for producing their liquor), the government announced plans in 2010 to quadruple the tax on vodka over the following three years, a hike that would double the minimum vodka price to about six dollars per half liter, roughly a pint. This time the aim appears to be less to fill the treasury's coffers—for which oil and gas are now far more important—than to finally do something about the drinking that's helping drive the average male life expectancy down to a level lower than North Korea's at at time when recent tax increases on cigarettes have helped push the number of smokers to historic lows in the United States.

However, few believe the authorities can withstand the centuries-old temptation to earn as much as possible from the new vodka taxes. Former Finance Minister Alexei Kudrin, long considered the government's leading liberal, recently encouraged his fellow countrymen to smoke and drink more, saying they were the best things they could do to help the economy emerge from the 2008 global financial crisis. "Those who drink," he said, "are giving more to help solve social problems [by] boosting demographics, developing other social services and upholding birth rates."

There may well be another major explanation for the government's failure to take effective measures to stop the rampage of alcohol: its unwillingness to face the crippling problem with anything like serious resolve or action. Or the authorities may believe, as Catherine the Great is said to have remarked, that it's easier to rule a drunken public.

In any case, higher prices prompted by the new taxes—along with restrictions on nighttime sales and advertising—are already driving more Russians to follow the old pattern of drinking dangerous and unregulated *samogon* and other poisonous liquor surrogates. Historian Alexander Nikishin is among those who maintain that establishing a monopoly is the only real way to fight the country's crippling alcoholism. But Nikishin also believes the lack of "enough honest people in government" would make it impossible to exert real control over alcohol production and consumption. "The more control there is in our country," he says, "the more corruption there is. Vodka can be your friend or enemy, depending on the authorities' attitudes. You can make a killing from it and lose your people."

But the government would have to do far more than simply control alcohol production and sales to seriously change the role drinking plays in Russia. Leaving aside the cold weather, that old justification for drinking to excess, alcohol abuse has partly been an "easy" escape from the individual's pawn-like role in society. More than just the physical difficulties of climate and geography, it's the state's crushing oppression, the corruption, the virtual lack of hope for change that are still contributing to Russia's traditional fatalism and resignation. The drinking done by the scientists I met in Novoi Urengoi surprised me at the time, but it was nothing unusual.

The morning I left, Victor, who'd drunk to the point of collapse, was in one of his rare sober moments. He apologized profusely. "Don't think badly of me," he appealed. My assurance that I wouldn't was genuine: I sympathized with him as a victim of his circumstances. Some of the drunks

I met in Russia, including several of my friends, were sensitive, intelligent people who'd lost control of their lives or never really had it.

As I was leaving for the airport, Victor repeated his invitation for me to visit his home in Khanty-Mansiisk. "We'll drink vodka together!" he promised as enticement.

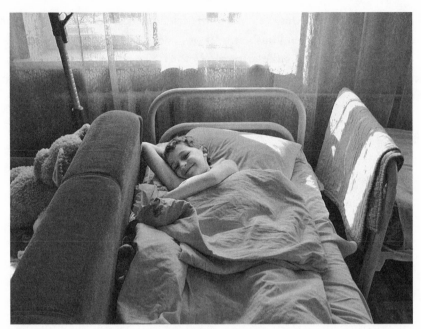

Internat No. 8.

A Nashi camp counselor passes propaganda images depicting opposition leaders Mikhail Kasyanov (left) and Garry Kasparov as prostitutes.

5

Intimates

Visiting friends is good, but home is better.

—Russian saying

The crushing uniformity of Moscow's dingy Soviet-era residential districts seems to lessen after sunset. The glow from countless windows, although generated mostly by ceiling lamps that cast an unflattering light inside the blocks of cramped apartments, can convey an almost cozy feeling. However illusory, they signify the haven of private life away from the gritty trials of the daily grind, especially because many of the apartments seemed lavish when they were first assigned to families that had been previously crammed into single rooms of dreaded communal apartments. Each abode became a testament to its occupants' resourcefulness. Every decoration—garish wallpaper, cheap lamps and gaudy velour furniture— represented a victory.

Of course there's far more variation today. Many of the apartments boast the latest foreign appliances to go with their *Evroremont* makeovers, as European-style refurbishments are commonly called (*Evro* for Europe and *remont* meaning "repair"). The new luxury heightens the sense of refuge, especially in winter, when streets layered with snow and ice are often barely passable, not to mention filthy. The patina of domestic tranquillity also belies the unimaginable suffering of recent memory.

Very many Russians have a dramatic, often appalling story of survival. Despite a current vogue for Stalin, the lawlessness of Moscow's streets is reminder enough of the violent, vindictive forces of human nature that continue to corrode society. Ubiquitous shopping malls and sushi chains give a gloss of Western-style normalcy to many districts, but step outside those oases of cathartic consumerism and there's no mistaking why Russians tend to believe that the individual is frail and security feeble. All the more reason the family was and remains a warm sanctuary that serves to widen the great cleavage Russians feel between themselves and the hostile outer world, despite many men's wretched treatment of their women at home.

Relatives of mine inhabit a little Soviet-era flat in a particularly smoggy Moscow district named Chertanovskaya. It belongs to my mother's second cousin Gera Kiva, whom I've mentioned, a mild-mannered, silver-haired man who lives with his wife, a gentle woman named Lucia, and his very elderly mother, Olga Sergeevna (my great-grandmother Polina's niece, whom everyone calls by her name and patronymic as a mark of respect). Now in her late eighties, Olga Sergeevna is canny, hardy and very frank. When she talks about her past, it's without rancor or regret. Her mentions of difficulties that would be intolerable to most Americans are no doubt offhand because they're nothing out of the ordinary for many Russians.

As I've noted, Olga Sergeevna's grandfather was a grain merchant in Kazan. Drafted in 1932, her husband was sent to southwestern Siberia as a food buyer for the Red Army and settled in the industrial city of Novosibirsk. Those years were among the worst of the Soviet famines, which were caused mainly by the collectivization of agriculture, and they were especially brutal in Kazan and other Volga River cities hit hard by Stalin's ruthless tactics and punishments. Since living was cheaper in Novosibirsk, where the chances of survival were also significantly greater, Olga Sergeevna soon joined her husband there.

In the late 1930s, they moved to Moscow, at first staying in the two-room apartment of my grandmother Serafima and her husband, Zhora, their lone family connection in Moscow. After World War II, when Serafima returned to Moscow with her new daughter, they, in turn, stayed in the Kivas' single room. Serafima and my mother may not have survived those years without such family ties, usually the most critical lifeline in a state that supposedly provided everything for everyone.

Of course, having the wrong connections could get you killed under Stalin, whose regime disrupted communication even between family members crammed together in single rooms. "No one ever discussed where you came from," Gera, a young boy at the time, recently remembered. One of his grandfathers had been a priest and other relatives were merchants. Worst of all, in the eyes of the authorities, part of the family had descended from gentry. "I knew almost nothing about any of that," he told me. "God forbid anyone had found out."

Travel abroad, work for international organizations and many other aspects of globalization have lessened the Bolsheviks' terrible legacy. Still, in some ways, family remains more important in Russia than it does elsewhere, even today. Although the Kiva family is not as tightly knit as it once was, Gera and Lucia's two grown sons spend much of the summer together at another Russian institution, the dacha, where Gera and Lucia help care for four grandchildren. Family ties remain central for them and most others in a country where institutions function poorly, the rule of law is weak and merit counts for far less in getting ahead than in other industrialized countries—all of which means it's often unwise to trust strangers. As in the past, practical considerations are more likely to dictate Russian behavior than differences in emotional makeup or beliefs.

————

It goes without saying that the Stalinist era wasn't the first time Russians or their ancestors faced an unrelenting threat to their existence. A need to overcome tremendous odds against survival has helped shape the Russian character since the first millennium CE, when the East Slavs, who gave rise to today's Russians, first migrated from Central Europe into the inhospitable northern forests around Moscow. The soil is poor in that region, swamps are numerous and winters bitterly cold. It is rarely mentioned that after settling in those forests, it took the Slavs many centuries to move south into the famed fertile Black Earth region. Crucially, that expansion came only after the foundation of their culture had been laid.

Scratching out a living from subsistence agriculture for many centuries provided the "womb" of Russian culture, shaping almost all aspects of life, as the Harvard historian Edward Keenan observed.[1] The Slavs—who quickly subsumed the indigenous, largely hunter-gatherer Balts and Finns—relied on slash-and-burn agriculture, chopping down trees, burning them and using the ash for fertilizer. That inefficient, wasteful method, which nourished crops for no more than a few years, required regular migration to new parts of the forest. One theory has it that slash-and-burn left an indelible mark on a people who have swallowed more territory than any other in the world.

No one family, let alone a single individual, could have survived very long under the brutal conditions in which the Slavs found themselves, according to Keenan, whose patient, rigorous dismissal of conventional wisdom about Russian history was a revelation for me and the many others who attended his lectures. A flooded field or the death of a cow could easily mean the difference between destruction and survival, he explained. Viable life required a larger basic social unit: the village, where relatively successful peasants could be forced to assume more responsibilities—such as taking care of a widow—while the less successful were saved from falling into complete ruin.

The central role of the communal village has made Russians hold "less confidence in human nature and its individual articulations than we do," Keenan has written about the effects of a millennium of subsistence farming. "They have learned that the individual is vulnerable and fragile."[2] Generally more pessimistic than their Western counterparts, Russians tend to be especially skeptical about "taking gambles on humans' moral virtue."[3] They're happier when group sanctions curb individuals' "harmful impulses."

Russia's perennial technological backwardness compared to countries further west kept reinforcing the tradition. The three-field system that laid the foundations for Europe's agricultural revolution in the twelfth century did not reach Russia until the second half of the fifteenth century. Mercantile towns became important only in the nineteenth century.

In the 1920s, idealistic Bolsheviks took the concept of the collective to its highest level by seeking to construct a utopian state that would serve as a new "family" for everyone. That required breaking apart the bourgeois family. Children would be educated not by their parents but by nurseries, schools and universities that would suppress reactionary, egotistical views about familial love left over from the old regime, instilling them instead with good communist ideals. The ideology originated abroad but grew well in fertile Russian soil.

The family structure faced its greatest threat under Stalin. Keenan believes the dictator's characterization of the state as the new basic unit that would supposedly protect the group from the harmful impulses of individuals remained within traditional ways of thinking. It was an all-encompassing endeavor. Art, literature and journalism were harnessed to shift self-identification from families to the Soviet collective. Stalin became the image of everyone's father, and the Motherland (*Rodina*) became their mother. People were instructed to forsake their own parents, as did the notorious and legendary Pavlik Morozov, the thirteen-year-old son of poor peasants who lived north of the Ural Mountains city of Sverdlovsk (now once again named Yekaterinburg).

Although there were countless other such cases, generations of Soviet schoolchildren were raised on the story of Pavlik Morozov, supposedly a model student and committed communist who headed his school's Young Pioneers group, roughly equivalent to the Boy Scouts. In 1932, he turned in his father to the OGPU, predecessor to the KGB, for forging documents to sell to "enemies of the Soviet state." The father, who headed the village soviet, or communist council, was sentenced to labor camp, then executed. Soon afterward, Pavlik's uncle, grandfather and other relatives took revenge on him and his eight-year-old brother by hacking them to pieces in the woods. All the perpetrators except the uncle were soon caught and shot as reactionaries.

Pavlik became lionized as a communist hero. Statues of him appeared throughout the country, composers wrote songs and even an opera about him and Sergei Eisenstein made a film about his story, cementing his status as a Soviet icon. For decades, teachers held him up as a model for the lesson that loyalty to the state must supersede loyalty to one's own family.

Virtually the entire story was invented. Details of the real one emerged only after the collapse of communism: Morozov wasn't a model student, a Young Pioneer or even called Pavlik, relatives said; rather, his name was Pashka, another diminutive for Pavel. As for his motives, one version has it that his mother may have compelled him to denounce his father after he'd left her for another woman. It's unlikely the truth will ever be known, not least because the Federal Security Service, successor to the KGB, continues to deny access to the relevant documents because it considers the case still open. The likeliest explanation is that the secret police or its agents murdered Pavlik and his brother to create a myth that would glorify informers and frighten residents of a region that was staunchly resisting the disastrous policy of collectivization.[4]

The building into which my mother, Tatyana, moved in 1945, when she was a toddler returning with her mother from wartime evacuation, housed doctors, senior nurses and other top personnel from my grandmother Serafima's tuberculosis dispensary. Built for wealthy bourgeois families, it had a splendid main entrance leading to a sweeping marble staircase and an elevator encased in ornate cast-iron latticework. The structure became a metaphor for life under communism. Its elevator, like many in Moscow, no longer worked—not that it mattered because the entrance, whose doors had been hammered over with boards, was irrelevant. As in countless other buildings, residents came and went through the "black" entrance in back, originally built for servants' use. That was partly because nighttime arrests were easier and less visible on narrow back staircases, which also made escape more difficult. The dusty main stairs were used only as a playground by Tatyana—Tanya—and her friends, who would sneak in there and pretend they lived in a mansion where they received guests in grand style.

Serafima and Tanya's apartment had four rooms, each occupied by a family, and a communal bathroom, a communal kitchen and a large entrance hall. Exposed pipes and wires ran everywhere. The families took turns cooking and hanging laundry to dry on lines over the stove in the depressing, grimy-looking kitchen. With no refrigerator or icebox, food was kept cool between the inner and outer windowpanes. Waiting lists dictated each room's occupancy; as Serafima gained seniority, she was rewarded with slightly larger quarters as they became available. By the time Tatyana was sixteen, their room was sixteen square meters—roughly 170 square feet.

Tatyana eventually stopped screaming, but she hated the institutions where she had to stay while Serafima was working long hours. She spent much of her first years in nurseries and state-run boarding schools called *internat*, where she would remain for several days running. After lunch, children would be put on cots outside for naps, swaddled in heavy sleeping sacks against the cold. Little Tanya found it torture—it was impossible to move, even to scratch an itch—but she quickly understood that protest brought worse punishment, therefore her displeasure poured out only when she was safe with her kindly, doting mother. However, dangers for the rebellious little girl lurked at home, too, including in the person of a new arrival she took to calling "the apartment hooligan."

Almost every communal apartment housed at least one usually feared and hated *stukach*, or snitch. The word comes from the verb meaning "to knock," itself a euphemism for informing derived from the supposed practice of knocking at officials' doors to deliver information. In Tatyana's flat, the informer occupied the largest room. Soon after his wife died, when Tatyana was in her midteens, he married a corpulent cleaning woman who moved in from her grim basement quarters in a nearby building. She was the embodiment of a peasant woman, a *baba*—the equivalent of a fishmonger's wife—with a large mouth from which issued very coarse language in a very gruff voice. Hardly believing her luck in having been elevated from rags to relative riches, she lost no time wielding her new power over her neighbors.

When hemlines began rising in the late 1950s, the *stukach*'s wife mocked Tatyana and her friends in colorful village dialect. "What's this?!" she'd bellow, standing in the kitchen. "Look at them walking around town, flashing their pussies!" (She used the term *pukhovka*, meaning "puff.") The girls proceeded to scribble caricatures of her holding a sign reading PUKHOVKA, which they scattered in the kitchen cabinets and on the stairwell. Livid, the apartment hooligan complained to the dispensary's director, which luckily for Tatyana had the effect of only spreading the mockery.

Tatyana's and Serafima's friends and relatives provoked hot fury from the *stukach*'s wife when they visited. Although Tatyana's father, the military surgeon Mutakhar Khuzikhanov, returned to his family in the Caucasus region of Kabardino-Balkaria after the war, he maintained contact with Serafima and visited occasionally. His youngest brother, Shamil, a gifted pianist who was almost certainly gay—and, needless to say, was tightly closeted in those days—studied at the Gnessin Institute, a musical college second only to the famed Moscow Conservatory. On graduating, he was assigned to the relative backwater of Yaroslavl, a city several hours northeast of Moscow, where he directed a choir. Desperate to return to the capital, he had little hope of doing so officially without obtaining a residence permit after his mandatory stint. Serafima's cousin Olga Kiva, who worked for a construction agency, eventually used her connections to procure him both the coveted documents and his own apartment. Meanwhile, he often stayed with Serafima and Tatyana.

The *stukach*'s wife castigated Shamil in archaic provincial speech at every opportunity. When he snuck into the kitchen to cook, she hustled in to bawl, *"Oslaboni gorelku!"* (literally "Weaken the burner!"—meaning turn down the stove). But it was jockeying over the single bathroom that caused the greatest friction between neighbors. In the rare instances when it was free, Shamil would hole up inside for long baths. Alerted to his presence there, his nemesis would lurk outside the door and growl, *"Moisia, moisia Tatarin, v poslendii ras!"* ("Wash yourself, you Tatar, for the last time!"). "Tatar" in itself was a derogatory term. Shamil, who liked to imitate the accents of the archetypal peasant characters who populate the plays of Alexander Ostrovsky, roared with laughter at her.

Privately, Shamil's fierce hatred of the Soviet order generated a steady stream of risqué and risky sarcasm and humor. And although he rarely thanked Serafima for her hospitality, he lavished praise on her cooking, especially her *shchi*, or cabbage soup. Her rice was never merely good, but "like white Persian lilac!" Eventually, he reciprocated by teaching Tatyana to play the piano.

———

Socialist realist literature, a term coined in 1932 to describe what had emerged as the single genre acceptable to the state, extolled privation in private life. Its protagonists—"positive heroes"—epitomized the ideal "new Soviet man," who recapitulated the official version of history, which invariably led to the triumph of Marxism-Leninism.[5] One of the classics, Nikolai Ostrovsky's novel *How the Steel Was Tempered* (1936), tells the story of a young Bolshevik wounded in the October Revolution. Overcoming his handicap, he becomes a writer who inspires workers building the new state. In Fyodor Gladkov's *Cement*, an earlier novel that served as a template for the standard socialist realist plot, the protagonist, Gleb, returns from the Russian Civil War to discover that his previously submissive wife has become a committed communist who sets an example by sacrificing her personal happiness. The couple leave their daughter at a crumbling children's home so they can help rebuild a destroyed cement factory. When Gleb wavers, his wife, Dasha, asks him whether he prefers "pretty flowers to bloom in the windowsill."

"No, Gleb, in the winter I live in an unheated room, eat in a communal kitchen. You see, I'm a free Soviet citizen."[6] The daughter eventually dies.

Under the strictures of socialist realism, the individual's freedom is inseparable from the fate of the state. Novelist Andrei Sinyavski, who castigated socialist realism in the 1950s, wrote ironically that absence of freedom posed no dilemma for people who believed.

> When Western writers deplore our lack of freedom of speech, their starting point is their belief in the freedom of the individual. This is the foundation of their culture, but it is organically alien to Communism. A true Soviet writer, a true Marxist, will not accept these reproaches, and will not even know what they are all about.[7]

Socialist realist art—some of it very good, especially when created by former members of the avant-garde—served the same purpose. Private interiors, the domain of bourgeois selfishness, were rarely depicted. Instead, crowds dominated, often outside the home, as they engaged in productive labor, harmonious street life and Soviet parades. As Harvard professor Svetlana Boym argues, one of the better-known exceptions to the rule illustrates how the distinction between public and private was minimized. Alexander Laktionov's *The New Apartment*, a painting completed in 1952, shows a beaming mother and son standing on the threshold of a new neoclassical Stalin-era apartment. The image of the proletarian salt of the earth, the mother has her head wrapped in a kerchief. Her hands are on her hips, and her son wears a Young Pioneers uniform. The boy is holding a portrait of Stalin, the eternally present father figure and benefactor. Around them lie some of their meager possessions, including stacks of books and a rubber plant. It's a scene of almost complete transparency: all the books, their titles visible on the spines, are by classic Soviet writers, and all the doors are open, so there's nothing to hide. Neighbors or the apartment's fellow residents—we don't know whether it's communal—look on. However, even that seemingly exemplary Soviet painting wasn't appropriate for the regime; it was censored after critics deemed the rubber plant too bourgeois.[8]

Communal living was one of the state's most effective tools for undermining traditional relationships. Besides the value of its economy when people were flocking to cities where housing was incredibly scarce, the communal apartment was intended to serve the ideological purpose of supposedly freeing women from the dictatorship of the kitchen by enabling them to share duties. In fact, the tight proximity bred suspicion and hatred. Nadezhda Mandelshtam, the wife of poet Osip Mandelshtam—who died in prison in 1938—observed that the Bolshevik regime cut social bonds between everyone. "Nobody trusted anyone else and every acquaintance was a suspected police informer," she wrote.

> Every family was always going over its circle of acquaintances, try-ing to pick out the provocateurs, the informers and the traitors. After 1937, people stopped meeting each other altogether, and the secret police were thus well on their way to achieving their ulti-mate objective. Apart from assuring a constant flow of informa-tion, they had isolated people from each other and had drawn large numbers of them into their web, calling them in from time to time, harassing them and swearing them to secrecy by means of signed statements. All such people lived in eternal fear of being found out and were consequently just as interested as regular members of the police in the stability of the existing order and the inviolability of the archives where their names were on file.[9]

Boym, who grew up under Soviet rule in Leningrad, describes the resulting practice of speaking "with half words."

> What is shared is silence, tone of voice, nuance of intonation. To say a full word is to say too much; communication on the level of words is already excessive, banal, almost kitschy. This peculiar form of communication "with half words" is the mark of belong-ing to an imagined community that exists on the margins of the official public sphere. Hence the American metaphors for being sincere and authentic—"saying what you mean," "going public," and "being straightforward"—do not translate properly into the Soviet and Russian contexts.[10]

———

My grandmother Serafima had a very small circle of friends who—thanks to the lack of restaurants and cafés, not to mention money to spend in them—would take turns hosting each other for tea and gossip in the relative safety of their rooms. Among the visitors was Serafima's childhood friend from Kazan, whom Tatyana called Aunt Rita. The visitor supplemented her income by sewing dresses for her friends, a service much needed during the clothing shortages, and for her own part took pains to wear lipstick and high heels.

Another frequent guest, Aunt Shura, was married to the brother of Serafima's husband, Zhora, still imprisoned after his arrest for being a member of the Tupolev aviation team. Anatoly Leimer, Zhora's brother, had also been arrested and almost certainly died. Aunt Shura, his wife or widow, lived in a small basement room with her teenage daughter Ella, a dark-haired beauty who had many suitors, including a boyfriend who later engaged in illegal "speculation"—trading goods for profit. This enabled him to provide Ella with foreign clothes that heightened her appeal to her admirers.

Although Tatyana knew very little about her mother's personal life, she did know that Serafima barely talked to anyone outside her little core group. When one or more friends gathered over *zakuski* and the occasional cake, there was much complaining. Whenever a voice raised itself in a hint of outrage, another voice shushed it with "Careful, the walls have ears!" At one point, Tatyana earnestly examined the walls to try to find them. Later, my mother would remember that "no one knew whether there were listening devices, but despite wanting to know what went on in every room, of course Stalin couldn't bug every apartment. But all of them had a *stukach*, and everyone knew who he or she was."

When Tatyana's father Mutakhar visited from southern Kabardino-Balkaria for several days once every year or two, he would appear in his military uniform, smelling of tobacco and bearing presents and otherwise unobtainable food he'd bought from shops for military officers: caviar, sturgeon, Georgian wine and sparkling water. Tatyana would race down the hall from her room into his arms at the apartment's entrance beside the kitchen. Tall, athletic and outgoing, Mutakhar died in 1954 from cancer.

Serafima as well as Mutakhar's younger brother Shamil, the cynical musician, were also close to an army colonel and his wife who, despite his status—or perhaps because of it—shared Shamil's barely hidden hatred for the communist regime. Alexei Panfilov had served in Vienna at the end of the war, when Soviet soldiers looted whatever they could lay their hands on. With utensils from a lavish pilfered silver service along with fine porcelain and other trophies, his wife, Tamara, taught Tatyana how to properly use a knife and fork.

Tamara took Tatyana under her wing partly because she had no offspring of her own and also because children were considered a special category of people, to be protected from the outside world even by strangers. Youngsters were a vessel of private life; shielding them from the state's manipulation and repression was the surest way to pass down alternative traditions and values. Even people who didn't see them that way treated them as a common good.

However, although Russians tend to treat other people's children well, anecdotal evidence is now emerging that many young Soviets suffered far harsher punishment and more neglect than commonly believed, according to some of the testimony from educator Marilyn Murray's moving columns in the *Moscow Times*.[11] I've seen mentions on Facebook of working parents leaving their children alone for hours and preschool teachers' threats to punish misbehavior by administering injections or forcing children to clean toilets. That's not surprising in a country where parents on playgrounds often act more kindly toward strangers' children than their own, whom they admonish as if they were exasperating, slow-witted adults.

Another member of Serafima's close circle, her cousin Olga (Sergeevna) Kiva, rarely displayed outward affection for Tatyana on the days she agreed to look after the mischievous girl. Beginning with stern lectures about what was allowed and what wasn't, Olga Sergeevna spent much of their time together suspecting misbehavior. That didn't stop Tatyana from violating rules by jumping on her relative's bed when she was away in the kitchen.

Olga Sergeevna behaved differently when it was her turn to visit Serafima's room. There she would exclaim, "Tanichka, Tanichka!" upon entering and Tatyana would be forced to kiss the woman, for whom she had no particular liking. Failing to display kindness to children in Soviet Russia raised suspicion. It was a signal that a person couldn't be trusted with the secrets of a family's private life. In a dangerous society where trust among family members was crucial for survival, exclusion could make life even more perilous.

No doubt Serafima's highly cautious nature, especially after her husband's arrest, made her especially protective of Tatyana. Her frequent warnings to be careful, to bundle up and to not get hurt often had the opposite effect on her rebellious daughter, whom she told nothing about the outside world and gave no direct hint about whether she believed Soviet rule was good or bad.

When Tatyana began school, she was bombarded with typical propaganda. Taught to be grateful to the Motherland, children were also inducted into Stalin's cult of personality. Like most, Tatyana believed Lenin was everyone's grandfather and Stalin was their father. On the most important official day of the year, the anniversary of the great October Revolution, Serafima—a woman who had suffered her share of privation and anguish under the communist system—presented her daughter with books inscribed with congratulations. "Perhaps she thought I was one of those with ears behind the walls," my mother said later in wistful reflection.

Other families hid far more: stories are legion about people lying to their spouses for decades. It was a matter of survival; the Soviet regime forced them to deny their thoughts, identities and histories to the extent that they began to doubt themselves, a widespread psychological trauma that has yet to be fully acknowledged, let alone dealt with. No wonder the culture of lying remains deep-seated today, when the daily denial of reality provides fertile ground for Russia's staggering corruption.

Some areas of normality existed under the Soviet Union, however. Although indoctrination was supposedly critical in Young Pioneer summer camps, many were surprisingly free of propaganda beyond the usual ideological songs, and even ardent anticommunists remember them fondly. Not all camps were the same. Tatyana initially pressed her mother to enroll her in one of those established for workers' children because that's where many of her school's bullies and rule breakers went, and she didn't want to stand out by being different. "They were bandit types," she said. "Their families drank heavily, the men swore, they were very crude and uncultured, and I was horrified by the children." Other summer camps were little different from their American counterparts: oases where boys and girls hiked in the woods, played volleyball and enjoyed their first crushes.

Lives in communal apartments continued more or less unchanged until 1961, when Khrushchev began erecting cheap five-story apartment blocks to alleviate the housing shortage. The structures were later called *Khrushcheby*—a spin on *trushcheby*, "slums." Serafima and Tatyana's move into their own apartment in one of those buildings occasioned great joy.

Although deep suspicion of strangers persists, attitudes toward personal relationships as well as the state began changing soon after Stalin's death in 1953. One of the qualities my father liked most about the Soviet Union when he traveled there in the 1960s and '70s was the nature of friendships, which led him to share an affection for Russia with other foreigners who also had some of their closest friends there. Ironically or not, George Kennan, the architect of the American policy of containment who served five months as a US diplomat in Moscow before his expulsion by Stalin, also loved Russia, a country he described in his memoirs as "in my blood… There was some mysterious affinity which I could not explain even to myself." For my father, there was nothing mysterious about the people he liked, the Western-leaning ones who read the same books and had the same political and cultural instincts. He once characterized their naturalness as a kind of freedom from fear of making fools of themselves. If Americans in restaurants hesitate to complain because they're afraid of appearing foolish and the English don't even dream of arguing, Russians wouldn't hesitate to plunge right in. On top of that, they were willing to do virtually anything, and at the drop of a hat, to help their friends. Like private life in general at the time, friendship was more important than work. And because most people were oppressed more or less equitably, meaning that ordinary striving rarely got you anywhere (unless it was done according to the Party's rules), Soviets seemed to value love and companionship, even if by default, more than most Westerners did.

There was also a very practical reason for the importance of friendship. As the authorities relaxed their grip on private lives, many people increasingly looked to turn the tables on the state by exploiting it for their own benefit. Growing nepotism, theft and other forms of corruption gave rise to networks and distribution systems for goods and services. Sociologist Vladimir Shlapentokh described the exploitation of state resources for personal interests as essentially "privatizing" the state, and he believes everyone came to assume that everyone else was partaking.[12]

Friends and family played the central role in what emerged as the Soviet "second economy," Shlapentokh writes.[13] You beat the system with the help of your friends. After the state confirmed people's right to own private plots of land in 1977, the dacha—an oasis away from urban life and Soviet strictures—became a center of leisure life. Because building materials often couldn't be obtained in stores, scrounging and stealing them from wherever they could be had became a key activity. Their disappearance from construction sites that were left unguarded caused work stoppages on many buildings, or so people said at the time. That channeling of state resources into private hands was illegal but accepted. And as more people bought cars—at the time, the only ones available were of Soviet manufacture—the constant need to service the rusting little disasters on wheels increased the importance of personal connections for acquiring spare parts.

Art and literature reflected the change. A new, more casual tone that arose during Khrushchev's de-Stalinization campaign in the late 1950s and early '60s idealized individual pursuits instead of the state. Poets Yevgeny Yevtushenko and Andrei Vosnesensky and guitar-strumming bards Bulat Okudzhava and Vladimir Vysotsky provided personal voices that undermined totalitarian generalizations and ideals.[14] In films, the nomadic geologist traveling vast expanses of empty land for the sake of furthering Soviet knowledge became an archetype. And for many citizens, travel within the Soviet Union and camping in the countryside became expressions of officially approved romantic individualism.

Although the Soviet Union had undergone a sea change by the time I first visited thanks to Gorbachev's *perestroika*, friends and family were still very much how one usually got things done even then, or perhaps especially then, since as I've described many store shelves were literally empty.

My cousin Ulugbek, who abandoned his promising academic career in 1993, and his wife, Natalia, relied on connections to survive. For example, a friend of Natalia's who worked in a grocery store would set aside a box of about twenty frozen chickens when deliveries arrived. "We'd thaw them, cut them up into pieces and try to figure out how long they'd last," Natalia explained. Such typical "under-the-floor" schemes of course made store shelves even emptier.

Many Russians had long made jam from fruit gathered or bought in summer so it would last until winter. However, a critical lack of sugar— much of it was used for making moonshine—meant that was no longer possible. Obtaining large quantities of food when it was available therefore necessitated freezers, which were in especially short supply. Unable to buy one in Moscow, Ulugbek used his connections to obtain something else, a new television set. After driving four hundred and fifty miles east to Kazan, he exchanged it at a freezer factory. "If you had a head for commerce,"

Natalia said, "you could get by." Another friend of hers who worked for a shoe company was paid in shoes—a common practice in the mid-1990s, when the economy was starved of capital, many wages were unpaid and barter transactions accounted for up to half of industrial output.[15] Natalia took some of her boxes of shoes to sell at factories and schools.

I'd already seen some evidence of the importance of connections when I met several Russians during a year I spent at Dartmouth College. They were among the first wave of ordinary Soviets who traveled abroad more or less freely, meaning no reason had been found to deny them permission to leave after they'd gone through the very onerous application process. At Dartmouth, they slept on the couches and floors of classmates they'd met during the Americans' semesters abroad in Leningrad, as St. Petersburg was then called.

They stayed and stayed. Those who were thrown out moved to rooms of new friends and acquaintances. The guests appeared to have not one iota of concern about their imposition and distracting effect on college students who couldn't easily afford either the time or the expense of caring for essentially helpless visitors. (With little English and no money, the Russians survived largely on food snuck from cafeterias.)

They succeeded because there was something infectious about their warmth, their eagerness to please and embrace of hedonism. I befriended one of them, a ne'er-do-well with long blond hair and a brilliant wit in his late thirties named Yuri, who after a few weeks had adopted the look and studiously unhurried manner of a California surfer. Thriving on company, he was game for anything, including swimming in the Connecticut River and especially guzzling beer at the parties held in one or another reeking fraternity basement most evenings. After I invited him to visit for a couple of weeks that summer, already knowing better, he stayed for months and became a devoted friend. I felt certain that if our roles were reversed and I were penniless in the Soviet Union, he'd do the same for me. In any case, no American I ever met had a tenth of Yuri's nonchalance or fatalism.

It was a friend of Yuri's, a waiter who had never previously heard of me before I showed up on *his* doorstep, who put me up when I arrived in Leningrad during the coup d'état attempt in the summer of 1991. He also used his connections to get pain relievers from a hospital because I was sick, then procured train tickets to Moscow that would have been impossible for me to obtain. However, those kinds of ties to friends of friends who were otherwise strangers began dissolving almost immediately with the Soviet collapse. Once the state's intrusion into private life more or less ended, so did the bonds engendered by the common plight. With everyone having to go out and hustle, there was far less time, energy and concern for others.

Although some found the new freedom to legally wheel and deal liberating, many couldn't make it in the new Russia. After spending almost a decade in the United States drifting from one job and/or friend's house to another, Yuri returned to his hometown, once again called St. Petersburg. Growing up under a system that provided most people with little incentive to work—unless you wanted to climb the Party ladder—he, like almost every other Soviet citizen, had developed a kind of passive resistance that consisted of doing as little as possible. Given a job to do—splitting wood in New Hampshire, for example—he would go at it until the job was done. But although he was brilliant with his hands and conscientious about even the most demeaning work, he seemed incapable of planning his future or otherwise acting to improve his lot. Russians have a special word to describe such behavior: *avos*, a desire to avoid hassles while maintaining blind hope for the best.

Back in Russia, Yuri took computer classes but couldn't be bothered to look for a job as a programmer, then tried trading money on the foreign exchange until he had none left. Unable or unwilling to hold down a real job for more than a few months, he continues struggling to make ends meet.

Like Yuri, the country itself is adrift in many spheres besides politics, its authoritarian regime sustained thanks mainly to the high oil prices that enable it to lavish money on whatever it wants. The American writer Richard Lourie calls it Zombie Russia.

Twenty years after the Bolshevik Revolution, there was no question about the nature and identity of Soviet Russia. Twenty years after the collapse of the Soviet Union, the new Russia has failed to forge a new identity for itself. It has no vision, no symbols and no values but to make hay while the sun shines. No single defining adjective has yet to adhere to its name—like Muscovite, Tsarist or Soviet Russia. No name has even been found for the 20-year period itself, like Thaw or Perestroika, which had caught on quickly in the past. No one believes in the country's future past the end of oil. There is a void at the core of today's Russia.[16]

In this Russia of little to offer apart from opportunities for the ambitious to grab whatever they can get, many rely on what's left of Soviet-era institutions, one of which is the grandmother: the *babushka*. Under communism, writes sociologist Shlapentokh, the housing shortages that forced young couples to live with their parents, combined with strict rules that pushed people into retirement at sixty-five and the need for financial and physical support from older relatives, enabled many young people to "exploit" their parents by imposing the care of their children on them. More than 40 percent of urban babies were cared for by their grandmothers, whose levels of activity increased after they retired, according to one study.[17] Although no statistics about current levels of grandparents' involvement exist, I have noticed that the parents of the majority of my friends spend much of their retirement helping bring up their grandchildren.

Among those friends is Kolya, the fellow journalist with whom I was traveling in Lithuania in 1991. Born in 1967, he was raised in an outlying Moscow neighborhood called Kuntsevo, in a typical apartment made of prefabricated concrete slabs. Six people, including Kolya's parents, sister, grandmother and great-aunt, lived in eighteen square meters—190 square feet. Like so many other boys, he grew up playing and fighting in the courtyard of his building, where residents gathered and talked. After his mandatory two-year army service, which he spent driving trucks at an air base near Moscow, Gorbachev's reforms enabled him to unexpectedly enter one of the Soviet Union's top universities, the Moscow State Institute of International Relations. MGIMO had been known for grooming future KGB officers and children of the Communist Party elite. After Kolya married in the 1990s, he sold his late grandmother's small apartment to help pay for a new one in Moscow's unfashionable outskirts, where his new wife's parents would live. Kolya's in-laws had given up their central Moscow home to his wife, a lawyer. Soon, in their new apartment, they took in Kolya and Olga's large dog. Several years later, they added Kolya's daughter. Despite having her own bedroom at home, that daughter—a precocious, energetic twelve-year-old—has grown up living with her grandparents. They take her to her nearby school and, in summer, to their dacha outside the city. Kolya and his wife usually see her only on some weekends. They are now divorced, far from unusual in the country with the world's highest divorce rate. According to the UN, five of every one thousand Russians are divorced.[18]

Although his salary is lower than those of his Western colleagues, Kolya unquestionably belongs to the Russian middle class. A well-educated urban professional with disposable income, he owns real estate and vacations on the Mediterranean—exactly the kind of person the Kremlin's critics hope will someday help support democratic reform. Despite the widespread signs of growth, however—including the mushrooming number of relatively affordable hypermarkets and sushi restaurants that cater to the demographic—definitions of the middle class and its size vary widely.

Signs of a post-Soviet middle class in the Western sense—very generally defined as including those with enough discretionary income to be able to afford consumer goods, health care and provide for their children's education—first surfaced in the mid-1990s. However, expectations for its rise were suddenly cut short by the economic crisis of 1998, when the precipitous drop of the ruble's value decimated people's savings. The numbers seemed to recover by 2002, when a benchmark study put the middle class at a quarter of the population.

But after a decade of steadily rising wages, stalled for two years during the global financial crisis of 2008, official figures still put the middle class—defined as consisting of individuals who earn at least the equivalent of twelve thousand dollars a year (or families earning that amount per individual) and also own a car and an apartment[19]—at 25 percent of the population, compared to around 60 percent in the United States. However, independent surveys put the figure at anywhere between 10 percent of the population when people are categorized by education and income to more than 80 percent when Russians are asked to identify the class to which they belong. Pollster Ludmilla Khakhurina told me that statistics issued by the state committee that compiles them may not accurately reflect real income, thanks to widespread tax evasion and the black and gray markets that continue to make up a large part of the economy. "Our social structure isn't clear because the criteria are changeable," she said. Russia's peculiar economy also differs from those of Western countries because housing was essentially distributed free after the end of communism and utility payments remain subsidized. Khakhurina prefers to look at consumer preferences and people's own evaluations of their status.

Russians' political apathy during the first decade of Putin's rule, when, judging by Western standards of engagement, the masses appeared to support a system that worked against their interests, led some to reject the term "middle class" altogether. "Consumer class" seemed more accurate.

Comparisons to the West are also misleading because many Russians' life-styles are made possible by enduring Soviet-era institutions and arrange-ments that provide stability in the face of upheaval by giving them a stake in the going system, as I've tried to describe. Although he doesn't support Putin, Kolya Pavlov also doesn't feel compelled to protest. Neither does his mother-in-law, who has often complained to me about her lot. Often tired and generally upset about having to bring up her granddaughter, whom she loves, she acquiesces nevertheless. Unlike grandfathers, who tend to be far more remote figures, grandmothers often accept their fate because it is expected of them, as it was under Soviet rule.

In other ways, *babushki* are anachronisms. Every block of apartments has its phalanx of them sitting on broken benches, where they while away hours with gossip and often dispense admonitions to anyone committing what they consider to be a folly, such as not wearing a hat in the cold. Women are sometimes upbraided for sitting on cold surfaces, which is believed to freeze their ovaries. The *babushki* are usually ignored. Despite their hard lot in life, they get very little respect.

The elderly have never had it easy in Russia, even when they're not dismissed as senile and weak. In the Soviet Union, life for most included not being able to travel abroad, speak freely, or even—usually outside of Moscow—find toilet paper to buy. But all citizens could count on at least one thing then: the state would fully provide for their retirements. No lon-ger, that support having all but vanished with the communist collapse more than two decades ago, leaving many to fend for themselves with little idea of how to get by, let alone experience at it. In the early 1990s, many thousands of elderly and very elderly people lined Moscow metro entrances, holding up clothes, household possessions and anything else they might sell, until they were banned from doing so. Although the average pension has more than doubled since 2002, many elderly are still forced to improvise.

Seventy-two-year-old Muscovite Lydia Kuznetsova, a former defense industry engineer, supplements her $130 monthly pension by selling clothes she sews. A widow, she also grows her own vegetables at a Soviet-era gar-den plot outside the city and pickles them for winter. Kuznetsova says she preferred life under the Soviet Union "because we grew up under that sys-tem. What's happening now is that prices are always rising. If pensions are raised even a little, prices for everything rise again." Kuznetsova shops at a special market on the city's outskirts, where prices for bruised fruit and defective goods are lower than elsewhere, a stark contrast to the conspicuous display of wealth on central Moscow's traffic-jammed streets.

The officials who acknowledge the discrepancy include President Putin, who occasionally gravely announces that society owes the elderly a debt. After he said that helping them was a top priority, he oversaw comprehensive pension reform in 2002, standardizing payments throughout the country and indexing them to inflation. Still, the average pension remains barely above the official subsistence level. The system, which runs at a deficit of more than forty billion dollars a year, faces crisis thanks partly to Putin's campaign promises to continue raising payments. Although the elderly continue to scrape by, falling oil prices or another financial jolt may leave the government unable to afford even the current level of help.

Older people aren't the only group to suffer en masse. Like many aspects of life, much rearing of young children is governed by superstition and tradition. Most babies are still swaddled at birth without being washed, then kept tightly wrapped for weeks. Often explained as necessary for the safety of infants who would otherwise hurt themselves, the practice reflects traditional views about individuals' harmful impulses. An old saw has it that swaddling helps explain Russia's outbursts of frenetic activity between the long periods of submission. Whatever truth lies in that, Russian children wave their limbs for all they're worth when the swaddling cloth is removed.

The popularity of a recent book titled *America—What a Life!*, which interprets American customs for Russian readers, highlighted the insularity of Russian life together with the success of state propaganda that depicts Americans as brutish imperialists. Written by Nikolai Zlobin, a political analyst who's provided some of the most trenchant criticism of Putin's Russia, it tapped a rich vein of general interest by explaining the American preference for teenage babysitters instead of *babushki*, the relative lack of lying in polite society and the preference for seeking out professional services— from plumbers to lawyers—based on ability instead of their closeness as friends or relatives.[20]

However, globalization is changing many aspects of life, including childhood. Hollywood films, American cartoon characters and pop music are helping assimilate new generations to a greater degree than ever before, at least on a superficial level. That will have a huge effect on a future Russian society that may no longer feel as alienated from Western culture (whatever its merits) as it has in the last decade. But while television and the Internet may be making that true for many children even in remote provinces, others are still suffering the consequences of a Soviet legacy that doesn't appear to be changing very much at all: the orphanage.

———

Moscow's Internat No. 8 is an unusual place. Housed in a neatly painted four-story concrete building in a leafy, residential part of town, the state boarding school for orphans is clean, its teachers are dedicated and the children, who sleep many to a room, appear genuinely happy. It's also open to visitors, which is why it's one of the very few such places I was able to observe.

Inside, every child has a heartbreaking story. A sensitive-looking thirteen-year-old boy named Sasha told me that he ran away from home at the age of six because his parents "behaved badly."

"They drank and took drugs and didn't take care of me," he said. That's a common story in Russia, where many of the nearly eight hundred thousand children identified as orphans have living parents. Another student, a smiling twelve-year-old girl with long red hair named Tatyana, was abandoned at birth. She said she liked drawing and sewing and wanted to become a doctor. She has a chance: the students at Internat No. 8 are incredibly lucky compared to most orphaned and abandoned children, and they know it. By all independent accounts, most other such institutions are depressing places that provide very few opportunities.

Despite Russia's vast number of institutionalized children, the government has only recently begun to encourage adoption. But very few Russian families want to adopt orphans because they are often seen as sick or otherwise damaged. Half of the fifteen thousand children adopted in Russia annually have been taken in by foreigners—many of them, until recently, Americans, who have adopted more children from Russia than from any other country except China and Guatemala, despite Russian policies that have made foreign adoption very difficult. An Education Ministry official named Sergei Vitelis told me the hurdles exist because Russian children should stay in Russia. "Adoption by foreigners isn't right," he said. "Any normal state should create conditions for children to grow up in their own country. That's what we're aiming for."

Children's rights advocates say such disapproval of foreign adoptions is more about national pride than any genuine concern for child welfare. In late 2012, Putin banned all adoptions by Americans as a response to President Obama's signing of the so-called Magnitsky bill, a human rights measure that instituted travel bans and other sanctions against Russian officials connected to the prison death of lawyer Sergei Magnitsky in 2009. Russian legislators settled on the adoption ban—part of a series of new restrictions aimed at reducing Russian cooperation with the United States—because it was one of the few measures that would have an impact on Americans. It followed public pressure prompted by several high-profile cases of abuse and death of adopted Russian children in the United States. There's "no need to go out and make a tragedy out of it," said Pavel Astakhov, a celebrity lawyer who is Russia's child rights commissioner and a major supporter of the ban, after announcing the new law would block the departure of almost fifty children already approved for adoption by Americans.

Although Astakhov has overseen a program to encourage foster care and adoption, the adoption ban's many critics say the attitudes behind it are condemning a growing number of children to a system of Soviet-era institutions desperately in need of reform, where they are living—and dying—in wretched conditions. The problems begin at birth, when hospital staff often try to persuade parents of babies with disabilities to give them up to state care. Poverty and alcoholism drive many other parents to abandon their children. Sergei Koloskov, who founded the Down Syndrome Society after a daughter was born with the condition, told me that far from providing support to disadvantaged children, the state hides them. Even normal children are at serious risk, he insisted. Contrary to government figures, he said, the number of orphans in Russia is growing and overloading the state's orphanage system.

Koloskov elaborated: "Healthy babies are lying in hospital beds all day as if they were sick, sometimes for months or longer. They're completely ignored. No one plays with them or provides any kind of stimulation. That happens because the orphanages where they're supposed to go after birth are full." I spoke to him after my son, a colicky baby, had just been born—perhaps the reason I found his testimony especially upsetting.

Of course the lack of attention at such an early age seriously harms child development. Elena Olshanskaya, a forceful young woman who has become one of Russia's most active children's rights activists, started a group of volunteers to help children in hospitals after she discovered abandoned babies in a room adjoining the one where she gave birth. "I was stunned," she told me. "They were completely alone. They were fed several times a day and that was it. After a while, they just stop crying."

Another new mother in a central Russian hospital happened on a room of abandoned babies who had their mouths taped shut to stop them from crying. Broadcast on national television, her mobile phone video shocked the country. Reports of babies tied down in their cots are also common. Bedsores and other wounds are ubiquitous, not least because hospital staff are seriously overworked. A veteran activist, Boris Altshuler of the group Rights of the Child, said the very few visitors who were able to trick or otherwise find their way into such places reported abandoned babies being left to "rot alive." "First of all there's the smell," he said. "The smell of unchanged linens or even children lying on bare plastic. The terrible smell because nobody changes the children's diapers, nobody cares."

Women give birth in maternity wards, where babies who are abandoned spend three days before being moved to nearby hospitals, which aren't equipped or staffed to care for them but are the only option available. Healthy children are then sent to so-called baby homes, institutions where they stay until the age of four before being moved to orphanages. There, their experiences differ widely. Unlike the relatively happy children at Internat No. 8, most end in establishments that are closed to the outside world. That's a legacy of the Soviet Union, which tried to isolate everyone not considered normal from the rest of society. "Many orphanages stand behind high walls and big gates, often somewhere on the outskirts of town," Olshanskaya explained. "People who live in such areas and pass by every day usually have no idea what's inside."

Children considered mentally or physically disabled are sent to special psychiatric institutions, where they can be twice as likely to die as children in regular orphanages, according to Human Rights Watch. Altshuler describes such places as "terrible." Evaluations deciding children's fates are often cursory. Misdiagnosis is common and sometimes even doled out as punishment for misbehavior. Altshuler described the recent case of a fifteen-year-old boy who began misbehaving after his divorced mother remarried. When she permitted a diagnosis of mental disability, he was taken to a psychiatric institution, "isolated from society." Children's rights advocates say such treatment is common and incomprehensible in a country facing a demographic crisis in which the birthrate has been decreasing for years.

Valentina Pavlova, who heads the Moscow office of Kidsave, an American organization that runs foster-care programs in Russia, told me that even in standard orphanages, the lack of contact with the rest of the world leaves children utterly unprepared for adult life. "When children leave those institutions," Pavlova said, "they enter another world they've seen only on television. Very few are able to cope because they've never owned anything of their own or experienced normal relationships. Above all, they've been deprived of love."

Many teenagers run away to live on the streets. "They don't like the life of hunger and starvation, boredom and cruelty," Altshuler said, adding that many still feel they have little choice. Most Russians' interaction with those children is limited to seeing them begging at train stations. Orphans who have children also tend to abandon their own offspring. Little surprise that the suicide rate for children, led by those who pass through orphanages and *internat* schools, is Europe's highest. Pavlova agrees with most other experts who say the only way to help abandoned children break out of life-long cycles of isolation and lack of education is to put them in the care of adoptive or foster families.

But Altshuler believes officials in charge of the country's state orphanages are obstructing new foster-care programs because they want to keep their state funding. "They don't use the best-known practices because institutions aren't interested in losing children." He describes the current system as an "orphan industry."

"We know only the tip of the iceberg because there's no government inspectorate for orphanages," he said, adding that the situation won't improve without public pressure. As long as the state keeps hiding orphans from society, he continued, attitudes about them won't change. "We know who Russia's real master is: the selfish, greedy bureaucracy, which is killing our country because it wants to make money from everything. From children's tragedies, orphans, anything."

———

As countless parentless children remain mired in lives of misery, the Kremlin is busy with other concerns, including indoctrinating young Russians to become loyal supporters of the government. For that, as for so much else, it looks to the Soviet past for inspiration. There has been no more visible, or absurd, example than a summer camp for thousands of teenagers and young adults located five hours northwest of Moscow. Situated on large, beautiful Lake Seliger in the Tver region, amid pristine pine and birch forests, it was started in 2007 by a pro-Kremlin youth group known as Nashi, or "Ours," which until then was best known for staging loud demonstrations outside foreign embassies. Under an earlier name, the group had conducted public book burnings.

The camp is a hive of activity on a typical day: campers kayak, play volleyball and sit around campfires at night, but there's a big difference from similar camps in the West. When I visited, large propaganda posters lambasting opposition figures hung from tree branches between campers' tents. One display compared the US president to Saddam Hussein. Some of the claims were clearly false, including one condemning European democracy by asserting that German police had killed eighty antiglobalization protesters during a G8 summit in 2007. In fact, one protester was injured. Elsewhere, slogans proclaimed Russia's greatness, some printed below pictures of intercontinental ballistic missiles. In another part of the camp, the faces of Russian opposition leaders had been superimposed over lingerie-clad female bodies and dubbed "political prostitutes." The whole affair would have smacked of the Soviet Union's Young Pioneer camps except that those much-loved institutions actually imparted relatively little ideology. In any case, the tactic appeared to be working on at least some participants, among them a baby-faced nineteen-year-old camper named Kostya Kudinov, who informed me with no trace of irony that the government's critics are "fascists."

"These people are against our Motherland. They're ready to do anything to cheat our country. We're against that. We're here to show our concern for Russia and discuss what we can do to improve its future."

But as campers drank tea around their campfires under the tall pines and posters celebrating Putin's manliness, it became clear many others weren't buying the messages. Twenty-three-year-old Irina Chechikova complained about the cult of personality the camp's mandatory political lectures were helping build around Russia's "national leader," Putin. Campers were also obliged to make career plans; state-controlled companies had set up tents where recruiters offered internships to the politically loyal teenagers. The camp organizers pushed a social message, too: alcohol was banned, and some displays exhorted campers to counteract Russia's alarming population decline by propagating.

That was the only message that appeared to be seriously taken to heart. Some of the campers described nights of promiscuous sex between participants who almost tripped over each other during their visits to various tents. The following year, Nashi's leader failed to dispel rumors that he had taken part in the escapades. But despite the camp's comic amateurishness, it was no isolated, crackpot endeavor. Although the same leader insisted it was solely the creation of his group, it had substantial government backing and no doubt funding as well. Putin, Medvedev and a host of other leaders paid visits.

Their laughable attempt to create an updated model of a Soviet-era institution for instilling values in young Russians reflects life under Putin, some of it a hollow shell. Despite his recent divorce, the president presents himself as an honest family man of action, a teetotaler in the mold of the young Soviet men communist propaganda upheld as models for an empire of huge drinkers. However, the camp was truer to its precedents than it would seem. Just as it did under communism, its propaganda masked a radically different reality: in Russia, corruption is the rule and mere lip service is paid to the notion of family values.

If Stalin wanted the state to lord over every aspect of private life, Putin is in many ways his opposite. The government that still grants cradle-to-grave social welfare on paper provides virtually nothing in reality, obviously not caring how people live in their own homes. While Russia remains a country where individual will is suspect, now no group represents the common interest. The state's interests are almost entirely Putin's. He manipulates public opinion to strengthen his power while Russians are left to fend for themselves in daily life. The family is still important for getting by or ahead, more so than in the West. But the leaders' essentially nihilistic attitude is helping perpetuate the sexism and violence that is tearing at the social fabric.

My parents at the 1959 American exhibition in Moscow shortly after they met.

My father (on the far left with microphone) lecturing at the Ford stand at the American exhibition.

6

Domestic Order

Women are long of hair and short of brains.
— Old Russian saying

A humorous 1980s television commercial for Wendy's restaurants reflected the Western view of Soviet life at the time: a grim fashion show with one dumpy model whose every outfit was the same shapeless gray dress. Most Americans were convinced Russians were also puritanical in those supposedly sexless days. But although the USSR hardly evokes an image of a sexual hothouse, that's what it often was. Attitudes toward sex were still very permissive when I first visited in 1991. Liaisons were made on the street, in shops, in the metro, on the escalators leading to the metro trains and pretty much everywhere else.

Official Soviet broadcasts and publications were prudish, to be sure. But although sex was taboo in public and government-approved literature and films presented a prim society, communism's crushing drabness didn't reach into the bedroom. Soviet realities, such as the difficulty of obtaining restaurant reservations and tickets to the Bolshoi, actually encouraged promiscuity by compelling people to look elsewhere for entertainment.

Such permissive attitudes emerged in the 1950s, partly thanks to the great shortage of men after World War II, when 40 percent of males between the ages of twenty and forty-nine perished among the thirty million Soviets who died in the conflict. With so few men around, women had little hope for marriage if they wanted physical release or a child. Competition was so intense that many women who longed to raise children often forwent the luxury of bothering with propriety or niceties. Sex often took place when and where it was possible and there was nothing shameful about it.

As so often in Russia, new views were imported from abroad, especially from early foreign tourists to the Soviet Union. Some of their very limited contacts outside officially approved channels were with enterprising young men who took risks by buying or trading anything that could be resold for several times its actual worth, from clothes to books and radios. Among the most popular items were glossy Western magazines that showed American and European fashions. Well-thumbed secondhand copies of *Vogue* and *Playboy* also provided glimpses of the budding sexual revolution in the West. They contributed to the change of attitude, which started with the young elite in Moscow and Leningrad who were increasingly less interested in the mores of their parents. For all the USSR's dictatorial aspects, sex there was very free by the early 1960s.

The biggest problem was *where*, even where to get things going. The lack of bars, let alone clubs or discos, meant that state restaurants were among the few places people could go to escape their communal apartments—that is, if they were wealthy, lucky or persistent enough to get in. Even on freezing nights, long lines routinely formed outside restaurants that were half empty because the employees inside were illegally selling produce, which made them as much as or more than they could make by serving customers. Supplies were always of questionable quality in any case. Visiting the resort city of Sochi, my father once took a table at a restaurant imaginatively called Fish that overlooked the Black Sea from the town's hills. When the waitress came along after a half hour or so in a typically surly mood, he asked which fish was fresh. "Young man," she admonished him, "stop clowning!"

The authorities generally frowned on restaurants, which many popular books and films portrayed as places where no-goodniks and criminals met to conduct their dirty dealings. But if you got in, you could dine while musicians performed popular songs and sometimes even jazz, although that remained risky until the mid-1980s. Anyone could ask anyone else to dance; refusing even highly intoxicated strangers was considered bad form. Splurging diners often ordered many dishes and left their plates largely untouched because they were really there for the drinking, talking and dancing.

But most partying was done at home. Among the experts in that during the 1960s was a friend of my parents named Sergei Milovsky. A gifted criminal lawyer who gave parties in his tiny apartment as well as in those belonging to his large circle of more privileged friends, Seriozha, as he was called, was much liked for his irrepressible good cheer and generosity, which extended even to distant friends of friends. The master seducer was also able to take advantage of the permissive attitudes of the day to maintain a steady stream of girlfriends. My parents once visited Milovsky's apartment when he happened to be entertaining three very young women. As my parents sat down, one of the three who had left for the bathroom emerged naked. Clearly trying to outshine her companions in the competition for their host's attention, she asked, "Do you want to see my pussy?" and didn't wait for an answer. That was typical.

"Everything was allowed then," my mother remembers. "There was no shame, nothing holding people back. Fellini was nothing; Russian girls could do anything!"

———

Life had become easier by 1959—six years after Stalin's death—when my mother turned sixteen and began going out by herself. Some consumer goods, such as shoes and even furniture, had begun arriving from abroad, mostly from Soviet Bloc countries but later even Germany and Britain. Exhibitions about life in other countries entertained and sometimes dazzled Muscovites, especially the fairs from Sweden, Czechoslovakia and Hungary. But the event that really shook the capital was the 1959 American National Exhibition.

That summer, more than two million people thronged leafy Sokolniki Park in the city's northeast, where a set of newly constructed, futuristic-looking pavilions brimmed with the latest American consumer goods. Braving a broiling sun—Moscow often suffers heat waves—people gawked at Polaroid cameras, the latest washing machines and a model house. The exhibition was an iconic episode of détente, one of the landmarks of rapprochement that came between the shoe thumping and nuclear brinkmanship of the Cold War. The Americans also intended it to astonish Soviets into accepting the superiority of capitalism over communism. On opening day, then–Vice President Richard Nixon escorted Khrushchev through the pavilions. Reaching a model kitchen, they stopped in front of surprised onlookers and faced each other in what would become known as the kitchen debate.

It was continued later in an RCA television studio on the exhibition grounds. There Nixon suggested to the portly, combative Khrushchev that the United States was ahead of the Soviet Union in some areas, using as an example the then-astounding development of color videotape, on which their meeting was being recorded. "This indicates the possibilities of increasing communication," he said. "And this increasing communication will teach us some things and it will teach you some things, too. Because after all, you don't know everything."

Khrushchev was having none of it. The Soviets were ahead in most areas, he insisted. Anyway, the tape would probably be used for propaganda back in the United States. "What *I* have to say here is being translated only into your ear," he said. "The American people will never hear it." Khrushchev could easily have been seen as having spent his entire political life preparing for that chance to demolish the apparent benefits of capitalism. At the time, however, most Americans believed, as they were inclined to, that Nixon won the debate. Either way, the major interest of many of the young Americans serving as the exhibition's guides was their once-in-a-lifetime opportunity to experience the Soviet Union, a state portrayed back home as America's fearsome, mortal enemy.

My father, George, was one of the guides. Two years after that first visit, he would return to Moscow for a graduate exchange year. He'd studied Russian during a two-year stint in the navy after his hopes of joining the Sixth Fleet headquarters in Naples—where he pictured himself wearing a summer uniform with a mandarin collar and carrying a sword—were dashed by the navy's consuming interest in Russian rather than Italian speakers, it being the height of the Cold War.

The choice fit my father's proclivities. As a high school student in New Jersey, he'd shocked his prosperous secular Jewish parents by announcing that he wouldn't attend college, then leaving home to apprentice himself at a farm in Vermont instead. After a miserable summer there, he eventually graduated from Harvard. Speaking to crowds at the Moscow exhibition's Ford display, he found himself spending far less time answering questions about cars than other aspects of American life, from the school system to the cost of bread. "Very surprisingly, there was a sea of affection for the American people," he remembered later. "There was also among those supposedly downtrodden and oppressed people, as we were incessantly told, a great deal of humanity and originality and humor." And there were questions, almost certainly from a corps of KGB plants, about why Americans lynched blacks, didn't have universal health care and surrounded the peaceful Soviet Union with military bases. But other voices emboldened by the crowd's anonymity sometimes shouted down the hostile questions.

That reaction came as a surprise to George, who, along with the other seventy-four guides, had been coached by the CIA on their voyage by ship from New York to Genoa, then by train to Moscow, on how to respond to challenges from Soviet visitors to the exhibition. On arrival in Moscow, he found it far more economically depressed than he'd expected. Countless men without limbs—the war had ended only fourteen years earlier—hobbled about on crutches or with empty sleeves. The model socialist city seemed more like a village in the sense that streets were dusty and many people were dressed in what looked like peasant clothes. Still, he was very quickly hooked. Although George and his fellow guides found Russians in groups difficult to deal with, they were very relieved to discover that individuals in America's enemy country seemed entirely human.

Visitors stood in line for hours at the front gates. Many of those who entered got their first taste of Pepsi-Cola. Tatyana came with a new boyfriend, a dashing cadet at one of the country's elite Suvorov military academies, who, after studying English, had been trained by his teachers to engage enemies of the communist order with arguments about the superiority of everything Soviet. Inside the park, Tatyana was drawn to the most crowded displays, where the American guides spoke openly about everything, and with humor. "I just somehow sensed how free that country was," she said of her first impression. "Through their gestures, through the way they behaved, through the way they were dressed. You could just see that they were free people, and we were not."

At the Ford display, my sixteen-year-old future mother asked my twenty-five-year-old future father (whom she'd tell she was nineteen) a question about American jazz that he, a lover of classical music, was unable to answer. But after following the microphone cord to the source of the voice and gaping at her beautiful face, he immediately announced a break in his question-and-answer session in the sun. Feigning an interest in a discussion with Tatyana's cadet, he got the couple to return the following day by giving them one of Moscow's hottest items that summer: exhibition tickets, so they wouldn't have to stand in an endless line again. More tickets for more days were required until she got the point and came alone.

When George returned to Moscow in 1961, it was to study the Soviet

legal system for his doctoral studies at Columbia University. He invited
Tatyana to the Bolshoi on one of their first dates. Late as usual, she rushed
from her communal apartment in the handsome old building I've described
into a big snowstorm. No car was in sight, let alone a taxi, which were per-
petually scarce in the best of circumstances. Hurrying to a larger street,
she engaged in a game of fatalism: if a taxi somehow saves me now, she
told herself, I'll marry George. It was just a way to comfort herself for a
moment: the idea of marrying a foreigner was much too far-fetched to take
seriously. An instant later, a car appeared at the end of the street. As it drew
closer, she saw it was a taxi. The green light behind its windshield meant it
was vacant.

She'd soon forget the coincidence. It would remain forgotten for many
years as their relationship evolved, but not for good.

———

Permissive attitudes toward sex ended with the fall of communism, when,
paradoxically, it was suddenly everywhere. Sexual images appeared in public with a vengeance prompted by reaction to the lifting of Soviet suppres-
sions. Mafia gangsters and their molls had the run of Moscow's loud new
nightlife. No self-respecting nightclub lacked for a strip show, while television channels showed an endless parade of B-grade Hollywood films containing plenty of nudity. Until recently, network TV broadcast the weekly
Sex with Anfisa Chekhova, hosted by a voluptuous young brunette who posed
nude in Russian *Playboy*. The show, which featured segments just this side
of soft-core pornography, addressed topics with its tongue held firmly in
cheek, including the pros and cons of sex in cars, whether blondes really are
dumber and reviews of sex toys.

Despite her youth and naive, if not exactly dumb, television persona,
Chekhova is well informed, well spoken and very ambitious. When I met
the elaborately dressed and made-up starlet in a trendy French café on Moscow's central Tverskaya Street, she said between sips from a glass of white
wine that the 1990s raised the curtain on sex, but not in a good way. "There
was sex, but no sex education. Rapes skyrocketed because men believed
women had no right to refuse their demands. And girls believed prostitution was something to aspire to." I remembered seeing advertisements for
secretaries in the help-wanted sections of the time that required women to
include their photographs and measurements with their applications.

Although there's no lack of prostitution today, a decade of oil wealth and authoritarianism has helped stabilize urban society, enabling increasing numbers of female lawyers, accountants, journalists and others to take top jobs in fields previously seen as male domains. Russia's capitalist boom is helping women make their own decisions about where to work and when, if ever, to marry and raise families. And although life in the mostly impoverished provinces remains largely unaffected, women's ever-greater role in society is slowly transforming perceptions in Moscow, St. Petersburg and a handful of other cities, especially among young men, who tend to be more exposed to global culture. Perhaps nothing more visibly reflects the seismic shift in that aspect of life than the number of female drivers on Moscow's streets. Whereas one could go weeks without seeing a single woman driver twenty years ago, there now seems to be one behind the wheel of every second car. When I spoke to a young Muscovite in her middle twenties named Lera Labzina, who'd been driving for two years, she said that made her "very, very happy."

"Driving represents another step toward women's independence," she told me. Not everyone is happy about that development, however. Another typical Muscovite, a young man named Nikolai Mukhin, complained that only men should be allowed to drive. "When I'm waiting at a traffic light," he told me, "I keep an eye on the light. But what do women do? They're putting on lipstick. For them it's normal to read a magazine at the wheel. That's dangerous for everyone."

Even women drivers believe women can't drive well. Elena Zdravomyslova, a gender studies scholar in Moscow, told me such attitudes reflect the growing disparity between a changing reality and deep-rooted sexism. "Women work in traditionally male professions," she said. "They drive cars and engage in business, but the public discourse is still about how they have 'different' brains, how their psychological differences from men prevent them from playing an equal part in society."

Popular culture offers two basic roles for women: housewife and sex symbol, both of which are presented in the hundreds of images that bombard Muscovites from billboards, television programs and glossy magazines. They are "aggressively sexualizing" the general idea of women's roles in society, Zdravomyslova declared.

Sex show host Chekhova told me the media portrayal of women in a society that provides few "constructive" roles for women to counteract it is seriously affecting their behavior. "Physical beauty is idealized to the point of hysteria," she said. "Women dress every day as if they're going to a ball. Moscow has beauty salons on every street, more than any other city. There's fierce competition to catch one of the eligible men throwing around large sums of cash." In a country where women still outnumber men by more than ten million—the highest disparity since the 1970s, according to a 2010 census[1]—the best options are to marry either an oligarch or a foreigner—"that is," she explained, "to live it up or leave." Despite her own show's relentless promotion of dressing up to attract men, Chekhova complained that the energy women spend on their looks comes at the expense of their intellect. "You go out at night and see women dressed to the nines and all looking like one another, like clones."

Moscow's reputation as a place where women dress up is well deserved, and it doesn't just apply to the wealthy. After midnight on any typical night, even during the depths of winter, young women in miniskirts and boots emerge from lines of cars parked up and down the streets surrounding the city's most "in" nightclubs. One is the international discotheque chain Pacha, which opened a branch a stone's throw from the Kremlin in 2009, at the height of the global financial crisis. Business boomed nevertheless. Pacha's manager, Basil Vasiliou, a large, bald Englishman with a penchant for shiny suits, assured me that far from putting a damper on the good times, the financial squeeze had left Muscovites with more free time to spend whatever money they had left. Oil prices having since recovered, any real concern was short-lived.

On a Friday night when I visited, crowds gathered around the club entrance's velvet ropes, guarded by burly bouncers rigorously enforcing the club's standards for those they deemed attractive enough to allow inside, a policy known as face control. Inside, svelte dancers wearing minuscule panties writhed on platforms above a crowded dance floor. Although reserving one of the tables that line the top-floor balcony costs thousands of dollars, all of them were packed, their patrons picking grapes from fruit trays, sipping Champagne and knocking back vodka. Most were highly conscious of the many eyes fixed on them, but this was Moscow, where ostentatious display is the norm. The neon-and-mirror interior below them was filled with a sea of mostly blond women, many wearing fur vests, the latest hot accessory. Most revelers would stay dancing under the laser lights until the club shut its doors the following morning.

Objectifying women is hardly unique to Russia. What seems to be different there is that as society grows richer, men are increasingly seeking respectability by marrying and settling down, and it's women who are on the prowl. Paradoxically, that trend reinforces increasingly traditional attitudes. Chekhova said that most women define liberation as having a strong man to take care of them and independence as the freedom to become a model or open a hair salon. Catering to those views, dating agencies that call themselves modeling agencies offer matches to wealthy male clients who take their pick from photos in glossy catalogs.

Chekhova's theory was borne out when I made a very unscientific test of young Muscovites' attitudes on Kamergersky Pereulok, one of downtown Moscow's swankiest shopping streets. While glamorous-looking women glided past Christian Dior and Versace boutiques, a well-dressed twenty-one-year-old named Yulia Gaidakova echoed views I'd heard again and again. Her marriage the year before, she told me, represented attainment of her life's most important goal. "Women want a good husband who's dependable, responsible and loyal. Everything else is secondary," she said. Men agreed. "Everyone should have his role in life," a bartender named Vladimir Shatilov told me after serving a brisk lunchtime crowd at a nearby restaurant. "If a man goes out and works, a woman has to take care of the home." But although Gaidakova typically praised Russians' attitudes toward marriage over those in the more egalitarian West, even she admitted not liking one aspect of relations between the sexes: men don't respect women.

Later I spoke to twenty-three-year-old Maria Kutsova, a friend's colleague whose hair was styled in a fashionable bob. We met at a trendy restaurant near the foreign law firm where she worked translating French and English into Russian. Inside, neither women nor men were shy about giving their fellow diners serious once-overs to the loud sounds of disco music. Kutsova complained that while Moscow's café society may resemble its Western counterparts, Russian women are forced to confront much more deeply entrenched sexism than women in the European countries she'd visited. Yes, women are more emancipated than at any time in Russian history, she agreed, but she insisted that attitudes toward their roles in society remain positively medieval. "If a woman has career, if she's smart and has a good education, she won't be able to find a partner who'd be at her level," she said. "Russian men can't compete with successful Russian women. They're just not used to it."

Kutsova added that dating is a challenge for other reasons. In a country where abortions are a common form of birth control, almost none of the men she met cared about safe sex, even though AIDS is spreading like wildfire. If she were looking for a long-term relationship, she continued, her most important goal would remain freedom. "Women like me are virtual outcasts in Russia. I can find a husband who will expect me to cook and clean and do everything for him. Maybe he'll earn a lot of money. But that's not what I want. I don't want to stay at home." She found Russian attitudes so oppressive, she said, that she'd decided to leave her family and friends behind to start a new life in Canada.

Relatively few women choose to confront sexism. When I spent a day driving across Georgia with journalist Olga Allenova in 2008 shortly before the Russian invasion, she told me she faced a near-daily struggle against sexist attitudes just to get her work done. A chic correspondent for the well-respected *Kommersant* business newspaper known for covering some of the most dangerous conflict zones in the Caucasus Mountains region, Allenova was nevertheless often denied permission to accompany male colleagues on press trips. "Sometimes I'm not allowed to ride in military helicopters on the 'principle' that women simply aren't allowed. You just have to learn to deal with those situations."

Although attitudes toward homosexuality have also evolved, there has been even less progress in gay rights than women's rights after a brief advance in the 1990s. Same-sex intercourse was illegal in the Soviet Union, punishable by up to five years in prison, until its decriminalization in 1993. Homosexuality was so far from the minds of most Russians that I was surprised during my first visit to Moscow to see men showing affection for each other by touching and even holding hands in public. Later I realized that rather than evidence of progressive thinking, the displays indicated that no one was interpreting them as sexual. Nevertheless, gay culture soon began emerging from underground. Although anyone who drew attention to himself that way risked beatings or worse, young Muscovites began to see aspects of the culture as avant-garde. Some gay nightclubs even became mainstream. One that featured men swimming in giant aquariums became hugely popular.

The retreat of those attitudes with Putin's emergence became very evident. In 2006, the controversial head of a popular gay website announced plans to organize Moscow's first gay pride parade. A well-spoken and apparently fearless young man, Nikolai Alexeyev appeared uncharacteristically nervous when I spoke to him shortly before the event. He told me his action was one of the only ways to draw attention to gay and lesbian issues. "The fact that we made the announcement and are discussing a parade, that it's being written about in the press and even shown on television, it all shows that society acknowledges that gays and lesbians are a real social group that can't be ignored," he said.

It also prompted a backlash. While politicians condemned the parade plans, skinheads and elderly demonstrators holding icons gathered in front of gay nightclubs to hurl insults and rotten eggs. Leaders of the Orthodox Church denounced homosexuality as a sin and the country's chief Islamic mufti opined that marchers should be flogged.

Soon the mayor's office said it would refuse to even consider an application to allow the parade to take place because the idea caused outrage in society. Subsequent attempts to hold unsanctioned parades ended quickly, after would-be participants suffered punches from homophobic protesters and rough handling by police. The swelling public homophobia was part of a larger movement toward intolerance, xenophobia and racism fanned by burgeoning neo-Fascist and other right-wing groups. Although a strong if less visible gay culture survives in Moscow, it's nonexistent in Russia's outlying regions, where gays live under threat of violent attack. A poll at the time, in 2006, reported that more than 43 percent of Russians believe homosexual relations between consenting adults should be prosecuted.

Although gay and lesbian leaders deplored the hardening resistance, they also criticized Alexeyev. Olga Suvorova, head of a lesbian organization called Pink Star, said Russia wasn't ready. "The announcements set off a war against gays," she explained. "It set us back many years in terms of the amount of homophobia there is in society."

Alexeyev dismissed such criticism, saying Russia will never be ready without being pushed. However, his strident public stance helped split the gay rights community. One prominent activist, Edward Mishin, the editor of a gay magazine called *Queer*, drew attention to himself by suing officials who refused his application for a same-sex marriage. Nevertheless, Mishin said plans for a gay pride parade had been needlessly provocative. "Even people in show business are joining a whole front against gays and lesbians," he told me. "This isn't just about the parade anymore. They're condemning homosexuality and believe it's something that should be combated."

Alexeyev's attempts to stage his parades continued prompting scuffles and attacks, including against visiting foreign activists, until 2013, when Putin enacted a new law banning "homosexual propaganda." Although it refers only to "nontraditional" sexual relationships, the purposefully vague measure essentially recriminalized expression of gay identity by outlawing gay parades and gay-themed events and banning dissemination of information about lesbian, gay, bisexual and transgender issues.

The law's supporters used the old argument about the need to protect the majority from individuals' destructive impulses by shielding what they called Russia's non-Western, conservative society from the foreign-influenced threat to its children. By 2013, the Levada Center found that almost two-thirds of Russians condemned homosexuality as "morally unacceptable" and almost a third believed it to be "an illness or result of psychological trauma."

Seen as part of Putin's drive to shore up his credentials among conservative voters, the new law made him mocked abroad as a caricature authoritarian who advocated discrimination. Critics focused on how officials would act at the upcoming 2014 Winter Olympic Games in Sochi. Gay bars in the West boycotted Russian vodka. At home, however, emboldened vigilante stepped up attacks against gays.

Russian attitudes toward women, like those toward homosexuality, are the legacy of a highly patriarchal society. Centuries of accepting that the head of the household made decisions for everyone, historian Richard Pipes has argued, were central to the development of modern Russians' behavior. Starting with medieval Slav tribal communities whose kinship clans formed their basic social units, people related to one another worked "as a team."

The head of the Russian peasant family, the *bolshak* ("big one"), had the final say in all matters.[2] Crucially, his decisions governed all tribal property, which was traditionally held communally. Those early communities, Pipes believes, laid the foundation for the later emergence of the legendary Russian peasant commune, the *mir*. The origins and importance of the *mir*, which acted as both a village government and a cooperative, have been subject to much fierce debate and mythologizing, especially during the nineteenth century, when socialist revolutionaries and other radicals saw it as proof that Russian society—unlike bourgeois European culture—was naturally predisposed to socialism. (*Mir* translates as "society" but also means "world" and "peace," concepts that have provided more fuel for the debate.) Pipes sees it as central to the rise of what he describes as Russia's "patrimonial" state, an autocracy under which the lack of private property enabled the tsar to consider everything his. Of course America also began with great patriarchal concepts and practices, but the burdens that had to be lifted on the way toward women's liberation were far less heavy.

By the time of the Bolshevik Revolution in 1917, Russian society seriously lagged behind Western Europe's. Although the country was industrializing faster than ever at the turn of the century, a government census conducted in 1897 found that at least three-quarters of the population still consisted of peasants, the vast majority of whom were illiterate.[3] Russia was very far from progressive.

Although the Bolsheviks promised radical change, they actually helped freeze social progress by cutting their subjects off from developments in the outside world for seventy years, a legacy that will endure for generations. On the surface, Soviet ideology condemned the traditional image of women as subservient to men and prescribed gender equality. The government used subsidies to encourage women to occupy the role of working mother, especially when the shortage of men left factory and other blue-collar jobs vacant. By the 1980s, more than 80 percent of women, many of them mothers, worked and even dominated some white-collar professions. They constituted 75 percent of teachers, doctors and dentists, according to the 1970 census—a far greater figure than in the United States. Nevertheless, social mores remained antediluvian. In the 1980s, Raisa Gorbacheva, Mikhail Gorbachev's glamorous and independent-minded wife, tried to provide a new model for women by playing a prominent role in her husband's affairs. However, she was widely disliked for it, and post-Soviet leaders' wives have since been much less visible in public, including Putin's former wife, Liudmilla, who was very rarely seen at all before the couple's divorce in 2013. Quoted in a biography of her husband, she described his "shall we say traditional ideas about a wife's place."

"A woman must do everything in the home," she explained. "You should not praise a woman, otherwise you will spoil her." His attitude made it extremely difficult to cook for her husband because "if he doesn't like the slightest thing" in a dish she'd made, he'd refuse to eat it.[4] When the former Aeroflot flight attendant announced the couple's divorce in an awkward, stage-managed interview on state television in June 2013, the news reignited long-running rumors that Putin was engaged in an affair with a former Olympic gymnast, now a member of parliament, who is half his age. It also prompted some to joke that Liudmilla is the "only Russian who managed to liberate herself from Putin."

Soviet rhetoric about women's rights, used largely to persuade women to work, did have some success in reducing bias. However, men continued occupying the highest posts, and behind the propaganda, attitudes toward women remained far more traditional than in the West. Gender scholar Zdravomyslova said that remains especially true in the provinces to this day. "Russians have much stricter limits in their perceptions about gender roles—what's a man, what's a woman," she said. "Society restricts its discussions to those limits."

The entrenched attitudes are helping perpetuate one of Russia's darkest secrets: domestic violence, which is so pervasive that many see it as normal. The government's own almost certainly low figures estimate that fourteen thousand women die annually from domestic violence. That's the death of one woman at the hands of her husband or partner every hour, more than ten times the number in the United States, whose population is twice the size of Russia's. Countless more women suffer violent abuse in secret. Although more than half the women questioned in a recent survey said they'd been beaten by their husbands, the real number is impossible to count because domestic violence, seen as a private matter not to be aired in public, remains hidden.

Elena Litvin, a soft-spoken Moscow woman in her late thirties, married a medical student in 1995 expecting to begin a happy family life. She gave birth to two children, but her marriage soon became a nightmare. "My husband began staying out late drinking," she told me. "He'd come home angry and beat me in front of the children. He hit me in sensitive areas, such as the stomach and chest, avoiding my face and hands so the bruises wouldn't be seen in public."

Litvin said her husband also threatened to kill her. Although desperate, she was too afraid to complain: a very common story in a country where victims of domestic abuse often have nowhere to turn. Moscow, with its more than ten million people, has not a single shelter for battered women. The one I visited outside the city was among only twenty government-run shelters in the entire country, and it had a total of seven beds. Like other officials, its director, a businesslike woman named Marina Nakitina, downplayed the issue of domestic violence, assuring me the problem is no worse in Russia than anywhere else.

The government has started to take action, but very slowly. Difficult as it may be to believe, Russian law still doesn't recognize domestic violence as a crime. Marina Pisklakova, who founded the Anna Center for Domestic Violence, told me that even the few officials willing to intervene in abuse cases are often prevented from acting until it's too late. Pisklakova's organization, which is located on the second floor of a small building in central Moscow and employs several people, is the highest-profile NGO combating domestic violence in the country. A petite, smiling woman who speaks flawless English, Pisklakova calmly recounted gruesome stories and shocking statistics.

"It's very difficult for them to do their job," she said of the police. "They know they simply can't intervene until victims' injuries are medium or severe or there's a murder." To be classified as "medium," she explained, an injury must prevent the victim from working for two weeks. Even many women able to prove they've suffered from domestic violence face other insurmountable obstacles. Restraining orders don't exist in the Russian legal system; women who file complaints against their partners often end by retracting them.

When Elena Litvin finally gathered the courage to go to the authorities, the police initially refused to investigate her claims, she said. It took them six months to initiate criminal proceedings against her husband, whom she finally divorced in 2004. Like many estranged Russian couples, they continued living together because they couldn't afford to move apart, an arrangement she said was "seriously harming" their young children. "They tell me it's difficult to bear his presence. He gets drunk and follows us around, finding fault with every word we say. His goal is to humiliate us."

After Litvin's ex-husband was eventually convicted of attempting to murder her, he was sentenced to a year of probation. "I have to go back to the same apartment," she said. "I have to hear the same threats and can do nothing about it."

Pisklakova said such stories are common in Russia, where an old saying advises women that "if he beats you, he loves you" and violence is often justified as a way of controlling women. "She must have done something wrong to deserve it," Pisklakova explained about the attitude toward beatings. "That mentality is still there, the mentality of women being basically created to serve men."

Some believe men's attitudes toward women are among the most direct vestiges of serfdom. Oppressed by their owners or other overlords, their lives circumscribed by the dictates of reactionary church dogma, male serfs had few outlets besides beating their women, or so the argument goes. Repression under communism perpetuated such traditional attitudes. "Physical violence and love is connected in Russia," Pisklakova added. She traced the association to a sixteenth-century domestic guide called *Domostroi*, "domestic order," that instructed the master of the house not to hit women in the face in order to avoid public embarrassment. It recommended whips as more effective than fists.

"No one spoke about domestic violence during the Soviet era," Pisklakova said, because the model of the Soviet family was presented as perfect. "Therefore, there couldn't be violence, period." Although attitudes are very slowly changing and new laws are being passed, and although the topic of domestic violence sometimes even appears on television talk shows, "it's still seen as up to women to make the home better," Pisklakova added. "Domestic happiness remains their responsibility."

Other convictions reinforce those attitudes, including the belief that men deserve more sympathy than women, partly because so many died during the last century's two world wars and also because their life expectancy is so much shorter. "Russian women are seen as very strong, which is true," Pisklakova said. "But the attitude is that they can deal with their problems while men need protection."

Domestic violence also continues to be accepted because Russians see themselves as emotional and passionate. The impetuous "Russian soul" is often invoked to explain "crimes of passion," however violent. A recent television drama billed as a tale about unhappy love featured a female metro employee who leaves her policeman husband after he beats her. After stalking her, he proceeds to kill her, then himself. "But the story wasn't about love at all," Pisklakova said. "It represented a classic case of domestic abuse, about power and control."

Change would almost certainly be faster under a political system that doesn't repress human rights organizations or undermine the independence of the legal system. Still, change would be slow even under a more democratic government. Attitudes toward women and their roles derive from the generally small place all individuals hold in a society where the strong rule and traditional arrangements govern most aspects of life.

Back on Moscow's streets, proud new driver Lera Labzina said that although she believes some attitudes toward women will continue improving, others will never change. "Men have never accepted women drivers," she said, "and I don't think they ever will." Even some women accept the stereotypes. Rear-window "warning" stickers that picture stiletto-heeled shoes are not uncommon on Russian cars. Others point to a larger lack of respect for the rule of law and human rights. "We never think about Russia as a country where *women* are oppressed," I was told by Irina Mikhailovskaya, editor of the Russian edition of the magazine *Forbes Style*. "*People* are oppressed, not just women. That was true about the Soviet Union, and it remains true today."

Mikhaylovskaya believes change will be very slow if it comes at all. "We're so far away from the West, it's not a question of a few years or even a generation."

Children play outside a derelict factory in southern Siberia. (*Justin Jin / justinjin.com*)

7
Indolence and Inefficiency

There is nothing petty about the Russian mind when it comes to the gap between the scale of conception and the amount of achievement.
—William Gerhardie, essayist (1895–1977)

S ince the dark days of communism, when many Moscow streets were unlit and the city as a whole was all but somnolent after dark, the capital has become known for having joined the ranks of cities that never sleep. Traffic jams persist, pedestrians clog its neon-lit sidewalks and shops and restaurants on every block bustle with customers. During the day, metro trains that arrive more frequently than every two minutes throughout the rush hours are packed to capacity. The frenetic, work-intensive appearance of things doesn't mean that activities are conducted efficiently, however. Nor should Moscow's resemblance to other major cities be taken as an indication that it functions as they do.

Consider the crumbling ZiL truck factory, a collection of hangar-like assembly plants that sprawls across acres of prime Moscow real estate on the banks of a canal off the Moscow River. The location is a legacy of the old practice, tsarist as well as Soviet, of building factories in the center of cities with little regard for aesthetics or urban planning, let alone residents' comfort. Founded in 1916, the complex cranked out more than two hundred thousand vehicles during its Soviet heyday, when ZiL was a pride and joy. The company also produced refrigerators and bullet-proofed limousines for Stalin. Today, ZiL trucks that look like they came straight out of the 1960s still roar from one end of the country to the other, their drivers bouncing and straining to steer the unwieldy vehicles without the aid of power steering or modern suspension systems. The Communist Party seemed to believe that only large trucks were necessary, even for hauling the smallest loads, and after the Soviet Union collapsed, ZiL continued building hundreds of thousands of obsolete hulks no one wanted.

Now the plant stands mostly idle, producing a mere thousand sorely outdated vehicles a year. It is kept alive mostly by orders from the city government, which took control of the premises in the 1990s, and a joint venture there that assembles Renault truck engines from imported parts. While many ZiL buildings are rented out to other companies, massive World War II–era machinery still stamps steel parts in one remote corner of the factory. When I spoke to several workers operating the equipment there on a frigid winter day, they were unwilling to talk for more than a few minutes for fear of being overheard. I had better luck outside the administration building, where a handful of brave workers held a meek demonstration to protest their pitiful wages, a bold move for state employees in Putin's Russia. One of the protesters was a stout, bleached-blond woman with short hair named Anna Fyodorova, who had worked at ZiL for thirty years and made the equivalent of three hundred dollars a month. That was her salary on paper. In fact, she said, she hadn't been paid since the previous summer, a situation for which she blamed company management.

"They take the money that's supposed to go to our wages," she said, "while they profit from renting out the factory premises. Capitalism is for our bosses, not for us honest workers because only those who steal get ahead." Fyodorova fondly recalled life in the Soviet Union, in particular ZiL's cradle-to-grave social support network, which included a hospital, stadiums, concert halls and children's summer camps. "ZiL used to be its own state," she said. "It owned everything, and everything used to be simple and easy."

Russia's recovery from the 1998 economic downturn promised to help reverse the industrial decline. The government's decision to devalue the ruble made Russian products cheaper, enabling new companies such as Wimm-Bill-Dann, which sold juice in Western-style packaging, to more easily compete with the flood of imports Russians craved. Then a surge in oil prices fed a consumer binge by buoying incomes. The GDP finally exceeded its 1991 level in 2004.

But the future remains bleak for many workers like Fyodorova in Russia's manufacturing sector. Despite being awash with oil and gas money, the government has failed—more accurately, it has declined—to use its riches for rebooting the country's mostly stagnant industry in any serious way. Life for factory workers in the old so-called worker's paradise has barely improved during the past two decades. Many employed in sectors kept alive by inertia, corruption and high import duties—such as the auto industry— put in their hours with a carelessness and disorder best conveyed by the word *bezalabernost'*, which means "lack of a working system." The work ethic remains so weak that apart from weapons and a few small civilian aircraft, Russia now produces virtually no manufactured goods that can compete in the world market.

However much that is a legacy of the Soviet Union, which famously pretended to pay workers who pretended to work, it is also an old trope in Russia, whose fairy tales teach that the lazy and bumbling will be rewarded as long as their hearts are pure.

The current lack of drive also derives from Russia's natural-resources economy, in which what really matters is how to take—including by theft— rather than how to produce. Despite endless official promises of change, there is little indication it will happen soon. The present system works well enough to sustain the ruling classes and, for the time being, enough of the great unwashed to keep them from thinking of revolt.

Not that some efforts to change haven't been serious. Some facets of education have improved since the 1990s, when there was no money to pay teachers, and a few entrepreneurs have been working hard to start new businesses, despite the government's choking regulations and demand for bribes. So is it Russia's fate to remain perennially underdeveloped? Or is it simply enduring bad luck, as it has been for centuries?

———

During the supposed rule of the proletariat, the main Soviet labor unions were weak organizations that actually represented the interests of management. Although that remains largely true today, a smattering of scrappy new workers' groups has emerged to speak for real workers. I dropped in on a meeting of one of them in a central Moscow basement one cold January evening. At the bottom of a set of narrow stairs, ten members of the Moscow Workers' Union sat around mismatched tables surrounded by busts of Karl Marx and shelves groaning with Lenin's collected works. The dusty relics seemed more comic than usual because the dogged earnestness of those present seemed intended to defy the consistency with which Russia's leaders have exploited its toiling masses. Solemnly agreeing that conditions for workers are increasingly miserable, the men nevertheless made no resolutions for action.

Vassily Shishkarev represented employees of ZiL. Tall, bearded and weary-looking, he argued that workers were far better organized in the past, even during the dangerous days before the Bolshevik Revolution of 1917, than they are today. "People don't discuss wages and factory work on the shop floor," he lamented. "Instead they talk about mushroom picking and potato harvesting like a bunch of farmers. That's because they're forced to survive on what they grow in their spare time and on food from relatives in villages back home."

Echoing Anna Fyodorova, the veteran ZiL worker who had protested at the cautious demonstration, he said those who live well in Russia are almost exclusively "those who steal state property, company shares and money." He questioned why the Moscow city government, which owns more than 60 percent of ZiL, hadn't fired its management for its "miserable" failure to modernize. Of course the question was rhetorical. "Ordinary people understand you can't survive by being honest," he said by way of an answer. "Putin and his gang are building no new factories," he said. "They're just taking for themselves and their cronies."

ZiL would surely have been shut down many years ago in any country with a competitive manufacturing economy. Its survival speaks volumes about the nature of business in Russia, which has much less to do with producing than expropriating—in this case subsidies from the city government. Shutting down the factory was also far from the union members' minds. On the contrary, Shishkarev criticized ZiL's cutting of Soviet-era social welfare, insisting wages be raised to compensate for reductions. How should ZiL boost salaries despite making no money? His answer was a shrug.

Back in the ZiL complex, mild-mannered spokesman Victor Novochenko admitted that his company is an anachronism. Despite workers' nostalgia for the good old days, he said, unloading Soviet-era social burdens and property is crucial to ZiL's hopes for reviving its fortunes. "We take up far too much expensive real estate in the center of Moscow," he added. He also pinned hopes on replacing the company's predominantly poorly trained pension-age workers by appealing to the government for help in training qualified personnel.

But the authorities' record in such matters has been miserable. Under Putin, the government's main strategy for assisting ailing industries has been to arrange takeovers by state-controlled companies or business groups close to the Kremlin. Investigative journalist Yulia Latynina, one of Russia's most incisive columnists, told me she's convinced state control is the worst way to encourage industrial restructuring. "In the best-case scenario, it results in the inefficient use of government funds to create unfair competition and stifle the market," she said. "In most cases, it means straight-out theft by the new managers."

Visiting another auto factory, the mile-and-a-half-long plant of Russia's largest carmaker, Avtovaz, is like stepping back in time. Until it was phased out in 2012, the most popular model of Avtovaz's signature vehicle—the Lada—had been based squarely on the Fiat that was 1966 European car of the year. The factory is located in the city of Togliatti, on the banks of the Volga River in the Samara region south of Moscow. Named after the Italian communist politician, the industrial eyesore is wholly dependent on Lada and the myriad auto-parts and tuning companies it helped spawn. It's also a center for organized crime where journalists who dare investigate the notoriously corrupt auto retail market are often killed. Until a third of its workforce was cut in 2009, the factory employed more than a hundred thousand workers—many of them women—who welded, screwed and hammered its products together, a massively labor-intensive process that required no less than thirty times the man-hours it took to build a car in the West. I spent less time than I wanted to on the factory floor because the midlevel directors accompanying my every step were far less interested in allowing the company's countless woes to be exposed than in hustling me to attend a vodka-soaked lunch—the usual blind for journalists. I barely managed to escape by claiming I had a plane to catch back to Moscow.

My friend Kolya once bought a Lada Niva, a small four-wheel-drive jeep. It needed service within a week because assembly workers had left metal shavings in the transmission. When I asked why he hadn't bought a much more reliable and comfortable used foreign car for the same amount of money, he shot me an exasperated look. "How long have you lived here?

Don't you know you can't expect a new car to work right away?" No wonder slightly used Russian cars—driven long enough for their owners to have hammered out some faults—often cost more than new ones.

Instead of shutting down such companies or forcing them to change, the government has kept them and the hundreds of thousands of jobs they generate on life support partly by keeping prices very low—a new Lada costs around five thousand dollars—and continuing to raise duties on imports of foreign cars. That alone would not be enough to keep the domestic car industry afloat, however. Pride has driven politicians, such as Moscow's former Mayor Yuri Luzhkov, to funnel huge amounts of government money into keeping it alive. When the global financial crisis of 2008 forced car factories to a standstill, threatening to deal Lada a long overdue death blow, it was Putin who rode to the rescue. Advertising efforts were redoubled, and, more effectively, import taxes were again raised, now to an average of 25 percent.

When Putin visited Togliatti in April of 2009 for a highly publicized meeting with Avtovaz workers, he vowed to do what was needed to keep the company going. The government soon announced it would spend billions of dollars on a bailout on top of the raised import duties. Now the company survives as a symbol of Putin's determination to exhibit himself as the defender of the Russian proletariat. Arguments about the steps needed for any real reform of the Russian auto industry aside, the Lada is such a bad car—and Avtovaz's executives are so bumbling—that it exposes Putin to ridicule every time he steps near one. In August 2010, the then–prime minister exchanged his chauffeured Mercedes for a tiny Lada Kalina he was said to be driving across Siberia. His publicity stunt, intended to display the car's reliability, achieved exactly the opposite.

Amateur video footage posted on YouTube showed Putin traveling with a massive convoy of cars, buses and trucks—which included three Kalinas, one apparently broken down on the back of a tow truck. Putin tried again in 2011, when he showed up at a Lada showroom to promote an ostensibly new model the government was billing as Russia's new "people's car." The then–prime minister failed to get the car to start, which he later very uncharacteristically blamed on himself, then failed to open the trunk until two company officials rushed to his aid. Nevertheless, Putin pronounced the new Lada a "good car."

While the authorities' penchant for propping up grossly inefficient state enterprises partly explains Russia's manufacturing failure, a more deeply rooted problem plagues new business owners. An entrepreneur named Vladimir Maltsev told me that the common scourge of corruption threatens the viability of his small wholesale trading company every day.

I met Maltsev when I was hailing a taxi and he stopped. (Russians often use their cars as gypsy cabs when times are tough. In the 1990s, several cars would sometimes screech to a halt the minute you stuck out a hand out and the drivers would argue about who would get the equivalent of the two- or three-dollar fare. Now it's usually quicker and cheaper to call a real taxi.) Although I'd spent years driving in Moscow and knew very well how the traffic police operate, I was researching the topic and asked Maltsev how often he was stopped. "Every day," he said with a sigh. When I went on to ask about other forms of corruption, he told me the tax police had recently frozen his company's bank account after claiming he had failed to file an apparently crucial document with his corporate return. When Maltsev—a stout, mustachioed man with dark curly hair—showed up at the tax police building with the proper paper, which bore a stamp showing it had indeed been filed, he was nevertheless made to wait in line at an office that never appeared to open.

"I kept returning," he said, "until someone approached me to say he sympathized because he saw me standing in line every day. The man then gently suggested I visit another office down the hall, where it was understood I'd pay a bribe and my problem would disappear. It did." Maltsev, who on that occasion coughed up five hundred dollars, said routine pressure like that is effective because it paralyzes companies. "Business owners will do *anything* to unfreeze their bank accounts," he said. Since the collapse of communism, officials have called entrepreneurship and small and mid-size businesses the keys to future economic success. At the same time, however, running one's own business has gone from merely extremely difficult to downright dangerous, and not only for Russians.

Among those who opened businesses in the 1990s were thousands of adventurous foreigners who came to Russia to make their fortunes in the country's wild new capitalism. Some struck it rich, but life has been far from easy for many of them. One is a dentist named Giovanni Favero, whose high-tech American-Russian Dental Center occupies plush quarters in the center of Moscow.

I met Favero in 2001, when I needed an emergency root canal and his clinic was the only one listed in the telephone book that answered on a weekend. That was the first of many regular visits I paid to the genial, white-haired man in his early seventies who speaks in a deliberate, indeterminate American drawl. Favero had run a practice in Sacramento for more than twenty years when he first came to Russia to lecture about American dentistry in 1991. He'd believed Soviet standards were advanced until he examined a Russian patient who'd just visited a dentist but still needed twenty-one cavities filled and a root canal. "When I saw the kind of dentistry that was actually practiced here, I said, 'Wow, I can really make a difference,'" he told me.

Favero eventually realized he could make an impact only by running his own practice. He also stood to make a fortune from newly wealthy Russians with very bad teeth. After opening his first clinic in 1995 and a second several years later, he now employs some forty people. Explaining why owning a business in Russia is more difficult than he'd expected, he began with a story: one morning, he found two thugs waiting for him outside his apartment.

"Instead of going to the elevator, I started walking down," he said. "But they ended by pushing me down the stairs, where I got into a corner and tried to defend myself." The thugs bloodied Favero and broke several ribs before running off. He believes they had been sent by the Russian he'd appointed to be his company's nominal director—something often required of foreigners. Apparently the man wanted to intimidate him into surrendering the practice. Having set up bank accounts and prepared all the paperwork necessary to transfer ownership of the clinics, the director needed only Favero's signature.

Although he went to the police instead and managed to maintain control of his practice, Favero said the authorities provide no guarantee of security. "You never know what's going to happen." Like so many others, he complained about constant demands for bribes by the tax police and other officials. The state's drive to reassert command over private industry is even worse. "They've taken back control," he said of officials under Putin. "Everyone wants to be a bureaucrat because that's how you make money. They let you work only if they think they can get you in the end."

Favero sees Moscow's glossy new buildings and bustling streets as a facade that hides the corrupt deals that stand behind everything. Advertisements for dental services plastered across Moscow are a symptom. "They advertise like crazy to get one-time patients, screw them and then close," he said of some of his competitors. "They don't need to care about doing a good job. With more than ten million people in Moscow, they don't need repeat customers."

Favero, who once caught a former partner secretly transferring money to the United States, said successful businesses like his are always under threat of being taken over by someone with better political connections. "If you go into partnership with somebody and the company is losing money, it's your company," he said. "If you make money, it's theirs. Believe me, they'll find a way to get it from you."

He attributes such behavior to the Soviet legacy of trying to "screw the system." "People will tell you what you want to hear to get what they want, and if you don't find out whether they're lying, it's your problem." Although he believes that when he leaves he'll have to abandon the investment he's made in his clinics during the past decade, he doesn't regret his time in Russia. "It's a real learning experience to find out just how lucky we are in America."

Far from showing any signs of waning, the informal economy of connections, agreements and favors, which was called *blat* in the Soviet Union, has relentlessly grown since Putin first took office in 2000. Among other authorities who have grandly acknowledged the problem, Dmitri Medvedev as president in 2008 claimed that corruption threatened Russia's very viability as a state. The government's own figures put the country's "corruption market" at an estimated three hundred billion dollars a year. In 2011, the police said the average bribe paid to officials was ten thousand dollars, while Transparency International ranked Russia 143rd out of 182 spots on its corruption index. The bribes inflate the price of everything from real estate to food as companies pass on the hidden costs of doing business. Maltsev told me he had no hope anything would change. "It's only words," he said of Putin and Medvedev's promises. "Corruption has always been all-pervasive. It's an integral part of our state."

Instead of tackling crime, the police spend much of their time falsifying statistics to meet Soviet-era quotas for cases they're required to solve, sometimes by framing innocent people. An ex-detective who spoke to me anonymously because he was afraid of reprisals from former colleagues said police even set up crimes they appear to solve as a cover for their real activity: using their official positions for profit. Police couldn't live on their meager official salaries, he explained, let alone afford the rows of shiny luxury cars parked in front of many police buildings. Those who don't agree to take part are fired or framed. "It's a business," he said, summing up. "And it goes all the way to the top."

The near-total nature of Russian corruption provided rich material for Nikolai Gogol, whose 1836 play *The Inspector General* is a brilliant satire of bureaucracy in the nineteenth century and one of the landmarks of Russian drama. In the comedy, the crooked officials of a small town mistake a visiting civil servant for a high-ranking government official whose inspection they desperately fear. Cottoning on, the young man takes advantage of the fawning local officials: he moves into the mayor's house, where he flirts with his wife and daughter while taking bribes from the town's merchants in return for promising to exile the hated town boss. The pretender skips town just before he's found out and the real inspector general arrives.

Recent accusations have placed Yuri Luzhkov, whom the Kremlin ousted in a political power struggle in 2010, among the country's most notoriously corrupt officials. Luzhkov was Moscow's mayor for seventeen long years, ten of them under Putin and Medvedev. Running the city like a personal fiefdom enabled him to sink hundreds of millions of dollars into ZiL in a futile populist campaign to revive the company. Medvedev fired him after a cynical state media campaign that accused him of making his wife Russia's richest woman by funneling city contracts to her construction company. But a year before his unceremonious removal, when the Kremlin was exhibiting no disapproval of his tight control of the city because it suited its needs, opposition leader Boris Nemtsov published a report about the mayor in which he put the price for a kilometer of road then under construction in Moscow at a whopping $570 million.

"If you compare the cost of Moscow's roads to the Large Hadron Collider in Switzerland," Nemtsov told me soon after his report was issued, "the particle collider is cheaper. So is the Channel Tunnel [between Britain and France]." It's no accident that the Russian capital remains one of the priciest places on earth: its costs reflect a closed political system in which construction companies enjoy close ties to political leaders. "In any country in the world, the Czech Republic, Britain, Germany, even Italy," Nemtsov said, "it would be cause for a criminal investigation. Those two"—Luzhkov and his wife, Elena Baturina—"would be sitting in jail. But not in Russia."

Nemtsov added that among the countless politicians up to their eyeballs in corruption, Luzhkov and Baturina were "so odious" that any move against them would send a loud signal to politicians and law enforcers across the country. The move came the following year, when Nemtsov's accusations—although never attributed to him or many other critics of Luzhkov in the opposition—suddenly found their way onto state television as part of its smear campaign. However, the allegations were no sign of a real battle against corruption. They were used to remove political rivals—in that case the last powerful regional leaders installed during the Yeltsin era.

Luzhkov fought back in a show of resistance exceedingly rare among top politicians; he was, after all, a founding leader of Putin's United Russia Party. But his inevitable defeat came when Medvedev used his presidential power to fire him. His replacement, a dour bureaucrat named Sergei Sobyanin, who had previously served as Putin's loyal chief of staff, put Moscow firmly under the Kremlin's direct control. But although Baturina's business interests have steadily declined since then, few Russians believe that she, Luzhkov or any other truly high-placed official will be formally called on the carpet for corruption. Sobyanin later faced accusations that he ordered Soviet-era asphalt sidewalks in the city center to be ripped up for replacement with concrete bricks. *His* wife owns a brick and paving business.

"Many have stopped believing it's possible to defend their rights if they're the victims of corruption," a lawyer named Yevgeny Arkhipov told me. Arkhipov, the director of the watchdog Anti-Corruption Committee, which operates hotlines throughout the country on which people can report abuses of office, said the lack of perceptible change following Medvedev's promise to fight corruption when he became president in 2008 disenchanted many people, according to the opinions expressed by thousands of callers. That feeling would swell into the protests of 2011–12. But in 2008, just as he was preparing to publish a report on corruption, Arkhipov and several other members of his group were forced to flee the country after he was warned they would be investigated. They released their findings in Ukraine, where they took refuge for two months, until they felt they could safely return.

Arkhipov confirmed that such intimidation is effective for frightening Russians into remaining silent. The authorities' marginalization of civil society, erosion of public institutions and crackdown on freedom of speech has been thorough enough, he told me, for many to no longer know even how to go about defending their rights. "The stricter their control, the more their activities are hidden from the public," he said, "and the more difficult it is for people to fight corruption. Better to pay a bribe than start a conflict with an official."

Not everyone has been cowed. In 2006, I visited a small plant in a non-descript brick building in residential northeastern Moscow, where dozens of workers were hunched over sewing machines and steam presses, producing uniforms for the likes of McDonald's, Pepsi and Procter & Gamble. The textile company had been started by one of the Soviet Union's first private businessmen to be allowed to operate legally, Ilya Handrikov, who launched his venture in the 1980s under Gorbachev's new laws after he was expelled from college for selling clothes he'd made himself.

No fat cat, the gregarious entrepreneur drove a humble Russian-made hatchback and worked out of a cramped office next to his shop floor, behind mannequins displaying the factory's products. When I first spoke to him, he told me that conducting business honestly was one of his main goals and highest obstacles. He said laws and regulations governing business were purposely vague and often difficult to pin down. Asked about his most frequent problem, he cited visits by fire inspectors and financial regulators who demanded bribes to stop them from reporting fabricated violations.

"When a fire code inspector comes by, he can 'find' any number of them," he said. "Which is of course why the majority of manufacturers have to pay bribes." When a drunk policeman appeared at the factory's front door, it turned out, after much barely coherent explanation, that he was looking for a different company. "Doesn't matter," he slurred after finally being made to realize his mistake. "You'll pay me, too."

Such visits prompted Handrikov to launch an organization to aid businesses like his. Now one of the country's most prominent corruption fighters, he told me that corruption is choking off hope for Russian businesses to compete globally. "Manufacturing has been destroyed," he said. "Small and midsize businesses have been trampled. How can you expect companies pressured by taxes, monopolies and political clans to create innovative ideas? They can't because all their energy goes toward simply trying to survive."

Forced to rent his factory's premises on the black market for years because city authorities refused to answer his myriad requests to lease it officially, Handrikov was also compelled to pay the fines their deputies stopped by to collect. He said the problem could have easily been resolved with one hefty, well-placed bribe but refused to pay it. For other companies that didn't have the money to comply with often arbitrary official demands, he said, submitting was cheaper.

"To our misfortune and unhappiness, the bribe is the main instrument of our daily life," he added. "And because our bureaucracy is the crucial main link between the state and society, things are getting worse and worse for the individual." Estimating that 30 percent of his expenditures were going toward kickbacks, he said he and other small manufacturers were barely able to stay afloat, in his case despite having big-name clients. "It's very hard to live by the rules. If you follow them all, pay all your taxes while everyone else doesn't, that's unfair competition."

In 2005, one of Handrikov's anticorruption groups collected the signatures of big-name legislators and heads of major unions on a petition that entreated Putin, then in his second term as president, to adhere to United Nations and European anticorruption standards. No reply ever came. "When they don't want to answer us," Handrikov said, "the question naturally arises: What's our dear presidential administration really busy doing?"

Partly in explanation, Handrikov described his association's effort to stop the sale of illegally imported clothes from China in 2005. Brought into the country on five thousand railcars the government had paid to transport, he said, the clothes were being sold by officers of the Federal Security Service, the country's security forces, who stood to make a huge, tax-free profit. When the Accounting Chamber—Russia's version of the IRS—sought to investigate the issue, the government barred it from proceeding.

Few who know Handrikov were surprised when he was finally forced out of business during the financial crisis of 2008, after the tax authorities demanded a fifty-thousand-dollar bribe. According to Georgy Satarov, that kind of corruption is a direct result of Putin's effort to consolidate power in his own hands. Bald, gravel-voiced Satarov co-chairs Handrikov's association and heads Moscow's INDEM (Information Science for Democracy) think tank, which studies corruption. One of Russia's leading political commentators, he told me Putin gave the bureaucracy a free hand by silencing the government's critics. "Corruption allows people to be easily controlled because it's easy to manipulate those who've been compromised. On the other hand, it also hurts the authorities because it sharply reduces the competence of state agencies."

Soon after Putin won a third term as president in 2012, state television began showing police confiscating massive piles of cash and jewels during raids on the luxurious apartments of high-ranking bureaucrats. The bread and circuses, part of the president's show of governing in the interests of the people, were part of the most visible anticorruption drive to date, which included the sacking of the defense minister. Far from praise, however, the campaign drew comparisons with similar drives under Brezhnev, which also had the unintended effect of exposing just how rotten the system was—especially then, when most people had to wait in line for basic goods. But in 2012, warnings that corruption threatened stability usually ignored the important fact that it's also central to how Putin exercises his power.[1]

One of my many personal experiences with official ineffectiveness took place in my apartment on the top floor of a small nineteenth-century Moscow building. One midmorning when I was working there, I heard the doorbell ring, followed by the voices of two men who said they were police officers checking on residents' registration papers. Annoyed by the distraction and eager to return to work, I opened the door without checking the peephole. In burst two unshaved thugs, one short and fat, the other tall and thin. The tall one was waving a pistol he claimed was loaded. Encouraged by their amateurishness and perceptible nervousness, which suggested they probably weren't hardened criminals—they hadn't even bothered to wear police uniforms, which were easily obtainable—I managed to fight them off, aided by my claims that video cameras were recording their break-in and by threatening reprisal from influential friends.

When I later phoned my wife, Elizabeth, an American who was working at the English-language daily newspaper the *Moscow Times*, she dismissed my arguments that informing the police would be useless. When the police arrived more than an hour later, the two detectives began by carefully inspecting the apartment for indications of wealth, then checking and rechecking my passport and residence permit, no doubt for any inconsistencies that would enable them to solicit a bribe. After listening to my story and laboriously writing a report, they handed it to me to sign. It contained very little of what I'd told them; instead it said only that I'd called the police after my doorbell was rung by two strangers who had left by the time the officers arrived. Their response to my incredulousness helped open my eyes to the effect corruption has on the state's ability to provide basic functions such as security: you have to understand the chances we'll catch the would-be robbers are very small, they said, and we have quotas for crimes we have to solve. Help us out, sign the paper and we promise to do everything to find them.

Many question how such effects of corruption can be measured or even defined in a society that sees it as a normal part of everyday life. Pollster Lev Gudkov, on the other hand, maintains that corruption is measurable and says the assessment must include far more than the amount of cash that changes hands. "Big business can only function by 'paying' with political loyalty to the authorities, for example," he told me.

Gudkov heads the Levada Center, Russia's only major independent polling agency. It was founded early in Putin's presidency after the state, upset about statistics that reflected badly on the Kremlin, forcibly took over a previous incarnation of the organization, in which a state-controlled company held a minority stake. That was a common tactic of the time: television stations, newspapers and other media were seized in Putin's drive to take control of the enterprises that shape public opinion. (Many Russians now compare their once vibrant national television news to Soviet propaganda broadcasts.) But the Levada Center's experts left their old employers and have since flourished, although in 2013 they began to fear the organization would be forced to close under a new law that requires all groups receiving funding from abroad to call themselves "foreign agents."

Gudkov blames corruption on Russia's "cynical climate of immorality." That can't be tackled as long as most Russians see a benefit in it, namely as a necessary means of getting things done, he said. "It's like oil in a car's engine. The system can't work without it. It makes up for the ineffectiveness of institutions." In that scheme, Gudkov said, the government's ongoing anticorruption campaign is "political theater." "It's not because Russians are deficient in morality," Gudkov concluded. "It's caused by how our practical social and political systems are structured." Real change, he said, must be seen as being in people's interests. "But who's going to deprive himself of his own bread and butter?" he concluded. "That's just not realistic."

———

Although many Russians believe corruption exists to a similar degree in Western countries—the source of much misunderstanding on both sides—most are well aware that their economy is very different. That's a very old story, the perception of economic backwardness having played a huge role in Russians' conception of themselves for much of their history. One of the reasons is that Moscow's models for a great number of important things have come from the West, a central aspect of a very complicated relationship.

Muscovites first began looking westward in earnest in the second half of the fifteenth century, when Tsar Ivan III (the Great) consolidated the formerly weak medieval state of Muscovy. Crucial for Ivan's success was that Moscow—previously one of many small warring principalities in the northern Slav forests—had recently instituted a change in its rules of succession that gave it a great competitive advantage. Previously, the throne had passed to the ruling grand prince's eldest male relative. That scheme prompted inevitable battles between brothers, cousins and others with claims to leadership and also spread wealth so thinly that ruling families' older branches often grew impoverished and weaker than those of new aspirants.

A ruinous civil war probably drove home the realization to Moscow's rulers that their system, like those of the other Slav principalities, worked less than satisfyingly well. In any case, they settled on primogeniture—passing the throne to the eldest son only—and developed a complex ranking system. One of the new rules forbade younger sons from marrying until the eldest produced his own heir.[2] That arrangement gave the principality some guarantee against the previously habitual infighting among senior members of the ruling clan and provided a degree of stability not enjoyed by other formerly more powerful principalities such as nearby Novgorod and Vladimir.

Moscow's advantage enabled it to absorb the neighboring principalities of Tver and Novgorod shortly after Ivan ascended to the throne in 1462. He soon renounced allegiance to the Tatar rulers of the Golden Horde, a remnant of the Mongol Empire to which Moscow still paid tributes. In 1493, Ivan began calling himself tsar—derived from the Latin word *caesar*—and naming himself sovereign of all Russia. (The title remained in formal use until 1721, when Peter the Great renamed himself *imperator*, emperor.)

Moscow's new wealth also prompted Ivan's newly ascendant court to search for an imperial style that would befit its grander status. Understandably, it first looked to the recently vanquished Tatars. So tsar and boyars—a rough equivalent of European nobles—dressed themselves in Turkic robes and called themselves "white khans" in their first correspondence to Italian courts.

When that failed to impress the crowned heads of Europe, it didn't take long for Muscovites to realize the going power lay not in the East but the West. At that point they quickly abandoned Turkic terms and styles. Instead, Ivan began copying European princes. He sent to Italy for architects who would rebuild the Kremlin. The walls that still stand today—then painted white—date from that period, and the main entrance, the Spassky Gate, still bears a Latin inscription praising the Italian Renaissance architect Petrus Antonius Solarius for its design. At the same time, Ivan's Greek wife, the Byzantine princess Sophie Paloelogue—who had been raised in Italy and was the niece of Constantine XI, the last Byzantine emperor— was helping Westernize Moscow's imperial style.

But as historian Edward Keenan points out, rather than slavishly copying its counterparts in the West, Muscovy's emerging culture was unique and dynamic. Despite talk of Moscow as the "Third Rome"—Constantinople, which fell to the Ottoman Turks in 1453, was the second—the cultural borrowing indicated not so much a lack of imagination on the part of the Muscovite princes as, Keenan believes, an ambitious search for their own imperial style. Not seeing themselves as successors to the Tatars, the fallen line of rulers, they were also not interested in the heritage of medieval Rus', the Kiev-based civilization that had preceded Muscovy by a couple of centuries and that some began perceiving as Russia's first incarnation only later. Keenan points to a list of 2,900 courtiers under Ivan III, ninetenths of whom had distinctly Muscovite names—Ivan, Dmitri, Vassily— as opposed to Kievan names, such as Vladimir, Yaroslav or Sviatoslav.[3]

But if Russia's early political culture started out as new and unique, comparisons to the West nevertheless soon came to play a very important role. Moscow's growth set the tone for its future relations with Western countries, historian James Billington argues, by propelling it into a world it was "not equipped to understand...The Muscovite reaction of irritability and self-assertion was in many ways that of a typical adolescent; the Western attitude of patronizing contempt that of the unsympathetic adult."[4] I feel that that dynamic continues shaping Russian identity today.

———

In the 1950s and '60s, Harvard economist Alexander Gerschenkron theorized that the farther east one travels in Europe, the more agrarian and backward the societies become. Born in the Ukrainian Black Sea city of Odessa and educated in Austria, Gerschenkron believed those levels of economic development deeply affected political regimes: the less developed a country, the faster it needed to catch up in order to keep pace with the constantly rising level of modernity in the West.[5] The only possible way for one as backward as Russia to accomplish that was to force change from above. Hence the tyrannical regimes.

Berkeley historian Martin Malia went further to explain the often severe nature of Russian autocracy. Disadvantaged by its meager natural resources (before the extraction of oil and metals began), and challenged by its lack of mountains and other natural obstacles that would help stop invaders, only "brutal state action from above" enabled imperial Russia to become a major European power in the eighteenth century.[6] The constant introduction of new agricultural techniques and technology that facilitated the Industrial Revolution was constantly helping the West raise the standard of what it meant to be European and modern. Russia's difficulty in implementing the increasingly complex adaptations necessary to help it keep up forced it to rely on some segments of the population for innovation. Thus the vanguard of modernization passed to growing sections of the gentry and merchant classes—still a tiny part of society—that became more Westernized than the peasants who made up its vast bulk. Over time, that gap threatened to destabilize a highly conservative society. Although change was necessary to keep up, change that came too fast could be highly damaging.

The most rapid bursts of industrialization in Russian history, together with urbanization and other forms of modernization, took place in the 1890s and the 1930s. The first led to a collapse of the ruling structure and revolution in 1917, but the second did not. Why the difference? Keenan asks, seeking to explain the nature of those changes in "Muscovite Political Folkways," one of the most seminal articles about Russian history.[7]

Normally, change among the elite—in education, Westernization, the absorption of foreign theories—is passed down to the rest of the population slowly over time. The end of the nineteenth century wasn't normal, however. In the 1890s, the reforming Finance Minister Sergei Witte— who oversaw the institution of the state liquor monopoly that would vastly improve the quality of domestic vodka—orchestrated Russia's greatest industrialization drive. That spurt was a response to Russia's humiliating defeat in the Crimean War of the 1850s.[8] Like the Great Reforms of Alexander II, who freed the serfs in 1861 and instituted the first jury system, industrialization was seen as imperative for survival.

Witte's modernization was massive, but not necessarily well thought out. With the push geared toward heavy industry, factories were built near the center of major cities, as I've mentioned. As with the Soviet modernization drives of decades later, its planners largely ignored light industry and the production of consumer goods. As Malia pointed out, another similarity was the peasantry being "squeezed through taxation to finance the whole undertaking without benefitting from it in any tangible way."[9]

Literature and art reflected the momentous change. At the turn of the century, Russia went from being a follower in culture to a global leader. In painting, modernist literature, dance and other forms of expression— Kazimir Malevich's Suprematist painting, Osip Mandelshtam's Acmeist poetry and Sergei Diaghilev's Ballets Russes, to name a few—St. Petersburg and Moscow took over from Paris and other capitals as the avantgarde's spearhead.

Governmental changes were also great. In the country with a tradition of highly centralized rule, representative politics emerged for the first time. However, Alexander II, who had instituted the zemstvo—an organization of local self-government—and taken steps to grow municipal institutions, was assassinated by revolutionaries in 1881. His son Alexander III was reactionary and suspicious of the masses, as was *his* son, Nicholas II, the last

Russian tsar. Nevertheless, one of Nicholas II's concessions following a short revolution in 1905 was permitting the founding and operation of the Duma, the empire's first parliament. It was a dramatic development. "This state and political culture," Keenan wrote, "in which political power had always flowed downward and outward through politically castrated military and civil bureaucracies, suddenly gave birth to, and tried to accommodate, new political formations that had, or claimed, a share of real political power: parties, assemblies, committees of industrialists, Dumas, city soviets [councils], soviets of workers and peasants, trade unions and innumerable leagues, societies and associations."[10]

Very unfortunately for Russia, however, Nicholas failed to avert a collision between the massive pressure for change and the more powerful inertia of historical continuity. Already barely able to keep a lid on a pot of boiling water, he stumbled badly in the Russo-Japanese War (1904–5), when Japan dealt Russia a huge humiliation by becoming the first Asian power to defeat a European one in modern times. Russia lost not only its Pacific but also its Baltic fleet, which had steamed all the way to the Far East only to be dispatched. The defeat proved the final straw that caused the revolution of 1905, but reactionary Nicholas soon backpedaled on most of his concessions.

Entry into World War I, in 1914, proved even more disastrous. Weakened by a woeful supply of weapons and ammunition, Russia suffered immense casualties. At one point in 1915, a quarter of the soldiers sent to the front were unarmed. Despite the troops' often heroic fighting, the incompetence of Nicholas—who was increasingly relying on his wife, Alexandra, and her spiritual adviser, the peasant Grigory Rasputin—and his top generals stoked the flames of the general disillusionment that culminated in another revolution in 1917.

Under times of such rapid change, Keenan stressed, the usual slow processes of "socialization and acculturation" of new ideas and practices from the elite to the masses weren't enough to maintain stability. The Bolsheviks, who seized power in November of 1917—following an earlier revolution in February, which gave rise to a provisional government led by moderate socialists—reinstated a traditional political culture. When the "spectacularly disruptive" rapid transformation destroyed the ruling elite, it was the peasant culture that provided stability—Russia's traditional "normalcy."[11]

The social culture stabilized once again by the end of the 1930s, evidenced by the fact that not even World War II, which took a far greater human and economic toll than World War I, unseated the political structure. A new political elite had reestablished extreme centralization. The Communist Party, which muffled, suppressed and rid society of the rising classes and groups that had threatened to upend the traditional political culture, became the new beneficiary of Russia's age-old system of closed, conspiratorial rule.

The new elite was composed of people of peasant or proletarian background whose attitudes derived from the centuries-old village political culture that grew from the need to survive extreme risk. Keenan described the continuity:

After a long period of social and political chaos, the great bulk of the Russian population shared with its leaders a conviction that only a powerfully centralized and oligarchic government can provide the order which they all crave. Having had little contact or experience with the notions of democratic electoral constitutionalism, they share the view that one can rely more confidently upon informal and personal relationships than upon those defined by the legalistic niceties so admired elsewhere. Having had decades of "wrong" government whose claims to legitimacy were generally considered within the political culture to be meaningless, they are more concerned that a government be "right" than that it be legitimate.[12]

Although there are many exceptions, Keenan's observations about Soviet reality hold largely true about contemporary Russia. After another decade of radical change that threatened to overthrow the traditional political culture—the post-Soviet 1990s—Putin, in essence, reimposed the old way of doing things. As always, it has been fear of disintegration and chaos, the eternal specter of anarchy, that has helped unite Russians in their support of him. Putin has gone to extraordinary lengths to paint the 1990s as a period of chaos and criminality, tacitly appealing to people's traditional anxieties. Despite the first major visible signs of public dissatisfaction among the urban middle class during protests in December 2011, a Levada Center poll conducted four months earlier showed that most Russians still believed order to be more important than democracy. Forty-five percent of respondents said the country needs democracy, but a "special" kind suited to its traditions.

"May God forfend a Russian revolt, senseless and merciless," Pushkin wrote, referring to a very destructive peasant uprising that took place during the reign of Catherine the Great in 1774. Paradoxically—and maybe also predictably—it was precisely that kind of revolt that led to the Bolshevik Revolution."

———

It's well known that forced labor is highly unproductive. Like serfdom, which lasted until 1861, the subjection of tens of millions of people to slave labor in the Soviet Gulag—the backbone of economic expansion under Stalin—did nothing to help Russian productivity. Although the Communist Party authorities may have put people to work very efficiently on paper, official statistics obscured the truth, just as government figures continue to do in Russia today.

Shortly after the Revolution, Lenin backpedaled on implementing economic centralization by adopting a temporary New Economic Policy, the NEP, in the 1920s to avert utter economic collapse by strengthening small private enterprises. After that experiment with limited "state capitalism," Stalin introduced full central planning and enacted the first of many Five-Year Plans in 1929. Its aim was to "scientifically" translate schemes for building socialism into targets for industrialization according to schedules drawn up by Gosplan, the state planning agency.

With the country facing mass starvation following revolution, civil war and state-induced famine, the first plan projected that the national income would rise by a staggering 500-plus percent within four years.[13] In fact, the scheme was a tool for aiding forced collectivization of the country's farmland, part of Stalin's "war" against the peasantry, which had disastrous effects on productivity. By comparison, NEP's policy of allowing farmers to sell surplus yields instead of having the whole lot confiscated by the state had been a stunning success. Nevertheless, the dictator's policies did transform peasant Russia into a largely urban society. A small part of the population before the Revolution, industrial workers doubled in number between 1928 and 1937, from 3.8 to 10.1 million, and later became the majority.[14] Malia called Stalin's industrialization the "Soviet experiment's only real achievement."[15]

The mechanism for achieving that change bred cruelty and paranoia. Less a real roadmap than a psychological tool for coercing loyalty, enslaving workers and justifying the elimination of anyone accused of obstructing the government, the Five-Year Plan also threw most Soviet resources at building heavy industry to the near exclusion of almost everything else. Coal, iron and steel production dominated, along with tractor and automobile manufacture. One of the signature projects was building a steelworks in the city of Magnitogorsk, roughly translated as "magnet city," in the southern Ural Mountains, to exploit huge reserves of iron ore. Much of the work was carried out by prisoners, who also built gold and nickel mines, oil wells and lumber camps in the vast stretches of uninhabited Siberia and the country's far north and east. Forced labor laid the foundations of many cities there, as well as the roads, railroads and other infrastructure they required.

All the construction was "carried out amidst constant crisis bordering on chaos," as Malia put it.[16] By 1930, industrial production was actually falling. Nine years later, the standard of living in the countryside was lower than it had been in 1913. Alexei Stakhanov—the miner who gave his name to the Stakhanovite movement, which encouraged "model" workers to achieve high productivity—was a favorite Soviet example, touted ad nauseam by propagandists. Stakhanov was reported to have mined fourteen times his quota in a single shift (102 tons in less than six hours). Actually, other workers whose efforts went unmentioned contributed to his achievement, however many tons he actually mined.

Far from becoming a model for socialist or any other kind of society, the inefficiency and shoddiness of Russian products had become legendary by the time my father began visiting the Soviet Union. On a Soviet collective farm in the southern Krasnodar region at which he spent some weeks in the 1970s, he reported that half the tractors, including the new ones, were under constant repair. Still, the director kept his farm in better shape than it would otherwise have been because he bought two tractors for every one he needed, a method of acquiring spare parts that spoke volumes about wastefulness and inferiority.

In Moscow, many brand-new buildings were ringed with nets to catch bricks that fell from their facades. Jokes were among the few things in which Soviet production excelled. One of them captured the spirit of sloppy work and shortages particularly well. It's 1978. A dentist who makes good money because he, like all competent dentists, is paid under the table finally saves enough to buy a car. Taking an immense stack of rubles—neither checks nor credit cards existed—he goes to an outlet (there were also no showrooms) where Volgas are sold. After laboriously counting the money, the manager pulls out a big ledger and flips through its pages. "Yes, you can have your car in 1986," he says. "April fourteenth. Do you want it in the morning or the afternoon?" The dentist thinks for a moment. "Better make it the morning," he says. "The plumber's coming that afternoon."

Overcoming the late-communist era's legacy of that kind of dysfunction remains one of Russia's greatest challenges. My first summer job in Russia, in 1991, less than a month before the attempted coup d'état, was as a translator for CNN. My very unglamorous assignment was to help put together temporary studios for covering a summit meeting between Gorbachev and President George H. W. Bush. Along with other television news channels, CNN set up some of its operations in the then astoundingly modern Mezhdunarodnaya Hotel on the Moscow River, which had been built in the late 1970s with help from the American industrialist and Soviet friend Armand Hammer. Having shown up in a blue blazer and harboring visions of not-too-distant stardom, I was happy to make the acquaintance of Kolya Pavlov but dismayed to find that my job would consist chiefly of lugging equipment from the basement to the conference rooms upstairs, where producers were setting up broadcast studios.

Nevertheless, all my interpretation skills were required. Despite the extortionary rates CNN was charged for storage, each visit to the hotel's dank depths necessitated negotiations with the men in overalls who kept the storeroom keys. They were rarely there. I'd find the door shut, a string sealed with wax attached across the door crack (as if that seventeenth-century method of preventing or at least recording theft would have discouraged thieves in any way). When they did happen to be available, the gruff doorkeepers would come up with one reason after another for not allowing CNN the use of its equipment. Needless to say, incremental bribes were the only way to get things in or out. That was the Soviet economy in a nutshell.

Trying to get things done could become overwhelming. After I began reporting for the local English-language newspaper the *Moscow Times,*

I broke a number of flimsy hotel telephones in provincial cities by slamming down their receivers. The frustration produced by hours of trying to reach one or another official is unpleasant to remember even now. Those were the Yeltsin years, when officials still spoke to reporters—if you could get through over the crackling lines, which produced mainly static. In the Volga River city of Samara, where I was trying to set up an interview with an up-and-coming young reformer type who was generating headlines after he'd modernized the local power utility, I spoke to any number of his secretaries before, during and after their boss's lunch. Each time, I received a promise he'd provide a yes or no response to my request if I called back fifteen minutes later—when the phone would unfailingly ring unanswered. When someone finally picked up hours later, it was only to lay the receiver down again. Anyone who has tried calling Russian consulates abroad for information about how to apply for a visa will confirm that I'm not exaggerating here.

Nevertheless, I was genuinely taken aback during a reporting trip for NPR years later when I arrived at a tiny provincial airport an hour ahead of the departure time for one of two weekly flights to find the doors chained shut. It was near a small town deep in the taiga forest of the far east, where an overnight snowfall had prompted me to call twice in the morning to confirm the time. Ten minutes of banging and yelling summoned the nonchalant airport director and his secretary, whose only explanation for why the plane had taken off earlier than scheduled was a shrug.

I didn't know whether to feel angry or desperate: the next plane wouldn't be leaving for days. Perhaps it was my own fault for having scheduled important interviews the following day in Khabarovsk, the nearest big city. There was nothing to do but check into one of two hotels. Turned away from the first by a woman who demanded, "What do you want?!" when I rang the bell on the concierge's desk, I managed to get a room in a crumbling hulk called the Youth Hotel.

If the airport staff members' refusal to admit any responsibility for having misinformed me was typically Russian, however, so was their transformed demeanor the following morning, perhaps because they hoped their unacknowledged guilt would be absolved when they offered good news. A private plane flying natural-gas pipeline technicians would be passing through and the airport chief had convinced the pilot to take me along. Now apologetic, the director gave me a half-hour lift to the airstrip in his ancient military jeep, in which he was barely able to negotiate the unplowed road. Inside, the young woman checking me in had never seen an American passport before. "Have you been to Hollywood?" she asked, beaming. "Bruce Willis lives there, right?" More than being able to keep my appointments, it was her friendliness that sustained my smile as I finally trudged out to the airstrip.

Western visitors to Russia have regaled their friends back home with stories of shoddiness, disorganization and graft for centuries. When the Marquis de Custine visited in 1839, his overwhelming response was dismay. "Seen from the Neva," he wrote of the river flowing though the grand imperial capital, "the parapets of the St. Petersburg wharves are impressive and magnificent; but from the first step on land, you discover that these same wharves are paved with inferior stones, inconvenient, uneven—as disagreeable to the eye as they are painful to pedestrians and treacherous to carriages."[17] Writing about the preliminary customs procedures—the full process would turn out to last days—de Custine described the petty officials he encountered on his first stop, the island of Kronstadt, in the Gulf of Finland just outside St. Petersburg.

> The profusion of small, superfluous precautions creates here a population of clerks. Each one of these men discharges his duty with a pedantry, a rigor, an air of importance uniquely designed to give prominence to the most obscure employment. He does not permit himself to say so, but you can see him thinking approximately this: "Make way for me, I am one of the members of the great machine of the State."[18]

In his description, the clerks make an inevitable mockery of efficiency and effectiveness. They also dehumanize those at the bottom of the ladder.

> At last we finished with the customs ceremonies, the courtesies of the police, were rid of the military salutes and a spectacle of the most profound misery which can mar the human race, for the oarsmen of the gentlemen of the Russian Customs are creatures of a kind apart. As I could do nothing for them, their presence was odious to me, and each time these miserable wretches brought to the ship officials of all grades employed by the Customs Service and

by the Maritime Police—the most severe police of the Empire—I turned my eyes. These ragged seamen are a disgrace to their country; they are a species of greasy galley slaves who spend their lives transporting the clerks and officials of Kronstadt aboard foreign vessels. In seeing their faces and in thinking about what is called existence for these poor devils, I asked myself what man has done to God that sixty million of the human race should be condemned to live in Russia.[19]

Quoting de Custine may smack of cliché because so many have done it during the century and three-quarters since he visited. But there's good reason: much of the spirit that depressed that eloquent observer persists, despite great changes in the urban landscapes. Although arriving in Moscow's recently modernized main international airport, Sheremetyevo, is less dismaying today than it was several years ago, it still gives a taste of the country that awaits your entry. Renovations that vastly improved the late-Soviet era's dark gloom have had little effect on the lethargic movements of the stern customs officials who take their time poring over the passports of visitors. Having just disembarked from their planes, passengers are forced to wait in jostling lines, sometimes for more than forty minutes. Emerging into the scrum of the arrivals hall, pivoting away from one dubious-looking taxi driver after another, one wonders why a country whose officials cite attracting foreign investment as one of their top priorities provides such a disheartening first glimpse to foreigners, many of whom are prepared to think the best of Russia. Of course that's an academic question.

Piotr Chadaev, considered the first of Russia's nineteenth-century Westernizers, famously pronounced that if his country had a universal lesson for the world, it was that its example should be avoided at all costs. "That is but a natural consequence of a culture that is wholly imported and imitative," he wrote. "There is no internal development, no natural progress, in our society; new ideas sweep out the old because they are not derived from the old but come from God knows where." Chadaev believed his country was isolated from the West; that it was a backward place with no past or future. By arguing that Russia must follow its own path of development to fulfill its historical mission, he also influenced a seminal group of nineteenth-century intellectuals called the Slavophiles, who had come to believe Russian isolation was a virtue.

Although the fictional character Ilya Oblomov represents a specific type from a certain era, he is among Russian literature's enduring archetypes. Young Oblomov, the product of a noble family who comes of age in the idealistic 1860s, is the embodiment of a generation of Russian intellectuals called the superfluous men. Generally young and aristocratic, they supported freethinking, often radical ideas, unlike most of their contemporaries. (Their later designation as superfluous arose because they appeared to have nowhere to channel their energies besides dueling, gambling and other self-destructive acts.) Oblomov plans to do great things that never materialize. Instead he spends his idle days living off a waning inheritance, a symbol of the demise of his class. Like the hopeless alcoholic Venichka Erofeev, whose tale of his train trip from Moscow to the suburban town of Petushki would lambaste the Brezhnev-era USSR a hundred years later, Oblomov is as comic as he is tragic. Published in 1859 by Ivan Goncharov, a St. Petersburg civil servant from a family of grain merchants, the novel *Oblomov* tells the story of the hugely lethargic Oblomov and his equally indolent valet, Zakhar, who live in self-imposed isolation in Oblomov's once grand St. Petersburg apartment, where the wealthy hero has settled after giving up hopes of a respectable career.

> Lying down was not for Ilya Illich either a necessity as it is for a sick or a sleepy man, or an occasional need as it is for a person who is tired, or a pleasure as it is for a sluggard: it was his normal state. When he was at home—and he was almost always at home—he was lying down, and invariably in the same room, the one in which we have found him and which served him as bedroom, study and reception-room. He had three more rooms, but he seldom looked into them, only, perhaps, in the morning when his servant swept his study—which did not happen every day. In those other rooms the furniture was covered and the curtains were drawn.[20]

Unable to bring himself even to read a book, Oblomov spends his days in his dressing gown, daydreaming. Among other plans, he envisions schemes to reform his ancestral countryside estate into a model of prosperous activity. Unable to achieve his arcadian ideal, however, he ends up justifying his inactivity. In the first pages, he receives an annual letter from the bailiff of his estate that contains the bad news of an ever-smaller income, which spurs Oblomov to decide yet again to overhaul its management.

> As soon as he woke, he made up his mind to get up and wash, and after drinking tea, to think matters over, taking various things into consideration and writing them down, and altogether to go into the subject thoroughly. He lay half an hour tormented by his decision; but afterward he reflected that he would have time to think after breakfast, which he could have in bed as usual, especially since one can think just as well lying down.
>
> This is what he did. After his morning tea he sat up and very nearly got out of bed; looking at his slippers, he began lowering one foot down toward them, but at once drew it back again.[21]

Oblomov's childhood friend Andrei Stolz, whose German name symbolizes his industriousness, represents his opposite. Productive and practical as he is, his efforts to prod Oblomov into action come to nothing. Nevertheless, the reader sympathizes not with the wooden Stolz but with Oblomov, who, despite his shortcomings, is warm, kind and imaginative.

Captivated by dreams of his once happy childhood, Oblomov personifies a state of mind: *Oblomovshina*, or Oblomovism, has come to mean a kind of inertia. He's not the first literary archetype to have done so. All children are familiar with one of Oblomov's best-known precedents, a fairy-tale hero named Ivanushka Durachok—Little Ivan the Sweet Fool—whose greatest desire is to while away his days lazing about on the warm tiled stove of his village hut. Like Oblomov, he is blessed with goodness and an easygoing nature. Unlike Oblomov, however, he manages to accomplish quite a lot.

Ivanushka often has two elder brothers who try to outwit him but whose greed and selfishness inevitably lead them to failure. In one tale, Ivanushka is fetching water at a river when he catches a magic pike. In return for its release, the fish grants him the power to make his wishes come true. Ivanushka's first act is to order his pails to walk home themselves. Commanded to chop wood in the forest, Ivanushka has an axe do it for him and a horseless sleigh pull the load home. Angered by the bizarre sight, villagers petition the tsar to arrest Ivanushka. Lured to the castle, he ventures there still lying on his stove, which walks there by itself. But he is saved from execution by the tsar's daughter, who falls in love with him. The tsar allows them to marry but has them sealed in a wooden barrel and set adrift at sea. After days of floating, the desperate princess begs Ivanushka to do something. When he wishes them to reach shore, the barrel instantly breaks open on land, where he conjures up a marble palace and they live happily ever after.

If fairy-tale characters that endure in the West—such as Aesop's dogged tortoise and the Grimms' seven dwarfs—tend to glorify persistence and hard work, Russian fairy tales often champion resignation to one's fate. The unlikely hero Ivanushka defeats his enemies, marries the princess and ends up living in a palace because he is compassionate and selfless.

Literary and fairy-tale archetypes that instill the notion that people without coarse ambition are the spiritually purest reinforce Russia's widespread fatalism, the idea that things will happen as they happen and nothing important can be done about it. However, today's workforce is more directly affected by systemic problems in a sphere that has long been seen as one of the country's great strengths: education. Like so much of Russian life, it is at the mercy of the self-interested bureaucrats and corruption that sap the strength of even those most committed to changing the Russian presumption that sloth conquers enterprise.

———

Russians and foreigners alike who are surprised the economy isn't more diversified and robust often point to the country's traditionally high educational standards. The Soviet Union used to boast that its system was the world's best, and while communism may have been disastrous in many spheres, it helped educate a land of formerly illiterate peasants. In addition to making literacy nearly universal by building on the impressive gains made before 1917, the Soviet Union produced some of the world's top physicists, mathematicians and engineers. Russian computer programmers and hackers remain some of the best anywhere, and with so many highly qualified people, the logic goes, surely Russian industry should have more to show for it.

However, closer examination of the schooling system gives a different

impression of the difficulties Russia faces in building a competitive economy beyond the segment based on mining natural resources. To begin
with, although technical training at top Soviet institutions achieved very
high levels, the education that most Soviets received under communism
failed to provide the basic curricula that are crucial for critical reasoning
and initiative, the kind the best American schools and colleges provide.
Heavy drilling in Marxism-Leninism discouraged creative thinking.

A handful of scholars, such as the literary theorist Yuri Lotman—of
Estonia's Tartu University, the Russian Empire's first institution of higher
learning, established under Swedish rule in 1632—were global pioneers in
the 1960s, '70s and '80s. But the Iron Curtain cut off most others, especially social scientists, from key developments abroad. Among the fields
that withered was psychology, which became a tool for justifying the incarceration of political prisoners in psychiatric wards, a practice that is showing signs of a resurgence under Putin.

Yevgeny Bunimovic, a poet and former teacher who is now a member
of the Moscow legislature, disputes the claim that Soviet schools were the
world's best. One of Russia's best-known experts on education, Bunimovic
works in an office in the newly renovated city Duma building on centrally
located Petrovka Street, where members of his staff are unusually cheerful
for Russian government employees. "It's a myth," he said of the idea that
Soviet education was among the world's best. "In mathematics and chemistry, yes, the teaching was good. But not in history, which was subject to propaganda. And the negative influence of Soviet control remains very large."

Another critic, Boris Davidovich, characterizes Soviet education as
"totalitarian." A mathematics teacher, Davidovich is also deputy director
of Moscow's School 57, located in an old neighborhood behind the Pushkin
art museum, close to the Kremlin. "The method was based on power," he
told me, "specifically the state's power over the teacher and the teacher's
power over the child, who was forced to learn."

Then came the Soviet collapse. An almost overnight disappearance of
nearly all education funding left schools to fend for themselves. Throughout the country, teachers were paid between five and ten dollars a month.
Following the example of other state employees, many continued working
despite receiving nothing at all. Most schools had no money for maintenance or new textbooks. Despite that, Bunimovic praises the Soviet legacy
for helping schools remain open during those very difficult years. In the

1990s, the Moscow school system somehow managed to keep textbooks free of charge, but "there was no money for library books or chemicals for chemistry experiments, let alone any kind of renovations. God forbid something went wrong."

School 57, which specializes in mathematics and is one of the country's best, struggled to survive. Since Russian schools are funded by regional and municipal governments, those living in Moscow, by far the richest city, are luckiest. With fierce competition to get in, many of School 57's students are gifted. But ten years ago, its green Soviet-era paint was peeling and the wooden floors were creaking and unvarnished. Deputy director Davidovich, a fast-spoken but philosophical man with graying hair and a short beard, exudes pride in the school, as do many others there, including the students. The end of Soviet-era controls "freed teachers," Davidovich said. "Now they can speak the truth without fear. It's a different mentality." But when the government left schools to do largely whatever they wanted, it also effectively stopped enforcing standards. With the Soviet coercion gone, there's been nothing to replace it. Davidovich believes the biggest problem now is students' lack of motivation. "It's very difficult to teach in those conditions."

In some respects, the situation has changed dramatically since oil and gas money began flooding state coffers more than a decade ago. With the government finally paying attention to education, there's been a sporting attempt to renovate School 57's old classrooms with earth-tone colors and new lighting, which make it seem like a different place. Davidovich said the government's decision to allocate a certain amount of money for each student has "transformed our situation." Teachers are now paid a thousand dollars a month, small by Moscow standards but a far cry from the pitiful salaries of the 1990s. Still, the city government covers only around 75 percent of the school system's budget, forcing directors to raise the rest themselves. Some comes from wealthy parents, many of whom demand special treatment for their children.

As competition for access to good public schools increases, parents complain about having to pay for their children to get into the best ones and then having to bribe teachers to give good grades. A middle-aged Muscovite named Tatyana Valentinovna told me she sometimes has to pay five hundred dollars. The prices increase for older students. In a 2011 poll conducted by an independent agency called the Public Opinion Foundation, respondents said higher education constituted the most corrupt sector of public life, even above the notorious traffic police.

Other systemic problems include government pressure to teach officially approved lessons, a consequence of increased spending on schools. Putin has called for a universal secondary school history textbook "free of internal contradictions and ambiguities." Previously suggested new versions have muted criticism of Soviet crimes and praised dictator Joseph Stalin an "effective manager." Bunimovic told me the education system is held hostage by a dichotomy between what the government says and what it does, as when Prime Minister Medvedev makes admirable speeches about the urgent need to improve education while heading a government that has very little tolerance for criticism.

"Medvedev has said our future depends on raising a new generation of critical thinkers, but how can you do that in a society in which newspapers are censored? You simply can't have both," Bunimovic said. He also criticized the government's historical revisionism. "We have a government that sees enemies surrounding Russia," he said. "That kind of thinking produces a certain type of student—not the critical, open-thinking type. Again, you can't have both."

Other schools, especially in Russia's much poorer regions, are in far worse condition. Many still struggle to survive, and the level of education is often miserable. Even in the relatively wealthy capital, most schools look run-down. The difference in levels of education is helping fuel the massive gap between the poor, who get most of their information from state television, and the elite, many of whose children read critical media in Russian and foreign languages on the Internet. Educators also say corruption and pressure to toe the official line, those hallmarks of Putin's Russia, are threatening the school system.

A medical student named Sasha Vitrogansky told me many medical school applicants pay thousands of dollars in bribes to pass their entrance exams and continue giving gifts to secure good grades. "Something wrong can always be found on our tests and reports," he said. "If you want to pass, you have to take along a box of chocolates and a bottle of liquor at the very least. You force yourself to smile when you hand them to your professor." Boris Davidovich told me that kind of bribery is seriously damaging even grammar schools such as School 57. "Corruption is lowering the level of education; it's one of our biggest problems," he said. "The state of our schools reflects society in general. It's our common woe."

Although the average Russian student now ranks close to the average American in world comparisons of educational achievement, Bunimovic concluded, neither country should be proud of that.

———

Since 1991, Russia has defied countless predictions and heartfelt hopes that its dominant way of doing things would change. Although travel abroad, the influx of foreigners, the freedom to read, the advent of the Internet and a new consumer culture have combined with other very powerful agents to produce some change, so far their influence hasn't been powerful enough. Under the Soviet Union, the Communist Party's monopoly on power enabled its leaders to embark upon, and often later abandon, grandiosely wasteful projects such as a railway through the largely unpopulated far east. Now vast income from the energy sector has replaced Soviet control and enables a less authoritarian regime to undertake similarly wasteful projects, such as funding the auto industry, for the sake of shoring up its power and glorifying itself.

Among the new initiatives was Putin's most audacious effort to present Russia as a modern place: his successful bid to stage the 2014 Winter Olympics in the popular Black Sea resort of Sochi, where the president spends much of the summer. Tens of thousands of mostly migrant workers toiled for miserly pay to rebuild the town's rickety Soviet-era infrastructure on a scale reminiscent of the old communist developments. The defiance of logic also approached Soviet levels, and not just because the city's subtropical climate necessitated hoarding the previous year's snow under thermal blankets on the surrounding Caucasus Mountains. Staging the world's premier international sporting event within a half day's drive of North Caucasus regions where Islamist militants carry out almost daily attacks did more to defy reason.

Sochi has become synonymous with Putin's crony capitalism because it enabled his associates at the top of Russian industry to reap billions of mostly taxpayer funds by helping build what have turned out to be some of the world's most expensive sporting facilities. Companies belonging to one man alone, Putin's childhood friend and former judo sparring partner

Arkady Rotenberg, earned more than seven billion dollars, more than the entire budget for the 2010 Vancouver Olympics.[22] Much of the work was shoddy, polluting and wasteful. The ski jump had to be rebuilt numerous times, until Putin himself fired the Russian Olympic Committee's vice president, whose brother happened to own the responsible construction company. The final cost estimate for the seventeen-day event surpassed fifty billion dollars, almost four times the proposed amount, making it the most expensive Olympic Games in history.

Nevertheless, the corruption and lethargy that come with Putin's system and its suppression of genuine enterprise may well continue sustaining the old way of doing things until the oil wells run dry.

Some of the thousands of soldiers sent to help put down opposition protests in central Moscow ahead of parliamentary elections in 2007.

8

The Avant-Garde

He who does not forget his *first* love will not recognize his last.

—from "A Slap in the Face of Public Taste," a manifesto of the Cubo-Futurist art movement, 1912[1]

Amid the old wooden dachas and new tin-roofed redbrick buildings that constitute Russian suburbia thirty miles northeast of Moscow, billboards and rudimentary strip malls selling construction materials give way to a rambling pine and birch forest. A two-lane road stops at a large metal gate flanked by a wall of neat concrete blocks and barbed wire. Behind them lies what used to be one of the Soviet Union's most closely guarded secrets: Star City. Built to train cosmonauts to fly into space, the area formerly called Closed Military Settlement No. 1 hosts astronauts from around the world as they prepare for stints on the International Space Station.

The aging compound, constructed around sprawling, typically Soviet paved central quadrangles, includes apartment blocks and a school together with massive brick buildings housing replicas of space station components. One section lies underwater at the bottom of a pool, where trainees in space suits float with the help of scuba divers. In another building, engineers fiddle with wires, pipes and panels of electronics in a very cramped residential module. Decorated with acres of wood and linoleum, the complex appears basic despite the highly advanced technology it houses. Although the engineers say their simulations are crucial to ensure the proper functioning of the space station, it's hard to imagine anything in the facility actually working in space, a perception heightened by the staff's defensiveness. Everything's better than at NASA, I was told, including the bureaucracy, which doesn't choke off progress as American officials do. The rivalry sometimes surfaces into public view. Although partly conceived as a showcase for what countries can achieve by working together, the International Space Station has prompted arguments between Russia's space agency and NASA that mirror Moscow's troubled relations with the West. Shortly before my visit, the station's commander confessed in a newspaper interview that squabbles about equipment and supplies were harming work in space. Since Moscow was charging foreign astronauts for using its facilities on the space station, he said, only Russians used the Russian toilets now and there was no more sharing of food. Other astronauts later played down some of the claims, but confirmed the general friction.

One of the loudest arguments was over the Russian practice of taking civilian travelers to the space station in exchange for tens of millions of dollars in fees. Vladimir Gubarev, a space industry expert who served as Moscow's spokesman for the joint US-Soviet Apollo-Soyuz mission in the 1970s, was pained by such disagreements. Speaking in the comfortable study of his central Moscow apartment, decorated with photos of Apollo-Soyuz and other Soviet milestones, he told me the American and Russian space programs do things differently. "They have different cultures, so it's a mistake to believe you can create a successful joint station in space," he said.

Gubarev placed most of the blame on Moscow. Instead of developing new technology, he said, the Russians were mainly interested in squeezing profit from seriously outdated technology, leaving their space program at mounting risk. In 2011, one mishap after another caused Russia to lose five satellites and a spacecraft, an ambitious unmanned probe that would have collected soil samples from a Martian moon. After it became stuck in orbit around the earth, the space agency's chief, Vladimir Popovkin, insinuated foreign sabotage. "I wouldn't like to accuse anyone," he told the newspaper *Izvestiya*, "but there are powerful [technological] means to affect spacecraft, and their use can't be ruled out." Although a deputy prime minister later admitted Russia's failures could have been caused by equipment "produced about twelve to thirteen years ago," other officials wondered whether American radar had disabled the probe.

To me, the space program vividly illustrated some of the paradoxes of

Russian life. Star City's jerry-rigged appearance reflected the legacy of a superpower with Third-World standards of living. Russia's backwardness has ensured that many of its achievements, in art as well as science, are inspired by and measured against advances in the West (when they're not largely stolen). The space program was also representative for another reason. In a society where many developments have been initiated by orders from above, the Soviet space program's early successes came essentially from below—specifically from the ingenuity and dedication of a handful of individuals.

In other areas, too, Russians have excelled at getting primitive machinery to work under extreme conditions, not only in the extraordinary circumstances that figure prominently in the national consciousness, such as victory in World War II—which is celebrated with what seems to be ever-greater pomp each year—but also in everyday life. Despite or because of huge obstacles and limited resources, they've displayed great originality and inventiveness in literature, painting, music, theater and cinema, and their feats during the last century would have been even more brilliant if Stalin hadn't killed so many splendid scientists and artists and driven so many others underground or abroad.

One theory holds that some of the very qualities that make largely undisciplined Russians relatively poor workers—lack of self-control, ambition and willingness to follow rules—also help liberate creativity. My relative Gera Kiva, a specialist in industrial automation technology who taught at Moscow State University, told me his field was seriously constrained because "we had no resources; we did everything by hand and the seat of our pants." Still, that wasn't the main problem. "Russians can think up anything—we swim in ideas," he said. "But we can't carry them out because we just don't have the patience to take things to the end."

With their dogged work, opposition leaders and human rights activists are spearheading some of the efforts to instill Western values in Russian society. One day, they may help change the relationship between the people and their state. Meanwhile, I believe the closed political system that inspires some individual creativity still stifles most achievement.

———

The Soviet Union trumpeted its launching of the Space Age half a century ago by sending the first man-made satellite into orbit around the earth. Far from the result of any government initiative, however, Sputnik was made possible largely by one man whose identity remained secret for decades.

Sergei Korolev, the father of the Soviet space program, began building rockets for military use after World War II, relying on German plans that came to light after the United States had captured the top German engineers. (Nazi technology was advanced partly because the Treaty of Versailles following World War I restricted Germany's production of weapons but said nothing about rockets.) The two-time winner of the Hero of Socialist Labor award—one of the Soviet Union's highest honors along with the Lenin Prize, which Korolev also won—had barely survived Stalin's Great Purge of 1937–38. He spent six years in the Gulag, partly in a Siberian labor camp, where he lost his teeth.

His longtime first deputy, a fellow rocket designer named Boris Chertok, first met Korolev in 1945 at a Soviet laboratory inside Germany. A frail ninety-five-year-old when he met a handful of reporters on the fiftieth anniversary of Sputnik's launch, Chertok was still wonderfully lucid. We gathered inside a museum dedicated to Korolev, surrounded by photographs and memorabilia of the space program, where Chertok said his former boss was not only a genius engineer but also a gifted organizer. "He had a great ability to persuade people," he recalled. "He was also exceptionally single-minded and ruthless with subordinates. Deep inside himself, he felt a great responsibility not only to his people but also to history."

Much of the Soviet Union was devastated after the war and many of its people were near starvation. But Korolev succeeded in persuading Communist Party leaders that rockets were worth funding because they alone could even the American advantage. The United States had military bases around the world, but the Soviet Union could deliver a nuclear warhead straight to the enemy. Gubarev, the former Apollo-Soyuz spokesman, believes it was "utterly illogical" for the Soviet Union to have been first into space, "but it happened because our rocket program was more closely tied to the military than the American one." Stalin had wanted bombers to deliver nuclear warheads, but Korolev prevailed, with support from military generals who had seen legions of their soldiers killed during the war.

After being given the go-ahead, it took years of intensive work for Korolev's rocket design bureau to have a prototype ready to fly. Chertok oversaw the missile assembly at the new Baikonur Cosmodrome, built on an isolated steppe in Kazakhstan, where conditions made the work grueling.

"Sleepless nights, temperatures soaring above one hundred and twenty degrees, dust storms, murky, undrinkable drinking water," he explained. "But I remember it as one of the happiest times in my life."

The first R-7 rocket crashed when it was tested in May of 1957, and a second prototype failed to launch. Only the fourth succeeded in becoming the world's first intercontinental ballistic missile. When the West failed to recognize the achievement, to the engineers' amazement, Korolev suggested sending a satellite into space. "He was the only one who understood the significance of a satellite," Gubarev said. Korolev went back to work and within weeks designed a simple, basketball-size sphere he called Satellite 1. It contained two powerful radio transmitters programmed to emit beeps over the course of three weeks. *Sputnik I* blasted off from Baikonur into Earth's orbit on October 4, 1957.

Although its beeps could be heard on radios around the world, its designers didn't immediately see the launch as a major accomplishment. So focused were the team members on the military aspects of their work, Chertok said, that they failed to recognize Sputnik's historical significance. "We prepared the launch with no great expectations," he said. "If it were to succeed, three cheers. If not, no big deal because our main task was to get back to building a missile capable of carrying a nuclear warhead."

The launch was first announced in a small item on the second page of *Pravda*, and the world reaction to Sputnik caught even the Soviet propaganda machine by surprise. "As for most of Sputnik's creators, it took us four or five days to realize that from then on, the history of civilization could be divided into before the launch...and after," Chertok said.

Despite the tremendous publicity Sputnik generated for the Kremlin, the names of its designers would remain state secrets for years. Even inside the space program, Korolev was known only as the Chief Designer, which caused significant anguish to the man who was also in charge of the effort that made Yuri Gagarin the first man in space in 1961. Sending scientists with no connection to the space program to take credit for its successes at international conferences—men humiliated by that role—was especially upsetting to Korolev, who was publicly recognized only after his death in 1966. Although other gifted pioneers contributed to the space program's historic achievements, the extent to which everything else depended on one man's ability to overcome outsize obstacles remains underestimated.

As they did with the space program, military strategy goals justified the funding of a large number of scientific institutes and projects. However, those aims weren't enough to save many of them from ruin after the Soviet collapse because the state was no longer able to pay for much of anything beyond its most basic needs. Thousands of scholars and technicians who had helped engineer some of the USSR's greatest feats lost their jobs. Many who didn't emigrate survived by driving gypsy cabs, trading in cheap consumer products and taking part in other small-time businesses—as some still do.

One result is that Russian science is declining dramatically despite the government's claim to be modernizing the country. A 2012 report by the well-connected head of the Russian Association for the Advancement of Science said a precipitous drop in funding—although not for government officials who oversee scientific institutions and earn far more than the scientists conducting research—has contributed to a "catastrophic" situation. Another study in 2013 listed no Russians among leaders in the world's one hundred top-ranked specialties in the sciences and social sciences.[2] An astute observer, Olga Khvostunova, points out that much of what money does go to science is channeled toward unrealistic projects to boost national prestige, such as the drive to develop nanotechnology. "The collapse of Russian science," she concludes, "will inevitably lead to a series of crises in the economy, social sphere, and public administration."[3] A recent plan to overhaul the Russian Academy of Sciences that would merge the hundreds of institutions it oversees under a single new government agency has prompted fears it will make matters even worse by putting scholars under the Kremlin's control.

Other members of the intelligentsia—including those who provided some of the strongest support for Gorbachev's reforms, which indirectly caused the end of their livelihoods—also continue to suffer. But prospects for some writers and artists have since improved with the rise of the consumer culture and its concomitant disposable income, which can be spent on diversions from the daily grind.

———

Comparing rocket science to art isn't a big stretch in Russia, where creativity and originality often come in sudden bursts and contrast sharply with the slavish imitations churned out in many other spheres. Some believe it is precisely the impediments in much of Russian life that feed wellsprings of

creativity. The religious philosopher Nikolai Berdyaev described two contradictory principles at the heart of what he saw as the Russian soul—"the
one a natural, Dionysian, elemental paganism and the other an ascetic
monastic Orthodoxy."[4] The opposition between those principles helps
explain such contradictions in Russian life as "despotism [and] the hyper-
trophy of the State" on the one hand and "anarchism and license" on the
other. Among those who see that kind of paradox as central to Russian
culture, one Moscow artist is especially skilled at dissecting and celebrating
the apparent contradictions.

Yuri Vaschenko, a smiling, mustachioed painter in his sixties, is a modernist fascinated by perceptions of open space, in which the Russian landscape is so rich. Although he spent several months each year in the United
States over the course of many years, he always returned to Russia "because
my inspiration is here," he told me. Some of it is born from the kinds of dis-
parities in which Russia is also very rich: the very wealthy versus the hordes
of the very poor; the terrible taste in most things versus the deep, almost
instinctive appreciation for the arts—music and ballet perhaps chief among
them—in a country where aesthetic considerations are very important.

Vaschenko's large studio lies under the eaves of a pre-Revolutionary
building off a small lane in one of Moscow's charming old neighborhoods.
He has illustrated many books, work that provided steady incomes for
artists during the Soviet era, when the authorities frowned on most real
creativity. Although the city provides the studio he works in, Vaschenko
almost lost it when a well-connected businessman one floor down decided
he wanted it for a duplex. Having surprised himself by persevering in court,
Vaschenko continues to dissect the vicissitudes of Russian life over tea or
vodka at a cozy round table surrounded by canvases, still-life props and
photographs of Boris Pasternak and his other intellectual heroes.

On a typical evening, he set herring, cold boiled beets, very dark Russian rye bread and vodka on his table: the substance of a delicious meal
over which we talked well into the night. I hadn't done that in a long time
because Muscovites—renowned under communism for their "kitchen
table" discussions of politics, metaphysics and anything and everything
else—now tend to go to bars and restaurants, where conversation has
become increasingly jejune. Despite Vaschenko's hospitality, however, he
sometimes complained about being interrupted at work by friends who
stop by unannounced, an old Russian practice and a staple of life when few

people had telephones. Friends and fellow artists insist they urgently need to speak for a few minutes and take offense if they're not invited to stay.

Moscow seethes with corruption and violence, he told me, "but I sometimes daydream that I'm walking down a dark street and suddenly the side door of a tall building opens and inside a large smiling pasha [an Ottoman lord] is presiding over a big party in an enormous, ornate hall. I couldn't conjure the image of abandon without the oppression. Maybe it could only happen here." One theory about why Russian literature and art abounds with grotesque images and mystical realism is that absurdity is a response to the country's history of unfathomable suffering. Vaschenko salvages significance even from the mediocre art that hardship often helps generate because he says bad work directs him toward useful visions. He told me that one evening, returning from a splashy exhibition of paintings mounted when the country's new oil wealth was first fueling demand for big and gaudy works, he realized that he had seriously enjoyed going. The affair's slogan, aping Soviet exhortations to "build communism," was *"Isskustvo— Pokupat!"* ("Art—Buy It!"). The exhibits included warmed-over surrealism, huge canvases depicting the universe and paintings of Rollerbladers as well as motorcycles that had been airbrushed to resemble reptiles. The best of the pieces were whimsical. One untitled photomontage, by a talented and controversial artist named Oleg Kulik, showed the massive Christ the Savior cathedral with a crashed BMW in front of it, symbolizing the new Russia's big spending and recklessness. "I didn't go there expecting anything great," Vaschenko explained. "I went to see artifacts. And it was incredible, like being on another planet!"

Although the Soviet authorities suppressed the work of many like Vaschenko, they invested in other creative spheres that also suffered when communism's collapse dried up their funding. The flagship of Soviet culture, the Bolshoi Ballet, suffered serious damage to its morale and standing in the 1990s following the ousting of its famed director Yuri Grigorovich, who had run the company with an iron fist for thirty years. After years of infighting under a string of directors, Mikhail Shvydkoi, then the culture minister, was appointed to rebuild the theater in 2000. A savvy manager held in high esteem by many creative types, he told me he found the ballet in ruins. "The Bolshoi lost a lot of the really big stars and needed new blood," he said.

Even in those years, when tickets were relatively cheap and some productions embarrassingly substandard, others were magical. Attending the ballet remains one of the great pleasures of living in Moscow, although music and theater are often no less brilliant. Some of the enchanting feeling surely must have to do with the soaring Bolshoi Theater itself, its gilded balconies and hundreds of chandeliers evoking pre-Revolutionary timelessness and grandeur. Founded in 1776, the ballet troupe long remained a poor cousin of the Imperial Russian Ballet—today the Mariinsky Ballet—in St. Petersburg. But it came into its own in the early twentieth century, before the Soviets advanced it as a showcase of communist achievement.

Shvydkoi hired the consulting firm McKinsey & Company, but his appointment of a talented new director who tried to reinvigorate the ballet in 2006 drew the enmity of Bolshoi veterans who accused them of destroying celebrated traditions. Thirty-seven years old at the time, Alexei Ratmansky forced the ballet to do more than restage classic productions; he hired new young talent and experimented with choreography by foreigners. One of his innovations that prompted vigorous criticism was his staging of a version of Sergei Prokofiev's *Romeo and Juliet* by British theater director Declan Donnellan.

Nikolai Tsiskaridze was prominent among the critics. A huge but aging star, the tall principal dancer with a trademark mop of long dark hair and a penchant for controversy told me that Ratmansky had trashed the Bolshoi's traditions and insulted its dancers. "I've been the main face of the Bolshoi for the past fourteen years," he declared in his spacious dressing room. "And suddenly he arrives from nowhere, someone who never danced here, and who couldn't even have dreamed of it. Now he's saying the Bolshoi has no good traditions and its dancers are old supporters of the Communist Party."

Not everyone agreed. Liudmilla Semenyaga, one of the Bolshoi's biggest stars in the 1970s, who had become a coach of prima ballerina Svetlana Zakharova when I spoke to her, told me that conflicts between dancers and choreographers were nothing unusual and praised Ratmansky for provoking controversy. "We need a breath of fresh air," she said. Nevertheless, Ratmansky left for New York's American Ballet Theatre a little more than a year into his tenure and has since become one of the world's most acclaimed choreographers.

The Bolshoi's deep divisions erupted into public view in 2013, when a masked man attacked one of Ratmansky's successors outside his apartment building by throwing sulfuric acid in his face. A former principal dancer, Sergei Filin suffered third-degree burns and serious damage to his eyes. His injuries astounded Moscow. In the preceding weeks, his car's tires had been slashed, his cell phones disabled and his e-mail account hacked. Some suspected that Tsiskaridze was a leader of the faction of dancers who railed against Filin's changes to the Bolshoi's classical repertoire. Tsiskaridze had been passed over for director and later lost an attempt to replace Filin. The Bolshoi's general director at the time, Anatoly Iksanov, went as far as telling a newspaper that even if Tsiskaridze had no part in the attack, "he led the situation in the theater to the state where someone else could have gone further." The contracts of both Tsiskaridze and Iksanov were later allowed to expire.

Soon after the attack, police arrested a dancer in Tsiskaridze's camp who was a staunch Grigorovich supporter and regularly clashed with Filin about money and roles. Pavel Dmitrichenko, who lived in Filin's building and is the son of professional dancers, confessed to organizing the attack. In a sign of just how deep suspicions run, however, many ballet members said they didn't believe Dmitrichenko alone hatched the plot and that someone else may have coerced him into becoming involved.

Whatever the truth, Filin wasn't the first to be so publicly targeted: a leading candidate for artistic director before him had resigned after sexually explicit photographs of someone who looked like him were posted on the Internet. Despite the Bolshoi's recent turmoil, however, ballet scholars say its artistic quality has continued to approach that of its chief rival, the Mariinsky, which added a modern new building in 2013 under its legendary director Valery Gergiev. In any case, Russian dance remains unmatched, a sphere in which Russian pride in mastering a foreign art form is truly deserved. Strict discipline is partly responsible. I've seen Bolshoi dancers perform astounding feats as if they were effortless even during their daily morning classes when I observed them in a large, airy room of the theater. Maybe because it's connected to art, Russians' mastery of ballet training appears to go against the general lack of discipline in other spheres. But that doesn't entirely account for, among other virtues, the unrivaled gracefulness in the way Russian dancers hold their hands, which conveys an impression that they have achieved emotional mastery over their bodies. The same is true for their ice dancing, which draws heavily from ballet.

The Soviet Union produced many of the world's top figure skaters until its Olympic training machine collapsed along with communism. But conditions have improved under Putin, who presided over a tenfold increase in funding for the sport. When I observed Russian champion Elena Sokolova prepare for the 2006 Winter Olympics in Turin by training in a well-outfitted Moscow ice rink, her veteran coach, Victor Kudriavtsev, told me that although training programs had undergone a sea change since the previous Winter Olympics, Russian figure skating had never really suffered serious decline. He said the consistency was partly explained by the difference in technique and choreography between the Russian school and its American and European counterparts. "We look at figure skating as art as well as sport. Russian athletes' programs are more than performances; they're spectacles."

In tennis, too, Russians believe their national characteristics have helped them excel. Although the Communist Party authorities viewed the supposedly bourgeois sport with suspicion, Ekaterina Kryuchkova, who trained Alyona Bovina and Vera Zvonoreva in a tennis center near the Kremlin, told me the sport has since exploded because emotions play a large role in the game. Russians are "colossally emotional" people, she said approvingly.

———

I've often overheard conversations on the street whose pathos was so moving it seemed unreal, as if straight from the pages of a great nineteenth-century novel. My father liked to say that Russia's celebrated realists, along with some of their twentieth-century successors such as Isaac Babel, were Russia's best reporters partly because they fashioned plots from news stories of the day. Although the scenarios may appear absurd and the dialogue over the top to Western readers today, the fiction was far less fanciful than many imagine, much truer to the kinds of anything-goes talk that really takes place.

"Since college, when I first started reading them, I thought the great Russian writers *invented* this kind of dialogue, where they all speak, few if any listen, and *non sequitur* piles joyfully or gloomily upon *non sequitur*," the celebrated correspondent Martha Gellhorn wrote. "Invent, my foot. They were reporting. Russians talk this way."[5]

Although the idea that suffering nurtures artistic creativity is hardly new, some believe there's something else about Russia that distinguishes it, something that prompts its intellectuals to think especially big. The historian and philosopher Isaiah Berlin pointed to the country's "intellectual vacuum," as he called that aspect of its backwardness—for which its lack of a tradition of secular education was partly responsible. It allowed new ideas, when they arrived, to take root as if people were intoxicated by them.

Although others have picked different dates, Berlin traces the birth of Russia's intellectual tradition to the country's literal entrance into Europe, when Russian soldiers flooded Paris following Napoleon's defeat at the beginning of the nineteenth century.[6] Russia's emergence as a great power coincided with the rise of Romanticism, the intellectual movement that turned its back on Enlightenment rationalism in favor of abstract mysticism. Among its main proponents were philosophers such as Hegel and other founders of German Idealism who credited an absolute spiritual force in nature, the *Geist*, with giving all aspects of life a single universal purpose. They believed the real and metaphysical worlds to be bound in one "organic" entity that was on an inexorable path toward progress.

Russian philosophers swallowed such ideas whole from the Germans. Friedrich Schelling, among the most influential, believed that people, as parts of the universal Absolute, can divine its patterns by using intuition to look within themselves. Such views informed attitudes toward literature and art, which came to be seen as parts of a whole. Berlin describes a supposedly Russian attitude toward literature in which private life and artistic work are inseparable. Thus the artist's "duty" to produce beautiful objects is not simply aesthetic, it is also moral. Russia's famous nineteenth-century writers, Berlin explained, "conceived of themselves as true craftsmen, sometimes as inspired servants of God or of Nature, seeking to celebrate their divine Maker in whatever they did."[7]

Even Ivan Turgenev—the most obvious example of a Westernized writer as opposed to a determinedly Slavic one, and thus supposedly more concerned with aesthetic than moral principles—believed social and moral issues were central to his work. His *Notes of a Hunter* (1852), a collection of short stories about rural life and the injustices of serfdom, humanized serfs by giving them complex characters, following his creed that "every being studied with sincere sympathy can free for us the truth which is the foundation of life." The book led to his arrest.

Nicholas I's reactionary reign further propelled the country's intellectuals toward the mystical. Assuming the throne in 1825, the notoriously suspicious monarch ordered executions and Siberian exile for members of the so-called Decembrists, rebelling soldiers led by a disparate group of free-thinking nobles who were opposed to autocracy and serfdom. They had hatched a quixotic plot to stop Nicholas's coronation, then carried it out in a confused attempt that one scholar described as "one of history's prime examples of how not to make a revolution." However, they later became venerated among the intelligentsia as the courageous fathers of the revolutionary tradition.

Nicholas's subsequent abolition of basic rights and liberties further enshrined romantic ideas about absolute truths. The intellectuals who didn't flee abroad abandoned overt discussion of dangerous political issues and retreated to their ivory towers to contemplate the kind of abstract questions the crown found far less threatening. "So far from inducing despair or apathy," Berlin wrote, Nicholas's crackdown "brought home to more than one Russian thinker the sense of complete antithesis between his country and the relatively liberal institutions of Europe which, paradoxically enough, was made the basis for subsequent Russian optimism. From it sprang the strongest hope of a uniquely happy and glorious future, destined for Russia alone."[8] The bourgeois European revolutions of 1848 only reinforced the tendency by ending in the suppression of the working classes that helped ignite them.

Reasoning along the same lines, the eminent critical theorist Boris Groys believes Russia's backwardness made it better prepared to accept upheaval in 1917. Revolution in the West can never take place on the same scale, he writes, because Europeans respect tradition. Since Russian intellectuals associated the idea of tradition, if not tradition itself, with backwardness, they were more willing to change by rapidly assimilating new ideas. More than that, the intelligentsia believed that only quick change could sufficiently compensate for Russian inferiority and allow the country to surpass the West.[9] It was partly a question of aesthetics. By being willing to organize all life in new forms, Groys writes, the Russians essentially allowed themselves to be subjected to a massive artistic experiment. True or not, Russian writers and artists led the modernist movement a century ago and created some of the twentieth century's greatest works.

———

Kazimir Malevich, the main originator of the Suprematist movement whose simple black squares typify Russian avant-garde painting today, believed "the artist can be a creator only when the forms in his painting have nothing in common with nature."[10] Echoing the language of the Bolsheviks, he denounced all realist art as "savage." Once in power, however, the Communist Party soon banned such subversive ideas. Then came socialist realism and, decades later, the Soviet collapse, which left most artists to fend for themselves. Russia's new wealth has since funded new galleries and fueled hopes that Moscow will once again play a major role in world art. However, Putin's political crackdowns, which have encouraged wealthy collectors to invest elsewhere, have clouded the immediate future for Russian contemporary art.

Vinzavod, a new center of Moscow's art establishment where gallery owner Marat Guelman briefly opened a showroom, is located in an old industrial site next to a train station. The sprawling former wine cellar was kept truly industrial: the tiled vaulted ceilings of its main exhibition space remained dirty, much of the floor was kept gritty, and the space is freezing even in summer. Opening night in 2007 attracted a large crowd of hip young Muscovites who spent time seriously contemplating the spotlit exhibits: a fountain constructed of cheap Soviet plumbing fixtures, a huge bulldozer covered in a black shroud and many video installations. Smoke machines helped evoke a sense of an incense-filled cathedral. The exhibition was called "I Believe."

Sitting on a shag rug in his incense-filled apartment, the long-bearded curator, Oleg Kulik—a major artist whose painting of a cathedral and a crashed BMW may have been the best installation in the gaudy "Art—Buy It!" exhibit that fascinated Yuri Vaschenko—told me the new show was meant to take back the sense of belief, or faith, from what he called the dogmatic contexts of religion and communism. "We don't know there will be a tomorrow, but we believe there will be," he said. "It's not certain, only a hypothesis. And we don't know it's not good to shout at people, but we believe we lower ourselves by doing so. The exhibit is meant to assemble various statements about the beliefs according to which we live our lives."

One of the works, Anatoly Osmolovsky's *Bread*, consisted of various boards of wood intricately carved to resemble slices of dark Russian bread then mounted in a series, some in bread-like outlines, others in the form of Orthodox icons. Kulik called it "part of the Russian tradition of religious iconostases, and the effect is strange." He said Osmolovsky's art was related to the works "field artists produced a thousand years ago, when importance lay not in the icon itself but in the feeling it arouses between the object and the viewer." Kulik thinks the discovery surprised even Osmolovsky. "Although he was simply making a formalist gesture, in doing so he realized that centuries of art history have been wrong," he explained. "The most important thing isn't the art, it's the consciousness it awakes. Its value isn't the price it commands, but the number of viewers who understand its qualities, who share a belief in it."

Kulik explained that each of the works in his exhibition was meant to contribute to a new belief system based on questioning. "We want a global revolution," he concluded—"to make people live correctly, to ensure happiness and wealth for everyone, to turn our rockets into flowering gardens." Although that call for a new moral order is typically messianic, its relatively elaborate theoretical basis also showed just how far Russian art had come since the 1990s.

Two decades ago, Kulik came to the art world's attention by staging street performances for which he stripped naked, went down on all fours and barked like a dog while an assistant led him around on a leash. That role represented the complete chaos brought on by the Soviet collapse. "Everything we understood was destroyed—the political system, the social system," he said. "I didn't know how to live. The only honest thing I could do was reflect my primordial state. It was an important part of starting over."

Yuri Vaschenko agrees that the Moscow art scene reflects a period of revolutionary change, but he feels there is still a long way to go. Moscow artists, he complains, are still too heavily influenced by their Western counterparts. But he believes the city's dynamism makes it one of the world's most interesting places for contemporary art. "Each time I return, I find something completely new," he said. "One building was demolished and another built right outside my window in a matter of months. Life is boiling and bubbling, and art reflects that hyperactivity."

However, Putin's reelection as president in 2012 after four years as prime minister caught the nascent art market off guard by encouraging the wealthy, wary of officials' mounting greed, to spend more of their time and money abroad. Collectors began turning their backs on local artists in favor of more established Western artists whose works they saw as safer investments. Some gallery owners, including Marat Guelman, turned to the government for support, but with artists and other intellectuals becoming increasingly politicized and joining the opposition to Putin, it's unlikely that state funding will do much to help Russian art.

———

Like much of its art, literature in the land of Dostoevsky and Chekhov was considered a wasteland in the 1990s, when readers flocked to buy pulpy romance novels and thrillers that had been banned under Soviet rule. Fiction writers are still struggling with the effects of decades of strictures against free expression, but authors and critics agree that Russian literature is coming back, its fresh inspiration partly provided by Putin's authoritarianism.

Dmitri Bykov, one of the country's most popular writers and a ubiquitous fixture on talk shows, dismisses the notion that Russia's great literary tradition was ever in peril. "Literature reflects Russian life," the rotund, curly-mopped Bykov, who is given to smiles and not afraid to criticize the authorities, told me. "Reality is in constant crisis," he added. "In that sense, people saying Russian literature is in crisis is the best sign it's actually alive and well."

The most prominent new writers became known abroad in the late 1990s mainly for their black humor, which mocked Soviet life and Russia's new wild capitalism and described versions of a dark, anti-utopian future. They included hermit-like Victor Pelevin—who declined to be interviewed—and Vladimir Sorokin, who told me that Putin's regime provided a treasure trove of subject material for his grotesque plots. We spoke on the porch of his substantial country dacha, surrounded by birch trees, near the celebrated Soviet writers' community at Peredelkino, fifteen miles southwest of Moscow.

Tall and thin with a goatee and a trademark mane of white hair, Sorokin had recently completed the sequel to his novel *Day of the Oprichnik*, which describes Russia in 2027. Separated from the West by a new great wall, the country is overrun by royal terror squads that indulge in gay sex and drug abuse: a metaphor for the kind of place Russia became under Putin, the author said. "Once again, the authorities in the Kremlin are completely closed off from the people," he said. "They're cruel, unpredictable and corrupt. They've taken the place of God and they're forcing people to worship them."

"In our society, the individual is repressed from birth on all levels," Sorokin continued, adding that fiction writing is one of the few pursuits in which completely free expression is still allowed. Nevertheless, Sorokin has run into trouble. Members of a pro-Kremlin youth group made headlines in 2002 by ripping up copies of his novel *Blue Lard* and throwing them into a mockup of a giant toilet. "I felt as if I'd become trapped in one of my own stories," he said. Charges of pornography, on which he was later taken to court, were subsequently dropped, just before a book fair in Frankfurt, Germany, at which Russia was the guest of honor. "They didn't want to lose face," Sorokin explained.

Although he and a handful of other writers are becoming increasingly well known abroad, Natalia Ivanova, the enterprising editor of the storied literary journal *Znamya*, told me the best Russian writers are younger and barely known. "Today's Russian literature is like a cake with many layers," she said. "We have popular mass literature and middlebrow literature, but we also have very good, complicated literature for the elite." *Znamya* publishes the latter kind of work, including novels by Mikhail Shishkin, one of the country's best writers. However, even as Russia's literary scene expands, Ivanova said, it's being threatened by a shrinking readership. Literature may have been the main form of escape from Soviet repression, she continued, but the proliferation of movies and television shows—many made available by the huge illegal pirating industry—threatens to turn a country of readers into one of viewers.

Although also under threat, drama, unlike literature, flourished during the 1990s. Moscow currently has more than 115 theaters, many of whose performances are packed by very discerning audiences. Among the top venues, the New Generation Theater stages plays by its director, Kama Ginkas, one of Russia's most acclaimed. I spoke to him during a production of his play *Rothschild's Fiddle*, based on Anton Chekhov's short story of the same name. The protagonist, a master builder of coffins, is consumed by anger because people don't die often enough. He ignores his wife and forgets the existence of his son until he is driven to despair by realizing too late he's let life pass him by. "The frightening paradox, that Rothschild starts becoming a real person only three days before his death, is absolute genius," Ginkas told me. "It's the closest Chekhov got to stating something directly, albeit through black humor." Ginkas's spare, inventive production, with brilliant acting, was compelling.

"There are lots of monsters like Rothschild in life," he continued. "People who are busy with business, art or whatever—but it turns out they, too, have wives and children, and they don't realize that life is much more than just their work. To put it another way, you don't have to be Raskolnikov in *Crime and Punishment* to realize there are no ideological, religious or any other justifications for killing. Everyone must realize that within himself."

Ginkas knows something about ideology, and not only from Soviet harassment. Born in the Lithuanian city of Kaunas in 1941, he survived its notorious Jewish ghetto after the Nazi invasion and began directing in Leningrad in the 1960s. He agreed to meet me in his massive studio in the theater, filled with props from previous productions, only after insisting I observe him directing a rehearsal for his next play, about the Grand Inquisitor in Fyodor Dostoevsky's novel *The Brothers Karamazov*. He often explores themes from literature, painting and music. "My challenge is to search for ways to express in drama material otherwise not meant for the stage," he said. "I think it's no more difficult than staging plays, but I don't believe in doing anything that comes easily. Your work isn't worth anything unless you have to struggle."

The American critic of Russian drama John Freedman is among those who rate Ginkas as one of the world's great directors. Freedman, who co-wrote the book *Provoking Theater* with Ginkas, traces the success of new Russian drama to the 1996 staging of a highly praised play called *Tanya-Tanya*, a comedy about love in post-Soviet suburban Moscow. But the popularity of theater is hardly new to Russia. Freedman cites Mikhail Shepkin, a nineteenth-century actor who called it "a cathedral."

"Russians go to the theater to worship," Freedman told me. "They go to the theater to hear the truth, to hear what's happening in their own lives." Marina Davydova, a young theater critic for the newspaper *Izvestiya*, agreed. Despite the Soviet era's censorship and isolation from the world, drama thrived even then. "It helped carry out the functions of a real parliament and a free press, which didn't exist," she said. "It took on a number of roles it otherwise shouldn't have."

Drama is again being politicized. One of the newest theaters, called TEATR.DOC, stages experimental works by young playwrights, often about topics in the news. A recent production described the prison death of lawyer Sergei Magnitsky, the anticorruption crusader. Drama critics say the best Moscow theater continues to prosper because it successfully reflects the country's rapidly changing society.

Still, both Ginkas and Davydova are pessimistic about the future. Davydova is concerned that outside the small circle of talented directors like Ginkas, middlebrow theater is deteriorating. "We could make rockets to send into space," she concluded, "but we could never mass-produce cars properly." Ginkas agrees, saying serious productions like his make up a tiny part of the theater scene, which continues shrinking as old intelligentsia give way to newer audiences who prefer expensive sets and sensationalized plots. "You can no longer put on a play that doesn't concern things like AIDS or prostitution," he said. "But what about the universal, everyday problems that matter to all of us? That we're all mortal? That we don't want to suffer, we want to love? That we're jealous, we hate, we want success and fear loneliness?"

I've often felt more exhilarated stepping onto the street after successful productions staged by Ginkas and other leading Moscow directors than after I've seen similar off-Broadway dramas in New York, perhaps because in Moscow life's inequities and brutality aren't hidden behind a veneer of civility or suppressed by a belief in a supposed equality of opportunity. In Russia, deriving some sort of catharsis, if not necessarily understanding, through art seems less academic or diversionary than it does in the United States—more necessary for coping with life's difficulties. Perhaps that helps explain why the bitter enmities between advocates of opposing solutions to Russia's enduring, generally unhappy condition have been a defining part of the country's history.

———

Although its relevance to universal problems was sometimes buried, no conflict defined Russian intellectual life as much as the nineteenth-century battle between the Westernizers, who believed Russia should look to Europe for its inspiration, and the Slavophiles, who wanted Russia to follow what they considered its own traditions. Among the Westernizing writers and philosophers who hoped Russia would abandon its despotic practices and adopt European ideas about individualism and liberty, the literary critic Vissarion Belinsky was especially influential. An idealist, Belinsky believed art should serve the overriding goal of combating the great evils of autocracy and serfdom as well as the resulting social ills of poverty, alcoholism and other afflictions. Content was more important than form for Belinsky, so it may have been no accident that even his supporters found some of his work unreadable. Nevertheless, his exile to Siberia, where he was crippled by malaria, helped burnish his reputation as a father of Russia's revolutionary tradition.

Belinsky heaped praise on Fyodor Dostoevsky in 1846 for his first work of fiction, *Poor Folk*, a novella that traces the relationship of a lowly, nearly destitute clerk and a woman he loves. Twenty-five-year-old Dostoevsky was a member of the Petrashevsky Circle, a group that met to discuss the works of French utopian socialists and other philosophers. It was named after the man who hosted the organization's secret meetings in his St. Petersburg apartment—a risky business. Infiltrated by some of the tsar's legions of informers, the circle was broken up in 1849, when its members were arrested and sentenced to death. Reprieved at the last minute, most were sent to Siberian penal colonies, where Dostoevsky's four-year incarceration helped transform him from an idealistic Westernizer into something close to a Slavophile, a conservative who came to believe Russia's salvation lay in adopting the Christian model of suffering and forgiveness.

By then, the European revolutions of 1848 had begun splitting the very loose school of Westernizers into two main camps: those who advocated bourgeois society as an ideal and those who adopted radical socialism. No one embodied the split more fully than Alexander Herzen, the philosopher many believe to be Russia's best. The father of Russian socialism emerged amid the generation of idealistic superfluous men of which Ivan Goncharov's character Oblomov was a caricature. Twice arrested and exiled to distant Russian parts before 1848, Herzen eventually settled in London, where he published a journal called *Kolokol*, "the bell." Initially a Hegelian, Herzen came to believe that no ideology or dogma could explain the human condition, a position that approached existentialism. His conversion began during the revolutions of 1848, when he happened to be in Europe and was shocked to observe the bourgeoisie's domination over the working classes who had helped it fight the old order. The disappointment prompted him to lose faith in his belief in inevitable progress. Convinced that life's purpose is life itself, he concluded that abstractions and general principles threatened to tyrannize society.

If progress is the goal, then what is it that we are working for? What is this Moloch who, as the toilers approach him, recedes instead of rewarding them; who, to console the exhausted and doomed crowds greeting him with *morituri te salutant,* can only reply with the ironic promise that after their death life on earth will be splendid? Can it be that you, too, doom the people of today to the sad destiny of the caryatids supporting the balcony on which others will some-day dance?[11]

Advocating nonviolent change over revolution, Herzen idealized the peasant commune as an answer to Russia's social problems. Believing the peasantry's "communism" superior to Western social structures, he aimed to reconcile it to Western individualism.

Back in Russia, some progress was about to be made. The death of the autocratic Nicholas I in 1855 brought his son Alexander II to power. A reformer who would come to be known as the Liberator for abolishing serfdom, Alexander instituted Russia's first jury trials and made other changes to combat Russia's staggering corruption and inefficiency, which were driven home by its humiliating defeat in 1856 at the hands of the British, French and others at the end of the Crimean War. Seen as the last best hope to stabilize the empire, liberalization had the paradoxical effect of further radicalizing the wing of the intelligentsia that believed in revolutionary change.

Many of its members came from a new generation of revolutionaries who emerged in the 1860s and split from their intellectual mentors, the men of the 1840s such as Turgenev and Herzen. Turgenev immortalized the divide in his novel *Fathers and Sons.* Unlike the "fathers," who mostly came from the gentry, the hard-bitten "sons" were usually *raznochintsy*— those of "mixed rank" background, many from clerical families—who harshly criticized their liberal, romantic fathers for being weak.

The new generation was well represented by Nikolai Chernyshevsky, the radical literary critic and social philosopher whose novel *What Is to Be Done?* celebrates young revolutionaries. Along with his protégé Nikolai Dobroliubov, Chernyshevsky believed all endeavors should be subordinated to politics. Denouncing bourgeois liberalism, he, too, idealized the Russian peasant commune as a model for his vision of socialist collectivism.

Arrested in 1862 and exiled to eastern Siberia, Chernyshevsky became a hero to many other radicals, including Lenin, who once credited Chernyshevsky's novel for converting him to revolution.

Chernyshevsky had an especially strong influence on the Russian populist movement that flowered in the 1870s. Radicalized students dispersed into the countryside to educate peasants, whom they believed to have revolutionary instincts. Deeply suspicious of parliamentarianism, which they saw as a tool of bourgeois domination, the populists opposed the call for a liberal constitution, which they were convinced would set back the revolutionary movement by strengthening Russia's wealthy capitalists. Some turned to terrorism. In 1881, an extremist splinter group called the People's Will killed Alexander II when it bombed his carriage as it drove along a narrow canal.

The tsar's reforms ended with his death. In an effort to save the empire from revolution, his son and successor, Alexander III, reversed many of his father's policies by strengthening his rule at the expense of the nobility and local government. Alexander's harsh despotism continued under his son Nicholas II, Russia's last tsar, whose shortsighted bungling helped set the conditions for revolution in 1917.

———

No serious Westernizer advocates violence today, although a popular street-art group called Voina, "war," has riled the authorities in St. Petersburg by producing a video of its members setting alight a police truck as a sign of solidarity with political prisoners and spray-painting a giant phallus on a drawbridge that rises opposite the headquarters of the Federal Security Service, the former KGB. The group also gave rise to the all-female punk band Pussy Riot. In general, the opposition leaders, human rights activists, lawyers and others advocating such still-foreign concepts as rule of law and free elections risk arrest and harassment by merely turning up for peaceful demonstrations that call for institutional transparency, freedom of speech and other ideals that would undermine the traditionally closed workings of state affairs. Some have taken up the mantle of Soviet-era dissidents.

Russia's new generation of human rights campaigners includes Tanya Lokshina, a slight Human Rights Watch activist with a grave demeanor who has risked her life documenting abuses perpetrated by security forces in Chechnya and other regions of the North Caucasus. When I traveled with her on a trip to Chechnya to record the abductions of young men in isolated villages in the Caucasus Mountains, she complained of similarities between her trials and what dissidents under the Soviet Union endured. "I'm a young professional of thirty, and I'm suddenly telling my staff what they have to do if the KGB walks in," she said. "This belongs in books. It shouldn't be happening."

The murder of journalist Anna Politkovskaya by an unknown gunman in the elevator of her Moscow apartment building in October 2006—one of dozens of unsolved killings of reporters and rights activists—dealt the group a serious blow. Politkovskaya's courageous investigations into atrocities in Chechnya had made her a household name, and Lokshina said her friend's death demonstrated the new level of impunity for those who kill Kremlin critics. "When Anna was gone, we all realized to what extent everyone else is vulnerable. If they could do it to her, everyone else is completely unprotected."

Two young Chechens, brothers of the alleged gunman, and a rogue former security service officer were acquitted of helping stage the shooting, which some officials blamed on foreigners and the exiled oligarch Boris Berezovsky. Other techniques for silencing critics have been more overt. In 2005, the head of an NGO that tracked abuses in Chechnya was charged with inciting ethnic hatred in what Lokshina called a "typical political trial." Soon after Russia's Supreme Court upheld the organization's closure, the Kremlin issued a bill increasing its already strict control over human rights groups and other nongovernmental organizations by forcing them to comply with draconian registration and accounting regulations. As legislators sped the bill to a yes vote on a freezing, gray November day, eight young activists tried to protest outside the imposing Stalinist parliament building next to Red Square. Ivan Nenenko, of an environmental group called Groza, told me he was taking part because the new bill would enable the Kremlin to further consolidate its power. "Every activity will be controlled from above, including even nonpolitical actions," he said before police dragged him away.

The following year, a loose alliance of rights and political groups called the Other Russia, headed by chess master Garry Kasparov, began staging demonstrations ahead of parliamentary elections and a presidential vote that would surely elect Medvedev as Putin's successor. Each time, officials denied permission before ensuring that many hundreds of riot police, backed by thousands of regular troops, broke up the crowds. Photos of young activists being hauled off to police trucks provided a revealing portrait of Putin's Russia.

Although reporters are permitted to cover such protests, they're never safe from police. I was never detained, but I've witnessed many arrests of journalists who were hauled off despite their visible credentials and other clear proof they weren't demonstrators. Attending such rallies is never fun. Expecting the worst, I've usually felt an unpleasant foreboding on top of the sinking feeling that the events were largely held in vain because, notwithstanding the attention they generated in foreign media, most Russians didn't care.

At one rally marking an anniversary of the Beslan school siege—when more than 380 people, half of them children, were taken hostage by Chechen rebels in 2004 and died during a shootout with troops who used grenade launchers and other heavy weaponry—police arrested Lev Ponomaryov, one of the first of many such detentions of leading protest organizers. In the 1980s and '90s, Ponomaryov, a veteran rights activist and protégé of dissident Andrei Sakharov—the brilliant nuclear physicist and Nobel Peace Prize laureate—organized mass demonstrations of hundreds of thousands of people in protest of Communist Party policies, events that helped bring down the Soviet Union. Ponomaryov, who spent three days in jail after the Beslan anniversary rally, told me in his cramped Moscow offices soon afterward that the former KGB officers who hold top government posts had revived Russia's police-state culture. "They're not able to conduct a political dialogue," he said. "They can only work according to the 'I'm the boss and you're the underling' principle. It's the way the military functions, and they've made the whole country like that." In 2013, police raided Ponomaryov's office and forced it to shut down after officials said the lease had expired. Ponomaryov, who insisted the rent had been paid through the end of the month, was thrown out on the street.

International organizations such as Freedom House in Washington put Russia near the bottom of the lists that rank countries' respect for political and human rights. Despite their difficulties, however, activists are still allowed to work. Liudmilla Alexeyeva, a dissident from the 1970s Brezhnev era who is the doyenne of the human rights movement, helped found the Moscow Helsinki Group, which she still chairs. Now very frail and in her eighties, Alexeyeva told me matters have never become as bad as the days when most dissidents were jailed, put into psychiatric wards, or forced to emigrate. "Back then, if you decided to publicly criticize official ideology," she said, "it meant you had to have decided to pay for it with your freedom." Today's authorities are more subtle. The government accused Alexeyeva of involvement with British intelligence soon after two British diplomats who were serving as liaisons to the Moscow Helsinki Group and other NGOs were accused of spying with the aid of high-tech communications equipment hidden in a fake rock—which the British authorities later confirmed. "It was done to blacken our reputation," she said of the accusation that her group was involved in the espionage. "It was based on false documents, and the lies were never punished."

Alexeyeva has also been threatened by nationalist groups, including one that put her at the top of a list of Russia's worst enemies. She said the Kremlin encourages such extremists with nationalistic policies such as occasional mass deportations of Georgians and police raids against foreigners working in street markets. Despite the pressure on them, Alexeyeva and other activists kept a tiny flame of protest alive by staging small demonstrations on the thirty-first day of each month, to symbolize the Russian constitution's article 31, which grants the right to free assembly.

Their doggedness was partly rewarded in 2011. That September, seemingly apolitical members of Moscow's middle class began grumbling after Putin announced he would follow his four years as prime minister by returning to the presidency for a third term, now extended from four to six years. Russia was starting to look like Brezhnev's stagnation-era Soviet Union, they said, a perception heightened by Putin's aging appearance. It was as if his many years in wealth and power had given him the impassive (probably Botoxed) sheen of a haughty dictator. One longtime acquaintance who works as a lawyer for a foreign law firm and whom I'd never heard utter a single word of criticism against Putin—perhaps because her firm profited handsomely from navigating the rising seas of paperwork required of foreign companies—now said she was thinking about moving abroad. Although she seemed more than content with her lifestyle, which includes several nights a week partying with affluent friends in exorbitantly expensive nightclubs and restaurants, she added that she no longer wanted to live in a place that appeared uncomfortably like the *sovok*, literally a "dustpan" and figuratively the Soviet Union, or *Sovetskiy Soyuz*.

"Those people want to stay in power for the rest of their lives," she complained. Putin's assertion that he and Medvedev had agreed to swap positions years earlier seemed especially insulting to many who had previously appeared unmoved by the widespread expectation that he would return to the Kremlin. After parliamentary elections in December, accusations of massive vote rigging—although no less rife than they were four years earlier—provided an excuse for tens of thousands to take to the streets for the first time since the early 1990s.

Two demonstrations were so big and attracted so many young, respectable-looking professionals in addition to no less respectable middle-aged and even elderly protesters that the authorities dared not refuse them permission to take place. The rallies helped open a new chapter in the Putin era: the protesters who said they were tired of their national leader after his more than a decade in power caught him on his back foot. Forced to react to rather than lead the political discourse for the first time, Putin employed a range of his old tricks, including insulting the opposition, subterfuge and blaming subordinates for corruption and ineptitude. Starting with a dismissal of the protesters as chattering monkeys financed from abroad, he retreated to backing a toothless Medvedev proposal for political reform and reshuffling some of his top officials.

Many took the removal of Vladislav Surkov from his position as the Kremlin's chief ideologue as a major concession. The wily and surly young official had masterminded the incorporation of fake opposition parties, coined the term "sovereign democracy" to characterize Russia's political system and justify its growing authoritarianism and devised the youth-movement campaign to denounce Vladimir Sorkin's novel *Blue Lard*. Reappointed to first deputy prime minister, Surkov said he would no longer involve himself in domestic politics. However, his successor Vyacheslav Volodin, a loyal enforcer in Putin's United Russia Party who would help oversee a major crackdown against the opposition, appeared even less democratic.

Another Kremlin ploy for sapping energy from protesters was to secretly back pliant opposition figures. Few were surprised, therefore, when the billionaire oligarch Mikhail Prokhorov announced he would run against Putin for president soon after the demonstrations. He later started a political party he said would give civil-society leaders a platform, but many saw that as another attempt to dilute the opposition; Prokhorov himself did not become a member. As 2011 drew to a close, however, Putin's tactics made him appear out of touch. For the first time in many years, there was hope that at least a small segment of the population, the urban middle class, would finally stand up for genuinely fair elections and other rights—the Western kind—that support their interests.

However, it has since been very rocky going for the opposition, whose strategy has been complicated by a new crackdown on the Kremlin's critics. One of the main symbolic events took place in May of 2012 after riot police blocked demonstrators from attending an authorized rally against Putin's inauguration for a third term. After some frustrated protesters ripped off police helmets and lobbed chunks of asphalt at the officers, some thirty police and more than a hundred protesters were wounded. Six hundred people were arrested. Evidence later surfaced that the violence was probably initiated by pro-Kremlin provocateurs organized by the police and was possibly meant to further polarize the opposition. Some began to worry that young, more radical protesters, frustrated by what they see as no options for enacting peaceful change, are becoming increasingly disillusioned—more evidence that Putin's self-interested authoritarianism is driving his country off a cliff. Few predicted that the authorities would arrest almost thirty of the protesters on charges of participating in mass unrest in what came to be called the Bolotnoye Affair, named after the square on which they were to gather. One of the protesters who pleaded guilty was sentenced to four and a half years in prison in what's seen as one of the most direct present-day parallels to political repression under communism. The liberal former Duma deputy Vladimir Ryzhkov compared the proceedings to Stalin's show trials of the 1930s.

Another well-known Kremlin opponent, the journalist and music critic Artemy Troitsky, was also a protest organizer. He describes the Kremlin's relationship to the country's creative classes as a "Cold Civil War." The crackdown has prompted many conversations among his friends about where to go when they flee Russia. "Young, smart professionals, the very people this country needs, want to go," he lamented. "They want to leave behind what's turning into a country of drunkards and corrupt officials who can steal all they want of Russia's oil wealth."

————

Mikhail Prokhorov was already the talk of the town in late 2011 for being forced from his leadership of the Kremlin-friendly, pro-market Right Cause Party. Because it had been assumed he'd taken the post at the

Kremlin's bidding, he surprised many by convening a meeting of supporters to denounce Surkov as a "puppet master" for attempting to control the party. Although no one could tell whether his accusation had been coordinated with Kremlin agents to provide the appearance of dissent, Russians watching video footage of the event were transfixed. The transgression of a top oligarch—whose continuing good fortune depended on the Kremlin's goodwill—in condemning a top ideologue injected longed-for drama into Russia's otherwise stage-managed politics. Not that anyone saw any of the news on television. The video showed on Dozhd, meaning "rain," a burgeoning Internet television site, while the main state-controlled news channels, which had regularly shown Prokhorov on nightly newscasts, barely mentioned him.

That was no coincidence. Much of the innovation taking place in Russia happens on the Internet, where serious newsmagazines such as Gazeta. ru publish uncensored news and incisive analysis of events. Well-designed culture-oriented sites—such as Openspace.ru, which helped lead the way until its recent closure—post reviews of Russian and international literature and art that are often more illuminating than, say, *The New Yorker*'s. Journalist Kirill Rogov—the founding editor of Russia's first major political news site, Polit.ru, in the late 1990s—credited the Internet with enabling reporters, scholars and bloggers to bring topics to public discussion outside the "controlled, traditional media." Indeed, social commentators divide the country between "Internet Russia," consisting of mostly young, increasingly globalized readers who can access whatever information they want, and "television Russia," which hears what the authorities want it to.

With roughly eighty million Russians—around 60 percent of the population, according to the Levada Center—already online, Russia has Europe's largest Internet audience, and readership dynamics continue steadily tilting in that direction. Surveys also show that the number of people going online every day, those who tend to use social media and get their news from the Internet, is growing fast. In April of 2012, the country's biggest search engine, Yandex, attracted more daily visitors than Channel 1, the most popular state television channel, for the first time. Forty-three percent of Internet users regularly use Facebook and Twitter, up from 33 percent the previous year, according to a Pew Research Center survey conducted in 2012, and the Russian version of Facebook, VKontakte, is even more popular than either of those sites. No surprise that the Federal Security Service demanded that VKontakte's young founder, Pavel Durov, close protest organizers' pages at the height of the demonstrations in December 2011, although it dropped the case after he ignored a summons and refused to answer when police rang his doorbell. That may have only bought him some time; shortly thereafter, two of Durov's founding partners were convinced to sell their shares in the company to a businessman who was rumored to be a Kremlin agent. After a police officer accused Durov of running over him in his car, he fled abroad amid predictions that the Kremlin aims to take over the site.[12]

With crucial media outlets constrained by Kremlin-friendly owners within certain editorial limits—chief among them a ban against outright criticism of Putin, Medvedev and the highest-ranking members of their circles—blogs are playing an increasingly central role in the national debate. Many originate on the country's most popular platform, LiveJournal. Embattled opposition leaders who are seeking to build on their support from largely educated, middle-class urbanites are also counting on social media to help mobilize Russians throughout the country to tackle the authorities in local politics. The first significant evidence of the effort took place during the presidential election of 2012, when thousands of monitors used Twitter to report widespread violations such as ballot stuffing and "carousel voting"—groups of people voting multiple times at various ballot stations. "People are increasingly skeptical about traditional political parties," a veteran newspaper editor and protest organizer named Sergei Parkhomenko told me soon afterward. "If social media can facilitate building nonhierarchical networks of people to disseminate information and coordinate activities, their role will become far more important." That remains to be seen.

Andrei Lipsky is a veteran editor at *Novaya Gazeta*, a stalwart independent newspaper co-owned by Mikhail Gorbachev. He, too, believes the dynamic is changing, thanks partly to the Internet. Lipsky, whose aging, cigarette-smoke-filled offices are home to some of Russia's best investigative journalists, said, "More people want an active part in life, for their voices to be heard. And that's the hope—the slow growth of civil consciousness." Kirill Rogov of Polit.ru told me that daily Internet use is driving up the number of people who get their news online. Before the election protests of 2012 began, just 5 percent of people got their news online, but the number is growing. "The Internet has started to become politicized," he said.

Although the authorities can monitor everything posted on Russian websites, they had long considered censorship unnecessary because control over the national media enabled them to influence the vast majority of Russians. That has begun to change. Nikolai Patrushev, a former Federal Security Service chief who now heads the Kremlin's security council, recently cited China as an example of "reasonable regulation" of the Internet, ostensibly for combating extremism.

Soon after Putin's reelection, parliament passed legislation enabling the government to close websites as part of a broad crackdown on the protest movement. Although the bill's backers said it was aimed at sites that display child pornography or promote suicide or drug abuse, critics feared it would pave the way toward censorship. *Wikipedia*'s Russian version protested by going offline for a day and Google said the bill "threatens users' access to legal sites." According to at least one human rights group, the year 2012 marked a turning point for the authorities, who now see the Internet as "the main threat to [their] well-being and stability."[13] The report cited 103 criminal prosecutions among measures across the country it said were aimed at censoring online information. The Kremlin also prevailed on Internet service providers to install software that enables officials to block sites banned for their supposed extremism. Still, statements by other officials, including Medvedev—who's called Internet censorship "impossible and senseless"—reinforce expert opinion that it is too late to impose controls without major political risk.

But the Kremlin has been fighting back in other ways. While the government backed friendly news sites, compromising videos appeared on the Internet alongside leaks of hacked telephone conversations and private e-mails from opposition figures' accounts. Some of the transcripts appeared on a pro-Kremlin tabloid site called Lifenews.ru, which falsely accused Boris Nemtsov of spending New Year's with a prostitute in Dubai. Other tactics came to light when hackers posted their own trove of e-mails from accounts they said belonged to overseers of the Kremlin-backed youth group Nashi. The messages discuss the deployment of abusive trolls—people who post inflammatory comments on websites—and the launching of distributed denial-of-service (DDoS) attacks against media sites. The e-mails suggest that journalists and bloggers were directed to extol Putin's popularity and attack his critics.

Despite the ardent hopes of many in the West that the Internet's rise would help undermine authoritarianism in Russia, observers say it hasn't happened, at least not yet. Alexei Simonov, head of the Glasnost Defense Foundation, a group that advocates freedom of the press, believes that's partly because most Internet use is for social networking and entertainment. "The Internet isn't a panacea," he told me. "It's only a medium, an opportunity to access information."

The rise of anticorruption crusader Alexei Navalny was among the Internet's most significant developments for the opposition. His site, Rospil.ru, where volunteers have exposed crooked deals by posting information and documents about state business transactions, helped make Navalny the leading voice among opposition figures before a suspended five-year prison sentence in 2013 made him Russia's most famous political dissident. A lawyer and blogger who held a six-month fellowship at Yale, he began his crusade against the corruption he said was choking his country by buying small stakes in some of the country's largest companies and then demanding information about how their managers spent their profits. He went after the giants of Russia's energy industry, including Gazprom and Rosneft, and published what he said was a leaked audit of Transneft, the state oil pipeline monopoly. The audit described shell companies that produced fake contracts and siphoned off some four billion dollars from funds intended for the construction of a pipeline to China. "When I read every day how those people are buying soccer clubs, flying on private airplanes, partying at luxurious ski resorts," Navalny said, "I understood it was funded by the money stolen from me. That's why I decided to do a very simple thing. If crimes are being committed so openly, why not just try to go to court or write prosecutors? It's simple enough; it's just that no one did it before me."

A blond thirty-seven-year-old who exudes confidence, Navalny runs his operation with a handful of others from cramped quarters rented in a Soviet-era building near a busy train station. Sitting behind a laptop in his office, dressed in a black T-shirt and jeans, he was relaxed, well-spoken, and lawyerly in developing his arguments. Official corruption is so widespread in Russia, he said, that even the government admits that more than thirty-five billion dollars is stolen from state contracts each year. "Corruption is so hardy here because it forms the very basis of the power structure," he added. One of his biggest successes was branding Putin's United Russia as the "party of crooks and thieves," which, along with Navalny's fiery rhetoric and apparent fearlessness, helped make him the biggest draw at anti-Putin protests. Although he's received almost no coverage on state television, one poll found his name recognition across Russia shot up to 37 percent by 2013.

He also became a leading Kremlin target. Convicted on embezzlement charges he dismisses as absurd and aimed to keep him from running for political office—although he remains free—Navalny has been compared to Khodorkovsky. Like the oligarch, he was sentenced after he refused to flee. "I want my children to live here and speak Russian," he told a reporter during his trial. "I want to pass on a country that's a little better." Some believe Putin's disinclination to mention Navalny's name when publicly criticizing him is evidence that he sees him as his main rival. Not everyone agrees that Navalny is the pioneer he claims to be, however. Galina Mikhalyova, a prominent member of the once popular social-democratic political party Yabloko, to which Navalny once belonged, reminded me that Yabloko members have been silenced in the past for campaigns against corruption that posed a threat to the authorities. "We know in our party how that kind of activity ends," she said. "One of our chairmen was killed, several of our members are under criminal investigation and others have been sentenced to jail." The death in 2003 of Yabloko member Yuri Shchekochikhin, a crusading investigative reporter who often guided me and other foreign correspondents toward the hidden sources of corruption, was among the most disturbing of Russia's many unsolved killings. He was looking into criminal allegations involving the Federal Security Service in 2003 when he suddenly fell ill and died from what his family says was poisoning.

No typical Westernizer, Navalny has extreme views about nationalism that have alienated would-be allies. Mikhalyova often sparred with Navalny before he was expelled from Yabloko in 2007 for his support of right-wing nationalist groups such as the militant Movement Against Illegal Immigration. He later helped organize annual marches of xenophobic groups, part of what appeared to be a new tactic among some young opposition members for attracting followers. He said Russia was swamped by illegal immigrants and plagued by "ethnic crime" that prompted conflicts, including attacks against the immigrants themselves. "Those are real issues today," he said. "But for some reason the liberal movement believes they should be made taboo because discussing them will unleash mythic dark parts of the Russian soul and result in the emergence of a new Hitler. That's idiotic."

Such bickering partly explains why the liberal opposition has been unable to mount a serious challenge to Putin. Clashes of ego have played a large role in its leaders' failure to form a unified political bloc that could contest parliamentary elections or rally behind a single candidate for president. Although some organizations have joined forces, Grigory Yavlinsky, a gifted economist and co-founder of Yabloko—who represents an older generation of liberal opposition leaders—is among those who remain steadfastly opposed to joining any other group. Aided by the government's multifaceted strategy to marginalize the opposition and prevent the emergence of a challenger to Putin—including propaganda, refusal to register parties on technicalities and banishment from state television—the failure to get along has dogged several attempts to forge a united movement.

In addition to stoking tensions among the opposition, Navalny's nationalism gives serious reason to worry about what Russian protesters may really want. Most of those who turned against Putin's regime in 2011 did so for some of the same reasons Russians have criticized their leaders for centuries: not necessarily because they want reform but because they perceive that their leaders have moral failings. Putin's return for a third term as president was a step too far, exposing naked greed that flew in the face of his professions of sacrifice and exhaustion (he once compared himself to a galley slave). Polls indicate that rather than a Western form of government, many of the disgruntled probably still want a strongman in the Kremlin—just a better one.

————

Regardless of Russia's immediate future—including Putin's possible return for another six-year term in 2018, which would make him the longest-serving leader since Joseph Stalin—the vast majority of Russians will continue to endure great difficulties, not least from the grinding bureaucracy and huge inefficiency that kills productivity. A Levada Center poll in 2013 reported that more than 70 percent of respondents said they would refuse to take part in protests against falling living standards or in support of their rights. Although the Communist Party's treatment of rocket mastermind Sergei Korolev and others of their best innovators lies in the past, government repression, waste, shoddiness and corruption remain prominent in the present.

The great contrasts they help generate have contributed to the creativity of artists and other intellectuals, including the opposition politicians and rights activists battling the odds to establish some of the universal values envisioned by Soviet-era dissidents and their nineteenth-century predecessors, the writers and philosophers—some of them, at least—who established Russia's intellectual traditions and hoped their country would join enlightened Europe.

The call is still being made, not for revolutionary change but evolutionary introduction of the institutions and practices democracies require. Among the civil-society initiatives to come out of the 2011–12 protests was Demokratiya2, a website enabling visitors to join groups taking part in, among other things, environmental activism, election monitoring and involvement in regional politics. Its organizers proposed a grassroots party that would elect leaders in regular direct online voting and be financed by its members, which Navalny once praised as the best hope for changing the dynamics of Russia's bickering, top-down party structures by drawing "real activists" into a bottom-up system of politics.

However, such Internet-reliant projects haven't fared well under the onslaught of new repression during Putin's third term. As the protest movement ran out of steam in late 2012, Navalny directed his energies toward the maintenance of apartment buildings. Seeking to sustain momentum, he set up a website on which users attacked the laziness and slovenliness of municipal plumbers and electricians by filing complaints about the lack of lightbulbs, broken elevators and other failures in the maintenance of communal areas. He has also continued to expose officials' hidden wealth by publicizing the work of bloggers digging up such evidence as registration forms for property held outside the country.

If such creative efforts help today's Westernizers draw enough support to challenge the status quo, they may eventually be able to help put Russia back on the difficult path from which Putin diverted it in 2000, after the short run of reforms following the collapse of the USSR. However, although predicting the future is futile, my observation of the deep-seated continuities in Russian behavior makes me pessimistic about the chances that my children will live to see Russia become a genuine part of Europe even if it abandons its current path in the near future. If the experience of the 1990s showed anything, it's that the country is too large and its character too ingrained to change more quickly. That's a deeply disappointing conclusion for those who, in 1991, hoped the transition would be far quicker—including me, my friends and members of my family, especially my father, who loved Russia thanks largely to the company of his long-suffering friends, almost all of whom were Westernizers.

The face of Putin's Russia: Police arrest another protester.

9
Cold and Punishment

Russia has no need of sermons (she has heard too many),
nor of prayers (she has mumbled them too often), but of
the awakening in the people a feeling of human dignity,
lost for so many ages in mud and filth.
—Vissarion Belinsky on the Russian Orthodox Church,
from a letter to Nikolai Gogol, 1847[1]

I have no memory of my mother complaining about the cold when I was
growing up in Connecticut except her saying that the worst moments of
her childhood were when she was so cold she cried. I, too, approached tears
more than once in Russia, including one memorable morning on the frozen
Taimyr Peninsula at the top of Siberia. In the ramshackle village of Khatanga, four hundred miles north of the Arctic Circle, an assortment of corrugated metal barracks, wooden houses and a scattering of Soviet-era brick
buildings are heated by steam pipes that would crack if they were buried
above the permafrost. They originate at a coal generator in the settlement's
center that blackens the snow and fouls the pristine air with dark smoke.
Beyond the village, stunted trees that form part of the world's northernmost forest give way to an infinite expanse of tundra. From a helicopter,
the only visible signs of life are occasional herds of reindeer: little specks
making their way through the snow accompanied by dogsleds driven by the
nomadic Dolgan tribesmen, a group of five thousand souls who live exclusively on Taimyr. From the ground on a crisp, sunny day, the beauty of the
flat, endless white takes your breath away.

Although Cossacks seeking the fur of arctic fox, among other animals, founded Khatanga in the seventeenth century, its sedentary population remained negligible until the 1930s, when the Soviet authorities began sending prisoners into the forbidding far north of Siberia to build a chain of Gulag camps that would help establish the timber and mining industries. Enslaved laborers constructed much of the nearest city, Norilsk, near the world's largest deposits of nickel, copper and palladium. The Norillag concentration camp held almost seventy thousand prisoners at its peak in the early 1950s.[2] (Today, oligarch-owned Norilsk Nickel, the world's largest nickel producer, subsidizes life on the peninsula.) Driving on isolated roads in such regions in summer, I occasionally came across crude dugout shelters used by the prisoners who built the roads decades earlier.

The camps near Khatanga required no barbed wire because trying to travel alone on the tundra brought certain death. Therefore I was surprised to hear some residents claim that a life spent struggling against the crushing elements is liberating, even exhilarating. Boris Lebedev, a deeply weathered, gregarious native of Ivanovo, a city near Moscow, told me he had made his way to Khatanga in the 1970s to "escape" the Soviet regime. "I came here to be free," he said of his life, which consists mainly of hunting and fishing. "Because only up here could someone truly belong to himself."

In Khatanga's canteen, dietary freedom extends to choosing between local reindeer meat and fish kept frozen in caves hacked out of the permafrost. Almost everything else is delivered by plane. For ten months of the year, Antonov An-24 twin turboprop planes carrying goods and produce arrive every two weeks or whenever weather permits them to land on the small airstrip that passes for a runway. It was there that I froze—on board one of the little planes in "only" minus-thirty-degree cold because it was just early October, not yet real winter. Lightly dressed passengers were kept violently shivering for almost two hours without heat because the crew members, who apparently had been celebrating the night before, had failed to show up. I was still cold hours later, when the plane, by then scorchingly overheated, finally landed in Norilsk.

But there's no need to venture to the continent's northernmost stretches to experience the kind of cold for which Russia is notorious. St. Petersburg's winters, usually only a few degrees colder than Moscow's bitter ones, feel much worse because they are very damp, thanks to the city's location on former swampland bordering the Gulf of Finland. A thick layer of frost often gives the city's magnificent buildings a sparkling white sheen.

Marveling at their beauty made my struggle to comprehend the will and sacrifice necessary to maintain civilization there more complicated.

Illustrating both, the Marquis de Custine described the reconstruction of the monumental Winter Palace under Nicholas I after it had been damaged by fire in 1837:

> In order to finish the work in the period specified by the Emperor, unprecedented efforts were required. The interior construction was continued during the bitterest cold of winter. Six thousand laborers were continually at work; a considerable number died each day, but, as the victims were replaced by other champions who filled their places, to perish in their turn in this inglorious gap, the losses were not apparent.

The practice of heating rooms to eighty-six degrees Fahrenheit to dry the walls more quickly during cold spells, when temperatures can plunge to minus twenty degrees, compounded the deaths. "Thus these wretches on entering and leaving this abode of death—now become, thanks to their sacrifice, the home of vanity, magnificence and pleasure—underwent a difference in temperature of 100 to 108 degrees."[3]

As my father wrote in 1982, such trials helped shape the country's history and character.

> A hundred writers have said it before and a hundred will say it again, but it is no less true for being a commonplace that the way to an understanding of Russian life lies through the ordeal of a Russian winter. *Russkaya zima*, the great depressant of spirit and water of animation. It is not a season of the year like other seasons, not merely a longer, darker, crueler span of time than that which annually slows the countries of northern Europe and America. It is a life sentence to hardship that prowls near the center of the Russian consciousness, whatever the time of year. As a prime cause and a symbol of Russia's fate, it molds a state of mind, an attitude toward life.[4]

Among those earlier writers, Chekhov lamented, "Cold to the utter limit...you go into a stupor, turn more malicious than the cold itself...[It] makes people mean, starts them slurping vodka."

Russians are expert in the various kinds of cold. Muscovites who loudly complain when it's twenty degrees say fifteen degrees is easier to take because it's drier. Shivering in fifteen-degree weather, they recall visits to Siberia when it was minus fifty and lovely because, naturally, you're bundled up properly there. There's always somewhere colder and better in the imagination, perhaps because it helps people endure the misery of the present. Today's Russians are far better prepared than they were even two decades ago for the type of winter that helped destroy the invading armies of Napoleon and Hitler. Gore-Tex, double-glazed windows and dependable foreign cars make life far easier. But climate and geography remain formative influences in a country where thousands of reindeer froze or starved to death in 1997 and the association of cold with punishment endures. Prisoners continue to be sent to Siberia, where the vast stretches of empty tundra, taiga and marsh contribute to Russia's "ungovernability." As an old Siberian lament has it, God is too high and the tsar is too far. The difficulty of policing the poorly controlled expanses also helps explain why punishment in Russia still appears draconian.

Unable to explain why such hardship was visited on them, Russians took to sanctifying it as a gift. Alexander Solzhenitsyn's proclamations about "intense suffering" helping Russia achieve a higher spirituality than the West are but some of the latest in a long line of Russian Orthodox champions of that argument for Russia's special fate and virtue.

———

Exile to Siberia or the far north naturally began with a journey there, often a punishment that was as bad as or worse than what followed. Under tsarism, the passage on foot used to take six months from Moscow. Under Communist Party rule, it still took months by train for those who didn't perish along the way. Among the tens of millions who endured the trip was Lev Mischenko, whom I first met in 2002, when veneration for Stalin was returning. I spoke to him in the kitchen of his small apartment in a sprawling concrete-slab Moscow suburb, where he lived with his wife, Svetlana. Razor sharp despite his frail appearance, he described the minutest details of everyday life in Siberia with Chekhovian irony.

Nine months old when the Bolshevik Revolution took place, Mischenko fled Moscow during the Russian Civil War along with the rest of his family to what his engineer father believed would be the relative safety of

Siberia. In vain: Bolshevik revolutionaries shot both his parents. Raised by his grandmother, Mischenko nevertheless graduated from Moscow State University and began working at its Institute of Nuclear Physics just before the Soviet Union entered World War II.

Sent to the front as a junior officer, he was captured and imprisoned in a series of German concentration camps before an escape attempt landed him in Buchenwald. When Allied forces were closing in on Germany in 1944, Mischenko escaped again, this time from a convoy of a thousand captives being evacuated elsewhere. Making his way across the front lines to an American tank platoon, he turned down an offer to remain in the West from an American officer who recognized his engineering skills. Unwilling to leave his sweetheart Svetlana behind in Moscow, he rejoined the Red Army.

Millions of Soviets taken prisoner by the Germans died in captivity. Mischenko didn't suspect that more than a million of those who survived would be sent straight to the Gulag. Still in Germany, he soon found himself under arrest, accused by the Red Army's ruthless SMERSH counterintelligence service of aiding the Nazis. When by chance the miraculous appearance of an alibi led to his acquittal, he was promptly charged a second time. After four months of nightly interrogations and a hearing that lasted less than fifteen minutes, he was sentenced to ten years in an isolated logging camp in the far northern region of Komi.

Crammed together with sixty others, Mischenko set off from Germany in a cattle car equipped with planks for beds. Such prisoners' journeys were called *etapy*, or "stages," because they stopped at many camps and so-called transit prisons for those en route to their final places of incarceration. Mischenko's trip took three months. It was December of 1945, but many of the prisoners, who had been arrested in summer, had no winter clothes. Much of what little they did have was stolen along the way by soldiers or *urki*, criminal—as opposed to political—prisoners, who received better treatment than the others. *Urki* traded with soldiers, usually for cigarettes or food. "We had practically nothing left by the time we got to the Soviet Union," Mischenko said. "The stealing continued anyway."

Prisoners—or *zeki*, derived from the Russian term for inmate, *zakliuchionnyi*—were "freezing all the time." German prisoners unused to Soviet suffering constituted a high percentage of those who died on Mischenko's train. During a stop, he caught sight of a former cell mate, an elderly

German engineer whom he had witnessed losing his mind during the inter-rogations. "He couldn't speak, even to his fellow Germans," Mischenko said. "Now he was shivering outside, wearing a thin jacket and no hat. It was January. He couldn't have survived." Mischenko, who, like many, had no shoes when he arrived at his camp near a town called Pechora, wrapped his feet in rags.

Despite his hardships, Mischenko believed he was incredibly lucky. His camp produced lumber for the railroad servicing Vorkuta, the center of a massive Gulag system that mined the Soviet Union's second-largest coal basin, four hundred miles to the northeast. During the two years before his arrival in Pechora in March 1946, almost two thousand prisoners had died, a staggering number for a camp that held fewer than a thousand *zeki* at a time. The major killers were hunger, cold, dystrophy and diseases such as pellagra, which is caused by vitamin deficiency. A fellow inmate who had been a military pilot later told Mischenko how chance had saved him from the brutal logging brigades. At death's door, the pilot was recognized by the camp's "technical director," a former prisoner from his hometown, who helped arrange his transfer to a different work brigade. Joining a burial crew that carted corpses into the forest—after guards had stuck each one through with bayonets just to be sure—the pilot slowly regained his health because his new detail was considered important enough to be fed survival rations.

The work regimen, worsened by guards' cruelty and neglect, eased for others after the war years, when it was acknowledged that the casualties were hurting NKVD secret police chief Lavrenty Beria's drive to squeeze as much produc-tivity as possible from the inmates. But although the death rate dropped to about one per month shortly before Mischenko's arrival, conditions remained brutal. Assigned to general logging duties, sometimes in twelve-hour shifts, he often helped haul out logs that had been floated down the Pechora River. That task, among the camp's most grueling, killed many *zeki*.

Keeping dry was impossible because the two sleeves from an old quilted jacket that had replaced his disintegrating foot rags got soaked through during work in the snow-covered forest and stayed damp even after nights in the "dryer"—a dugout whose very hot stove only made it drippingly humid. So Mischenko was hugely fortunate when his expertise earned him work maintaining the camp's power generator. That was "heaven" because the premises were warm and the work was relatively easy. The plant even had its own shower.

Freed nine years later, Mischenko joined hundreds of thousands of prisoners streaming back from labor camps in 1954, the year after Stalin's death. However, his sentence banned him from coming within a hundred kilometers of Moscow for another five years and he was unable to secure work as a physicist for another fourteen. Svetlana had waited for him during his thirteen-year absence, trekking thousands of miles to visit him in Pechora several times. Now reunited, they finally married and raised a family.

My question to Mischenko about how he interpreted the growing nostalgia for the Soviet Union prompted him to describe running into an old childhood friend several years after returning from the camps. "When I told him where I'd been, he began to shake with fear of being seen with me and quickly left," he said. "That's how much people were enslaved by the system." Society's failure to acknowledge the crimes of communist rule, Mischenko said, was perpetuating their catastrophic effect on the Russian psyche.

―――――

Incredible as they may seem, the twists and turns of Mischenko's story reflect common experience because the Gulag played a central role in the Soviet economy while enabling Stalin to perpetrate terror by incarcerating tens of millions of innocent people. They included my grandmother's husband, Zhora.

More than three months after his arrest at the height of the Great Terror in November of 1937, Serafima received a short letter from him. It had been sent from another logging camp, near a town called Ivdel in the Ural Mountains region of Sverdlovsk. Sentenced to ten years' hard labor—with the "right" to correspond—he was one of Ivdellag's first inmates, an especially difficult fate because most early arrivals had to build their own camps with rudimentary supplies in the middle of nowhere. Serafima immediately wrote back, then sent three more letters before finally receiving a reply:

May 10, 1938

My dear, dear, darling, wise one,

How joyous it is to get letters here, especially yours! I feel I'm not alone, that somewhere there's a kindred heart. But my dear, kind little wife, why are you worried that I'm smoking *makhorka* [low-grade tobacco] under the influence of bad people? How little you know the real situation! Here are my friends: the rector of a Leningrad university, a senior scholar from the Belarusian agriculture academy, the assistant to the director of a perfume enterprise. They are the members of my work brigade and my friends, and we are not an island amid the general mass. These people give you an idea of the general contingent—and we all smoke *makhorka...Makhorka* is nothing! Much more serious is that I haven't had a bite of protein for several months now. We get mainly water and dry cabbage and sometimes bread dumplings, but no trace of protein. Even lousy, old protein would be welcome.

My dear, kind Simusia, why were you crying when you were writing your first letter and maybe your second one, too? I could recognize the tear streaks I know so well. I remembered them from the letters from Alupka [in Crimea where Serafima was treated after the death of their daughter Natasha] and I felt very bad and couldn't hold myself back.

Zhora went on to answer Serafima's questions about what had happened to him. There had been no trial, he said, only interrogations that repeated questions he'd already answered the previous summer, when he had been questioned at his aircraft design bureau.

"Why do you have a German name? When did you arrive from abroad? If it was your grandfather's name, when did he arrive? Whom do you know abroad?" No one, I repeatedly replied. "Do you correspond with anyone? Who are your relatives here and what do they do? Where have you worked?"...Two days later, around the 27th or 28th of November, I was brought in again to hear information about me even I myself didn't know. It turns out I was a spy recruited by the Gestapo to conduct counterrevolutionary Fascist activities...There was no word about who recruited me or which foreigners I met. No word about the name of the counterrevolutionary organization to which I belonged. I got the impression they didn't really care about my activities, just that they wanted me to understand those things about myself I didn't know.

It was all very polite. Not a single word was spoken in anger. I wasn't even directly named an enemy or counterrevolutionary or a spy. It all took about forty minutes. Then on the night between November 30th and December 1st, I was sent to [a prison on Moscow's central] Taganka [Square]. I was held there four days in an overcrowded basement because the cells were overflowing, until I was finally put in a cell on December 4th. On December 15th, I was ordered to sign a little piece of paper titled "Protocol," then the results of a "hearing," my name and a declaration that I was to be sentenced to ten years in correctional work camps for my counterrevolutionary activities. I was sent to the Urals on March 1st, along with a group of Germans and Latvians, and remain here today. That's it, the answer to your question.

As you can see, I was never tried...There were no concrete accusations, no witnesses, no confrontations. Finally, there was no investigation and no trial. If I'm a spy, I should have been tried by a tribunal. If I'm an agitator engaged in counterrevolutionary activities, I should have been tried by a special collegium of the Supreme Court...I treated everything that took place with suspicion and disbelief, like many here...But because everyone is sentenced for exactly the same thing and to the same term, you don't feel lonely and lost amid all these people of your level—engineers, pilots, chairmen, managers, directors...

Apologizing for not having replied earlier to Serafima's four letters, he explained that he'd spent three months away from Ivdellag in a brigade that floated lumber down rivers. "It's not the imprisonment and labor that's frightening," he wrote, "but the terror of stupefaction from a slow death of exhaustion."

The graveyard has been growing from the first day of our arrival, along with the cases of periodontitis and broken-off, frostbitten extremities. Oh well, you can never foresee where your fate will take you. My dear one, my joy, let's hope for the best. Everything will find its right course...When I was out with the brigade, I would often sit at night on the plunging bank of the gloomy taiga [forest] river and remember and kiss you, my dear wife. I wanted so much to caress you and to be caressed.

I don't need anything for the time being, especially please don't think of sending underwear. If you do, however, please include a towel, but not our towel from home, that would be very difficult for me to bear. Better a new one, and a piece of soap, cheap, of course, because expensive soap is useless here.

My dear one, we'll be together again someday. I'm no criminal, after all, and have done nothing wrong. All this is temporary; we just need fortitude and time. Often while walking along taiga paths—how wild the taiga is!—I would while away my time remembering moments from our life, especially the winter of '36 and '37...the table, the lamp with the blue shade, the warm stove. Something warm and soft would begin flowing inside me out on the freezing taiga and my soul would glow. Only the death of another of my slow-plodding comrades would distract me from my dreams. Because he was remembering his own table, his own stove. Otherwise we didn't say a word to each other, didn't dare intrude on those memories.

———

The degree of civilization in a society," Dostoevsky wrote in *The House of the Dead*, "can be judged on entering its prisons." Far as Russia's current penal system is from the KGB-run Gulag, the legacy of its sadism and neglect very much endures. Prisoners in pretrial detention are still tortured into giving confessions, as the notorious case of Sergei Magnitsky showed the world in 2009. Arrested by the same police investigators he had exposed, those who had committed tax fraud worth hundreds of millions of dollars, Magnitsky was beaten, became ill, was denied medical care and left to die on a cell floor after refusing to retract his accusations. Some of the officials involved later received awards and promotions, and the less prominent killings that regularly surface continue to illustrate the same sad points, even after Medvedev signed highly publicized legislation aimed at fighting the widespread lawlessness among police.

The majority of the country's six hundred thousand prisoners are incarcerated in penal colonies, where they live in barracks that differ little from the Gulag's. Russia has only seven large prisons, including Vladimir

Central, a collection of solid brick structures in the medieval city of Vladimir, east of Moscow. Conditions there—one of the few prisons foreign
journalists can visit without having to file more than the usual reams of
paperwork—are relatively good. Nevertheless, very little inside the thick
walls seems to have changed in the two centuries since they were built.

In one cramped, wood-floored cell, four prisoners with shaved heads
and downcast eyes said they had no complaints about their treatment.
That wasn't surprising because they spoke under a guard's watchful eye.
Elsewhere, it was hard to miss signs that the prison authorities were hiding the real conditions. Across a courtyard, in a building they declined to
show, faces peered from the windows of what appeared to be cells jammed
with many more inmates. Although Russia's prison population, second
in size only to that of the United States, has significantly diminished in
recent years thanks to new sentencing rules, conditions inside remain little
changed, and former prisoners speak of raging disease together with the
overcrowding.

Women's prisons are little better. Reports describe an almost complete
lack of privacy—including no partitions between the holes in the ground
that pass for toilets—humiliation and punishment for soiling sheets, even
accidentally, with menstrual blood.[5] Much more than men, women convicts
tend to be treated as outcasts in society, even after their release.

Some describe far more disturbing conditions. Among them is a
youthful-looking, soft-spoken former inmate named Vladimir Gladkov,
who spent a total of fifteen years in Vladimir Central and other penal institutions, including a so-called torture prison: Kopeisk, a transit prison—
for the temporary incarceration of inmates bound elsewhere—in the Ural
Mountains region of Chelyabinsk, where Gladkov said guards systematically abused prisoners.

Gladkov, a former driver who said police framed him for murder,
described regular mass beatings that began with his arrival: "They'd force
us from our cells, order us to spread our legs and put our hands against
the wall, then whack us with batons until we had to help drag each other
back to our cells." Guards exerted psychological pressure through a steady
stream of insults directed especially at dark-skinned minorities from the
Caucasus and Central Asia. Gladkov met an ethnic Tajik whose skull was
fractured when he was thrown against a wall. Apologizing and begging him
not to complain, the guards delayed his transfer until his skin had healed.

"The most frightening is hearing others scream while you're waiting your turn," Gladkov said. "The fear turns you into an animal." Doctors routinely refused to record injuries. Prosecutors accepted complaints before dropping investigations for a supposed lack of evidence.

The journeys between prisons and penal colonies, still called *etapy*, are also still made in the same kind of train cars that took inmates to Gulag camps. Traveling in winter, Gladkov froze in his light tracksuit and slippers. Later devoting himself to studying the judicial code, he appealed and complained at every step of his incarceration—risky behavior because most who make trouble that way are singled out for especially harsh treatment. "We'll rape you if we want and we'll kill you if we want," Gladkov said a prison warden in another prison had told him. "Nothing will happen to us because prisoners are meant to be punished."

Another former Kopeisk inmate named Yuri Skogarev corroborated Gladkov's account. During his four years in solitary confinement, he told me, "guards would take me out, handcuff me to a shower, then beat and kick me until I fainted and woke up back in my cell." Skogarev told me prisoners were regularly stripped and made to clean filthy toilets with a single rag. Much of the abuse was doled out by prisoners who were enticed to beat their fellow inmates by perks, including drugs as well as extra food and cigarettes. Use of such enforcers and informants, called activists, is an integral part of the discipline system, meant to generate constant fear.

Skogarev said prisoners regularly die. Four inmates were killed at the Kopeisk prison in 2008 when the authorities accused them of attacking guards. But human rights groups said their black-and-blue corpses indicated they were probably beaten to death for having protested their treatment. Nevertheless, hundreds of other Kopeisk inmates made headlines in late 2011, when they revolted against cruel treatment and extortion. Failing to provide the prison authorities with regular payments, usually made by relatives, was said to result in more beatings and torture.

Such conditions are no secret. Rights groups have posted smuggled videos of prison torture on the Internet. In one clip, what appear to be guards dressed in riot helmets and face masks force cowering inmates to strip outside, then beat them with rubber truncheons. Inmates often attempt to escape such beatings by mutilating themselves with cuts or by swallowing pieces of wire. Hundreds of them sometimes slash their arms and wrists in mass protest. Others commit suicide. News of such events barely registers in a country where there's virtually no sympathy for prisoners, who are seen as deserving of their fates.

The human rights activist Lev Ponomaryov described dozens of torture colonies like Kopeisk throughout Russia. "The system of incarceration is meant to destroy people psychologically," he told me. "They're told they're not human. They're punished for trying to defend their dignity." The Soviets, he added, used to say the system turns people into "Gulag camp dust."

Sitting at his desk in his cramped office on an old Moscow side street, Ponomaryov showed me a page-long letter carefully handwritten in what looked like brown ink but was actually the blood of an inmate who had no pen. Pleading for help in his smuggled appeal, he said he feared for his life.

Denying the existence of torture prisons, the authorities claim that all penal institutions are regularly inspected by government officials and all complaints investigated. But Ponomaryov said there was a clear rationale: spreading fear and compliance among the general prison population, a style of enforcement that is integral to Putin's authoritarianism. "Torture prisons are places in which totalitarianism rules," he said. "That's why it's so important to stop it: that kind of system spreads to other parts of society."

Some former prisoners estimate that 70 percent of the people incarcerated in Russia's prison system are abused. "God help you," an ex-inmate told me, "if you end up in a Russian jail."

The difficulty of governing the mostly inhospitable land of the world's largest country in area may partly explain the brutal nature of Russian punishment as well as its penchant for authoritarianism. According to Slavic legend, based largely on the *Primary Chronicle* of Kievan Rus'—a highly untrustworthy source primarily written by monks in the twelfth century—quarreling Slavs asked Scandinavian Viking warriors known as Varangians to rule them in order to establish some form of order and prosperity. In fact, trade was responsible for the initial expansion of nonindigenous settlers into the states that preceded Russia. Archaeological evidence shows that Scandinavians sailed down Russian rivers to trade with the Byzantine Empire in the ninth century and established control over the various settlements along the way. Historians have argued that the Varangians, who probably called themselves Rus', gave rise to the state of Kievan Rus' and established the Riurik dynasty, which ruled Moscow until the death of

Fyodor I, son of Ivan IV (the Terrible) in 1598. Real events notwithstanding, the appeal to a strong ruler to rescue the people from enemies and chaos is rooted in Russia's cultural tradition. Citing the Varangian legend in *Anna Karenina*, Tolstoy's semiautobiographical character Levin praises the merits of political submissiveness by calling their rule a "privilege [the people] had bought at such a high price."

When Slavs first began crossing the Ural Mountains into the Turkic Siberian Khanate in the middle of the sixteenth century, very few indigenous people lived there to slow their expansion.[6] As usual, trade, especially in furs—chiefly sable, fox and ermine, which were central to Muscovite finance and foreign transactions—drove the explorers into virgin lands. The Stroganov merchant family would soon dominate the business. Granted estates by Ivan IV, it sponsored Cossack-led expeditions into Siberia in the seventeenth century before enlisting a Cossack leader named Ermak to defeat the Siberian khan. Scoring important victories before their leader was killed and his men forced to withdraw, Ermak's soldiers opened the way for others who followed. Then expansion began in earnest and took only decades to reach the Pacific Ocean.

Once territory was "settled," provincial governors charged with enforcing Muscovite law had too few resources to do so in any comprehensive way. The Kremlin relied on a harsh code of punishment, mostly for "political" crimes, to keep the lid on chaos by reinforcing fear. *Slovo i delo*, the sovereign's "word and deed" legislation, called for a series of punishments, usually against peasants and other low-ranking subjects, who had been accused of maligning officials. Singing a song impugning the tsar's reputation was enough to prompt flogging, breaking on the wheel or subjection to other heinous torture. Denunciation by others often served as evidence.

Rather than the terrible wrath of an almighty tsar, *slovo i delo* reflected something closer to desperation. Unable to punish most lawbreakers, the governors protected the myth of his power by making examples of a few.[7] Tellingly, the punishment system was most used under relatively weak tsars, such as the first Romanov, Mikhail I, whose coronation at the age of seventeen in 1613 ended the Time of Troubles, which followed the end of the Riurik dynasty. Although Catherine the Great formally ended the system in 1762, the practice of making examples of a few in a country where lawbreaking is frequent lived on.

Randomness was a hallmark of Stalin's Great Terror, too. Unlike Hitler's Holocaust, which killed clearly defined groups of people, Soviet repression swept up victims who didn't understand why they were punished. That also applied to society at large: many people didn't know why their relatives had been taken or whether they'd be next. Although its proportions are vastly smaller today, fear still functions as the glue in Putin's system of top-down administration, partly by helping to ensure that widespread lawbreaking doesn't extend beyond prescribed boundaries.

Foreigners jostling in line at the so-called passport control booths in the arrivals sections of the country's international airports aren't exempt from that system. I'd believed that the long, hard stares the sour-faced border-guard officials train on each discomfited passenger were meant mainly for show until one encounter after a trip from Washington. The young woman behind the glass was clearly trying to identify me before she silently reached across her desk to push a button. I was traveling with my wife, Elizabeth, and our one-year-old son, Sebastian, whom the guards allowed to pass through before two of their thick-necked colleagues materialized to escort me away.

"You're leaving on the next flight back!" they barked. Their response to my demand for an explanation was, "We don't have to tell you anything!" After they'd left me next to a group of dejected-looking Pakistanis at a wall in the rear of the arrivals hall, frantic calls to the US embassy and the Russian Foreign Ministry confirmed that the officials *were* legally obligated to explain. That was a tense time in late 2007, shortly before parliamentary elections that a number of foreign election observers were barred from monitoring. My cell-phone battery died. I was left to wonder which of my broadcast reports the authorities may not have liked or whether I'd been targeted by an official who had overstepped his powers in an attempt to show his zeal.

After four hours of arguing and waiting, during which the American ambassador told me the Kremlin had been informed that expelling an NPR reporter would be a serious mistake, I was allowed into Russia minutes before the scheduled departure of the Washington-bound plane I'd nearly been forced to board. I never learned the reason for my treatment.

———

Lack of uniformity in the enormous bureaucratic machine that runs the Russian state has much to do with the selective punishment and enforcement that is often left to the whims of local leaders charged with maintaining order. The same was true under communism, when terrible inefficiency in the Gulag often left its prisoners unable to "fulfill the norms" of work calculated by the system's directors. That put well-qualified engineers like Zhora Leimer in great demand for their skills, which they used to help build roads, railroads and other infrastructure. My grandmother's husband was even able to obtain a temporary permit to leave the "zone"—the camp territory where prisoners lived—unescorted, a coveted privilege he described in letters written over periods of weeks and months.

Ivdel, December 8, 1938

My golden Simulinka,

Happy New Year's once again, my dear one! Tell me, how did you greet it? How I met it is clear—I was utterly with you. I decided to lose myself in dreams and went to bed at ten, drifting into a nervous sleep. As I was falling asleep I thought about life and of you... I woke before dawn and went outside into the frosty night. I looked at the stars and absently thought that they are also shining where you are. I remembered how they shined for me in childhood...Then it began to snow and I lay down in the predawn silence while others were sleeping...

Simulinka, how beautiful life really is; it's only that people seriously dirty it with all kinds of "isms" and complications. Apparently it's a result of their becoming ultracultured: they forget life is the most important thing we have. Of course, everyone must contribute to culture and live for the betterment of society, but without forgetting about one's own life...No one has the right to build godliness by feeding on people's lives, on fresh human blood. I tell that to myself when a cloud of gloom passes over me.

> *Why are my brows so sullen,*
> *To what end is my heart burning?*
> *My end is an Asian truth,*
> *A little muffled shot point-blank*
> *And September will cry rain*
> *Over my hillside grave.*[8]

Apologizing for being too gloomy—the result of "depression and a temporary loss of perspective"—Zhora said the camp's atmosphere had taken a turn for the worse. "Pressures have unexpectedly begun, repressions and all kinds of harassment," he wrote. "Wild, senseless, and unnecessary."

Probably it's being done just for the sake of it, just in case. There's an apparatus for exerting pressure and it must earn its bread.

Did you give my statement to the Supreme Soviet Presidium? Of course I don't have high hopes for a fair analysis of my case. Now isn't the time to be dealing with such nonsense as fairness and truth in practice. It's enough they exist in theory...

But I've been distracted trying to reason things over and haven't finished describing my New Year's. I celebrated it on the following day. Andrei Fyodorovich [a fellow engineer] and I sat down in our barracks, made some cocoa and drank it with crackers he was sent from Moscow. He got a touching New Year's package with an evergreen twig and congratulations. We sat in front of that twig to drink our cocoa. Then the days followed each other with no changes.

In another letter two and a half months later, Zhora transcribed for Serafima the words to a fox-trot called "Counting the Hours," which he said was "very characteristic of our mood."

Ivdel, February 23, 1939

We're parting, perhaps forever
On an autumn day, deliberately and simply
But I remember years past
And feel sharp, tormenting pain.

Counting the hours, to measure by hours,
I'll learn to live in separation
I will await you, I will believe,
I will remember, and I will love.

You're my only lighthouse,
Where my hopes fly in the spray
Fate will decide
When and where and how
We will be close again.

What awaits is unknown,
The past foggy and forgotten.
But the heart feels we'll meet again
On life's journey sooner or later.

That's the way it is, the sum of me.

A certain young woman here arrived from Harbin [the Chinese city where many Russian émigrés settled], who was of course arrested as a spy. She sings that song with a very good voice. What feeling she conveys, and what oppression we feel listening! Lambs put on skewers by those punitive organizations, abundantly coated with seasonings: spying, terrorism and other nonsense. And you say my case will be appealed!

By the summer, Zhora's description of some of his plans for construction projects appeared to suggest he'd at least partly reconciled himself to his imprisonment.

August 18, 1939

I remember how I sat during the fall and winter evenings and days, reading and thinking how best to build them. Because nothing like them has ever before been built according to my plans; in the past I just did student work. Now I see rows of machines in the workshops brought in to realize my projects. Those machines are building foundations I drafted. Now cars are driving on an overpass I remember planning. When it was first under construction, I was afraid about what would happen if my work was good for nothing. No, everything functions and it seems they're happy with them. Apparently I'm good for something.

When Anton Chekhov undertook to visit a notorious penal colony on the far-eastern island of Sakhalin in 1890, he traveled more than two months from Moscow by train, horse-drawn carriage and river steamer to reach his destination. Although he praised parts of Siberia for their beauty and relative freedom from tsarist repression, what struck him most was the squalor he encountered. "Poverty, ignorance, and worthlessness that might drive one to despair," he wrote about the far-eastern region of Primoriye.[9] He saw Sakhalin as a "perfect hell."

Together with advocating reform, Chekhov's motive was to study "unbearable suffering, the sort of which only man, free or subjugated, is capable."[10] He described the flogging of a prisoner sentenced to ninety lashes, when "after only five or ten blows his flesh, covered with weals from former beatings, turned crimson and deep blue; his skin peeled with each blow. 'Your Worship!' we heard through the screams and tears, 'your Worship! Spare me, your Worship!'"[11] Chekhov dreamed about the incident for several nights.

The brutal tsarist penal system was nevertheless far kinder to inmates than what would follow under the Soviet Union, when millions died building the cities and mining and lumber industries of the far east.

Logging remains a major occupation today. Much of the poorly regulated industry is illegal, including the clearing of vast swaths of timber sold very cheaply to China, Japan and elsewhere. Finding workers willing to undertake the backbreaking work of filling even legal quotas remains a problem, so some companies rely on another Soviet legacy: cooperation with North Korea. During the Cold War, Pyongyang sent prisoners to logging camps in remote stretches of the Russian far east to help pay its debts to Moscow. Two decades after the collapse of communism, North Koreans are still a source of very cheap labor for Russian firms. No longer prisoners, they continue doing dangerous work, isolated from the local population. Hoping to learn at least a little about their working conditions, I traveled to a timber camp in the Amur region on a cold day in March.

Boarding a train in the dilapidated city of Blagoveshchensk, across the Amur River from the Chinese city of Heihe and its shiny skyscrapers, I headed north through endless forests and taiga. Watching the totally unpopulated landscape pass by my window was alternately exhilarating and monotonous: you wouldn't want to be stranded there. My destination was the snowbound town of Tynda, a collection of Soviet-era concrete-slab buildings built to serve as the main crossroads of the Baikal-Amur Mainline, a colossal railway project intended to help develop the region for no discernible reason other than settling it. Considered one of the great follies of the late Soviet era, the so-called BAM railway remains unfinished. Nestled among gently rolling forested hills, isolated Tynda was only thirty years old when I visited, but seriously decrepit. That didn't make it much different from many other Soviet-era settlements except for its compound of long, single-story wooden buildings on the edge of town: barracks for North Korean workers.

The complex stood at the end of a narrow road, where a tall gate next to a guardhouse and a big searchlight blocked the entrance. It was surrounded by an old wooden fence topped by a string of rusting barbed wire. Inside, conditions looked very basic. A large North Korean flag flew at the top of a tall pole, near banners and monuments bearing slogans written in red Korean characters. Occasionally, the gate opened to allow laborers through, usually in groups of three. Sitting on the snow-swept road, they looked bedraggled and weather-beaten. When I tried to speak to one, he told me in broken Russian that he didn't understand me. Others appeared to want to talk but were visibly afraid.

Residents of nearby houses seemed oblivious to the foreigners living among them. A kindly middle-aged woman named Liudmilla Alexandrovna told me that the workers keep to themselves. "When we come across them in the forest, they're afraid of us. We used to feel sorry for them, looking very poor, dressed in their black work clothes. Now we're used to them."

Despite rumors of abuses, frequent accidents and food shortages in the camps, local police don't concern themselves with the North Koreans' affairs unless they learn of murders and other serious crimes. The few officials who agreed to speak to me said the government's agreement with North Korea gives them no jurisdiction over the camps. However, it was clear that the authorities in Tynda were receiving a steady stream of fees and, by many accounts, payoffs for issuing work permits. Before being unceremoniously ejected, I glimpsed stacks of North Korean passports waiting to be processed inside the local office of the Federal Migration Service, which implements immigration policy. An official later told me that sixteen hundred North Koreans work in the region, usually for three-year stints, but others said the number was probably far higher. A former manager of Tynda's main logging company estimated that his one firm alone may have employed more than six thousand people.

At a processing plant I managed to visit in the forest twenty miles south of Tynda, massive saws cut logs into boards. It was desolate and freezing, and the situation was little better in summer, when the hot and humid forests swarm with mosquitoes. Unlike the members of the few Russian work brigades around Tynda, North Koreans cut and clear wood by hand, without the help of timber harvesters and other heavy machinery. A local who had worked alongside them told me that conditions were dangerous and workers were under constant surveillance. Nevertheless, life in Tynda, however punishing, gives circumstantial evidence of the much worse conditions back home: only those in good standing with the North Korean authorities are allowed to travel to Russia.

The need to cope with the cold helps explain Russians' abiding love of one of their great pleasures, the public baths called *banyi*. From homemade wood-heated huts ubiquitous in the countryside to large establishments in cities, *banyi* provide escape from the drudgery of daily life, especially the seemingly endless stretches of freezing, overcast weather, when roads are dangerously icy and bundled-up pedestrians look weighted with grim determination.

Under Soviet rule, the *banya* fulfilled another important function by providing the millions living in crammed communal apartments a place to bathe, and some have kept prices low as a kind of social service. Every Moscow neighborhood has at least one *banya*, usually housed on the first or second floor of an ordinary-looking apartment building. Most are single-sex. Patrons typically enter a large room filled with high-backed benches, where they undress, wrap a sheet around themselves and head to the baths. They return to the main room between sessions in the steam room to relax, drink tea or vodka and talk.

The steam room itself, or *parilka*, resembles a sauna, although it's larger and more humid. An employee called a *banshik* regulates the furnace, usually fueled by gas, and produces the desired amount of steam by throwing in ladles of water, often infused with mint, eucalyptus and other scents.

Some *banshiki* have fan clubs that come at the same time every week to sit on the wooden platforms or beat each other with dried birch-leaf besoms, which may sound masochistic but feels much like a massage when done by experts. Heading out of the *banya* after a session in a typical Moscow establishment called the Donskiye Baths, a regular named Gennady Novitsky described the process as "a whole science."

"You use the birch leaves to draw the steam close and open your pores," he explained. "That helps you sweat out the poisons." True or not, it's supremely relaxing. After the scorching-hot *parilka*, many jump into a pool of cold water—or, in the countryside, into snow—before heading back to the steam room to repeat the routine. Novitsky said the feeling of absolute abandon erased all concerns about daily life, including its hierarchies. "There's no such thing as a general in a *banya*," he said. "Everyone's equal." Another patron claimed the *banya* routine is as necessary for Russians as eating and drinking: "They say church purifies the soul and the *banya* purifies the body."

Little has changed in *banyi* since Soviet days except the prices. Although many at the Donskiye Baths considered the ten-dollar fee high, Muscovites can pay hundreds elsewhere for slightly better surroundings and a few beers. Moscow's oldest and fanciest *banya*, the gilded Sanduny Baths, near the Kremlin, was built for nobles in the nineteenth century and said to have been frequented by the likes of Pushkin and Tolstoy. The main room has an ornate Gothic wooden ceiling and mosaics depicting idyllic Black Sea scenes; marble pillars surround the large pool. Before the rising price of attendance limited our visits, I would often go with my friend Kolya, whose father had regularly taken him when he was a boy—and with my own *banya*-devoted father when he visited me in Moscow.

Although my wife, Elizabeth, often questioned why Kolya and I would voluntarily spend hours sitting in steamy rooms staring at other not-very-fit naked men, it was there where we relaxed enough to develop our most unrealistic ideas for journalistic collaborations: journeys across Russia to document the best vodkas; larks to Afghanistan—whose landscape and cuisine Kolya and I both loved—to research a book I was writing about the Soviet war. When I dared question our chances of accomplishing our most fanciful plans, I was rebuked for raining on the spirit of our parade. "Of course we'll do it," Kolya admonished me. "How could we not? We're the best! Now lie flat!" Kolya's skill with the birch besoms on my back, along with the beer and steamed shrimp we devoured afterward, made our visits among the activities I've most enjoyed in life.

Despite its many renovations, however, Sanduny maintains a noticeably seedy look and its employees are as gruff as their Soviet predecessors. Explaining the exorbitant cost, a *banya* director told me customers demand the high prices "because they want fewer people to jostle them." That failed to impress Gennady Novitsky back in the downscale Donskiye Baths. He said it doesn't matter which *banya* you visit: "When you emerge on the street afterward, you feel so light that you think you might float away."

Many foreigners who agree find another winter tradition, that of plunging into swimming holes sawed out of ice-covered ponds and rivers, less tempting. The popular custom, which has made a comeback since Soviet days, takes place en masse at midnight on the Russian Orthodox observation of Epiphany, in January, and according to superstition brings very cold weather called the Epiphany frosts. I observed one session five days into the coldest winter in twenty-six years, in 2006, when the temperature was minus twenty-five degrees Celsius and an Arctic freeze was pushing mercury levels in Siberia down to minus fifty. In Moscow, automatic teller machines were malfunctioning and electric trolleybuses ground to a halt. Traffic was greatly reduced since it seemed that only the lucky few with heated garages or those who kept their cars running all day were able to get on the road.

First-aid workers who stood by a tributary of the Moscow River lined with elite dachas admitted that its icy water conferred only negative health consequences. Nevertheless, dazed-looking swimmers wrapped in towels after bathing said they felt exhilarated. Some insisted that more than just a physical sensation, their experience of the cold was a rite of passage important to their identity as Russians.

———

The cold and other hardships have persuaded generations of Russians that they behave a certain way because they think differently from others, as a much-quoted passage from Vassily Aksyonov's semiautobiographical 1980 novel *The Burn* describes.

> In Europe there are frivolous democracies with warm climates, where an intellectual spends his life flitting from the dentist's drill to the wheel of a Citroen, from a computer to an espresso bar, from

the conductor's podium to a woman's bed, and where literature is something almost as refined, witty and useful as a silver dish of oysters laid out on brown seaweed and garnished with cracked ice.

Russia, with its six-month winter, its tsarism, Marxism and Stalinism, is not like that. What we like is some heavy masochistic problem, which we can prod with a tired, exhausted, not very clean but honest finger. That's what we need, and it's not our fault.[12]

Aksyonov, who was later expelled from the Soviet Union, presents a typically idealized picture of Europe, laden with envy. As Edward Keenan has pointed out, the passage also reflects a belief that the Russian concern with deeper matters bestows moral superiority.[13]

Forty years earlier, a prominent Soviet educator named Anton Makarenko decried Russian intellectuals' "passionate love of slovenliness and disorder...Perhaps they had a special taste that could discern in this disorder a gleam of something higher, something attractive, something that touched them deeply—a precious gleam of freedom."[14] But Aksyonov—the son of journalist Yevgenia Ginzburg, whose *Journey into the Whirlwind* remains one of the best accounts of life in the Gulag—undermines such views by blaming Russians for their own plight. "Not our fault? Really?... Who cut themselves off from the people...licked the boots of Europe, isolated themselves from Europe...submitted obediently to dim-witted dictators? We did all that—we, the Russian intelligentsia."[15]

The passages tap into the central nineteenth-century debate that, regardless of its merits, came to define Russians' conception of themselves: Who is to blame for the country's ills? That leads to another eternal question—What is to be done?—that has prompted one grandiose solution after another. If the Westernizers sought to rescue Russia by imposing foreign values—often with a very Russian call for revolutionary upheaval, as I mentioned—their rivals, the Slavophiles, looked inward. Emerging in the late 1830s, they believed Russia's problems lay in having abandoned its patriarchal traditions and Orthodox Christian principles in favor of Western rationalism and individualism. Peter the Great bore the greatest blame for derailing Russia from its supposedly natural path toward harmony and salvation based on the values of the Slavic peasant commune, a view based on nostalgic yearning for an imagined "lost" country.

The Slavophiles drew on an old tradition of dissent begun in the fifteenth century in the monasteries of principalities such as Novgorod that were conquered by Moscow. Their monks influenced the sons of elite families exiled there in disgrace, who continued to share in many of the assumptions central to the "dominant" culture. Among them were the same despairing, conservative views about the weakness of man's nature. Rather than seeking to overthrow the tsar, they criticized his moral imperfection, often using a traditionally religious vocabulary.

Russia's first historian, Nikolai Karamzin, helped lay the foundation for the Slavophile tradition by attacking constitutional reforms drawn up by Alexander I's adviser Mikhail Speransky, a founder of Russian liberalism who in 1809 advocated the establishment of a series of legislatures to check the tsar's powers. Although Karamzin—a conservative who defended autocratic monarchy in the wake of the French Revolution—didn't believe Russia to be fundamentally different from Western countries, later Slavophiles argued for Russian exceptionalism. Most were products of wealthy families who attended universities and traveled abroad. Like the Westernizers, they came of age under the spell of German Idealism; its emphasis on mysticism and intuition for divining universal truths naturally appealed to those who argued against the belief that Russia was inferior. The Slavophiles believed their country was no worse than the West, just different. More than that, Russia's deeper spiritual principles would eventually triumph.

The chief Slavophile philosopher, Ivan Kireevsky, who believed that Europeans' "logical reason" had reached "the highest possible level of its development," credited them with the awareness that "the higher truths, the living insights, the basic convictions of the mind all lie outside the abstract circle of its dialectics."[16] Luckily for Russia, he continued, "the essence of Russian civilization still lives on among the people and, what is most important, in the Holy Orthodox Church. Hence it is on this foundation and on no other that we must erect the solid edifice of Russian enlightenment, built heretofore out of mixed and for the most part foreign materials and therefore needing to be rebuilt with pure native stone." Among those who took up the Slavophiles' rejection of Western modernity, Dostoevsky, in his novel *The Devils*, depicts the radicals of the 1860s as devoted to blind self-destruction by following foreign ideas they didn't really understand.

Another fellow traveler, Tolstoy, advocated a return to the values of the patriarchal peasantry. The "great writer of the Russian land," as Turgenev called the author of two of the novels widely considered among the greatest ever, *War and Peace* (1869) and *Anna Karenina* (1877), was a complicated figure. Known for his moralistic philosophy and prescriptions for social reform, Tolstoy respected anarchism and advocated nonviolence, positions he derived from his literal interpretations of the Bible. No other literary shrine compares in hallowed status to his modest family estate at Yasnaya Polyana, about a hundred miles south of Moscow, where he set up a school and experimented with farming methods.

Descended from old Russian nobility, Tolstoy began writing in 1852 soon after joining the army to earn money to pay off gambling debts. His experience fighting in the Caucasus would later provide him with material for his brilliant novella *Hadji Murad*. Defying simple characterization, *War and Peace* explores his theory about individuals' powerlessness against the forces of history. Partly an account of Napoleon's invasion in 1812, it includes almost six hundred characters, historical as well as fictional. The sweeping novel moves from the lives of two aristocratic families to the tsar's St. Petersburg court, Napoleon's headquarters and the battlefields of Austerlitz and Borodino.

Anna Karenina tells parallel stories of two marriages. One is of the well-regarded title character, who begins an affair but—unable to bear society's deceit and hypocrisy—becomes trapped by social conventions. The second involves an independent landowner prone to philosophizing whose character mirrors Tolstoy's. Also concerned about the tension between the individual and society, the semiautobiographical character Levin works in the field with his peasants and seeks to reform their lives.

Tolstoy's later works explore his radical Christian philosophy, which resulted in his excommunication from the Russian Orthodox Church in 1901. Although many of his works were censored, his literary fame helped ensure his freedom from arrest. But the end of his life was marked by ill health and an inglorious struggle for influence between his disciples and his longtime wife, Sofia Andreevna. Her nighttime searches of his papers are believed to have finally driven Tolstoy to abandon Yasnaya Polyana for a life of ascetic wandering in the middle of winter. The year was 1910; Tolstoy was ninety-two years old. He got as far as the train station at the nearby town of Astapovo, where he fell ill and soon died of pneumonia. Thousands of peasants lined his funeral procession.

Alexander Solzhenitsyn, who believed the Bolsheviks hijacked Russia from its true path, was among those who continued the Slavophile tradition half a century later. The dissident who exposed the Gulag's horrors in his best-known books, *The Gulag Archipelago* and *One Day in the Life of Ivan Denisovich*, later shocked the audience at a Harvard University graduation ceremony in 1978 by delivering an infamous address that railed against Western culture. People in the West, he said, lived in overly legalistic societies made morally weak by prosperity. "Through intense suffering our country has now achieved a spiritual development of such intensity," he thundered, "that the Western system in its present state of spiritual exhaustion does not look attractive."

Solzhenitsyn, who called for a restoration of the monarchy after his return to Russia from exile in 1994, was hardly unique among Russian intellectuals for being inflexibly dogmatic. His heroism in attacking the Soviet Union blunted criticism of him in the West, however. My father, who co-wrote a biography of him shortly before he was exiled in 1974, had communicated with him through secret notes passed through relatives of Solzhenitsyn's first wife, Natalia Ryshatovskaya. The relatives would burn the notes after my dad had read them. Despite that implicit authorization of the book and all the information in it, however—my father smuggled the manuscript back into Russia so that Solzhenitsyn's relatives could criticize it—Solzhenitsyn later accused him of publicizing KGB lies about him. "That was very Russian," my dad told me. "Here was another prophet fighting for truth by lying. He denounced my book without having read a word, and I stupidly thought I was helping him by increasing his fame in the West, his only real protection."

Earlier, Solzhenitsyn's friend Ilya Zilberberg had risked his young family's safety by hiding some of the writer's manuscripts in his communal apartment. They were eventually discovered, evidently because Solzhenitsyn—although usually enormously cautious—had mentioned them over the telephone. Nevertheless, Solzhenitsyn blamed the mistake on Zilberberg, because, my father said, "Solzhenitsyn could do no wrong, he had to be a saint. In that way, he was much like Lenin whom he so fiercely opposed."

———

Despite their conservatism, most Slavophiles called for the abolition of serfdom and scorned the state ideology under autocratic Nicholas I. Drawn up in 1833 by the education minister, a count named Sergei Uvarov, the doctrine of Official Nationality propounded three pillars for the Russian state: orthodoxy, autocracy and nationality. Chief among them, autocracy meant the tsar's absolute power, which the other two components served to support. Nationality—*narodnost* in Russian, which also means "populism"—signified the Russian special "national spirit." Orthodoxy stipulated obedience to the Church's values.

The formulation reflected the Orthodox Church's traditional role as a subservient enforcer of state authority, sealed by Peter the Great, who first established the Synod, the governing church council, as a state department in 1721. That function, critics believed, helped explain the Church's repressive nature. "The church has always favored whips and prisons," wrote Vissarion Belinsky, the literary critic who is considered the main father of Russia's revolutionary tradition, in a famous letter to Nikolai Gogol. Responding to Gogol's growing support for autocracy late in his life, Belinsky assailed his assertion that Russians were innately religious. The Church "has always groveled to despotism," he wrote. "But what has that to do with Christ?"

Richard Pipes later interpreted the Church's basic doctrine as "the creed of resignation." Russian Orthodoxy "considers earthly existence an abomination, and prefers retirement to involvement...preaches patient acceptance of one's fate and silent suffering."[17] The lack of independence, Pipes argued, was responsible for the Church's rapid demise under the Bolsheviks, who were able to strip and destroy thousands of churches and subject tens of thousands of priests and monks to torture, arrest, and murder in a country of millions of supposedly devout believers.

Still, the Russian Orthodox Church, as the historian James Billington has argued, was central to developing the first recognizably Russian culture by providing the mediums for artistic expression, attacking secular literature and music and focusing painting on the icon. "The Orthodox Church brought Russia out of its dark ages," he wrote, "providing a sense of unity for its scattered people, higher purpose for its princes, and inspiration for its creative artists."[18] The Church also reinforced the Russian claim of a special destiny. Inherited from Kievan Rus', which adopted Christianity in the tenth century, Byzantine Orthodoxy had the effect of helping isolate Moscow from the West following the decline of Byzantium. At the center of its ideology, Billington argues, is the belief that "Russian Christendom represents a special culminating chapter in an unbroken chain of sacred history" and that "Moscow and its rulers are the chosen bearers of this destiny."[19] Orthodoxy remains especially hostile to the Catholic Church, which it often accuses of seeking to convert Russians.

For centuries, the Church and nationality were considered virtually synonymous: Russians were unquestioningly Orthodox. The word for "peasant," *krestianin*, is a version of "Christian," *khristianin*. Little surprise, then, that after almost a century of turmoil and state-enforced atheism under communism, the Church's resurgence has played an important, if mostly superficial, role in the ongoing quest for a national identity. Onion domes and icons are instantly recognizable as Russian around the world, symbols of a religion with a powerful aesthetic appeal. Even Pipes praises the "beauty of its art and ritual." Standing under the vaulted ceilings of one of Moscow's old churches during a daily service today imparts a serene sense of timelessness, as if nothing has changed for centuries. The air is usually thick with the smell of incense and smoke from candles crackling in front of gilded icons. There are no pews; worshippers stand, coming and going as choirs sing and priests recite centuries-old texts in Church Slavonic.

Although church and state remain formally separate, many Russians now see Orthodoxy as official in all but name. In the 1990s, Yeltsin gave the Church tax breaks on trade in alcohol and tobacco, enabling it to do very lucrative business. Patriarch Alexiy II, who spearheaded the Church's revival before his death in 2008, was often seen on state television with Yeltsin and, later, Putin. His publicly intimate relationship with the former KGB officer turned president was not as unlikely as it may have appeared. Like most Soviet-era priests, Alexiy is believed to have been a KGB agent; his code name was Drozdov.

The Church continues to flourish under Putin, who attends services regularly, wears a cross and claims to have hid his faith under communism. State officials and businessmen have endowed religious orders, built new churches and restored old ones. Alexiy in turn endorsed Medvedev's presidency in 2008, then blessed his inauguration, as he did Putin's in 2012. But although the alliance between Orthodox Church and Kremlin has served both well, some members of the Church, which is now flush with wealth and influence, have shown signs of trying to forge a measure of independence—most visibly during the street protests against parliamentary elections in December 2011, when various Church authorities temporarily joined demonstrators in criticizing the rigging of votes.

However, the Church has been hobbled by a lack of devout supporters. Although more than two-thirds of Russians, almost a hundred million people, claim to believe, only some 10 percent regularly attend services. One opinion poll revealed that a mere 4 percent of those questioned said they look to religion as a source of moral values. Most of those who identify with religion appear to be motivated chiefly by nationalistic views that extol Orthodoxy. Some conservative voices in the Church blame its ongoing attempt to cultivate political influence with the Kremlin for undermining its authority among Russians.

Among them is a young but prominent deacon named Andrei Kuraev, who teaches philosophy at Moscow State University and a seminary in Sergiyev Possad, site of Russia's most important monastery. When I spoke to the youthful-looking bearded priest with long brown hair in the study of his expensively decorated Moscow apartment, he was dressed in a traditional black cassock and round wire-rimmed glasses and kept glancing between two mobile phones on his desk and a flat-screen television mounted on a wall, which was broadcasting news on a state-run station. He told me the Church had been forced to sacrifice its independence. "It must serve the people, not the authorities," he said. "Without an independent Church that plays the key role in society, Russians will lose their power in this part of the world and become just another ethnic group." Russia was on the threshold of becoming an "Islamic state," he concluded, never mind that only 6 percent of the population is believed to be Muslim.

Seeking to boost the number of young believers, the Church has successfully lobbied to make classes about Russian Orthodoxy mandatory in state schools. It has also railed against foreign missionaries and campaigned against reconciling with the Vatican, partly because Russians for centuries saw the Polish-Lithuanian Empire, a once powerful Catholic state, as an existential threat. But critics say the Church's leverage against the government is still limited by its general lack of concern with serving ordinary people. Although some individual priests have worked hard to help the needy, the hierarchy leaves most charity work to foreign aid organizations, its official position being that those who do not succeed don't deserve pity.

Yuri Samodurov, a soft-spoken human rights activist who is the former director of Moscow's Sakharov Museum, told me the Church was bent on "monopolizing" Russians' religious beliefs. "It insists on dictating our morality and ideology," he said, "because its main goal isn't helping people but increasing its own power." Church leaders denounced Samodurov for organizing a controversial art exhibit in 2003 called *Caution! Religion*, which featured works such as Jesus's face on a Coca-Cola logo with the words "This is my blood." After Orthodox believers vandalized some of the works, a court cleared them of "hooliganism" charges. The Church then sued Samodurov and other organizers, who were found guilty of "instigating religious and ethnic hatred."

The current Russian Orthodox patriarch is a sharp-tongued former Church spokesman who has criticized "human rights" as "a cover for lies and insults to religious and ethnic values" and praised Putin's rule as a "miracle of God." Although billed a modernizer when he took over in 2008, Kirill I has done little to satisfy supporters' hopes that he would oversee a regeneration of the Church by transforming it into a real moral ballast for Russians still battling with communism's terrible legacy. When bloggers noticed in 2012 that an official photograph of Kirill had been doctored to remove a Breguet watch worth more than thirty thousand dollars—although its reflection on a well-polished table remained visible—public anger at the patriarch, who had denied rumors he owned a Breguet, prompted more accusations the Church is little more than another corrupt government department.

Kirill's response to the arrest of members of the feminist punk band Pussy Riot helped seal that image. Dressed in bright neon dresses and balaclavas, the women—more a performance-art group sustained by a rotating cast of about thirty women than a traditional rock band—became an icon of protest after creating videos of impromptu public appearances during which members cavorted and profanely criticized Putin before his reelection to a third term in 2011. After they'd managed to perform for several minutes in Moscow's main Orthodox cathedral, Christ the Savior—where they called on the "Holy Mother, Blessed Virgin" to "chase Putin out"—three of the women were arrested and sentenced to two years in prison for "hooliganism," a common catchall charge used against dissidents. One member was later released.

Thanks to their stoic demeanor and eloquent, even literary statements during their trial, the young women have come to be seen as true inheritors of the Soviet dissident tradition. Although they apologized, saying they'd been making a political statement about the government's ties to the Church, prosecutors sought to build a broad spiritual indictment against them by accusing them of inflicting moral damage on Russia and inciting religious hatred. Outside the courtroom, nationalist groups burned pictures of the group's members. Abroad, however, Pussy Riot—which had emerged from the street-art collective Voina—generated a chorus of support from pop stars and politicians. Amnesty International described the women—two of whom had small children at home—as "prisoners of conscience."

Nevertheless, one particularly outspoken minister responded by calling the singer Madonna—who had supported the defendants during a concert in Moscow—a "whore." Such behavior appeared to provide another striking sign of the Kremlin's blindness or indifference to the terrible press it all but courted by making the previously unknown group an international cause célèbre. However, prosecuting Pussy Riot appeared to fit Putin's drive to split society by stoking his version of a culture war. Unwilling to respond to calls for change with anything other than a crackdown, the authorities banked on support from the majority of conservative Russians by portraying a minor disturbance as an assault on Russian Orthodoxy. For his part, Kirill, leader of a church with which many still sympathize after its repression under the communist regime, accused Pussy Riot of blasphemy and doing the devil's work. The following year, Putin enacted a so-called blasphemy law that punishes "public actions expressing obvious disrespect toward society and committed to abuse the religious feelings of believers" with fines and up to three years in prison.

The affair provided more evidence of the Church's closeness to the authorities and reinforced its reputation for remaining rigidly hierarchical, intolerant of dissent and wary of competition. After a Gorbachev-era Soviet law declared all faiths equal in 1990, the Church successfully lobbied to marginalize other religions. It also continues to help isolate Russia from the West by advocating a vision of the country's future that is rooted in nationalism, opposed to liberal democracy and little changed in the last thousand years.

———

Much like the enduring Slavophile-Westernizer debate, Russia's ongoing, sometimes tortured search for its place in the world will continue to be influenced by Church leaders, advocates of a Russian-led "Eurasian Union" and others who make various claims for the country's exceptionalism. Their views will keep feeding Russians' ideas about themselves and their country, which also remain affected by its difficult climate and geography.

Hundreds of deaths from cold each winter help reinforce a sense that life is cheaper in Russia than in the West together with the very old corollary that individuals aren't suited for making it on their own. And although Siberians exhibit fierce pride in their region, Siberia and the far north still loom large in the collective imagination as places of involuntary exile, where the cold is additional punishment.

The notion of individual weakness has helped buttress Russia's age-old fatalism. In the summer of 1939, just after the height of Stalin's Great Terror, when the Gulag system was approaching its full size, Zhora wrote Serafima that something was "hanging over the camp's atmosphere" in Ivdellag: "People are suffering from evil so much they're trying to convince themselves it's for the better."

Ivdel, July 22, 1939

Let the end come quickly. Some kind of end, freedom or death, to the happiness of healthy human life or to the bloody wall of murder— forward to humanism or backward straight to Robespierre's slaughterhouse. Let mine be a lonely, unnamed grave under the Urals cliffs or the parquet floor of a jolly dance hall. I don't care. To the end, to the end!

Ivdel, August 23, 1939

Dearest one,

I'm writing my last letter to you. This morning we received a tele-phonogram [message dictated by telephone] about sending me from Ivdellag together with an engineer...No one knows anything about where I'm being sent or why. It just said there was an order that I be sent away immediately. Others disappeared in such cases. They promised to write, but not a single person has.

I'm probably being sent to another camp. Oh, how I don't want to go, how difficult it is to travel to a strange new place! Nothing good comes of winters in unfamiliar places. The battle is not over survival but death. You're put in the worst situations doing the hardest work. All your friends are left behind in the old place. Indeed, I have a privileged position here, and who knows what awaits me there. Maybe I'm being sent where I'll have no contact with the world. Whatever happens to me, remember that I love you and will be with you. Even if I disappear without a trace for years, I'll immediately find you the moment I free myself...

I embrace you and Mother. Love and remember me.

My mother in Moscow, 1963.

10
Clan Rules

The law is like a cart—wherever you point it, that's where it rolls.

—Old Russian saying

W hen Alexander Bulbov's plane touched down in Moscow on a cold October night in 2007, the deputy head of Russia's drug control agency was doing nothing more unusual than returning home from a law-enforcement conference abroad. So the masked commandos who stormed the plane and snatched him away as he was getting ready to leave caught him very much by surprise. Accused during the following days of abusing his office by authorizing illegal phone hacking on behalf of private companies, he appeared to be the newest casualty of the government's latest anticorruption campaign. However, it soon became clear there was more to his case.

No ordinary antidrug official, Bulbov masterminded wiretapping operations for several high-profile criminal investigations into the activities of Federal Security Service officers accused of making millions of dollars through smuggling and tax evasion in connection with an expensive furniture store called Tri Kita. The veteran investigative journalist and member of parliament Yuri Shchekochikhin had been looking into the same allegations when he died, almost certainly from poisoning. He was one of more than a dozen reporters who have been killed—probably assassinated—since Putin came to power.

Far from a crusading liberal, however, Bulbov was directly plugged in to the political power structure as the right-hand man of the drug control agency's chief, Victor Cherkessov. A former KGB officer, Cherkessov was a close Putin associate and reputed leader of a powerful Kremlin political "clan" of former security officers. How could the ally of such a loyal figure have been arrested? The answer would shed light on the mystery of what went on behind the Kremlin's high walls.

Just as in Soviet days, the doings in the corridors of power remain a closely guarded secret. Analyzing Russian politics, which Winston Churchill compared to watching "dogs fighting under a carpet," again requires Cold War–style Kremlinology. With competing conspiracy theories planted by rival groups among the weapons in the struggle, anything is possible, any rumor might be true.

It was significant that Bulbov's arrest was made by a new agency called the Investigative Committee, which had been launched by Putin months earlier and was headed by Alexander Bastrykin, a former law school classmate of the president's. Formally subordinate to the prosecutor general, Bastrykin had been repeatedly accused of overstepping his powers but never censured. When I met Bulbov's lawyer Sergei Antonov soon after the arrest, he intimated that the charges against his client were fabricated to punish Bulbov's boss, Cherkessov, for crossing a line by authorizing eavesdropping on people who weren't meant to be subject to it, at least not by him. A large, genial man who spoke to me in his sprawling downtown office, Antonov said Bulbov's phone taps had resulted in the arrests of FSB generals and contributed to the dismissal of the general prosecutor himself. All were connected to an even more powerful Putin ally—the president's deputy chief of staff, Igor Sechin, the shadowy KGB veteran who also chaired Rosneft, the massive state oil company.

Antonov said Bulbov fell victim to a power struggle between Kremlin rivals who were operating competing intelligence agencies, both of which reported directly to Putin. Bulbov's arrest, he added, was aimed at fueling fear. "Stalin used to arrest the wives of his top officials, even Molotov's," he explained. (Vyacheslav Molotov was Stalin's foreign minister.) "They became hostages, to ensure people like Molotov didn't act out of line. That's happening again, not to family members but to deputies and allies." A former KGB officer named Alexei Kondaurov, who knows more than most about secret intrigues, told me that Putin's role as the ultimate arbiter between clans loyal to him inevitably provoked competition between them. "It's obvious Cherkessov and Bulbov didn't assign their own tasks," he said. "Their orders came from the very top and carrying them out helped provoke the clan war."

Rather than chaotic infighting, Bulbov's arrest appeared to show the president carefully maintaining his power by playing rivals against each other. The struggle intensified after the arrest, when two officers from his drug control agency died mysteriously from radiation poisoning. Bulbov's boss, Cherkessov, soon published an open letter warning that the stand-off threatened to tear the country apart. "There can be no winners in this war," he wrote.

Continuing its campaign nevertheless, the Investigative Committee proceeded to arrest a professorial deputy finance minister. But then a former detective named Dmitri Dovgi appeared to lift the lid on the group's operations. His revelations came in a newspaper interview in which he claimed he had been ordered to open the investigations into Bulbov, the deputy finance minister and others he said were innocent of any wrongdoing. He, too, was promptly arrested, accused of accepting a million-dollar bribe to drop a probe into a businessman suspected of embezzlement.

Hoping to glean more details, I attended Dovgi's trial, held in a small courtroom in northeast Moscow. The youthful, dark-haired defendant claimed the bribery charge was punishment for his exposure of the truth about his onetime employers but revealed nothing else about the committee's activities. On the day of the jury's deliberation, a juror who had shown signs of intending to vote for acquittal was delayed by a traffic policeman on her way to court.[1] Ignoring her special juror's document, the officer kept her long enough for the judge to appoint an alternate juror. Found guilty, Dovgi was sentenced to nine years in jail. Bulbov, later released on bail, still faces trial. The Investigative Committee's influence has continued to grow and grow.

The infighting cast a sinister pall over Moscow, adding to the uncertainty surrounding Putin's expected exit from the presidency the following year. Unsurprisingly, the intrigue ebbed after the election of Putin's protégé and four-year placeholder Medvedev. Few saw a coincidence: the clash had made crystal clear to the various Kremlin clans that they risked losing everything if any of them conspired to back a new leader. By enhancing his personal authority over men already loyal to him, Putin ensured he would remain Russia's supreme leader even after stepping down from the country's most powerful office.

Such clan politics explain a good deal about often seemingly inexplicable Russian behavior that ignores all manner of instructions, directives and regulations. Doors open to personal appeals, exceptions are made for friends, sweetheart deals violate supposedly ironclad prohibitions and the rule of law seems among the least admired of Western values. "Again and again through the centuries westerners who have been brought into contact with Russia have been shocked and baffled by the relative lawlessness of Russian life," the legal scholar Harold Berman wrote in 1950. Although Berman believed the Russian system to have originally derived from the same Roman law that gave rise to Western codes, Russians "did not particularly want a western legal system." Understanding what they did want requires looking at a side of Russian heritage that "has been obscure to westerners because of their very preoccupation with law and legality."[2]

Refusal to go by the book, or even read it, is more than a reflection of the anarchy Russians are known to fear. It's actually a manifestation of one of the most hidden aspects of their way of life. Official institutions—the kind Western countries depend on for governing—function so inefficiently in Russia because their actual role is largely to serve the workings of a different system, essentially the collection of informal networks of crony arrangements I mentioned at the start of this book. I believe they make up the real governing structure, whose beneficiaries carefully suppress the transparency and legality they perceive as threatening them. The supposedly mystical respect for authority and obsession about *besporiadok*—literally "without order"—Russians are believed to share is actually driven in part by interest in maintaining a system in which many hold a stake. Kirill Kabanov, a former security service officer who heads the nongovernmental National Anticorruption Committee, compares the scheme to feudalism. "A system of vassals headed by a group of high-ranking 'untouchables,'" he explained. "Each group has its own network, a criminal structure in which loyalty is bought."

Of course Russia displays a facade of quasi-democratic government. But just as ideas imported from the West have for centuries acted as a veil, those foreign institutions largely serve to conceal more enduring arrangements. Little as they contribute to an efficient economy, fair governance or other goals generally prized by Western societies, they are very effective for perpetuating the traditional Russian values of stability and aversion to risk, and they rely on a carefully constructed image of Putin as a wielder of great power.

Foreigners are unlikely to know that Russia has had more weak rulers than strong ones and that Ivan the Terrible and other ogres in popular Western images were actually far less potent than they seemed. The historical record is important because despite Russia's reputation as a country ruled by iron-willed despots, it has more often been governed by a group of oligarchs whose ability to function under relatively flimsy tsarist authority became a lasting trait of national political life.

Besides the very important job of producing an heir, the tsar's main role in medieval Muscovy was as a mediator or allocator of authority among leaders of the ruling clans, the most powerful usually being those closest to him. Relationships were based on kinship and power was obtained through engagements and marriages. "It was the brothers, uncles and fathers of the lucky brides who formed the innermost circle of power," Edward Keenan explained.[3]

The dearth of Russian historical records, Keenan argued, partly explains the obscurity of those oligarchs' roles and why virtually nothing is known about how a painful, debilitating bone disease called ankylosing spondylitis all but crippled Ivan the Terrible. Soviet forensic scientists who exhumed his remains in the 1960s discovered the condition, which rendered many of the stories we know about Ivan being terrible—his violent rages, kinky sex, throwing of cats from Kremlin towers—highly unlikely. Far from the mad despot official histories make him out to have been, Ivan was probably desperate to abdicate and vacated the Kremlin in favor of a palace outside Moscow, something many historians have been at pains to explain.[4] That it often mattered less who the tsar was than that someone occupy the position probably accounts for why the ruling boyars—a rough equivalent of nobles—were willing to submit themselves to a series of false successors after the death of Ivan's son Fyodor in 1598 brought about the end of the Riurik dynasty, soon to be followed by the more truly terrible Time of Troubles.

After the Troubles ended with the advent of the Romanov dynasty in 1613, Muscovy entered a period of expansion that required a growing bureaucracy to manage its acquisition of new lands. Originally recruited from foreigners, clergy's sons and merchants, a group of leading clerks called *diaki* began to influence the behavior of the ruling clans, which increasingly depended on them. So when Peter the Great launched Russia's imperial age at the close of the seventeenth century, his reforms were less a radical departure than a formalization of changes that had already taken place during the previous hundred years. Peter established ministries to govern the state, modernized the military and instituted compulsory education for the gentry. But rather than upend the political system by Westernizing Russia, as most believe, he rationalized it. For Peter—whose exile from the Kremlin as a child meant he wasn't steeped in the court's conservative culture—forcing the shaving of beards and other reforms were aimed at finally breaking the old kinship-based system in favor of the newer bureaucratic one, which displayed some characteristics of a meritocracy.

However, the deepest foundations of "Russianness," as Keenan put it, didn't radically change even amid the upheaval of modern times. Rather, "they have combined and reintegrated themselves in new forms, reaffirmed by political and social chaos and dizzying change."[5] Among the constants was an "authentic distrust of the unpredictable and risk-laden workings of electoral democracy," which threatened to destabilize the going system. Notoriously corrupt, inefficient and cumbersome as it was by the end of the nineteenth century, Russia's government nevertheless succeeded in maintaining social and political order in an enormous and poorly developed country. Far from being fated, the political culture was the product of a practical order that enabled the state to survive adverse conditions against great odds. In other words, it succeeded in accomplishing goals that happened to be different from Western ones.

———

The collapse of the Soviet system—which, revolution notwithstanding, developed into an extreme version of the traditional, risk-averse political structure—offered a chance to change that culture. If Western influence had previously affected mainly the elite and intelligentsia, now far more Russians had access to foreign ideas through books, magazines, television and travel abroad than ever before.

Several fundamental 1990s reforms gave hope for real political transformation in certain areas, including Moscow's governance of the regions.

After centuries of administrative coercion, for the first time in history the Kremlin began exercising control though fiscal policy—bargaining over taxes and the federal budget. Many criticized Yeltsin for enabling governors to act like corrupt princes: after telling them, famously, to take as much power as they could swallow, he allowed them to negotiate separate treaties. However, his decentralization actually represented an overall advance. It facilitated the rise of new elite groups and interests led by rival oligarchs and politicians who included various powerful regional leaders, the highly influential founders of Gazprom—including the longtime prime minister, Victor Chernomyrdin—and members of the dominant group: Yeltsin's inner circle, called the Family.[6] Although their rivalries set the pattern, those opponents also showed some signs they wanted to begin abiding by a set of common rules for their mutual benefit.

Those and other 1990s developments weren't fated to fail; they were brought down by a coincidence of contingencies, including a severe economic crisis in 1998, outrage over NATO's bombing of Yugoslavia the following year and Yeltsin's ill health. By weakening his ability and resolve to provide political protection for the government's Westernizing technocrats, the convergence of crises unleashed a political struggle that Putin eventually won by exploiting mounting popular anger over a decade of upheaval, humiliation and nostalgia for the USSR's superpower status. Lauded for ensuring stability, Putin used it to reinstate the old political culture—far from the first time that has happened in Russian history.

Aided by the boon of skyrocketing oil prices once he took power, the new leader restored the Kremlin's administrative control. He immediately set about replacing elected governors with presidential appointments, instituting controls over the national media and removing his rivals from government—and he continues tinkering with electoral and other laws to maintain his control over the country and its officialdom. It's worth repeating that his innovation wasn't cleaning up Russia's various Mafias but instilling a kind of order by making the Kremlin the main Mafia.

One hallmark of the current arrangement is that very few officials are fired, even for the most egregious behavior, as long as they remain loyal. Instead they are reshuffled into various parts of the vast state bureaucracy. When Putin's sneering young ideologue Vladislav Surkov was relieved of his duties as deputy presidential chief of staff—apparently to placate street protesters in 2011, although the move in fact appeared to be a long-expected result of clan realignments—he was given the title of first deputy prime minister before being reinstalled as deputy prime minister and chief of government staff after Medvedev become prime minister in May 2012. He was finally removed a year later, only to be reinstated as Putin's aide soon after. Stacked with the likes of Surkov and other Putin loyalists, Medvedev's cabinet was engineered to enable Putin to continue controlling the government, which he also often criticized. Few of its officials' job descriptions said much about their actual roles because administrative positions rarely reflect merit or real degrees of power.

That was especially evident under the Soviet Union, when Party bureaucrats were rotated through a variety of agencies and state enterprises with little or no regard for their knowledge and expertise, if they had any. Rather, they were appointed based on their informal relationships with other officials. Similarly, Dmitri Medvedev's four years as a president who supposedly had vast formal powers belied his real role as one of Putin's oligarchs, and not the strongest. During his tenure, *Forbes* magazine was astute enough to name a mere deputy prime minister the country's real second-most-powerful person: the Rosneft CEO Igor Sechin. He is a member of a small, shady group dominated by natives of Putin's hometown, St. Petersburg, that controls the real levers of power—and profits from them. Although he no longer formally handles the government's energy portfolio, Sechin continues to wield huge influence through Rosneft, whose $55 billion acquisition of BP's Russian joint venture in 2013 made it the world's largest publicly traded oil company, responsible for around 5 percent of global production. Sechin is also chairman of the state energy holding company, Rosneftegaz, which owns three-quarters of Rosneft and more than 10 percent of Gazprom. If there were any question about his role, his position as secretary under Putin of an energy commission conceived in 2012 effectively undermined the deputy prime minister officially in charge of energy, Medvedev's close ally Arkady Dvorkivich.

Among Putin's other cronies, several newly fabulously wealthy members of a St. Petersburg lakeside dacha cooperative, which the future president joined in the 1990s, are believed to ultimately disburse some of the riches from sales of Russia's oil and gas. They include shareholders of the deeply obscure but hugely powerful Bank Rossiya, which has been accused of using secret offshore companies to channel state loans intended for the acquisition of a jaw-dropping collection of Gazprom assets. Former bank insiders have said shady privatizations of companies such as Gazprom's Sogaz insurance firm enabled Bank Rossiya to suck billions of dollars' worth of value from the parent company.[7] Anders Aslund, a Swedish economist who is a keen observer of the hidden aspects of Russia's economy, says the Putin circle's "sheer asset-stripping" includes huge capital expenditures—$52 billion in 2011—on pipelines and other projects that cost far more than they would in other countries because much of the money is skimmed off.

Another firm, a Netherlands-based oil trading company headed by a former refinery manager named Gennady Timchenko, suddenly became the world's third-largest oil trader thanks to contracts to export oil from Rosneft and Gazpromneft—Gazprom's oil wing—in amounts equal to a third of Russia's seaborne production. Now one of the world's richest men, Timchenko was rumored to be operating on behalf of Putin, whom at least one well-connected observer has accused of amassing a secret forty-billion-dollar fortune.[8] Putin, who claims an annual income of one hundred and fifty thousand dollars, has denied the accusations.

When Timchenko lost his agreement with Rosneft in 2011, reportedly after balking at having to pay a premium, it was taken as a sign that Putin's authority was crumbling as his cronies fought for spoils. Igor Yurgens, a wealthy businessman and leading Medvedev adviser who served as a mouthpiece for the liberal reforms he supposedly supported, used the occasion to issue his latest prediction of Putin's demise. The new development reflected a "real crisis of management," he said.[9]

In fact, the competition has been constant. "You shouldn't assume there isn't jockeying behind the scenes just because Putin's in charge," one mid-level official told me. "That's the nature of the system." Despite the rumors about his decline, *Forbes* put Timchenko's worth in 2013 at more than fourteen billion dollars, a staggering rise from four hundred million dollars just four years earlier. He was only one of a new group of billionaires whose obscure but clearly very close connection to Putin has enabled them to displace some of the old oligarchs at the top of the ladder. Characterizing Putin's ruling elite as "Politburo 2.0"—after the Communist Party's governing body—a Russian think tank identified eight political and economic bosses who run the country under the president's arbitration, Timchenko and Sechin among them.

As for Medvedev—another longtime associate from St. Petersburg who as president often mouthed tough Putin-style rhetoric and adopted a version of his patron's swaggering walk—he never shook his much-ridiculed schoolboyish image. Unlike his surly mentor, President Medvedev grinned from ear to ear when he appeared next to the leaders of foreign countries, suggesting disbelief of his incredible luck. But his manner helped him succeed in his main role of deflecting domestic anger at corruption and mismanagement and misleading the West into believing he was serious about outlandish promises to end what he called Russia's "legal nihilism" and modernize the country.

His least believable exhortations came in a sweeping online screed that passed for a political platform in 2009. Titled "Go Russia!" it denounced the country's "primitive economy based on raw materials and endemic corruption." The new political system will be "extremely open, flexible and internally complex," he wrote. Admonishing his "brilliant and heroic" fellow Russians to drop their old "paternalistic attitudes," he issued a detailed list of actions that would make the country a "leading" one. Its experts "will improve information technology and strongly influence the development of global public data networks, using supercomputers and other necessary equipment." Moreover, "legislators will make all decisions to ensure comprehensive support for the spirit of innovation in all spheres of public life, creating a marketplace for ideas, inventions, discoveries and new technologies."

Medvedev's failure to enact a single significant initiative for achieving even one of his goals did little to quell four years of speculation about whether he was serious—a spectacular achievement. Political expert Stanislav Belkovsky, a former Kremlin insider who initiated the rumors about Putin's personal forty-billion-dollar fortune, told me that any perceived differences between Medvedev and the Kremlin's hard-liners were part of a deliberately constructed myth aimed at obscuring their real nature. "All those influence groups are actually business groups, and Dmitri Medvedev and Igor Sechin are part of it. They don't differ from each other either in their philosophy, their ideology or their life purposes."

After he stepped down to become prime minister, Medvedev was subjected to a series of public attacks and insults, including some delivered in a state television documentary that virtually accused him of treason for delaying Russia's attack against Georgia in 2008. While Putin rolled back one after another of his symbolic initiatives, Medvedev gamely accepted his new role as public whipping boy—yet more bread and circuses, some believed, or a strategy to pave the way for his sacking, or both.

More than that of a pawn, however, Medvedev's function has also been to act as a boss of the young, supposedly liberal officials who had close ties to some of the most powerful businessmen not plugged into Gazprom or otherwise directly tied to the Kremlin. The wife of Medvedev's one-time chief economic adviser chaired the boards of two companies controlled by the billionaire oligarch Suleiman Kerimov—who is also close to the influential First Deputy Prime Minister Igor Shuvalov.[10] A lawyer with a say in economic regulatory policies, Shuvalov earned tens of millions of dollars, partly through investments in Gazprom made by one of Kerimov's companies a year before the lifting of restrictions on foreign ownership of the stock sent the share price skyrocketing by 700 percent in three years.[11] Although Alexei Navalny and other opposition bloggers briefly put the Kremlin on its back foot by publicizing the news after it was exposed in the spring of 2012, Shuvalov was promoted to be Medvedev's number two in government soon after. His wife was also the subject of media revelations—about her stakes in offshore companies in the British Virgin Islands after Putin had ordered officials to divest themselves of such foreign holdings. The interests of those supposed liberals surely lie less in reform than enabling the private business of their associates to boom, aided by massive loans from state-controlled banks.

––––––

Putin's rise wasn't simply the result of a fortuitous or disastrous alignment of contingencies, crucial as they were for helping enable it. The government has never successfully refuted signs of complicated political engineering, including circumstantial but convincing evidence of a pivotal plot to bomb residential buildings that killed more than three hundred people in 1999. Although the authorities blamed Chechen rebels, many Russians suspect the security services staged the explosions as part of a secret plan to bring Putin to power the following year.

Most of the residents of an apartment block in southeast Moscow were asleep when the first blast on the ground floor tore through the front of their building one night that September. It killed ninety-four people and injured almost two hundred fifty. Five days earlier, another bomb had killed sixty-four people in the southern city of Buinaksk. In the coming weeks, two more explosions would kill more than a hundred thirty in Moscow and Volgodonsk, another southern city.

The shock waves set off fear throughout a country gripped by a savage political struggle to succeed ailing President Yeltsin. Although no Chechen took credit for the bombings, Putin, still prime minister, used them as a pretext for launching a second war in Chechnya. Seething with expertly displayed anger, he vowed to kill Chechen militants wherever they were hiding. "If they're in the airport, we'll kill them there," he said in a video clip that sealed his tough-guy image. "And excuse me, but if we find them in the toilet, we'll exterminate them in their outhouses."

That was the public's first taste of his now infamous prison-inflected slang, which won huge approval in a society humiliated by losing its first war in the tiny region on its southern border. As an incisive political analyst named Vladimir Pribylovsky told me, the bombings "changed the situation" by enabling Putin to present himself as a decisive man of action. "Two things brought about his victory: the bombings and the phrase about wiping out terrorists in the outhouse."

Serious questions surfaced from the start, including why bulldozers cleared most of the debris mere days after the bombings, far too soon to allow anything like proper investigations. Then a mysterious episode directed attention toward the FSB. It began late on a September night, when residents of an apartment block in the city of Ryazan, in central Russia, noticed a suspicious-looking car parked near a basement door. They informed the police, who discovered large bags of white powder connected to a detonator in the basement, its timer set to go off early the following morning.

The police said tests showed the powder was hexogen, a World War II–era explosive that had been used in the Moscow explosions. Although the local authorities announced they'd narrowly averted another blast, just as they were about to make arrests two days later, FSB chief Nikolai Patrushev appeared on national television to report that the sacks actually contained only sugar. Patrushev said they'd been used as part of a safety drill, and the FSB quickly cleared the basement of all remaining evidence.

When the authorities refused to investigate the bombings further, a band of liberal legislators formed their own independent committee. Twelve months later, in April 2003, its vice chairman, a prominent Kremlin critic named Sergei Yushenkov, was gunned down outside his Moscow apartment. Before his death, he told me the committee's findings pointed toward the security services. "These special forces, which have giant opportunities and secrets, can manipulate public opinion and direct the course of events using all kinds of illegal methods at their discretion," he said.

Mikhail Trepashkin, a lawyer representing two sisters whose mother died in one of the Moscow explosions, began his own probe. I had a long talk with Trepashkin shortly after his release from four years in prison—punishment, he said, for investigating the crime too closely. Gregarious and disheveled, the seasoned former KGB counterterrorism investigator displayed what seemed to be a photographic memory for names, dates and times as he described a complicated network of individuals and groups connecting politicians, police, security forces and criminals.

Trepashkin had been fired from the FSB in 1995 after helping catch high-ranking military officers in Moscow selling weapons to Chechen rebels, their ostensible enemies. (A rocket grenade fired at the US embassy during the bitter protests against NATO's bombing of Yugoslavia in 1999 was later traced to the cache.) Three years later, he took part in a now legendary news conference alleging that rogue FSB death squads had put him and Boris Berezovsky—who was still a Kremlin power broker and Putin patron—on a hit list. Among the security service officers also participating in the briefing was Alexander Litvinenko, who would be fatally poisoned in 2006 by a radioactive substance in London, where he was living in exile. Litvinenko's supporters say he was killed because he, like Trepashkin, had accused the FSB of criminal activities, including responsibility for the apartment bombings. Roman Shleinov, then the head of investigative reporting at *Novaya Gazeta*, later told me he believed Litvinenko's killing was ideologically motivated. "He would often call us from London with tips that never led anywhere," he told me. "He had no worthwhile information. He just represented the tragedy of an ordinary person caught between opposing groups."

Trepashkin said it was ironic that Putin is believed to have helped organize the news conference in 1998, when he was still an unknown presidential administration official. His goal was to assist in sidelining rivals who stood in the way of his promotion to FSB chief in July of that year. Litvinenko had recently appeared in an extraordinary videotape in which he claimed his FSB bosses ordered him to beat Trepashkin, who had sued the agency over his dismissal. "I was to plant weapons on him or even kill him because he knew something they were frightened he'd publicize," he said. In the video, Litvinenko claimed his bosses were acting on their own, and that he was risking his life by speaking out against them. "If these people aren't stopped now," he warned, "this lawlessness will swallow the entire country." Trepashkin said that after Litvinenko fled to London, he was approached with an offer to clear his own record by agreeing to spy on Litvinenko there.

Trepashkin also echoed widespread opinion that the official confusion over the Ryazan incident was evidence that the FSB indeed organized the operation—not as a counterterrorism exercise but to blow up the building. Many also believe that Putin, who headed the FSB until August 1999, surely knew about the plot.

Trepashkin claimed to have found ample evidence contradicting the official version of events but was prevented from presenting it in court after police stopped his car shortly before his case was to begin. "They searched it twice and found nothing," he explained. "But as they were closing the door, they threw in a bag containing a pistol. I said it wasn't mine, but there was nothing I could do." Arrested on a charge of illegal possession of firearms, he says he was promised it would be dropped if he stopped investigating the apartment bombings. He was eventually sentenced to four years in prison. Tortured and held in filthy, cold Siberian cells—conditions he said seriously affected his health—Trepashkin called the judges who convicted him "bandits" for upholding clearly fabricated charges. They did so "only because, as I was told, the order came from up high." It showed Putin's regime "was based on a team that showed loyalty only to him, above the law." Although six Muslims from southern Russia, none of them Chechens, were eventually sentenced in connection with the 1999 bombings, the case remains unsolved a decade and a half later.

The details that later emerged about the apartment bombings were unknown when Putin first took power. Nevertheless, the nature of his leadership was already crystal clear to those who cared to examine the record. His first weeks and months in office were a great personal disappointment to me because his every action seemed to reverse the gains of the 1990s and encourage society's basest inclinations toward nationalism and lawbreaking. It was also frustrating that few foreigners saw his presidency that way until many years later.

My mother's first conscious sense of the official deception that has played a key role in Russian history came when she was thirteen years old. Arriving at school one morning, she noticed a group of boys using more than their usual amount of determination to pelt each other with crumpled pieces of paper. Unfolding one, she was taken aback to see Stalin's portrait. It was 1956, shortly after Khrushchev delivered a momentous unpublicized "secret speech" at the Twentieth Party Congress in which he denounced Stalin as a brutal murderer and blamed his cult of personality for crippling the Soviet Union with fear. The tyrant's portraits were soon taken down around the country, propaganda was softened and those who were bold enough went so far as to begin criticizing some aspects of their lives under communism.

The thaw coincided with Tatyana's growing rebelliousness. Responding to Serafima's doting and caution by doing or trying to do whatever she was told not to, she also skipped class and sometimes paralyzed her mother with fear by disappearing from their little room for days without warning. Tatyana's independence fed her contempt for Soviet strictures and deprivation. "She protested by the way she lived her life," her cousin Gera Kiva recalled. When he swallowed his nervousness and decided to attend one of the international exhibitions that began appearing in late 1950s, he spotted her having her hair styled in a replica of a French hairdresser's salon. She pretended not to see him, he said, because "she'd taken herself to the West."

Blossoming at the age of sixteen, Tatyana, with her dark beauty, began attracting a flood of admirers, including, briefly, the Soviet hockey champion Stanislav Petukhov as well as my future father. Although she maintained contact with him after the American exhibition in 1959, their romance had cooled by the time he returned to Moscow for graduate study in 1961, and they drifted apart. Settling on studying foreign literature, she enrolled at the prestigious Moscow State Pedagogical Institute for Foreign Languages, housed in a sprawling neoclassical building across the river from Gorky Park.

Studying English emboldened her to frequent some of the city's fanciest cafés, of which there were extremely few, such as those in the Art Nouveau–style Metropol and National hotels, off Red Square. Since meeting foreigners there was exciting but risky—or exciting *because* it was risky—she wore handmade clothes that weren't easily identifiable as Soviet and made certain never to speak Russian. However, she forgot her cardinal rule one evening when talking to a classmate in the Metropol lobby. A large woman in a drab gray suit materialized and grabbed her arm. *"Devushka!"* ("Girl," a standard form of address), she growled. "Come with me!"

After leading Tatyana along a corridor and into a dimly lit room containing a table and several chairs, she proceeded to grill her. "What are you doing here? Whom are you meeting?" Recovering from her shock, Tatyana felt queasy from a sinking feeling that the KGB would open a file on her, ending her carefree life. "Who do you think you are?!" the woman barked, clearly taking Tatyana for a prostitute, thanks to her unusual clothes and foreign boots, a gift from a well-connected suitor. She fixed her stare on Tatyana's pillbox hat. "And where did you get *that?!*"

"It's Soviet!" Tatyana protested, the only thing she could think of to say as the woman snatched it away. To her great good fortune, the hat *was* Soviet-made, which embarrassed the woman. *"Khorosho"* ("okay"), she said with a sigh. "Now, tell me what you're doing here." Tatyana's luck extended to having remembered to carry her student identification. Many of her classmates who were studying to be interpreters were also being groomed to spy on foreigners, and her interrogator either took her for an agent or decided not to risk finding out because her manner suddenly transformed. "I'm sorry, my dear one!" she said in apology. "Let's forget all about this." Tatyana knew that getting off so lightly would have been impossible a few years earlier.

Immersion in literature soon began transforming her from an impetuous party girl into a resolute young woman with intellectual ambitions. After meeting a young painter named Yuri Kuperman in the National Hotel's café, she fell in with a group of artists and other bohemian types. Most of the painters supported themselves illustrating books, but some—including Kuperman and his friend Ilya Kabakov, who would become Russia's best-known conceptualist—were experimenting on their own, often starting by imitating pictures of Western art brought by visiting foreigners.

Although Tatyana rarely saw George—who eventually settled in London and made reporting trips from there to Moscow—they came to share mutual friends. Among them was Sergei Milovsky, the skillful Moscow lawyer whose unrivaled connections and sparkling charisma enabled him to live a highly atypical life as a kind of Soviet playboy. Not that one would have been able to tell by his appearance: there was nothing particularly distinctive about the middle-aged man with close-cropped graying hair. Milovsky's epiphany had come during his service as a young conscript in the bitter Winter War with Finland in 1939–40, when Soviet forces attacking with three times as many men and a hundredfold more tanks were repelled by the far better equipped and trained Finns. Crack Finnish snipers picked off Soviet soldiers with frightening ease, often on open territory because the Red Army's generals relied on their ability to sustain heavy losses as a favored tactic for overwhelming the enemy. Many who weren't killed froze to death during that exceptionally frigid winter because they lacked tents.

Desperately cold and exhausted one especially freezing night in the open, Milovsky battled sleep for fear he would die and wondered why Soviet soldiers were kept in the dark about their every move. Envying the vilified enemy's soldiers, glimpses of whom showed them to be far better dressed and equipped, he decided the war was a monstrous error that exposed the huge lie that life in the USSR was better.

Returning to civilian life, the natural charmer became expert in dispensing and soliciting favors and built a list of acquaintances that came to include privileged diplomats, journalists, actors and children of high-ranking Communist Party officials. Among them was a son of Anastas Mikoyan—a Party leader and close cohort of Stalin before becoming an important supporter of Khrushchev's thaw—who brought Danish cheeses and salami to Milovsky's legendary parties, which attracted legions of women bored by the monotony of their lives. Many came to him for help and advice, with which Milovsky was unstinting. It was thanks to him that Tatyana and George eventually reconnected and married a decade after their first meeting.

––––––

Milovsky was a shining example of someone who could work the system, an activity in which almost every Soviet engaged. Such schemes, in which unofficial networks are paramount, have required maintaining elaborate fictions, especially about the country's leaders—a pattern set far before the seventy years of Soviet rule.

In medieval Muscovy, noble families whose wealth and power were sustained by the idea of a divinely appointed tsar wielding absolute power were disinclined to "leak" information to outsiders.[12] The old adage "Don't carry garbage out of the hut" helps explain why foreigners, who often found Russians' activities puzzling, tended to attribute their behavior to their uniqueness and inscrutability. The absence of genuine evidence about the inner workings of Russian politics also fueled speculation and propaganda.

Ivan IV's reputation as "the Terrible" was enhanced by foreign visitors not privy to the clan struggles behind the facade of his absolute rule. One of the main sources of information was an English merchant named Jerome Horsey, who became Queen Elizabeth I's envoy to Moscow. Describing Ivan's sacking of the independent principality of Novgorod—secondhand information at best—Horsey wrote that his cruelty bred intense hatred and inspired many plots to kill him. Sniffing them out, Ivan proceeded to "ransacke and spoill and massacre the chieff nobillitie and richest officers, and other the best sortt of his merchants and subiects; his hands and hart, now so hardened and imbrued, did put many of them to most horrable and shamfull deaths and tortors."[13]

Such accounts fed a myth that probably developed after the accession of the first Romanov, Mikhail I. Seeking to reinforce the legitimacy of a weak ruler whose family hadn't been among the most powerful, its supporters encouraged an account of Ivan's reign as divided into two stages. During the first, he built up the principality under the influence of a wise tsarina, Anastasia. According to the conventional wisdom, her early death sent him into a deep depression that led to madness and earned him the moniker *grozny*—which is actually best translated as "fierce," not "terrible." Anastasia, of course, was a Romanov.

The foreign stereotypes reinforced domestic fictions. Russians "imitated European historical reasoning for the same reason that they imitated wigs and portrait painting and ballet," Edward Keenan argued. "Because their own was, or seemed to them to be, somehow deficient. In particular they acquired, and developed, an obsession with the juxtaposition of native and foreign culture that has distorted their perception of both."[14] In the nineteenth century, Keenan added, Russians developed "more complex forms of rejection of the European treatment of history," including the idea of the Russian "soul," which foreigners were deemed unable to understand. So it went and so it goes.

———

Despite the appearance of his great personal authority, however, Putin's ability to govern in the Western sense—to institute structural economic reforms that would help wean Russia from its dependence on natural resources, establish a rule of law, rebuild infrastructures and generally act in the interests of the state and its people—is feeble at best. Outside Moscow, regional leaders govern their provinces largely as they see fit, acting with impunity as long as they remain loyal to the Kremlin. In that sense, the Russian state is weak because the center has little leverage beyond its administrative coercion and is rarely serious about doing more than that. However, as the gap between Putin's promises and reality has widened, maintaining the central fiction of his all-powerful rule has become a growing challenge.

It was still relatively easy in 2007, when Putin's United Russia Party won more than 70 percent of the vote in parliamentary elections. (Some regions, such as Chechnya, gave the party the old Soviet-era 99 percent.) Although independent monitors reported systematic abuses—including harassment of opposition campaigners, stuffing of ballots and forced voting—very few voters seemed to care. Young Russians, including some I interviewed at a popular industrial-looking hangout for Moscow's artsy young crowd, told me they weren't concerned about the lack of democracy. "Russia is stable and on the right path," a museum curator named Katya Kaytushina told me. "Anyway, I'm not really interested in politics." A few tables away, an eighteen-year-old student named Alexei Aksandrov said he'd voted for United Russia. "I was a little concerned about the cult of personality being built around Putin," he admitted. "But I like the president's course. I mean, he looks good on television, and he's respected. Maybe there is a dictatorship in Russia, but I'm not worried about it."

The mood was very different at a roundtable discussion across town between some embattled Kremlin critics. Among the morose participants was the veteran corruption expert Georgy Satarov, who said he'd come to the conclusion that society was afraid to voice, or vote for, its own interests. "Russian public opinion no longer exists," he declared. "People vote how they're expected to. They say what they believe they're expected to say."

Medvedev's nomination to succeed Putin hinted at how little the prime minister's ascent would change the status quo. The president formally appointed the successor he had personally groomed after receiving the heads of four political parties, all essentially pro-Kremlin, in his office so they could unveil "their" unanimous choice. Saying that their pick of Medvedev represented the opinion of a wide variety of Russians wasn't simple hypocrisy. The imitation of democracy was central to Putin's maintaining power. Since no observer could have believed it was legitimate, the importance lay in the display. As he prepared to leave office in 2008, he took part in more of the publicity stunts for which he was widely ridiculed abroad: riding horseback shirtless, flying in fighter jets, shooting wild leopards with tranquilizers. They helped burnish the perception of his personal authority that would be crucial for maintaining power. When he stepped down, an astounding 80-plus percent of the population said he'd done a good job.

From the beginning, the cruder his persona became, the tighter was his connection to the conservative majority on whom he increasingly depended. During a 2002 news conference in Brussels, he responded to a reporter's critical question about Chechnya by inviting him to come to Moscow to be circumcised. Later, he dismissed newspaper reports about him as gossip "picked out of someone's nose and smeared onto little bits of paper." Rude as such outbursts appeared to foreigners, and even to many Russians, they were popular. When I attended several annual Kremlin news conferences for more than a thousand reporters crammed into a Kremlin auditorium, Putin owned the room, keeping the increasingly weary journalists fixated for hours by alternating between threats, jokes and flirtation.

Natalia Muraviova, the rector of Moscow's Academy of Communications and Information, sees such performances as coming from a highly talented actor. "He uses a lot of repetition that builds to a crescendo," she told me. "And his widely reported aphorisms are like gems. They're few and far between, and everyone remembers them." Muraviova praised Putin's speechwriters for enabling him to connect emotionally with his supporters by using images to support his statements. "He understands how language is used," she said, "and does it very consciously."

Putin's skills have enabled him to play the part of political pundit in addition to his other roles. Inevitably, after corruption scandals and airline and other disasters that reflect very poorly on government oversight have come to light during his many years as leader, he has appeared on television dressing down one or another minister, or all of them, as if he himself had had nothing to do with the failures. Doing so has helped presumably outraged viewers to identify with him as well as place him within the traditional image of Russia's rulers: "good tsar, bad boyars." That is, the leader's beneficent intentions are undone by the self-interested maneuverings of his crafty advisers.

In 2011, however, after more than three years as prime minister, Putin's pumped-up persona began deflating. An archaeological diving excursion from which he emerged holding antique vases obviously planted earlier appeared ludicrous, as did later missteps. To make matters worse, his stern but relatively youthful visage, one of his biggest assets, seemed to be aging—paradoxically the result of Botox injections, many believed. Dorian Gray–like, his face took on an artificial-looking, impassive gloss reminiscent of a well-fed but declining dictator. When he appeared at a martial arts fighting match, an audience that would normally have been expected to support him booed. New accusations that he was out of touch, living in a bubble surrounded by sycophantic advisers, dented his authority.

Putin didn't stand idly by. After opposition leaders scored a rare coup by rebranding United Russia with Navalny's slogan—the party of "crooks and thieves"—he promptly launched a new vehicle called the Popular Front that all manner of organizations and celebrities were strong-armed into joining. The language of military mobilization extended to a newly manufactured social-networking group called Putin's Army that juxtaposed the martial symbolism with sex by producing bizarre Internet videos of buxom young women preparing to rip open their tank tops and staged events with models in bikinis washing cars "for Putin."

Their hero nevertheless continued compounding his public relations blunders by bungling the announcement that he would run for a third term as president. The widely expected announcement came during a televised United Russia conference, during which Medvedev humiliated himself by announcing he would step down. Then Putin declared that the two of them had agreed on the decision years earlier. It was a watershed moment. Its level of cynicism insulted ordinary Russians who had previously played along with the facade of democracy. Even though United Russia won 20 percent less of the vote in parliamentary elections that December than it did in 2007, tens of thousands of protesters who weren't willing to ignore the blatant rigging this time around took to the streets holding white ribbons, mimicking the "color revolutions" that had recently overthrown old administrations in Georgia and Ukraine.

Nothing if not consistent, Putin responded by taking another page from his old playbook, insulting the protesters by saying he thought the white ribbons were condoms. Maintaining that only he could steer his country through the shoals of anarchy and stagnation, he dismissed opposition leaders' wise decision to advocate clear steps toward gradual reform through fair elections and other measures that would reintroduce political competition, characterizing the call as an urge for revolution, a "constantly recurring problem in Russian history."

He proceeded to use much of his political toolbox to try to discredit, disorient and undermine the opposition. President Medvedev, paying condescending lip service to the opposition's demands, was trotted out to issue another call for easing restrictions against political parties. That served only to draw attention to his central dilemma: crack down and risk bigger demonstrations or ease up and undermine the carefully cultivated perception of authoritarian dominance. The discerning political columnist Yulia Latynina pointed out that Putin's apparent belief that concessions to public opinion displayed weakness meant "you actually do show weakness when you compromise, something the public perceives just like a shark senses the blood of a wounded fish."[15] Putin nevertheless won reelection in March of 2012 with more than 60 percent of the vote amid a huge police presence on the streets. Protests continued but were greatly diminished.

Still, reaction to the two elections showed that civil society continued to display some vital signs after a decade of steady decline. It also showed fixing elections to be Putin's main challenge. Almost thirty thousand people turned up at polling stations to observe the presidential vote. They were joined by formerly compliant politicians, television personalities, journalists and activists, who blogged and tweeted about many instances of fraud, especially schemes to bus factory workers and provincial residents from one voting station to another so they could cast multiple ballots. For once, a small grassroots opposition raised the prospect, however distant, of a struggle for the country's future.

The Kremlin's concessions were largely for show. One of Medvedev's electoral reforms, the return of direct gubernatorial elections—which Putin abolished in 2005—allowed the president to hold "consultations" with candidates and regional lawmakers to ban independents from running, which virtually neutralized the measure. A new law effectively rescinded it altogether in 2013 by allowing each region to revert to Kremlin appointments. However, another change, which lowered the number of signatures required for new parties to qualify for registration (it used to be forty thousand; now it's five hundred), gave hope by easing a rule previously used to sideline rival political groups. As opposition leaders scrambled to form new parties and alliances, jailed oligarch Khodorkovsky praised it as a "step forward, which could change something in Russia, but most important possibly become the main catalyst for a change of political generations."[16]

The Kremlin undoubtedly hoped the reform would facilitate the rise of multiple new parties that would further fragment the already eviscerated opposition. However, the opposition hoped it would help institutionalize the nascent protest movement by allowing new groups to take part in regional elections in the fall. Among the promising developments was the merger of the liberal Republican Party—led by the dynamic young former legislator Vladimir Ryzhkov—with Boris Nemtsov's Parnas movement, which took place after the government allowed the former to register for elections. In the end, the authorities made the next regional elections irrelevant by stepping up efforts to strong-arm, cajole and undermine opposition candidates back to the political margins. After pro-Kremlin candidates swept to victory in voting that opposition leaders said was rigged, Putin declared that the results confirmed he was pursuing the right course.

Faced with the need to transform his regime to ensure its long-term survival, he instead resorted to the old tactic of superficial reappointments and nominal changes. Soon after his election, he resigned his chairmanship of United Russia, a party he never formally joined—a clear symbol of his disdain for any institution that would constrain his power, even one whose real raison d'être was to support him. "The president is a consolidating figure for all political forces, for all citizens," he explained. Medvedev—also not a party member at the time, despite having headed its voting list in parliamentary elections—took his place.

Dmitri Travin, a keen political commentator from St. Petersburg, stressed that United Russia wasn't a real party. He compared it to the Soviet-era *nomenklatura*, which he said did nothing to try to preserve communism when it collapsed. "The *nomenklatura* used its privileges to privatize part of the state enterprises, and to make big money doing so, rather than save the USSR. In other words," he wrote, "the *nomenklatura* lived well in

Soviet times under a totalitarian system and exploited the crisis to make sure it was well set up in the new, market-economy Russia...United Russia is doing exactly the same."[17] Were Putin's regime to collapse, Travin concluded, "these people wouldn't lift a finger to preserve it: they would prefer to go into business (or even to go and live in the West) with the capital they are busy accumulating through corrupt practices."

Putin has since continued tweaking electoral rules while setting about compensating for United Russia's declining popularity by turning to his Popular Front, which developed into an official mass organization directly subordinate to him. The Kremlin fought back in other ways that reflect the dirty nature of politics in a state headed by a former KGB officer, including on the Internet. While the government backed friendly news sites, the notorious Kremlin youth group Nashi deployed online "trolls"—abusive comments—and bombarded Internet sites with distributed denial-of-service attacks that temporarily shut down critical media sites. As noted earlier, compromising videos appeared on the Internet along with transcripts of hacked telephone conversations and private e-mails from the accounts of Alexei Navalny and other opposition figures. Many of the transcripts appeared on the pro-Kremlin tabloid site Lifenews.ru.

The authorities' attempts to discredit the opposition by manipulating Internet sites have often backfired, however. When bloggers noticed that a photo of Navalny had apparently been doctored by a newspaper to make it appear as though he were standing alongside the Kremlin's archenemy Berezovsky, an outpouring of online ridicule compared the tactic to clumsy Soviet propaganda.

Some of the practices came to light in 2012, when hackers calling themselves the Russian wing of the Internet hacker group Anonymous posted their own trove of e-mails from accounts they said belonged to Nashi's overseers. Many of the messages appeared to be from the head of the Federal Youth Agency, Vassily Yakemenko, and its spokeswoman. They were shown directing journalists and bloggers to extol Putin's popularity and attack his critics. The e-mails describe price lists and payments and discuss schemes to file hundreds of comments on websites and create a video cartoon comparing Navalny to Hitler. Yakemenko stepped down soon afterward to found a new political party he promised would attract young "creative or middle-class" people because the old generation, "whose thinking remains weighed down with ideas from Soviet times, must be squeezed out of the ruling elite."[18] After that especially transparent attempt to co-opt opposition-party supporters failed, he opened a café.[19]

But even those who found Yakemenko laughable were deeply troubled by the Kremlin's renewed crackdown on protesters. Putin took the oath of office in May, virtually snarling his words in a lavish coronation-like Kremlin ceremony after police emptied roads and swept the city center for protesters. Some, including Nemtsov, were beaten and arrested in a popular opposition hangout, a French café called Jean Jacques. Nemtsov said the empty streets exposed Putin's fear of his own people. "This is not how you celebrate a holiday," he scoffed. "This is how you celebrate seizing power."[20]

As the opposition settled into what has become a long-term struggle, demonstrators took to playing cat and mouse with police by staging impromptu rallies and "promenades" around the capital. Parliament, where a handful of critics displayed symbolic stirrings of dissent against the pro-Kremlin majority, proceeded to take action. Fines and other penalties for protesters accused of violating public order are now almost ten thousand dollars, or sixty times what they used to be. The following month, legislators passed a series of bills restricting civil society, free speech and launching what appeared to be an opening salvo against Internet freedom. NGOs that receive funding from abroad are now required to declare themselves "foreign agents," a term clearly meant to associate them with espionage.

Soon afterward, Putin appeared to signal yet another campaign against NGOs in a speech that ordered the FSB to boost scrutiny of such groups—which he accused of "putting pressure on Russia." Many had refused to register as foreign agents. Teams of officials from departments ranging from the tax police to fire inspectors soon began harassing human rights groups, charities and even the offices of foreign think tanks with raids and audits. Golos—which threatened the authorities as no other group did because it was the country's only independent election monitoring agency—became the first to be charged under the new law and fined ten thousand dollars.

The Investigative Committee—the group set up by Putin and headed by his close former KGB crony Alexander Bastrykin—took the lead role in the crackdown. Russians had been shown a glimpse of Bastrykin's character during his clash with a newspaper editor in 2012. Angered by an article in the crusading investigative paper *Novaya Gazeta* that called him and Putin "servants" of organized criminal groups, Bastrykin had the journalist driven to a forest outside Moscow. There he ordered his own bodyguards to

leave, and—the newspaper later reported—threatened to cut off the journalist's head and legs. Then he joked that he would investigate the murder himself. A public outcry forced Bastrykin to apologize, but no censure
followed.

Soon afterward, on the day before a mass protest in June, Investigative
Committee officers raided the homes of not only Navalny but also Ksenia
Sobchak, a TV host turned protester and Russia's chief "it girl," as well as
other opposition leaders and their families. "I never thought we'd return to
such repression in this country," Sobchak tweeted.

In October, the Investigative Committee placed another young opposition leader, the outspoken leftist Sergei Udaltsov, under house arrest on
charges of plotting a violent uprising after investigators escorted by masked
commandos searched his apartment for more than five hours. The authorities later charged him with the more serious indictment of "staging" riots.
His trademark dark sunglasses, austere military-style jackets and many
arrests for dogged protesting had burnished his reputation as a brave young
radical. Now state television aired a documentary alleging he was plotting
a violent uprising against the government with the help of an exiled banker
and Chechen militants. The film included blurred footage, allegedly taken
by a hidden camera, that recorded him plotting a coup in Russia with a
Georgian member of parliament. Later, a member of his Left Front movement who criticized the authorities before trying to apply to the UN for
political refugee status in Ukraine was kidnapped from a Kiev street by
masked men and sent to jail in Siberia.

Another dissident whose work as a rocket engineer gave the FSB even
more reason to suspect him hanged himself in a holding cell in the Nether-
lands after the authorities there rejected his asylum application. His death
brought attention to a growing list of Kremlin critics, many of them minor,
previously unheard-of figures, who have had difficulties seeking refuge
abroad.

Navalny, however, refused to flee, even after it became clear he would
be tried on the on-again, off-again embezzlement charges against him that
were revived after he embarrassed the Investigative Committee's Bastrykin
by disclosing that he secretly owned property in the Czech Republic, then
further angered the Kremlin by attending an unsanctioned rally in front of
Lubyanka, the FSB headquarters. Accused of stealing around five hundred
thousand dollars' worth of timber from a state-controlled firm in 2009

while serving as an adviser to the governor of the Kirov region, northeast of Moscow, he went on trial in April 2013. Navalny dismissed the accusation against him—one of four, and the first to reach the trial stage—as an attempt to silence his criticism, and he declared he wanted to run for president.

His trial was a first of such a prominent opposition leader. The case against him was based largely on the testimony of one of his alleged conspirators, who worked with the prosecutors. During the trial, the man provided contradictory evidence, and the judge refused to allow Navalny's lawyers to cross-examine him. The defense was also blocked from calling a dozen witnesses. The judge found Navalny—who spent most of the trial blogging and tweeting—guilty and sentenced him to five years in prison. However, he was unexpectedly released on bail after the verdict prompted angry protests in Moscow and other cities.

Navalny had already begun campaigning for Moscow's first relatively free mayoral election in almost a decade. His release prompted speculation about whether it represented a small breath of democracy, a split within the ruling elite, or an attempt to bestow legitimacy on the vote. Although the unbeatable incumbent, the dour Putin ally Sergei Sobyanin, clearly wanted the legitimacy of a clean vote, the Kremlin's main motives probably included the desire to keep outsiders confused about the extent of Putin's authoritarianism: The speculation distracted from the inevitability of Sobyanin's victory.

Navalny proceeded to cement his image as Putin's main rival by mounting an energetic, Western-style grassroots campaign in which he addressed voters on stages and streets across the capital. After he won an astounding 27 percent of the vote—losing to Sobyanin's 51 percent—a judge suspended his five-year sentence. More than to appear unpredictable, that decision also reflected Putin's longtime strategy of backing off when his actions appear highly unpopular. In that case, the Kremlin probably saw more repression as less productive than freeing Navalny. His conviction bars him from running for office again, and the threat that the authorities can drag him back to jail at any time still hangs over his head.

Whether or not he remains free, the charges against him were so flimsy that they appeared to signify a return to Soviet-style justice against political opponents, demonstratively showing that the facts matter far less than the state's determination to eliminate its critics. Still, the authorities had launched the proceedings only when few were inclined to object. By early 2013, much of the blog traffic and op-ed discussion about the protest movement concerned the disillusionment that had set in among opposition supporters and the moral crisis among its leaders. The hounding of a prominent economist cemented the sense of hoplessness. Sergei Guriev, the well-connected rector of the leading New Economic School and board member of Russia's largest consumer bank, was a key supporter of some of then-President Medvedev's highest-profile projects. After he annnouncd he'd donated money to Navalny, however, the Investigative Committee repeatedly interrogated him about his contribution to a report criticizing Khodorkovsky's prosecution years earlier. After fleeing to Paris, where his family lived, he said he feared arrest.

The pro-Kremlin analyst Sergei Markov appeared to make the government's case when he went so far as to allege that the New Economic School is a tool for "the Western political and economic elite to exert its influence on Russia's ruling circles ... Sergei Guriev was the intellectual center of that group that developed and implemented a project to replace Putin with a more easily controlled politician."[21] Like similar Soviet-era attacks, they hid deeper political motives: impugning Guriev was a way for hostile clans to assert themselves and weaken Medvedev.

Although such measures to stifle displays of public dissatisfaction blunted the movement, they have also added fuel to its fire, which will burn as long as Kremlin critics are prevented from expressing their views. What kind of country the new-old president ultimately bequeaths will partly depend on how far he is willing to go to cement his legacy. Even if he steps down at the end of his current term in 2018, no doubt he will seek to install a loyal successor to guarantee his security, as he did Yeltsin's.

Rumors about possible replacements are a staple in Moscow. Among the top candidates, in theory, are Moscow Mayor Sobyanin—a former Putin chief of staff—and a nationalist deputy prime minister named Dmitri Rogozin. Both have been singled out as possible compromise figures who may appeal to enough political clans to assume the president's role of arbiter. Insiders believe the engineering of Medvedev's election in 2008— when the clan wars first emerged in public—will provide the model for the second succession.

No development can be ruled out, however. One observer who compares Putin's system to Fascist regimes believes it shares their brittleness partly because leaders' cults become unsustainable as they grow old and decrepit.[22] Infighting between fragmented elites and a growing refusal among the educated, young and middle class to submit to unconditional authority and humiliation also contribute to the serious risk of breakdown, a possibility that will no doubt increasingly beset the authorities. Putin's health became a concern when he skipped a number of scheduled events in late 2012 after having been photographed grimacing at a conference and clutching his chair. After denying anything was the matter, the Kremlin said he'd hurt his back practicing judo.

Putin soon returned and if he remains healthy, the critical question for Russia's future will probably be whether his political system can consolidate by uniting the competing political clans following the transfer of his personal power when he finally steps down. Among those who have stacked government agencies with his protégés, Sergei Ivanov—a steely former KGB general who lost to Medvedev as Putin's pick for president in 2008—has since regrouped and made inroads against his rivals. Meanwhile, some opposition leaders hope that emboldening disaffected voters to reject Putin will enable them to convince the rich and powerful that their positions would be more secure under a more moderate leader. A recent Levada Center poll showed a solid majority still supports Putin—who has said he hasn't ruled out running for a fourth term in 2018. But it also showed a growing number of Russians believe he represents only the narrow interests of those in power.

Whatever happens, the real battle for the country's future will require more than merely installing a new group in power. It will mean addressing the old behavior Putin did so much to reinforce in so many facets of life. Conventional wisdom long held that his great popularity rested on a tacit social contract: as long as booming oil prices buoyed living standards, most Russians were willing to close their eyes to authoritarianism. But the uncomfortable reality is that at least half of what is called the middle class, that great hope for Russia's future, consists of government officials. More than that, even progressive-seeming professionals and entrepreneurs who admit to preferring life in the West nevertheless profit from the abuses of office that have crippled major institutions at home. They may not want real reform. "These people who dine, dress and holiday well want the quality in Russia's political kitchen to correspond to that of [restaurateur Arkady] Novikov's [fancy] restaurants," Yulia Latynina wrote during the height of the protests in 2011. "Their problem with the authorities is aesthetic: they don't want to go out for oysters then have to come home to last century's spoiled gruel."

One of the main prerequisites for genuine reform is overhauling the institutions Putin's crony establishment has done much to undermine, not least of which is the legal system. In the early 1990s, when laws were in flux, White and Case's John Erickson represented several Russian companies along with his Western clients. Among them, the Salyut Design Bureau, a former Soviet agency that oversaw satellite launches into space, sought Erickson out when a foreign investment bank attempted to overcharge it for advisory work. Such fairly common behavior, which reinforced the going view of capitalism as a predatory activity, appalled Erickson, who was therefore gratified to witness Western executives occasionally learning lessons about how business was conducted in Russia.

Describing a typical deal in those days, Erickson told me that important meetings with CEOs and their lawyers would often begin in the standard way, with negotiations about a list of open points. The two sides would settle each by compromise, usually until "about point number seven, when it would be clear from what the Russians were saying that they felt they really hadn't agreed to anything on points one to six."

Even signed contracts remained open to interpretation. "The Russians viewed them not as binding agreements," Erickson said, "but simply guidelines about how they might act in the future. Maybe they'd comply, maybe they wouldn't. Of course they didn't have to care because you really couldn't sue them effectively in the courts." When Erickson drafted Western-style commercial regulations, versions often came back from government offices with roughly 10 percent of the text remaining. "It made me realize very quickly that Russia wasn't America or Germany. It was a different country with its own system, its own way of doing things."

Although the failure to properly overhaul the Soviet legal system has had disastrous consequences under Putin, some successes have been achieved. The introduction of a jury system in 2003 for the first time since the Revolution provided the best hope for fighting widespread corruption in the court system. Statistics show why. While judges presiding over non-jury trials find defendants guilty more than 98 percent of the time, juries have acquitted some 15 percent of defendants.

So when the directors of one of the country's largest cigarette importers were accused of fraud soon after the reform passed, they opted for a jury trial. The lead juror, a soft-spoken deputy director of a small publishing house named Liudmilla Barabanova, told me the prosecutors presented reams of documents during the trial but not a shred of evidence to support their charges. Worse than that, each juror was offered a bribe of as much as five hundred dollars to find the defendants guilty. "We were all very tense," she said. "But we didn't dare complain to the judge because we knew it would be used as a pretext to dismiss us. We had to remain silent to see the trial to its end."

Barabanova and the other jury members came to believe the accusations were false, cooked up by a rival to put the defendant company out of business, and that the prosecutors were playing along. But the jurors had no chance to acquit the defendants: they were sent home three days before they were due to reach a decision. "We were dismissed because we weren't going to reach a guilty verdict," Barabanova said.

The case went to a retrial. The new head juror, Yevgeny Danilov, told me it emerged that the plaintiff company was registered in the United States under a false name, something prosecutors assured the jurors was standard practice. "We understood something was wrong, that documents were being fabricated," Danilov said. "We also realized we had to protect our own integrity, so no one could compromise us." The jurors found themselves sneaking in and out of the courthouse to avoid being trapped into meetings with prosecutors who could later be accused of influencing them. This time the jury persevered in unanimously acquitting the defendants. Unlike American practice, however, Russian law allows acquittals to be appealed, and the prosecutors took their case straight to the Supreme Court, which overturned the not-guilty verdict and ordered another trial.

A young lawyer named Ekaterina Stavitskaya represented the defense during the third trial. Speaking in her small, plain office, she told me such trials were a way to get ahead in business. "Lawsuits have replaced the contract killings of the 1990s as a more humane way to get rid of competitors," she said. In that case, it didn't work: the third jury acquitted the defendants a second time. Later, however, the prosecutors again appealed to the Supreme Court.

After the first trial, its jury members tried to make sense of their experiences by meeting with the defense lawyers. They later realized they were spied on because photographs of them appeared in newspaper articles that accused them of obstructing justice. One paper called the jury members "secret terrorists." The prosecutors appeared on television to denounce some of them as homeless, unemployed and mentally deficient. "I felt like my soul was being spat on," juror Danilov told me.

Critics of the jury system complain that unlike Britain and the United States, Russia is a young, undeveloped democracy whose population can't be expected to make important legal decisions. That was the opinion of the stolid justice minister, Yuri Chaika, who later became prosecutor general. "From the point of view of our society's understanding of the legal system, of the level of our legal culture, it's probably too early to have introduced juries to Russia," he said.

Supporters of the jury system counter that jurors aren't meant to be experts but peers who consider specific issues. A leading legal expert named Sergei Nanosov told me that judges routinely ignore egregious procedural violations to rule in prosecutors' favor. They are kept in line by such a large array of institutional arrangements, including bonus pay doled out by regional officials, that "it's fair to say our legal system is utterly dependent on the state."

A rare Moscow city judge who refused to follow orders became a cause célèbre. Olga Kudeshkina was presiding over a trial against a customs official who had launched criminal proceedings against the owner of the infamous FSB-connected Tri Kita furniture shop, central to the 2007 Kremlin clan battle that prompted the arrest of the drug control agency's Alexander Bulbov. The prosecutor general himself quashed an investigation into the smuggling of four hundred tons of furniture before going on to charge the customs official who initiated the probe with abuse of office. Kudeshkina was fired when she refused to convict him.

When I spoke to her later, the smiling, elaborately coiffed former judge explained that officials called chairmen of the courts, who assign judges to preside over trials, are expected to select loyal people for sensitive cases. A deputy chairwoman had selected her for the furniture trial "by mistake" because the chairman was on holiday.

The authorities essentially control the courts, Kudeshkina said, but "it's much more difficult to do that with juries, so of course the authorities want to get rid of them by saying our citizens aren't ready." Judges' dependence on politicians is so great, she concluded, that apart from cases involving political matters, Soviet practice had generally been fairer and less corrupt. Although Soviet judges were very occasionally fired for unjustified convictions, "that never happens today."

Pro-Kremlin legislators have continued calling for the jury system to be limited to cases not involving national security or hate crimes, something legal experts believe is part of a strategy to chip away at the few surviving remnants of judicial independence.

In many other institutions, the informal patronage system behind the Kremlin's ruling structure has seriously undermined the government's oversight, including in the regions outside Moscow. Besides the Caucasus, perhaps nowhere has that been more visible than the crime-ridden port of Vladivostok on the Pacific coast, where massive smuggling industries enrich officials who help criminal groups spirit illegally caught fish, timber, cars and many other goods in and out of Russia. No profitable business is exempt, a local law professor assured me. For most of Putin's tenure, the region's governor was a square-jawed former used car dealer named Sergei Darkin, who made his fortune selling the secondhand Japanese cars that sustain the local economy. Victor Cherepkov, a former Vladivostok mayor who waged an epic battle against corruption, told me Darkin also became part of a criminal group involved in prostitution, poaching and racketeering. He rose to power after the boss's death, which was made to look like a scuba-diving accident. However, Darkin—who later cemented his position by marrying the millionairess wife of a rival named Igor "the Carp" Karpov after his death from a sniper's bullet—assured me there were no improper connections between business and politics in his region.

Shoring up the Kremlin's role as the ascendant Mafia-type group by appointing such men has also deepened Russia's greatest security threat: instability in the North Caucasus, including Chechnya, which is led by Ramzan Kadyrov, another top tough who used to be a rebel fighter. What's happening there may be an extreme illustration of Moscow's relationship with the provinces, but is instructive because it mirrors the state of affairs across the country.

Russia launched the first military campaigns to conquer the mountainous region on the southern edge of its expanding empire in the mid-1700s.

Organized largely by kinship clans, ethnic groups and language, the fragmented collection of Islamic societies that populated the North Caucasus offered fierce resistance to tsarist troops. By the nineteenth century, Pushkin, Mikhail Lermontov and other poets were romanticizing the dangerous region as a beautiful object of Russian manifest destiny.

Sporadic resistance continued well into the Soviet era, especially in Chechnya, where traditional kinship clans called teips helped keep society together under repression by Stalin, who in 1944 exiled all Chechens to Kazakhstan and elsewhere for allegedly collaborating with the Nazis. By the 1950s, however, popular Soviet comedy films depicted the Caucasus as an exotic tourist destination where communism was modernizing an amusingly backward people. Such patronizing attitudes seem almost quaint today.

Many Russians now associate the Caucasus primarily with horrific television news images of the aftermath of bombings—corpses strewn about Moscow's airports, metro system and streets. The predominant view of the region as little more than a seat of terrorism and poverty is fueling deep suspicion and hatred. In 2012, protesters in the capital began rallying under a banner that read STOP FEEDING THE CAUCASUS, demanding that the government end the funding of a region they saw as irredeemably corrupt.

When I visited Chechnya's capital, Grozny, in 2009 during one of many trips to the region, the city I first saw as a bomb-flattened wasteland four years earlier had been rebuilt with lightning speed. Expensive cars sped down Putin Prospect, a name some acquaintances could not bring themselves to say. Cafés bearing French and Italian names, a sushi restaurant and a branch of a Moscow luxury shopping mall lined the main thoroughfare. Giant posters of the thirty-three-year-old Kadyrov loomed everywhere, and everyone I spoke to on the street recited stock phrases about his greatness. Privately, residents complained bitterly of Kadyrov's rule by fear, enforced by abductions, torture and killings. "We have to live like this, like it or not," a friend named Heda Saratova explained. "We're forced to say things we don't believe." A brave human rights activist, Heda is one of the few people who have continued documenting abuses after the grisly murder of her colleague Natalia Estemirova in 2009.

I'd traveled to Grozny with several fellow journalists on that occasion to interview Kadyrov. Summoned from our threadbare hotel to his heavily fortified compound in the dead of night, we passed a horse-racing track and a man-made pond outside its main entrance. Inside, lions prowled in cages, part of Kadyrov's extensive zoo housing rare animals and birds, and there was a rumor that the complex also contained a prison where he tortured and killed with his own hands. Passing a sleek black Mercedes near the front door—a relatively modest example from Kadyrov's fleet of luxury cars—we stepped into a massive, marble-floored palace lined with ornate columns and luxurious silk wallpaper.

Playing billiards with one of his men, the Chechen president was dressed in slippers and an Armani tracksuit. Although the squat bear of a man with a short beard and the jovial manner of a frat boy had been president for more than two years, he greeted us with a display of bashfulness, as if he were embarrassed by the opulence of his fantasy playground. By the time we sat down, it was 2:00 a.m.

Although Kadyrov shares apparently close personal ties to Putin, he began the first Chechen war as an anti-Moscow rebel and chief bodyguard for his father, Muslim imam Akhmad Kadyrov, a separatist leader who switched sides during Chechnya's second war. The Kremlin later installed the senior Kadyrov as the Chechen leader before his assassination in a bomb blast. Today, the son praises Putin for "wise policies" that kept Chechnya a part of the Russian Federation. "If we would have been given independence, it would have been the end of our people. We would all have died," he said in brusque, heavily accented Russian.

When I asked about Estemirova, whose death a leader of Memorial, the human rights organization that employed her, had blamed on him, Kadyrov accused her of having no honor or shame. Insisting his only concern was for the welfare of ordinary Chechens, he boasted, "I'd lay down my life for my people." True or not, his fealty to Moscow obscures an irony not lost on most Russians: Kadyrov—who advocates strict Islamic codes, including polygamy—effectively governs his region independently of Moscow. His critics wryly note that the young leader has achieved the kind of de facto self-rule that had eluded Chechnya's former separatist leaders by doing what he wants inside the region in exchange for maintaining outward loyalty to the Kremlin.

Kadyrov's brutally enforced pacification of Chechnya has had the effect of spreading violence to neighboring regions. I traveled to the Caucasus again in 2011 to investigate the growing perception that a certain, perhaps managed, level of instability there suited one or more groups among the authorities in Moscow. That time my destination was the currently most volatile region, Dagestan, where I drove to the village of Gimry, a scattering of tin-roofed houses nestled between jagged peaks and accessible only by a narrow dirt road.

Fall arrives late in the green valleys, where the pervading smell of burning leaves is especially strong. You would think the subtropical region, with its abundant possibilities for growing fruit and other crops, along with the locals' reputation for fine craftsmanship, should be booming economically. In fact it's depressed, mired in corruption and seething under the Kremlin's heavy boot. But although most of its population barely ekes out a living, Gimry's deep isolation didn't preclude the enrichment of some residents, including the owner of a large new house where I was invited to lunch. My hosts included the son of the village chief, who drove a fancy Volkswagen Touareg. When we sat in the courtyard over several courses, finishing with sweet grapes from vines hanging overhead, I couldn't know they were half joking among themselves in the local Avar language about the benefits of kidnapping me for ransom. Later the local journalist who escorted me there earnestly told me not to take it personally. "That's their business, you see."

In a province so remote that children speak only Avar and residents use the word *Russia* to describe the country's other regions, not their own, one could be forgiven for forgetting we were in Putin's Russia. But despite its location on the southern fringes of the country's vast landmass, the spread of violence from Chechnya has been a central symbol of rule under a president who has used the threat of terrorism as a main justification for his attack on his country's democratic institutions. Far from the stability he's claimed, however, his policies have encouraged traditional society to tear at the seams.

Gimry's elders described how soldiers had recently sealed off the village during a so-called counterterrorism operation that lasted almost two years. An elderly man with a long white beard named Nabi Magomedov broke down as he described how it began with militants luring his son, a prominent member of the Dagestani parliament, out of his house with a request to talk. They proceeded to shoot him sixty-two times. Chechen rebel leader Doku Umarov later took credit for ordering his death, accusing the younger Magomedov of betraying Islam by participating in politics. But if the ensuing police operation was meant to combat extremism by smoking out separatists among the villagers, it did the opposite. In addition to their daily searches of houses, soldiers had carte blanche to cut down apricot trees for fuel—"Otherwise they'd have frozen," one farmer admitted—and to steal livestock and kill residents.

Villagers said they were protesting by refusing to observe Russian law and adopting Sharia instead—or at least their understanding of it, which included blood feuds and other centuries-old forms of remediation. Many became Salafists, conservative Muslims who denounced the Sufi Islam traditionally practiced in the Caucasus because it is supposedly under state control. On a small plateau above the village, workers were constructing a large madrasah said to be partly financed by "outside" money, perhaps from Saudi Arabia. Some hoped the new institution would replace the village's state school.

Such opposition to rule from Moscow is an old story in Gimry, the birthplace of the Imam Shamil, one of the legendary leaders of resistance to the tsarist empire in the nineteenth century. But the religious radicalization is exacerbating new divisions in a region whose many ethnic groups previously coexisted more or less peacefully. When a budding relationship between a young resident of Gimry and a woman in the neighboring Sufi village of Insukul resulted in a shootout that killed seven people, the conflict was soon perceived as religious in nature. Both villages were girding for revenge when I visited.

In the months that followed, the violence rang alarm bells when gun and bomb attacks killed a number of moderate Sufi leaders, not only in Dagestan but also in other regions previously not known for such violence. The top Muslim official in the Tatarstan region, more than a thousand miles from the North Caucasus, was wounded in a car bomb attack and his deputy was shot dead on the same day. In August 2012, the country's most senior Islamic cleric warned of a looming civil war in Dagestan, which lies several hundred miles from Sochi and the 2014 Winter Olympics. Putin's response was to tell security forces to "outsmart and outmuscle" Islamist militants to ensure security during the games.

However, locals in Gimry also told me the mounting tensions were pointing toward a larger confrontation, which some ominously welcomed as a means of establishing formal independence. It would be led by young men who regularly leave their homes and go "into the forest" to join militant groups performing weekly bombings and shootings.

Outside a ramshackle brick mosque—where young men, some sporting dark beards and military fatigues, gathered for midday prayers—one worshipper named Abu Magomedov, who had served in Chechnya as an FSB officer, told me that killings such as the assassination of Dagestan's interior minister in 2009 were justified as justice and retribution. "I was ordered to kill innocent Muslim boys 'to control their numbers,'" he said of his time in Chechnya. "How am I supposed to take that?"

The anger is helping estrange increasingly radicalized young people from older generations that were made less devout by centuries of loose adherence to Islamic customs even before the suppression of religion under Soviet rule. The effects are sometimes felt beyond Russia's borders, as Americans learned during the Boston Marathon bombing in 2013, when two young Chechen-Avar brothers who had lived in Massachusetts for a decade set off bombs that killed three and wounded more than two hundred fifty people. Evidently grappling with the pressures of belonging to two cultures, the elder, Tamerlan Tsarnaev, began holding increasingly radical Islamist views to the dismay of his father, who separated from his wife and returned to live in Dagestan. Assimilating in the United States must have been especially hard for a family from a highly patriarchal culture of warriors. Although the brothers were almost certainly radicalized in the United States, where they learned about Islam from the Internet and had little if any known connection to militants in Russia, their search for identity was not unlike those of many young men in the Caucasus who express their alienation through violent acts.

Near Gimry, the village of Balakhani was home to a twenty-eight-year-old schoolteacher named Mariam Sharipova, who came to national attention in 2010 as one of two suicide bombers who killed forty people in the Moscow metro. Inside the modest house clinging to a mountainside where Sharipova had lived with her parents, her father, a devout, bearded teacher named Rasul Magomedov, said he couldn't explain why his daughter blew herself up. But he told me the Kremlin encourages such actions by using the threat of terrorism to consolidate its power. "Moscow pours all its blame for everything wrong into the Caucasus, to justify its actions and failures before average working people," he explained.

It was difficult not to be moved by Magomedov's stoic manner. Describing his daughter as a hard worker who had earned a degree in psychology and planned to study for a doctorate, he said the authorities should have

heeded her act as a wake-up call. "Change your attitude toward us Dages-
tanis," he concluded, predicting there will be more such attacks in the
future. "Don't think we're stupid people," he added. Magomedov disappeared without a trace a month later, the apparent victim of a kidnapping.

Three days before I spoke to him, twin explosions killed a police officer and injured sixty civilians outside a liquor shop in Dagestan's capital,
Makhachkala, a hundred miles east on the shore of the Caspian Sea. In a
hospital a short walk from the street's mangled buildings, people wounded
in the blast lay bandaged on cots in a hot, crowded room. Among them
was a young man named Magomed Getinov, who told me he was leaving a
friend's apartment when the blast went off, sending shrapnel into his side.
Although he called the bombers monsters, he blamed the region's massive
unemployment for prompting many young men with little to do to turn
to violence. "They're confused," he told me. "They lose their morals, start
turning into religious extremists and blow up innocent people because they
believe they're going to take over the world."

Despite its poverty, Makhachkala's society is cosmopolitan and open
in comparison to much of the North Caucasus. At a dinner with the gregarious head of the official journalists' union, a veteran political operator
named Ali Kamalov, he raised his first shot of vodka to Allah. A typical
representative of older generations, Kamalov had the benevolent manner of a patriarch from the North Caucasus—part tough guy, part Jewish
mother—and insisted I not leave the table before stuffing myself with at
least three servings of kebabs. He told me the root of the region's problem
was the pervasive corruption choking the economy. Huge funds for developing agriculture, infrastructure and social services were being pilfered by
officials in Moscow and Makhachkala. Some of the money was spent on
luxury cars and an expanding ring of suburban brick houses going up outside the capital. Distributing the Kremlin's largesse enabled the powerful
former Mayor Said Amirov—who is confined to a wheelchair after having
survived more than a dozen assassination attempts—to build a patronage
system so entrenched that when the Kremlin recently decided to oust him
after fifteen years, it sent a team of special-forces commandos in armored
personnel carriers to bundle him onto a helicopter bound for Moscow,
where he faced murder charges. His fate, after having twice earned the
title of best Russian mayor, is reminiscent of powerful Communist Party

bosses such as Uzbekistan's Rashid Rashidov, whom the Kremlin was able to unseat only by using satellites to photograph cotton fields, then estimating how much he was faking production figures.

Across town in an outlying, concrete-block neighborhood, Svetlana Isayeva runs the group Mothers of Dagestan for Human Rights from a tiny ground-floor office. She started the organization after her twenty-five-year-old son disappeared from the street outside her home in 2008. Stoic, dark-haired Isayeva told me many young men detained by security forces had been forced to confess to terrorism, after which some were killed. "Law enforcers burn them alive in their cars," she said. "Then they're accused of blowing themselves up by accident." She said the abductions began taking place regularly when troops were moved to Dagestan from Chechnya in 2007, after the war there wound down. "All that equipment, all those soldiers. What was the military supposed to do?" she said. "They need conflict to continue surviving. That's the only way I can explain it."

Half a day's drive west through Chechnya lies the region of Ingushetia, which is also crippled by corruption and bears the country's highest official unemployment rate, a staggering 57 percent of the able-bodied population. During one of my trips there, in 2011, the threat of violence hung heavily over the dusty main town of Nazran, which was little more than a chaotic crossroads near a market and a bus station. Years of shootings and explosions by Islamist militants convinced most restaurants to close soon after dark, and it was nearly impossible to find alcohol served anywhere. Young people drank tea in a popular café near the market, one of the few such places where I saw women spending leisure time in public. Marina, a quick young medical student who declined to give her last name, told me that although she didn't go out after nightfall, she'd grown inured to violence. "The first time a friend is killed, you grieve for maybe a year or more," she said. "But after twenty times, you get used to death. We hear explosions one day and forget about them the next."

Locals say although only some two hundred militants remain active in the region, the military stokes the conflict because soldiers get extra pay for combat and officers get promotions and special powers to control local life. Moscow-based Memorial still keeps extensive records about human rights abuses in Nazran. In its cramped, bare-bones office there, along a row of shops selling clothes, housing supplies and mobile phones, researcher Abubakar Sechayev told me that many young men disappear because the slightest suspicion of knowing a militant is enough to get them arrested or worse. "A person can be suspected today and easily killed tomorrow, and his house burned down," Sechayev told me. "If the security services had any real proof, they'd go through the courts."

Despite its obvious failure, the Kremlin's Caucasus policy isn't likely to change soon. A recent poll showed that most Russians believe the authorities should undertake harsher measures to fight militants there, such as reviving the death penalty and punishing militants' relatives. During my latest visit, soldiers carrying out a counterterrorist operation in a town near Nazran arrested six suspected militants. The following day, an elderly woman and her daughter told me that "federals"—interior ministry troops—had broken through their front gate and searched their house. When the mother protested, the soldiers' response summed up the Kremlin's attitude. "Shut up, old woman: we do what we want here!"

A canal next to the Hermitage gallery in
St. Petersburg flows into the Neva River.

11

Grandiosity and Bombast

Russian maximalism, hurling us from one extreme to the
other, is a sickness of spirit, a metaphysical hysteria, an
inward slavery.

—Nikolai Berdyaev, 1917

In late 2008, the state television channel Rossiya aired "the project of the
year," a series called *The Name of Russia* that it said would identify
the greatest Russian in history. Over the course of three months, some of
the country's best-known conservative figures appeared weekly on a slick
set to debate their choices in a whittling-down that would culminate in
an online vote. The future Orthodox Church patriarch, Kirill, then still a
bishop, lobbied for the thirteenth-century prince Alexander Nevsky, whose
legendary battlefield victories over Swedish and Germanic knights, the
bishop claimed, had saved Russia from annihilation. Comparing the battles
to Russia's invasion of Georgia that year, Kirill said both military efforts
had signaled the country's rebirth as a great power. Peter the Great and
Lenin also ranked among top candidates, but the loudest controversy was
generated by Internet voting that temporarily pushed another name to the
top of the list. The leader for a time was Joseph Stalin, born Iosif Vissari-
onovich Dzhugashvili.

Although the show's creator, a veteran television personality named
Alexander Liubimov, dismissed the embarrassing development as the
work of computer hackers, the dictator came in third in the final results,
behind the winner, Alexander Nevsky, and the number-two finisher, Piotr

Stolypin, a reforming nineteenth-century prime minister to whom Putin would soon compare himself.

Unfathomable as it may have been to foreigners, and unscientific as the poll was, its outcome coincided with more rigorous surveys that reflect a very sobering trend: more than half a century after his death, a majority of Russians praise Stalin's policies. Dismissing the irony that the tyrant was Georgian, not Russian, a Muscovite in his sixties named Igor Stepanov told me the prime overseer of the Soviet purges and other mass atrocities deserved serious consideration. "Whether the consensus is that he was good or bad for Russia remains to be seen," Stepanov reasoned. "But failing to acknowledge Stalin's role in history wouldn't be right." At the same time, a thirty-four-year-old accountant named Syleia Daripova praised Stalin for his feats. "Not everyone can accumulate power like that," she said. "People say he murdered half the country, but you can't deny he was a unique personality." In 2013, a Levada poll put Brezhnev at the top of a list of "most positive" leaders in the twentieth century, according to 56 percent of respondents. He was closely followed by Lenin and Stalin.

The country's leaders encourage such attitudes. Russian historians conservatively estimate that at least twelve and a half million people died from execution, famine and imprisonment during the seventy years of Soviet rule, although the figure of twenty million is more commonly agreed upon. But that record didn't stop Putin from calling the communist collapse the greatest catastrophe of the twentieth century. Although he was referring to the trauma the event inflicted on ordinary Russians, his carefully chosen words were purposely ambiguous. In heaping praise on his old employer, the KGB—among other exercises in the exploitation of nostalgia for the stable Soviet past—he was more straightforward.

Liubomov told me in polished English that his main purpose in producing the television series had been to excite Russians' interest in history, whatever the results. But critics assailed his program for muddling the past by ignoring prodigious state crimes. "Can you imagine a German show debating Hitler's merits?" asked Yan Ratchinsky of Memorial, which has done more than any other organization to document Soviet abuses. Speaking in Memorial's old redbrick building several blocks from Moscow's once feared police headquarters, Ratchinsky told me Liubomov's program would have been "fine" in democratic countries, where archives are open and history's problems are freely discussed. "But Russia's not that kind of country," he observed. The show helped glorify the state, he said, by perpetuating the official view of history as a string of great victories under strong leaders. Putin's administration encouraged that line, he added, because it helped convince citizen masses that they have no influence on the will of the state. "The only thing left for them to do," he said, "is to hope for a good tsar."

After dozens of years compiling files on victims of Soviet repression, Memorial's directors estimate that completing the task will take six to eight more decades at their current rate, which official obstruction is slowing. Once a year, some of the group's members assemble outside Lubyanka, the KGB's forbidding old headquarters in central Moscow, to read the names of people the Soviet authorities shot. The organization's chairman, a venerated former dissident named Arseniy Roginsky, who served four years in the Gulag in the 1980s, told me the exercise was necessary because the city that brimmed with monuments marking Soviet achievements in war and science lacked a single official memorial for victims of the communist era. Since reminders of the country's bloody past undermined Russia's new official identity, he said, the vast majority of Soviet archives, including informers' names, remain secret, and only a quarter of the USSR's mass grave sites are known.

Unlike postwar Germany, the Russian government never acknowledged the previous regime's crimes, Roginsky continued, because Communist Party officials remained in power after 1991. "After all," he said, "Moscow wasn't conquered by enemy forces; Yeltsin was a Politburo member. Unlike other former Soviet republics, we couldn't blame outsiders and collaborators. We cooked up the Soviet system ourselves and we must judge it ourselves, for which our leaders simply don't have the political will."

The failure to acknowledge Soviet crimes also pained the man most responsible for ending the USSR. Although Mikhail Gorbachev has steadfastly maintained that Russia would have been better off if communism hadn't collapsed—despite his central role in the process—he worried that his place in Soviet history was being "written out" of school textbooks. Very much at ease in his role of elder statesman, the aging politician supported Putin for many years after he began systematically undermining the country's democratic institutions—in order to preserve his status as head of his Gorbachev Foundation, some believed. However, at a conference in the organization's late-Soviet-era brick building, he pontificated that "a new history is being created, one in which Stalin's rule is seen as a golden age,

Khrushchev's as utopia and Brezhnev's as a continuation of that golden age. None of that is happening accidentally."

But beneath the surface of Kremlin controls and its elaborate show of purpose and unity, the government has shown itself to be fragile by Western standards, as I've mentioned—even when its power appeared huge and menacing. Putin's current project has undermined Russia's stability not only by failing to draw elementary lessons from its own history but also by encouraging nationalist attitudes that have fueled racism, xenophobia and a rising wave of violence against minorities that, in the same old cycle, ultimately threaten the Kremlin's grip on power.

An old saying has it that while no one anywhere can divine the future, Russia is the only country with an unpredictable past. Rather than grapple with history's difficulties, its leaders, like many of their predecessors, have attempted to forge a new ideology from a schizophrenic pastiche of symbols from tsarist as well as Soviet history that have been lifted out of context for the purpose of legitimizing their own rule. Even the most prominent Soviet critic, Alexander Solzhenitsyn, is praised by the leaders who laud the great achievements of the regime he reviled. At the same time, virtually nothing is said about the immense cost of the vast projects—such as building cities from scratch and invading Afghanistan—launched at great sacrifice in the sprees of searching for The Solution to Everything: megamessianic undertakings, many of which ended in failure, destruction and death.

———

Grandiose projects have played a central role in Russian history and identity since the launching of the greatest tsarist architectural feat in 1703. Built largely by forced serf labor on marshland beside the Gulf of Finland, the city of St. Petersburg represented an immense act of will. Peter the Great wanted the capital moved from Moscow to a port closer to the rest of Europe, mainly so it could serve as a bulwark against the Swedish Empire, which had dominated the Baltic Sea for centuries. By the time the Peter and Paul Fortress was completed, however, Peter had vanquished the Swedes, who no longer posed a threat to his new capital. Subsequent rulers expanded it along a plan of radial streets whose rational layout was meant to display the reach of the tsar's empire. Up went ornate, sometimes outlandishly decorated baroque buildings, many conceived by Italian architects, most prominently Bartolomeo Rastrelli, who designed the fabulous Winter Palace.

But if building St. Petersburg represented an all-out bid to create a European city, as many suppose, the project missed the mark in at least one telling respect. Whereas most capitals developed over centuries from small settlements to include layers of Romanesque, Gothic and baroque architecture, Russia's new metropolis was distinctly different. It represented Europe at a single stage of its development, with a distinctly un-European uniformity that remains a monument to the Russian penchant for using foreign forms for its own purposes and characteristic creations.

The new capital provoked extreme reactions. Alexander Herzen described it as having no history, Western or Russian—a place where nothing was original. Myths filled the vacuum, starting with apocryphal folktales about floods and other forces of nature avenging the creation of a foreign city whose granite banks straitjacketed the water flowing through its canals. Pushkin drew on those themes to give St. Petersburg its central literary work. His 1833 epic poem "The Bronze Horseman" describes a statue of Peter on horseback by the French sculptor Étienne Falconet. Erected by Catherine the Great, it depicts his mount rearing above the snake of treason next to a malevolent Neva River.

> *November's breath of autumn cold;*
> *And Neva with her boisterous billow*
> *Splashed on her shapely bounding-wall*
> *And tossed in restless rise and fall*
> *Like a sick man upon his pillow.[1]*

The poem follows the story of a young clerk named Yevgeny, whose betrothed is swept away during the great flood of 1824. Driven to madness, he threatens the statue, then imagines it coming to life to pursue him through the city in a narrative that immortalized the image of Peter as a symbol of ruthless will. It established the tension between his creation's grand facades and nature's dark forces as a major literary theme.

Although "The Bronze Horseman" depicts Peter's vision for the city as a "window on the West," Pushkin didn't invent the metaphor. As the Harvard literary scholar Julie Buckler has argued, a nobleman first used it in a

1739 letter in which he described St. Petersburg as something very different from a conduit to Europe: a *shop* window. With the city representing *all* of Europe *inside* Russia, according to that logic, Russians had no need to go to the West. There it was, on display for them in St. Petersburg.

The earlier understanding of "window" lies closer to another metaphor that later came to describe the city: a theatrical stage. The Marquis de Custine, among others, described St. Petersburgers as actors. "I do not blame the Russians for being what they are," he wrote.

> I blame them for pretending what we are...In Petersburg everything has an air of opulence, grandeur, magnificence; but if you judge reality by this appearance, you will find yourself strangely deceived. Ordinarily the first effect of civilization is to make material life easy; here everything is difficult; crafty indifference is the secret of the life of the great majority.[2]

St. Petersburg's deceptive image reflects the importance of fiction for running the huge empire that could barely keep an infrastructure in place. The need to maintain an appearance of order enhanced the perception of theatricality and artifice. In that way, in the primacy of its facade, the city that is usually seen as a foreign plant on Russian soil is actually quintessentially Russian. Ironically, the new capital's perception as alien to Russia's true nature became integral to its culture. Moscow continued to represent Russia's big heart: a sprawling, seething, overgrown village that Gogol compared to an old housewife cooking *blini*. By contrast, St. Petersburg was German—meticulous and narcissistic.[3]

Cracks in its facade—seedy dark alleys, grinding poverty and the hyperobsession with rank and groveling outward obedience against which Dostoevsky's protagonist rails in his seminal *Notes from Underground*—also undermined its grandeur. *Petersburg,* a 1913 Symbolist novel by a highly intellectual writer named Andrei Bely, provided one of the ultimate expressions of those dark themes. It follows a wealthy young revolutionary ordered to assassinate his father, a high tsarist official. An assemblage of fragments and references that describes a surreal city of double agents, chaos and paranoia, the book portrays the wrenching social changes brought about by the rapid industrialization and urbanization of the early twentieth century. Apocalyptic visions from the St. Petersburg tradition appear on almost every page, including historical and fictional characters from "The Bronze Horseman," Dostoevsky's underground man, and Gogolian overcoats and noses.

After the Revolution, the Bolsheviks transformed St. Petersburg's symbolic role by returning the capital to Moscow. Deprived of its official function, the theatrical stage became a museum. After more than a million inhabitants died during the Nazi blockade in World War II, mostly from starvation, the city was rebuilt, then saved from the ruin of Soviet development largely by neglect. The poet Joseph Brodsky saw his native city as a cultural vessel.

> I must say that from these façades and porticoes—classical, modern, eclectic, with their columns, pilasters, and plastered heads of mythic animals or people—from their ornaments and caryatids holding up the balconies, from the torsos in the niches of their entrances, I have learned more about the history of our world than I have subsequently from any book.[4]

Crime-ridden and very poor compared to Moscow—roughly a quarter of the population stills inhabits communal apartments—St. Petersburg remains very different in its core and spirit. Rarely able to fully relax in the seething capital, I took the overnight train as often as I could for therapeutic strolls along St. Petersburg's stunning canals and in its down-at-the-heels gardens. It was especially appealing during the white nights season in late June, when the sun never fully sets and the glee of young residents carousing on the streets until early dawn becomes infectious.

Finally, however, New Russia's oil money began trickling down to the former capital, threatening its architectural unity with Kremlin plans to relocate various state agencies there. Poorly regulated new construction by developers who began pushing residents from the city center in order to illegally rebuild or simply raze old homes has been more destructive. Although many buildings are protected by law, a prominent historian and preservationist named Alexander Margolis believes few are safe. "Under our style of capitalism," Margolis said to me in despair, "developers bribe officials to condemn sound buildings and allow them to build whatever they want. It's not clear how much of the old St. Petersburg will survive." Meanwhile, the city retains its old role in the national consciousness, at least for now. The head of the Moscow Architectural Institute, a scholar named

Vyacheslav Glazychev, told me it has helped preserve a "natural European-ism" that remains a strong antithesis to the rest of Russia. "I always talk about a binary pattern," he said. "That means two capitals of Russia, not just Moscow."

If St. Petersburg is the product of a unified vision, Moscow is a cacophony of conflicting, unfinished projects. As Muscovites themselves like to point out, their city, despite its estimated thirteen million residents, retains the feel of a provincial village whose various parts reflect different priorities and ideolo-gies. Large swaths of Moscow's mostly nineteenth-century neighborhoods were bulldozed as part of the communist aim of building a model socialist metropolis with broad avenues of totalitarian grandiosity. The seven so-called Stalin skyscrapers, massive neo-Gothic edifices looming over their districts, are the most visible fruits of that effort. But the project progressed in fits and starts. Stalin's tastes fluctuated and war interrupted construction before his death in 1953. While the heavy neoclassical Stalinist structures, with their aus-tere pillars and spires, still dominate a number of thoroughfares—including Tverskaya Street, a kind of main drag—pre-Revolutionary Art Nouveau and baroque buildings still provide welcome contrasts.

Khrushchev later imposed a cut-rate, glass-and-concrete vision of modernity. The best examples—on a sprawling, impersonal street called Novy Arbat, roughly parallel to Tverskaya—were outdated even before their completion, although those efforts are luxurious compared to the brutalist concrete-panel eyesores that went up almost everywhere else. But even their construction had virtually halted in the decaying city by 1991.

The subsequent capitalist boom brought new layers of eclectic, mostly garish new office and apartment buildings built during a construction spree tightly controlled by former Mayor Yuri Luzhkov, who combined free-market economics with a Soviet command-style administration that micro-managed most aspects of city life until his ouster in 2011. Luzhkov was also among the first post-Soviet politicians to begin appropriating symbols from Russia's past to glorify his rule.

The Christ the Savior cathedral, the world's largest Russian Orthodox church, was among his most ambitious projects. First constructed in the late nineteenth century to mark the victory over Napoleon in 1812, it was dynamited in the 1930s to make way for a colossal Palace of Soviets that was never built. The site eventually housed a giant outdoor swimming pool until Luzhkov commissioned the construction of a copy of the original cathedral. The gaudy new version, a symbol of Russia's supposed spiritual rebirth after seventy years of communism, was decorated by Luzhkov's "court artist," a Georgian named Zurab Tseretelli. Luzhkov also had Tseretelli design an underground shopping mall in Manezh Square, adjacent to the more famous Red Square, where garish, cloying statuettes of characters from Russian fables decorate a set of fountains. Tseretelli's contribution to the city's Victory Park, which commemorates the fiftieth anniversary of the end of World War II, include a gargantuan spire that can be seen for miles.

However, Tseretelli's most controversial work is a towering statue dominating a central bend of the Moscow River. Erected to commemorate the three hundredth anniversary of the Russian navy, it shows Peter the Great standing on a supposedly eighteenth-century ship whose above-deck structure consists of St. Petersburg buildings. Whether its many levels of historical nonsense were intentionally or unwittingly ironic, the twenty-five-million-dollar structure is a mountain of bad taste. Ignoring St. Petersburg's artificiality and the seeming contradictions of Peter's image—paradox itself being a dominant feature of the national character—Tseretelli's take on the *Bronze Horseman* sculpture was an odd choice for Moscow. Luzhkov, whose chief interest was surely underscoring his power, made nonsense of the sea, Russia's infant navy and everything that linked Peter to St. Petersburg as few people have ever been to any city.

Around the same time, Boris Yeltsin commissioned committees of scholars for a much-derided attempt to develop a "national idea" that would help fill the ideological void left by the disappearance of communism. But it was Luzhkov who set the tone for what would come later by harking back to tsarist history, including by occasionally dressing himself up in a knight's costume to portray Yuri Dolgoruki, Moscow's supposed twelfth-century founder. It's no accident, as the Marxists used to say, that Stalin erected a statue to the same warrior outside what is now the city hall. The Soviet dictator often appealed to Russia's sense of patriotism by way of its history, especially after the onset of World War II. Trying to do the same, Luzhkov later provoked controversy during a failed attempt to erect billboards depicting Stalin in honor of the Soviet victory over the Nazis.

Putin has since taken the lead in adopting symbols from pre-Revolutionary and communist history to generate a nostalgia-fogged vision of Russian identity that has helped camouflage the nature of his rule. He appropriated the music for the Stalin-era Soviet anthem for Russia's use and—a mere week after having announced that Russia had "no elements" of Stalinism—introduced a Hero of Labor award, another relic that first appeared under Stalin as the Hero of Socialist Labor. The president also likes to compare himself to earlier doers such as the ruthless Stolypin, Nicholas II's prime minister, whom Russians remember today less for introducing his important land reforms than for inspiring "Stolypin wagons," a type of train car that still carries inmates to Siberian penal colonies. Putin has also invoked Prince Alexander Gorchakov, one of Russia's most respected foreign ministers, whom he quoted in the title of his 2012 election manifesto, *Russia Is Concentrating*, an allusion to the country's renewal following its devastating defeat in the Crimean War in 1856. Revealing his vision of democracy in another publication, Putin said Russia had no need of "the circus of various candidates competing with each other to give more and more unrealistic promises." Purporting to criticize his opponents, the harangue was startling for its description, again intentional or unwitting, of his own system of elaborate pretense.

> We don't need a situation where all that is left of democracy is the facade, where democracy is understood as a one-time entertaining political show and a candidates' casting call, where substance is forgotten for the sake of shocking statements and mutual accusations, where real politics is reduced to shady deals and decisions made behind the scenes but never discussed with voters. We should avoid that blind alley.

Putin's projects have been as remarkable for their hollowness as for anything else. As Europeans debated the EU's future amid the euro crisis in 2011, he proposed a new alliance that would resurrect a form of the Soviet Union by bringing its former member states into a "Eurasian Union." This one would be bound not by ideology but trade, building on an existing customs union with Belarus and Kazakhstan that Putin has described as "the most important geopolitical integration in the post-Soviet space since the breakup of the Soviet Union." Having done as much as anyone to stifle regional economic cooperation by banning goods imported from Georgia and Moldova and cutting off gas to Ukraine, Putin now voiced hope that the union would supersede the Commonwealth of Independent States, a toothless alliance of eleven of the original fifteen Soviet republics.

The new plan evokes Eurasianism, a hard-line nationalist movement conceived by 1920s émigrés who believed Russia to be closer to Asia than to Europe. Resurrected in the 1980s, it has recently been led by Alexander Dugin, a strident ideologue who envisions a strategic bloc that would join the former Soviet Union to Middle Eastern countries, including Iran, in order to rival the American-led Euro-Atlantic alliance. It fits well with Putin's oft-invoked "multipolar" world order—as opposed to the "unipolar" US-led version—although rather than building international institutions, his main goal is strengthening Russian power. Whereas the communists distributed cheap oil, gas and other subsidies as a way of bribing allies and clients, Putin has engaged in hard-nosed bargaining aimed at increasing Moscow's influence and has issued credit to countries such as Belarus, Ukraine and Kyrgyzstan, which have been willing to buy Russian commodities in return for ceding control over pipelines and other infrastructure.

In a 2013 apologia for Putin published in the *Financial Times* that had all the hallmarks of official propaganda, Dugin explained that having been abandoned by the liberal elite during the recent mass protests, the president was now following his true beliefs by becoming a Russian "conservative modernizer" who would save the homeland from a "single, encroaching world order."[5] Comparing Putin to a pantheon composed of Peter the Great, Stalin, Lenin and Ivan the Terrible, Dugin said his mandate was his appeal to the Russian masses and that his actions represented a "rethinking of what comes at the end of the transition" from communism. "Having lost the cold war," Dugin wrote, "Russia will try to revise the status quo using all available opportunities."

Some see Eurasianism's rhetoric as a salve for the trauma of the communist collapse. As Richard Pipes has argued, countries such as England and France, which had created national states before forming overseas empires, found it easier to deal with the end of colonialism. The Russian nation-state, by contrast, developed concurrently with an empire it directly bordered. "As a result, the loss of empire caused confusion in the Russians' sense of national identity," he wrote. "They have great difficulty acknowledging that Ukraine, the cradle of their state, is now a sovereign republic and fantasize about the day when it will reunite with Mother Russia."[6]

Without Ukraine, moreover, the largest market for Russian exports, Moscow can have no real hope of establishing the Eurasian Union. So when Kiev was preparing to sign major agreements with the EU—a possible step toward eventual membership—in late 2013, Moscow issued an ultimatum that it couldn't choose both and threatened economic sanctions. Russia's anger had the effect only of hardening Ukraine's resolve to sign the EU deals.

Even more damaging for its interests, the Kremlin has been hard at work squandering its greatest instrument of influence, the Russian language. Picking fights with Ukraine, Moldova, Estonia and other former Soviet republics—whose populations, subjected to Russification sometimes for centuries, have spoken the language as a second mother tongue—has encouraged them to want to forget Russian. Some three hundred million people spoke the language in 1990, but it's projected that only half that number will speak it by 2025 as former colonies cement their own national identities by focusing on their native languages.

Putin's grand visions include doubling Moscow's size to alleviate its mind-numbing traffic jams and rebuilding Sochi for the Olympics. In that gaudy symbol of postcommunist Russia, where moneyed vacationers go to swim in the murky sea or ski in the Caucasus Mountains, prices are as high as New York's. Like Peter the Great in his day, Putin has coerced billionaire businessmen into supporting the undertaking. One built a new airport and a seaport; another dropped two billion dollars into the nearby mountain resort.[7] Putin farmed out another scheme, building a Russian Silicon Valley in a suburb called Skolkovo, to Medvedev. Dismissing those plans as fantasy, *Vedomosti*, a leading business daily, wrote that "the way [the authorities] speak, they are practically past accomplishments, and it would seem that Russia should share its successful experience of modernization with all backward countries still struggling to develop."

"In the Kremlin's imaginary utopian world," the paper continued with more than a little irony, "Russia is already the core of a powerful regional alliance stretching from the Atlantic to the Pacific Ocean. That union is a force with which the whole world must reckon, especially because the

Russian military will be armed with cutting-edge technology and weapons and will overwhelm the entire world."

———

Britain was only just establishing its empire when Alexis de Tocqueville famously predicted that two relatively unnoticed countries of the time would one day compete for world domination. Russia and America, he wrote in *Democracy in America*, published in 1835, would follow different paths to become great powers. "The principal instrument of the former is freedom," he argued, "of the latter, servitude." Each "seems marked out by the will of Heaven to sway the destinies of half the globe."

Almost two centuries later, Russians and Americans are often likened to each other for their informality, easy hospitality and other qualities less frequently encountered in the more stratified European societies. They are also similar for their attachment to reinvention as a cultural theme, although in very different if not opposite ways. The American dream includes escaping the past and its European roots. Russians dream of being respected in Europe if not accepted as part of it. It bears repetition that Russian culture tends to be reactive in the sense of borrowing Western ideas and transforming them to fit native patterns and conceptions. Some ideas are inventive and original, such as the culture magazine Openspace. ru and the television channel Dozhd—Internet sites that are lively reminders of the 1990s, when media outlets were raw and vital. However, most initiatives are anything but.

Among them, Putin's project to cast Russia as a great power has heavily relied on good old-fashioned nationalism. No different from other varieties, which seek to create an imaginary community of "us" against "them," the Russian version is also anchored on the perception of a past injustice. It's no accident that after a decade of Russian flirtation with the West, the United States is again chief among villains. Moscow's imagined rivalry with the world's most powerful country not only encourages fond memories of Soviet might but also enables the Kremlin to punch above its weight on the world stage.

Although some foreign policy experts maintain Putin genuinely wanted to ally with Washington following September 11—not least in order to justify the conflict in Chechnya as part of the global "war on terror"—anti-Americanism has been part and parcel of his stance from the beginning.

In regular barrages, he has charged Washington with spreading violence and extremism around the world and with seeking to foment discontent in Russia in order to weaken and even dismember it, then steal its natural resources. He once compared American foreign policy to Nazi Germany's, saying "new threats" in the world, "as during the Third Reich, contain the same contempt for human life and same claims of exceptionality and diktat in the world." He also accused Washington of encouraging Georgia to attack its pro-Moscow breakaway region of South Ossetia, which purportedly prompted Russia's invasion in 2008.

Putin has made some of his accusations on Russia Today, the three-hundred-million-dollar-a-year English-language satellite channel founded in 2008 to broadcast the Kremlin's views, often in the form of denunciations of American imperialism and greed and other supposed signs of Western decline. In a 2013 interview in which he publicly offered political asylum to Edward Snowden—the ex-CIA whistle-blower soon after granted temporary refuge in Russia—he went on to criticize the United States for being founded on the "ethnic cleansing" of its native population and for using the atomic bomb on Japan, which he insisted even Stalin wouldn't have considered.

Choosing George W. Bush's scheme for a missile defense system as its main bugbear, the Kremlin objected most strongly to plans for stationing a radar system in the Czech Republic and ten missile interceptors in Poland, two former Soviet Bloc countries. Although Washington affirmed that the rankling installations were directed against Iran and North Korea, Moscow insisted their real purpose was to neutralize Russia's nuclear weapons deterrent, its intercontinental ballistic missiles. Never mind that the ranges of American interceptors are too short to threaten Russia's missiles during any time in flight and therefore pose no threat to Moscow's nuclear deterrence. Or that experts ridiculed Bush's plans to deploy untested radar technology. Putin threatened to retaliate by directing nuclear missiles at Europe. For the first time since the Cold War, he also resumed international bomber sorties on aging Soviet-era aircraft and sent naval ships to South America.

For all Medvedev's supposed liberalism, he picked up Putin's mantle by greeting Barack Obama's election victory in 2008 with a threat. As congratulations were pouring in from around the world, the then–Russian president labeled American policies "egotistical and dangerous" in a state of the nation speech delivered in front of top officials gathered in a massive

Kremlin hall. Lashing out against the missile defense plans, Medvedev said Moscow would be forced to respond by stationing new missiles of its own near Poland, something even the Soviet Union had refrained from risking. The message—that any expectations that the new US administration would have an easier time dealing with the Kremlin were misguided—was the latest in a string of rants that moved Moscow's relations with Washington back toward Cold War lows.

Celebrations marking Victory in Europe Day have seemed to grow longer and larger—and the trumpeting of the USSR's defeat of Nazi Germany as evidence of Russian greatness ever louder—every year since Putin's ascendance, even after he revived the Soviet tradition of driving tanks and missiles across Red Square during the annual military parade. American children barely register the date, if at all, but their Russian counterparts are incessantly reminded of that supposedly central part of their national identity in a fashion very much in the mold of the constant Soviet advertising for one or another glorious anniversary of the Revolution. The practice of decorating car antennas and door handles with orange-and-black striped ribbons—called the St. George's Ribbon, which adorns military medals—became widespread at roughly the same time.

Although the Kremlin toned down its rhetoric after Obama canceled the missile-shield installation in the Czech Republic, it continued to threaten retaliation against the new scheme. Seeking to undermine the Kremlin's so-called zero-sum view of foreign policy—the idea that a benefit for one side necessarily constitutes a loss for the other—the White House's top Russia adviser, Michael McFaul, a Stanford professor appointed to the National Security Council, led an attempt to engage Russia with a nuanced "reset" program of cooperation on mutually beneficial issues. The realist approach facilitated the signing of a nuclear weapons treaty and a significant boosting of diplomatic ties on various bureaucratic levels. But after the scholar—who advocates democratization in Russia and other countries—was appointed ambassador to Russia in 2011, he was greeted in Moscow with a withering attack on state television that accused him of seeking to overthrow the government. Alluding to the Soviet use of secret sleeper agents, Putin chimed in by blaming Secretary of State Hillary Clinton for orchestrating that year's public protests against him. She set their tone, he said. "They heard the signal and started active work."

The government ordered the US Agency for International Development

RUSSIANS

to shut down its Russia operations soon afterward for what the Kremlin characterized as meddling in its internal affairs. Some of Russia's most active civil-society groups, which Putin once characterized as "Judases," were among beneficiaries of the fifty million dollars that USAID distributed in Russia each year. They included Memorial and Golos, the vote-monitoring group whose thousands of volunteers played a central role in documenting the mass fraud during the parliamentary elections of 2011. A foreign ministry spokesman explained that the American funding had sought to "influence the political process, including elections at various levels, and civil society." During the first parliamentary hearing on US human rights abuses since the Soviet collapse, lawmakers used the opportunity to lash out against the United States again by criticizing Americans for waterboarding, abusing children and issuing "anti-Russian propaganda."

Responding to criticism about such rhetoric, Putin said he regularly followed public opinion polls to ensure he understood the opinions of "not just the intelligentsia, which I respect, but also the native Russians." Such nationalistic fantasy, which pits "us" true Russians against a group of malevolent "others"—a lumping together of intellectuals, opposition leaders and foreigners—is aimed at redirecting public anger over a government unable to address the country's widespread poverty, corruption and mounting predictions of economic downturn because its overarching concern is with preserving Putin's power.

Not to be outdone, a new parliament convened in January of 2013 to propose a list of initiatives to curb foreign influences in Russia, an absurd surge of patriotism meant as a display of loyalty during increasingly repressive times. Having recently banned adoptions of children by Americans, legislators proposed a complete ban on all foreign adoptions, along with a requirement that Russian officials who have children studying abroad lose their posts if their offspring fail to return to Russia immediately afterward. Another initiative would have barred them from studying abroad at all. Other proposals included a bill to prevent foreigners, as well as Russians with dual citizenship, from criticizing the government on television and a bill forbidding officials to marry foreigners from countries outside the former USSR.[8] No such measures were ultimately adopted.

If legislators believed their zeal would protect them from the president's mounting anti-Western campaign, however, they were mistaken. After pledging that the country would "de-offshorize" its economy, Putin sent them a bill banning officials from holding bank accounts abroad and investing in foreign government debt. A provision outlawing the ownership of any property abroad was toned down to stipulate only that foreign assets be declared, an alarming prospect nevertheless for an elite whose ownership of foreign property is legion. "Managing a foreign property without a foreign bank account is hardly possible," wrote a young opposition legislator named Ilya Ponomaryov. "But that's the whole point of the new legislation: to turn more people into criminals."[9]

Alexei Navalny leaped at the opportunity by publicizing revelations that no less a figure than the head of the Duma's ethics committee, a United Russia founder, had failed to declare apartments and other property in Miami Beach worth more than two million dollars. Although Vladimir Pekhtin initially dismissed the allegation as "unmerited," he was soon forced to resign by colleagues who were worried that his denial would expose the party to a public backlash. The standing ovation in parliament he received on leaving no doubt reflected relief instead of the supposed restoration of respect for political morality for which he was lauded. That would have been premature. Another United Russia member deputy, a billionaire, soon also resigned, for "health reasons," and Navalny continued helping expose other United Russia leaders—lawmakers, governors and others—as "liars and hypocrites" by publishing their patriotic-sounding public statements denouncing corruption and the West next to foreign property registration documents and Google Maps photos of their luxurious villas on the Riviera and other holiday destinations.

No one could have seriously believed the party purges represented a real opposition victory, however. The applause for Pekhtin was closer to the standing ovations Stalin received from Communist Party leaders quaking in their boots. If Putin's rule had been relatively benign for loyal members of the elite, it was now becoming dangerous even for them. The new campaign, which included a presidential decree ordering more than a million officials to declare their expenses as well as their income and assets, did much to reestablish the traditional threat of arbitrary punishment that had attained its most extreme form under the totalitarian dictator. However, the new version was much closer to the more predictable Brezhnev system, under which the Party kept some of its corruption in check by punishing those who stole too much. It gave Putin even more leverage over the globe-trotting elite while making a show of cracking down on their excesses and doing ever more to further his drive to isolate Russia from the West. Taken together, such recent actions have pushed the Putin system of rule toward fully formed maturity.

In other quarters, the anti-Western feeling that has ebbed and flowed in Russia over centuries has diminished since foreign travel and uncensored Internet use made the West available to the Russian people for the first time ever. But while popular sentiments continue to be shaped and channeled from above, a wellspring of nationalism has risen from the grassroots, perhaps also for the first time in the country's history—and it is complicating our understanding of its society. For example, a Pew Research Center poll conducted in 2012 reported that only 31 percent of respondents were satisfied with how democracy was working in Russia—an indication that more and more Russians recognize a gap between democratic values and their perception of Russian reality. Nevertheless, 72 percent of those same people said they held a favorable opinion of Putin. It's probably no coincidence that 73 percent believed Russia deserves more respect in the world.

The most intense hatred of Americans I've witnessed in Moscow had come a dozen years earlier, in the backlash to NATO's bombing of Serbia. The desire for revenge it prompted was mixed with admiration, envy and feelings of rivalry that came partly from an older, collective sense of inferiority and shame for Russia's backwardness and place in the world. To put it crudely, people's first unfettered look at the outside world during the 1990s made them realize that mammoth reforms were required for genuine competition, and it activated an easy excuse for why they weren't undertaken. It was a short jump from "we're different" to "we're better!"

Within a few years, I began noticing fewer Russians at parties given by foreigners and fewer foreigners at Russian parties. By 2005, the trend was unmistakable. Although troubling, the de facto segregation lightened the atmosphere among fellow Americans by enabling us to speak more freely because things had become stickier in mixed company. Instead of being able to bemoan local and national problems with sympathetic Russian friends, I found myself watching my words for fear of appearing to insult their country.

Even many young people, including those in their teens and twenties who were studying foreign languages and had traveled abroad, shared Putin's near-xenophobic chauvinism. A visit to an eleventh-grade history class at one of Moscow's most prestigious schools shortly after Obama's election seemed typical in that way. A friendly, well-spoken student named

Dima Osafkin condemned the United States for meddling in the affairs of other countries. "America has pursued anti-Russian policies in Georgia and other former Soviet countries on our border," he told me without rancor. "That's unfair, and we don't like it." A classmate named Danil Kuznetsov said Medvedev was right to threaten to deploy new missiles. "It wasn't just tied to the American election. It was a smart move because the United States has been surrounding us with its own missile bases."

Widespread suspicion of the United States troubled Georgy Mirsky, a veteran foreign affairs specialist. Apart from the intelligentsia and urban middle classes, "our people are much more nationalistic, chauvinistic and antidemocratic than Putin himself," he told me. "So the current regime is by no means the worst we could have." Mirsky said that unlike the masses, however, Russia's political elite—whose members continue to regularly travel to the United States, send their children to study in British and American universities and still keep their money in foreign bank accounts despite Putin's anti-Western campaign—doesn't hold store in its own propaganda.

He believed the elite exploited popular anti-American feeling in order to blame the United States for Russia's problems. "Who could be a better scapegoat?" he asked. If there was Marxism-Leninism under the Soviet Union, the eminent scholar concluded, "Russia's ersatz ideology today is patriotism. And it's interchangeable with anti-Americanism."

———

In the 1990s, reporters could call on any number of liberal Duma deputies for interviews. Even high-ranking officials of Yeltsin's administration such as Boris Nemtsov and other young reformers were sometimes willing to shed light on how the government carried out its decisions. And while it was easy to dismiss their main opponents—the communists who controlled parliament—as retrograde obstructionists, even they could be enlightening. Although one of their leaders, a former Soviet prosecutor named Victor Ilyukhin—who led an effort to impeach Yeltsin on charges of genocide against Russians and helping to end communism—sometimes appeared to embody the party's worst aspects, he spoke intelligently, with empathy for his electorate, and appeared to be trying to do the right thing by them in his own way.

Putin's rise caused almost instantaneous change. During the rare instances they agreed to engage, officials reverted to Soviet-like stoniness they sometimes leavened with saccharine, paternalistic manners. I resorted to gleaning scraps of information about attitudes among the great and good in government during lunches and other informal meetings with one or another of a small handful of low- and middle-level officials I knew. Otherwise, Moscow bureaucrats generally took their cues from the president, whom I once questioned during one of his annual news conferences, held in front of a thousand-plus journalists crammed into an aging Kremlin auditorium. I asked him to explain a recent rant of his about foreign countries he had accused of seeking to portray Russia as an enemy. "Do they include Washington and London?" I inquired. "Otherwise who specifically do you believe wants to damage Russia's image?" Since I'd submitted a different question to his spokesman a week in advance, Putin's answer wasn't entirely unprepared. Having been late to join the hours-long line to get into the auditorium, however, I found myself sitting on a distant balcony beside a powerful stage light that obscured the view of me from the stage below. Ignoring the frantic hand-waving of more visible reporters next to me, the moderator managed to pick me out.

Putin adapted his answer with the menace he often reserves for foreign journalists. "There's a dishonest attitude to the interpretation of events," he lectured, glaring up in my direction. "That's the work of Russia's ill-wishers. If you write those kinds of things, you're among their number." Uncomfortable as it made me feel, I found his response instructive for appearing to confirm that the news conference had been choreographed to appear spontaneous while enabling Putin to control his responses.

Although I found that and other aspects of reporting in Russia similar to what had been required under Soviet rule—for example, having to ignore loathsome officials' anti-American barbs for the sake of opening doors for important interviews—nothing I experienced approached the games my father had to play to remain in good enough standing to be allowed to visit the USSR.

Fiercely critical of the Communist Party authorities as he was, he never shared the common Western impression of the Soviet Union as little more than one big labor camp. The topics he covered, mostly involving people's lives and thoughts beyond politics, enabled him to describe some of the "normal" and even positive aspects of life, from ballet to mushroom picking. Therefore he was taken aback and a little hurt when an especially plodding Soviet publication called *Molodoi Kommunist* ("young communist") ran a scathing denunciation of him. Rashly deciding to complain, he visited the journal's editorial office, where the staff had no idea what to make of him and his protest. Seemingly chastened, however, the editors asked him to return for lunch several days later, apparently to get rid of him before reporting the incident to higher authorities. At the lunch, which was typically grand for a semiofficial occasion, the friendly as well as apologetic editors suggested more mutual understanding could be achieved in a second, smaller meeting. Toward the middle of a third lunch, supposedly a heart-to-heart with a single man who hadn't been present at the previous meals, it dawned on George that the man was no editor but a KGB officer.

More invitations followed, usually to the upscale Aragvi restaurant, which was known to serve the KGB as a kind of listening post and reception place for foreign visitors. Its private rooms were perfect for bugging conversations. "My flesh crawled the minute I saw him," George recalled. "But I assumed he had the power to have me kicked out of the country and prevented from returning, so I had to be very careful." Short and stubby, with an ugly, glowering stare and a country accent of which he was ashamed, Bastard, as George silently called the man, oozed envy of Western freedom and privileges even when he was spouting Marxist-Leninist slogans and pressuring his "guest" to "join the struggle for world peace" by supplying information about his fellow Americans. George had to walk a very thin line between pretending he'd be willing to do that one day and saying nothing that could be used to blackmail him. Despite the liters of vodka the Bastard downed on the KGB's expense account, he sobered up the instant his prey slipped enough to utter something that might have been construed as anti-Soviet.

The KGB officer—who, my father later learned, indeed had the power of admitting and expelling him—"made life a thousand times easier" by not calling him during several reportorial trips to Moscow from his base in London. But his luck ran out when he went to research his biography of Solzhenitsyn, by far the most powerful Soviet dissent of the time. Returning from an interview with one of Solzhenitsyn's closest Gulag friends to his room in the Rossiya Hotel, a brutalist box next to Red Square, George was shocked to find Bastard sitting on the edge of a chair, his fury "enough to burn a hole in the door." After years of George's game of being a friend of the Soviet Union, "now he'd obviously found out I was gathering material about Solzhenitsyn, meaning I'd double-crossed him. No doubt that was a blow to his personal standing. After all that work he'd done on me, what would his bosses think of him?"

He shouted that the road was now "closed" to George. "Entry to the Soviet Union is forbidden to you!" In his nervousness, however, George mistook the word "entry" (*vezd*) for the very similar-sounding "exit" (*vyezd*).

"'Holy shit,' I thought. 'I'm stuck in the Soviet Union for the rest of my life!' No doubt I turned white, which is just what he wanted. He marched out, very satisfied," my father recalled.

Nevertheless, George managed to return to Moscow ten years later. Arriving in early 1980, when the United States was boycotting the Moscow Winter Olympics in response to the Soviet invasion of Afghanistan the previous year, he noticed what appeared to be a remarkable new development about which he hadn't read: many people, including the relatively straight and patriotic, had started complaining. Not about politics, which were rarely discussed openly, or about any high principle, but about the shortages of consumer goods, the low standard of living, the sense that society in general was no longer working. It was the start of a revolution of rising expectations and lowering hope that they'd ever be met—a revolution scarcely described in the West, where fear of the Soviet Union continued to dominate in the media. Although living standards had risen under Brezhnev, the Soviet people were increasingly aware of how poorly they lived compared to people in other countries, and they were sick of it. Returning to London, George published articles in the London *Sunday Times* and *Harper's Magazine* describing Soviet society as "sick."

I noticed something very similar about Russia when I returned to Moscow for a reporting trip in 2011 after more than a year away: everyone was complaining. No longer around their proverbial kitchen tables, as they did under communism, but in the sushi chains and fancy department stores that made life appear very different from the way it was in what my father likes to call his "day." Before every taxi trip, I girded myself against harangues from the driver about how the greedy bastards at the top were stealing everything.

In another development that suggested similarities to Brezhnev's USSR, a Levada Center poll conducted the same year revealed that 22 percent of adults wanted to leave the country for good—three times the number that had said so four years earlier and significantly more than the 18 percent who had said they wanted out as the waning USSR was spiraling toward dissolution in 1991. The poll surveyed people between the ages of twenty-five and thirty-nine who lived in large cities and earned five to ten times the average income—i.e., the young middle-class people who would soon take to the streets to protest.

Authoritarianism was among the least of their concerns. What bothered them most of all were high prices, crime and corruption. Of course no one had liked those features of their lives earlier. The difference was their growing impatience with the stagnation behind the high-flown rhetoric, a sense that Putin's imminent return meant that nothing would change for the foreseeable future.

———

The ever-stauncher nationalism Putin used to help weather the growing dissatisfaction fed the deep-rooted racism and xenophobia coursing just beneath the facade of a society that comprises more than 180 ethnic groups and is still grappling with the consequences of the Soviet collapse. Communism had once promised to wipe out national boundaries and ethnic distinctions. Actually, the imperialists in the Kremlin relied on a poorly defined Soviet "nationality" to veil the dominant Russian nationalism. A rhyme about Yuri Gagarin conveys the flavor of that racialist spirit.

> *Kak khorosho shto nash Gagarin*
> *Ne Evrei i ne Tatarin*
> *Ne Kalmyk i ne Uzbek*
> *A nash Sovetskii chelovek!*
> *(How good that our Gagarin*
> *Isn't a Jew or a Tatar*
> *Not a Kalmyk or an Uzbek,*
> *But a man of our own Soviet stock!)*

Like American congressmen endlessly gerrymandering state districts, the Soviets drew and redrew national and regional boundaries to finesse their rule over territories, including the khanates and emirates of Central Asia, which formerly had no such borders. The practice fanned long-suppressed ethnic disputes that, when unleashed by the crumbling of communism, resulted in bloodshed and so-called frozen conflicts in former Soviet republics such as Georgia, Armenia and Azerbaijan.

Although Russia remained remarkably cohesive following the Soviet collapse, bitter enmity broke out between its various neighbors, too, including the Ossetians and the Ingush in the Caucasus. Their brief war in North Ossetia in 1992 resulted in hundreds of deaths and the expulsion of sixty thousand Ingush, and simmering tensions still show no signs of abating. Ossetians venturing into Ingushetia, and the other way around, still say they risk beatings and murder. In late 2011, when I wanted to take a taxi from Nazran in Ingushetia to the nearest airport, half an hour away in North Ossetia, my driver agreed only under the condition that a police sergeant accompany us to insure against trouble. Although none occurred, I sensed mass violence could easily break out again if and when the Kremlin relaxes its draconian security measures.

The most prominent antagonists by far, however, are the white Slavic Russians who have joined the ranks of various nationalist groups since the 1980s. Among the politicians seeking their support who have long become fixtures on the political scene is Vladimir Zhirinovsky, the clownish "ultranationalist" leader of the fiercely illiberal and utterly undemocratic Liberal Democratic Party, who once presented me with a bottle of Zhirinovsky brand aftershave, boasting that even the US president didn't have his own line of toiletries.

Zhirinovsky and others have played on the dislike of millions of migrant workers who, during the past two decades, have streamed to various parts of Russia, especially Moscow, where they work on municipal sanitation crews and construction sites, providing very cheap labor for the building boom. Although an astounding 60 percent of Tajikistan's working population is believed to live in Russia, migrants are rarely seen on the streets except when they're sweeping them. Central Asians form part of a virtually segregated second class of residents who do the various kinds of dangerous, backbreaking work that most Russians reject.

During a visit I paid to the construction site of a typical updated Soviet-style residential block, Tajik workers, who slept on a rough concrete floor without access to running water or a working toilet, told me they earned the equivalent of eight hundred dollars a month—and that the police demanded bribes even though they had legal permits. "Tajiks in Moscow are slaves in the twenty-first century," one soft-spoken worker named Said Chekhanov remarked. "We're treated like animals. The police insult us, and our employers forbid us even to talk at work."

Everyone at the construction site had stories of attacks by masked men in the middle of the night. Another Tajik I met, a timid twenty-eight-year-old named Sukhaili Saidov, described an assault outside the metro by five young men wielding knives. He escaped after being stabbed in his stomach. However, he said another attack, on a young Central Asian woman, haunted him more. "She was killed right in front of me," he said. "Three men grabbed her outside the metro, where there were lots of people around. She was screaming, but the police did nothing. Then the men smashed her head with a brick."

After suffering three attacks, Saidov was afraid to venture outside after dark, which cost him his job as a security guard. But he didn't want to return to Tajikistan, where the average wage was around fifteen dollars a month. With work in Moscow enabling him to support ten family members back home, he decided to stay and look for another job.

Karomat Sharipov, the head of a support group for Tajiks, blamed greed for fueling racist attacks. "Construction companies are making huge sums of money," he said. "And so are the authorities, who are secretly paid to help 'organize' the migrant labor system. Spreading fear is profitable for them."

Although Putin has denounced racist attacks, he has also fanned the attitudes that animate them by exploiting nationalism for his political gain. During his first term as president, the Kremlin launched a nationalist party called Rodina ("Motherland"), partly to bleed communists of votes, before pulling the plug because Rodina's leader, Dmitri Rogozin, was becoming genuinely popular. At its height, the party was banned from competing in Moscow's municipal elections after broadcasting anti-immigrant advertisements urging "Let's clean the city of garbage!" The aborted venture illustrated Putin's attempt to walk a fine line between attracting nationalist voters and encouraging the virulent nationalism that has threatened to undermine his support.

The balancing act seemed to start unraveling in 2006, when locals in Karelia, a forested region next to Finland, attacked houses and businesses owned by Chechens and other Caucasus natives before running them out of town. I flew there a few days after the incident had raised alarm bells in Moscow. The backwater industrial town of Kondopoga, whose name is now a byword for racism, was hardly unusual in that Caucasus natives owned stores and restaurants there and ran the local market, many having fled economic collapse and instability back home. On its dusty main street, residents told me usually nothing happened there.

The violence began when several ethnic Russians celebrating their release from jail beat an Azerbaijani bartender after refusing to pay for their drinks. Witnesses told me the restaurant's owner called in a group of Chechens wielding knives and clubs who attacked the Russians, killing two of them. The deaths prompted residents to call for the expulsion of Caucasus natives from Kondopoga. "They do whatever they want, act like they own everything," a local named Victor Pavlov told me, echoing many others. "They've bribed our corrupt officials, bought out our stores and are dispossessing the Russian people."

Activists from Moscow arrived to organize protests. Among them was Alexander Belov, a young member of parliament and extreme nationalist who heads a notorious and vocal group called the Movement Against Illegal Immigration. When two thousand protesters met to draw up a petition addressed to the local mayor, Belov called for all Caucasus natives to be expelled within twenty-four hours, although he later denied having incited the crowd. "I just said, 'The land belongs to you Russians,'" he told me. "'You've been robbed and that will soon be remedied.'" After the protest broke up, a mob of some two hundred mostly drunk young men rampaged through Kondopoga's streets, throwing rocks and Molotov cocktails at stores, restaurants and houses belonging to Chechens and other Caucasus natives. Roughly sixty people fled.

When I spoke to some of them in the gym of a nearby summer school, where they were under police protection, a middle-aged Chechen woman named Taisa Gazikhanova told me the rioters had threatened to kill them. "I was born here," she declared. "Nevertheless the people I've lived around my whole life suddenly turned on us." Her plight failed to impress Karelia's governor, Sergei Katanandov, who told me he sympathized with unhappiness over what he called ostentatious displays of wealth. "Everything would be fine if new arrivals in our region respected our principles, our views about life," he said. "And if they didn't insult people with their behavior."

Back in Moscow, Putin revealed his sympathies in language whose code wasn't difficult to crack. The government, he said, had a duty to protect the "native population" from criminal groups "with an ethnic flavor" that control street markets. Then he proceeded to restore Soviet-era quotas on foreigners working in shops and markets. Alexander Verkhovsky, an expert on racism who runs Moscow's Sova think tank, told me such behavior encouraged extremist violence. "What's more, officials often use hard-line rhetoric to win public favor," he said. "They say the country is surrounded by foreign enemies. But since the average Russian can't fight foreign countries, he targets people around him."

Although few explosions on the scale of Kondopoga have followed, the nationalist movement continued growing. The killing of a young Slavic soccer fan during a 2010 fight with a native of the Caucasus region Kabardino-Balkaria prompted five thousand fellow fans and nationalists to riot in central Moscow. Placing roses at the grave, Putin said the young man's death was "a great tragedy" and promised more restrictions against immigrants. Another killing of an ethnic Russian—this time allegedly by an Azerbaijani man in an industrial Moscow district—prompted outraged locals to join hate groups in storming a shopping center, beating migrants, and attacking police. The authorities responded by targeting the victims. Seeking to stem the tide of anti-migrant anger, police raided a vegetable warehouse, where the arrested more than a thousand people under the pretext of investigating crime by migrants. Mayor Sobyanin pledged the crackdown would continue—the response that promises to fan the flames. The Levada Center recently found that 60 percent of Muscovites supported the rallying cry "Russia for Russians!" That does not bode well for a country whose Muslim population is expected to expand as more immigrants arrive from the Caucasus and Central Asia and internal migrants move from the North Caucasus to other parts of the country.[10]

———

The relationship between Russia's Slavs and Jews is no less complicated but perhaps more paradoxical. Americans often have a hard time understanding why Jews, *Everei*, aren't considered Russian and still tend not to identify themselves as such even if their ancestors have lived there for centuries. While others may not find that unusual in a generally xenophobic former empire that co-opted hundreds of ethnicities, Russian anti-Semitism does have some unique characteristics. Historian James Billington traces their development to the advance of Muscovite self-identity in the fifteenth century, when an "anti-Jewish fervor" was "built into Muscovite ideology."[11]

Muscovite pretensions to being "chosen," he explains, bred hostility toward older Jewish claims to the same distinction, made more acute by envy of the more cosmopolitan culture of Jewish groups that interacted with the Slavs, mainly at the edges of their territory. They included Jews from Western Europe as well as the Turkic Khazars in the Caucasus, whose leaders converted to Judaism.

Nevertheless, Russia's small population of Jews escaped serious persecution until the late eighteenth century, when Catherine the Great acquired large swaths of Lithuanian and Polish land heavily populated by Jews after Russia conspired with Prussia and Austria to partition the once powerful Polish-Lithuanian Empire.

Catherine marked off a territory that included parts of Lithuania, Poland and Ukraine exclusively for Jews. Heavily taxed, they were forbidden to leave without permission. Poverty in the shtetls of the so-called Pale of Settlement was dreadful, and its inhabitants were never free from fear of repression and violence, especially under the conservative Nicholas I in the mid-1800s. However, their oppression began in earnest at the end of the century, when they faced waves of anti-Jewish pogroms (derived from the Russian word meaning "to storm" or "destroy") that swept the empire after a period of relative calm under the reforming Alexander II, liberator of the serfs.

The reactionary new tsar, Alexander III, was a staunch anti-Semite whose conservative adviser Konstantin Pobedonostsev believed Russia's "Jewish problem" would be solved by the conversion to Orthodoxy of a third of Jews, the emigration of another third and the death of the rest.[12] Alexander progressively tightened laws against Jews, banning them from the countryside and from participating in local elections even within the Pale. Jews were also ejected from Kiev and Moscow. More pogroms followed after a nationalist newspaper in 1903 published what it said was the text of a Jewish plan for world domination. Possibly written with the help of the secret police, the so-called "Protocols of the Elders of Zion" purportedly documented the minutes of a meeting between Jewish leaders to plan their global hegemony, which would be achieved by controlling the world's press and economies.

By the turn of the century, the Russian Empire held more than five million Jews, most inside the Pale, roughly half the world's Jewish population. But millions were emigrating, many to the United States. The misery of shtetl life also motivated Jews to become prominent in revolutionary politics, whose promise of "internationalism" offered a path to assimilation through a new, common identity. Many Jews became prominent Bolsheviks. Others were leaders of the rival Menshevik faction of the Social Democratic Labor Party, whose founders of were also Jewish. Life improved very little for most Jews after the Revolution, however. Tens of thousands died in pogroms during the civil war, many in Ukraine. Still, the Pale's demise prompted the migration of almost half its Jews to locations elsewhere in the Soviet Union, where they were able to attend school and settle in industrializing cities.

Although Stalin's repression didn't overtly target Jews over other groups—the Communist Party ostensibly opposed anti-Semitism—his barely concealed prejudice surfaced near the end of his rule, when he accused a group of predominantly Jewish Moscow doctors of conspiring to assassinate Soviet leaders. Hundreds were arrested for allegedly taking part in the so-called Doctors' Plot. What would have almost certainly become another mass purge involving arrests and executions, this time directed at Jews, ended with Stalin's death in March 1953 and was quickly declared a hoax.

Increasing numbers of Jews tried to emigrate to Israel and elsewhere during the decades that followed. Although the authorities attempted to limit the flow, international pressure, increased by American sanctions under the Jackson-Vanik amendment of 1974, forced Moscow to raise its quotas. In 1989, a record number of Jews—more than seventy thousand— left the Soviet Union, mostly for the United States.

To his credit, Putin has publicly fought discrimination against Jews and made the opening of a Jewish museum in Moscow a priority. However, hearing otherwise apparently informed people explain their dislike for Jews by assigning them characteristics of the old stereotypes has darkened some of my many days in Russia. Although dark-skinned people bear the brunt of Russian xenophobia today—"black" refers to people from the Caucasus as well as Africans—anti-Semitism remains strong.

————

The recent anti-migrant riots have encouraged speculation that Putin's greatest political threat comes less from the liberal opposition than from nationalists doubting his devotion to their hard-line patriotism. Among them, MP Belov—who would soon thereafter be sentenced to six months in a penal colony for inciting racial hatred—informed a British reporter that "normal societies" boast active civil societies. "But in the period of Vladimir Putin's rule," Belov continued, "everything was done to get rid of civil society and revive aspects of Soviet totalitarianism. The elites are corrupt, and not working in the country's best interests."[13] Large groups of nationalists who joined the 2011 protests against Putin made many other participants, most from the equivalent of the left, uncomfortable.

Putin responded in one of his election manifestos with contradictory criticisms and prescriptions. His favoring of harsher punishments for internal migrants committing crimes outside their native regions harked back to tsarist laws restricting the movement of Jews. A week later, one month before his reelection, the same Dmitri Rogozin who had briefly headed the Kremlin's short-lived nationalist Rodina Party sought to portray the candidate's ramblings as part of a long tradition of grand visions for the country. A savvy young politician, Rogozin had achieved prominence in the 1990s by leading a lobby group called the Congress of Russian Communities, which advocated the rights of Russians abroad. Following his stint with Rodina, Putin named him ambassador to NATO in Brussels, where his saber rattling earned Rogozin a high-powered job back home as deputy prime minister in charge of the defense industry. Some believe Putin is grooming the sharp-tongued politician to succeed him.

In a newspaper article, Rogozin lauded Putin's manifesto as an "unprecedented event" that would have "long-term consequences for the development of our statehood." Russia's great calamities in history, he wrote, took place when past leaders failed to cater to the needs of ethnic Russians, the country's "state-forming people." Although Nicholas II sensed looming catastrophe in 1917, he helped provoke revolution by appealing too late for support "from Russian patriots and conservatives." "Traitors" led by Gorbachev, Rogozin continued, contributed to the collapse of the USSR seventy years later by allowing the pressure of "ethno-nationalism" in various Soviet republics to tear the union apart. Painting a picture of impending global doom in a tract that could have been written by a nineteenth-century Slavophile, he accused the United States of hatching "hegemonic plans" that would divide the world in a new struggle for resources. A "fifth column" of liberals was doing Washington's bidding by working to split the "great Russian people." Rogozin praised Putin as the only European leader "who has not been run over by the steamroller of American hegemonism."

Election-season fearmongering, perhaps, but with serious implications. By the end of the year, a presidential commission had proposed a theory of a special Russian "civilization" that is separate from the West. Drawing a distinction between the description for ethnic Russian, *russkaya*, and the word that pertains to the Russian state, *rossiiskaya*, it openly derives from nineteenth-century philosopher Nikolai Danilevsky, a highly conservative nationalist who promulgated a theory of "historical cultural types."[14] The chest thumping that passed for ideology wasn't really prompted by a fear of Russia's collapse—which the rabble-rousing rhetoric only encouraged—as much as by worry that what *would* collapse was Putin's regime. I have to say that my years of observation cause me to see it very differently from Rogozin, as do most of the relatively small numbers of Russians who think like most educated Westerners. The attempt to co-opt the nationalist vote by legitimizing and glorifying the current authorities with yet another contradictory whitewashing of the past can only encourage the destructive forces that have made Russia a dangerous place to live if you're not a white Slav.

Isolating Russia as its own civilization has enabled Putin not only to brand his opponents as traitors but also reinforce his authority over possible rivals within the elite by threatening to accuse them of the same offense. His critics have had a hard time responding partly because Russia lacks a tradition of loyal, constructive opposition. That helps explain why the majority seems to have accepted Putin's painting of his rivals as radicals together with his seemingly grand, uncompromising visions, cynical and hollow as they may be.

That's not to say that advocates of gradual reform have no precedents apart from the towering figure of Alexander Herzen. Among the others was a group of liberal intellectuals whose attack against the intelligentsia in *Vekhi* ("signposts"), a collection of essays published in 1909, unleashed a storm of controversy. Conceived by a gifted economic historian named Piotr Struve, *Vekhi* hit a nerve by laying into what the writers believed was the dogmatism and radicalism that were fanning destructive revolutionary activities. After the initial three thousand copies of the succès de scandale sold out almost overnight, four more printings quickly followed, along with a virtual industry of books and articles repudiating its premises.

It was all about another lasting problem of Russian governance—the obstacles to compromise, the intransigence, that developed under absolutism. The Vekhiists believed the reforms Nicholas II had been forced to adopt after the 1905 revolution obliged the intelligentsia to try working with his regime. That position was more controversial than it may sound because even moderate groups rejected compromise with the otherwise rigid tsar, including the Constitutional Democrats, or Kadets, who would lead the revolutionary provisional government in 1917 before the Bolsheviks hijacked it. The philosopher Nikolai Berdyaev decried revolutionaries' withering attacks on their rivals as assaults on knowledge. The intelligentsia, he wrote, "did not have an interest in truth itself: it demanded that truth become an instrument of social revolution, of popular welfare, and of human happiness."[15] Berdyaev charged that the imposition of populist but despotic standards in the name of "love of the people" was subjecting Russian spiritual and cultural values to political interests. Sergei Bulgakov, a former Marxist like Berdyaev who became a controversial Orthodox Christian theologian, contended the intelligentsia's worship of the people was really self-worship.

Struve—a brilliant editor and politician who helped found the Marxist movement before going on to help lead its repudiation—accused the intelligentsia of "virulent fanaticism" and a "murderous logic of conclusions and constructs."[16] Another Vekhiist, the legal scholar Bogdan Kistiakovsky, criticized its lack of interest in the basic Enlightenment principles of individual liberty and rule of law, crucial ideas borrowed from the West. "Where is our *L'esprit des lois*, our *Du Contrat social*?" he asked about the seminal works by Montesquieu and Rousseau.[17] Instead, "supremacy of force and seizure of power" were paramount.

Needless to say, history vindicated the *Vekhi* essayists. After helping beget the Revolution, the intelligentsia went on to abet the establishment of a fanatical dictatorship that would quickly become far more murderous than the tsarist regime it had found so oppressive. In other words, the left, in a manner of speaking, shared the psychic and even emotional qualities of the right, both formed by the same absolutism. *Vekhi*'s metaphoric talk of despotic ideology became reality for the millions who lost their freedom.

Among them was Zhora Leimer, my grandmother Serafima's husband, who feared the worst when he wrote his last letter to her in 1940 because he didn't know he would soon be returned from his Ural Mountains Gulag camp to Moscow. There he was reunited with Tupolev and other aircraft designers in a minimum-security camp called a *sharashka*. Immortalized in Alexander Solzhenitsyn's *The First Circle*, such institutions exploited imprisoned scientists and engineers, many of whom considered themselves lucky to be able to continue conducting research for the military as a form of forced but relatively normal and well-fed labor. Permitted to visit her beloved Zhora, Serafima even hoped for his early release. Although Tupolev and others were indeed soon freed to better help the war effort, however, Zhora disappeared again. His German surname virtually sealed his fate after the Nazi invasion of 1941.

Thirty years later, Serafima wrote the Moscow city prosecutor to request his rehabilitation, as absolving people of political crimes was called. "They were scheduled to finish working on a project to develop an airplane," she said of his group, "and were waiting to be released, as he told me during a private meeting." Instead, she said, "I received a statement from the Moscow city council interior affairs department saying that my husband, Georgy Ludvigovich Leimer, died in 1942 in a prison in the Kirov region."

The determined rebelliousness of Serafima's daughter, my mother, against Soviet restrictions suggests she shared some of the same reactions to despotism. In 1967, Sergei Milovsky, the popular lawyer and man-about-town, took her aside to inform her that George was due to visit the following year. She should marry him, he said. "It's your chance to leave this godforsaken country, and I doubt he'll stay unmarried very long." Tatyana didn't agree. Common as the fantasy of escaping the Soviet Union was, she'd never seriously considered it. Besides, she'd recently broken off a serious relationship, and starting a new one with someone she'd already dated had little appeal. "Then you're a fool," Milovsky said sadly. Both my parents would soon be mourning his early death from cancer.

But Tatyana didn't dismiss his advice outright. Although she rarely saw George during his visits, he made certain to meet her at least once, sometimes to give her books he'd brought for her dissertation on nineteenth-century American literature. And just before he arrived in August of 1968, something had changed that encouraged her to reconsider. The Soviet invasion of Czechoslovakia that crushed the Prague Spring killed the last chance to possibly make a variety of Soviet socialism work—a terrible irony, some believed—and dashed the remaining hopes of those who had admired it. Some had dreamed the effort to build communism with a human face might become a model for reform. Tatyana and her friends sank into a black mood of futility and helplessness.

When George invited her to the Aragvi restaurant, where he would sometimes meet his KGB tormentor, her announcement about wanting to leave took him aback. "That's like a bomb in my lap," he told her, partly because he'd come on assignment from the *Sunday Times* of London and knew that what he'd be writing about the country's retreat toward what was called neo-Stalinism would make trouble for them both if his articles appeared with his byline. But marrying Soviets to get them out was hardly unusual for foreigners, and he promised to do his best. Before his articles and the book they comprised, *Message from Moscow*, were published (anonymously), and before the biography of Solzhenitsyn, George was still in decent favor with the authorities, who were not beyond believing that granting Tatyana permission to marry might help induce him to write more positively about the Soviet Union. He was also set to return the following year for another assignment, and Milovsky had pledged to use his connections to help.

After more struggles with the authorities—and after considerable anxiety because Tatyana would have a big black mark against her for wanting to marry an American if their application had been denied—they celebrated good news. Serafima and a handful of relatives and friends, including Milovsky, attended their ceremony in one of Moscow's palaces of marriages. During the dinner that followed at the Praga restaurant, the husband of one of Tatyana's childhood friends used his toast to say, regretfully, that "our best things always go for export." Photographs of the dashing couple carrying a wedding present of a shiny samovar on a traditional visit to Red Square soon appeared on the front page of the British Communist Party's newspaper *The Daily Worker*, purporting to show that Russian women could indeed marry Westerners without trouble. Tatyana soon discovered that that issue of the paper had been withdrawn everywhere in Moscow, surely because such mixed marriages were not to be encouraged.

Since it would have been difficult to arrange a honeymoon afterward, George and Tatyana had already taken theirs: a cruise up the Volga River for an article he would write. Although they were far from strangers, Tatyana was not the girl of sixteen who had met George a decade earlier, so both were delighted to find themselves falling back in love during their two weeks together on the great river. She remembered telling herself she'd marry George soon after they first met, when the taxi materialized to take her to the Bolshoi. "Maybe it was part of some grand plan," she'd later muse about their long separation. "It let me grow up by leading my own life, to mature in my own way. Nothing good would have happened if we'd stayed together during those early years."

She finally joined George in London on the warm, sunny afternoon of May 1, 1970. Despite her friends' delight at and envy of her departure from Moscow, the fact that she'd left her old life and everything she'd known didn't register until, halfway to Britain, her plane's captain announced they were flying over Copenhagen. "Suddenly it seemed unreal. Really? Copenhagen? That's it, I thought—I've actually left! It was an incredible feeling— I was somewhere in the sky and my dream was coming true! I was so lucky, so happy."

———

Tatyana found Moscow transformed almost beyond recognition when she first returned to visit more than two decades later, in the 1990s. "It was night and day. People were no longer afraid. They dressed well, expressed themselves freely and had opportunities. We'd had none of that."

But the Russian psyche remains heavily influenced by the Soviet experience. The stultification of the social sciences under communism, cut off from developments in the West for so long, may be partly to blame. Edward Keenan believes the lack of analytical tools that might have enabled people to understand their roles in a changing society helped breed deep cynicism about the contradictions between official ideology and their personal experience. The cynicism encouraged pilfering, alcoholism, violence and other antisocial behavior that served to reinforce the traditionally pessimistic view of human nature.

Widespread cynicism endures, together with much antisocial behavior. And despite signs that Russian attitudes were again changing with the protests of 2011, a Levada Center poll conducted soon after Putin's reelection a few months later showed him retaining overwhelming support, chiefly among stay-at-home mothers (69 percent) and workers (55 percent). Among them were gray masses of uniformly older, mostly working-class people who had attended pro-Putin rallies, many paid or coerced to do so by their employers. What they lacked in outward enthusiasm for the candidate who painted himself as their protector they made up in numbers: tens of thousands of representatives of a vast, vulnerable population for which stability remains more important than change, with its possibility of yet more upheaval.

Still, the growing contradictions between rhetoric and reality will inevitably threaten the president's ability to dominate the ideological battle for Russians' hearts and minds. The sweeping prescriptions and grandiose visions have done nothing to stem the soaring corruption, worrisome demographic trends, growing alcoholism and other signs that serious crisis may threaten. My mother, who is among those Russians optimistic that their country will someday join the civilized world, believes the similarities between the Putin and Brezhnev eras make such a transition all but inevitable. She cites a friend who liked to predict in the early 1970s that the then-unsinkable-seeming Soviet empire would eventually collapse under its own weight, "a colossus on clay legs."

The government is highly attuned to one dynamic in particular: the price of oil. Yegor Gaidar, the prime minister who oversaw Russia's drastic economic reforms of 1991 and 1992, argued that oil exports enabled the Communist Party authorities to offset serious structural problems in the 1970s and '80s, including the need to buy vast volumes of foreign grain to make up for stagnating production at home.[18] The arrangement lasted until a glut in global oil production sent prices plummeting to less than ten dollars a barrel in 1986. The ensuing decline in Soviet production hastened economic collapse by starving Moscow of the hard currency it desperately needed.

Others disagree about the importance of oil's role in the Soviet collapse. However, one point is clear: the government today is far more dependent on energy than the Soviet Union ever was. Since the economy recovered from the economic meltdown in 1998 that sent the Yeltsin administration into crisis, the quadrupling of oil prices enabled various governments under Putin to increase federal budget expenditures ninefold in real terms in a decade, while wages almost tripled.[19] But economists predict the government will eventually run into trouble. Although its 2008 budget was calculated to balance with oil at sixty dollars a barrel, the level necessary for balancing soon rose to $120, and even that may not be high enough in the future, thanks to Putin's pledges to increase, by hundreds of billions of dollars, federal wages and other expenses aimed at generating support from the masses. And although energy sales have brought annual trade surpluses of almost eight hundred billion dollars, Russians' huge desire for foreign products has driven an inexorable rise in imports that may one day surpass exports.

The country got a taste of what may happen when cash starts to become short in late 2011, when Putin lashed out at several cabinet members for failing to fund his election promises in a new budget. Some ministers, including Medvedev, had the temerity to snipe back for the first time in recent memory, prompting temporary speculation that Putin's authority was declining. That exchange took place when oil prices were still climbing to record highs. With new drilling techniques increasing global production, that may not last. Even if prices stay level, the Russian oil industry is still largely living off Soviet-era investment. To maintain production levels, which are expected to decline by 2020, the government will have to invest far more—which will probably prompt bitter battles over oil profits. Lack of investment and failure to reform the economy have added urgency to predictions of dramatically slowing growth and worries about looming recession that have heightened anxieties about the future.

If civil society fails to topple Putin's regime—or that of a chosen successor—perhaps economic decline will. With corruption also taking ever-larger slices of the national wealth, the masses who continue supporting Putin—because they feel the government provides them with more benefits and stability than they would otherwise enjoy—may not do so indefinitely.

To truly join the Western world, however, Russians will have to do more than change their political establishment because the obstacles lie not just in Putin but also in the formative factors of geography, climate and history, which remain powerful shapers of Russian behavior. Among other vital things, the people will have to move beyond looking to the state to compensate for the country's traditional backwardness and resulting insecurities.

Real change would require fundamentally new ideals. "After a brief period of declaring allegiance to Western values in the 1990s, we've moved away from them," Arseniy Roginsky of Memorial reminded me. "We said we would respect the individual, but it never happened. That path was far more difficult than we ever imagined." Instead, he said, "the search for stability and a Russian national identity led right back to the old Soviet anti-Western sentiments."

The foreign affairs scholar Georgy Mirsky, who taught at Princeton and New York University, told me he believes the process will take generations. "Whenever my American students asked why bad news was always coming out of Russia, with its great culture, I'd tell them to imagine being put into a psychiatric asylum when they were three years old and released at thirty. Could you be a normal person? Of course not. After seventy years of Soviet rule, one of the most antihuman regimes in history, how can you expect the next generation to be normal?"

Russian forces outside the Georgian city of Gori in August 2008.

Kolya Pavlov (right) and I in Chechnya, in front of a bus to Grozny.

12

Future Delayed

Russia has only two allies—her army and navy.
—Alexander III, reigned 1881–94

The sun was baking the Mediterranean-like landscape that stretched out below the foothills of Georgia's Caucasus Mountains when I passed through in August of 2008. The military truck in which I was riding belonged to a Russian convoy rumbling toward Gori, the faded provincial city Moscow had occupied after Tbilisi tried to seize back its Russia-supported breakaway region South Ossetia. The truck bed's metal sides were supposed to prevent the handful of reporters within them, who were being hosted by the Russian military, from witnessing the destruction outside, but I managed to peek through a rip in the canvas top. Chipped by tank treads, a two-lane road lined by stately rows of tall poplar trees traversed golden-brown fields. We passed burned-out Georgian military pickups and cars abandoned on the edge of the asphalt. Some were still smoldering, together with patches of fields that were sending up black smoke in the distance. Apart from an occasional elderly man or woman who stared at the invaders roaring through their empty villages, no one was visible.

The countryside seemed even more eerie because I'd traveled some of the same roads during a reporting trip barely two months earlier. Seeing the familiar landscape under such very different circumstances filled me with depression. Entering Gori, we passed bullet-riddled buildings and shop windows broken by looting South Ossetian separatists. The convoy halted on the barren main square, where Russian soldiers emerged from their personnel carriers near a statue of Stalin, who had been born there.

Wary residents jostled in a nearby line for bread handed out by Russian forces, who boasted that they'd brought security to the city. Most locals were hungry, very frightened and didn't know what to expect. One jittery man, drunk like many others, couldn't recall his last name for a beat. Finally remembering it with relief, Lyova Mazmishvili told me Georgians *wanted* to live under their former Soviet masters again. "We never should have split from Russia," he stuttered unconvincingly, within earshot of the Russians. "We're brothers." Away from the main square, opinions were very different. A middle-aged woman named Dali Neberidze told me she was afraid of losing her mind. "It was a nightmare," she told me of the Russian aerial bombardments. "The Russians just want to show their might. Look what they've done to our city!"

Back on the central square, the lounging soldiers seemed relaxed, as if on a lark. A swaggering colonel named Andrei Babrun shrugged and smirked when I asked how long he expected Russian forces would stay. "There has to be peace in this region!" he lectured. "We must answer Georgian force properly." Others joked about awaiting orders to move on Tbilisi, just fifty miles away.

Fellow reporters who had covered the first war in Chechnya remarked how much better the Russian military looked now, starting with the sober, or at least not visibly drunk, privates. Still, their unwashed appearance inspired little confidence. Although Moscow's scattering of the puny Georgian army had showcased Russia's resurgence, the campaign revealed important weaknesses. Faulty intelligence, poor coordination and a reliance on aging Soviet equipment reflected badly on the Kremlin's long-running effort to reform a military characterized by vicious hazing among conscripts and massive corruption in the officer corps.

The government's ancient military doctrine was partly to blame. Moscow had to stop pretending it was a global counterweight to the West, military analyst Pavel Felgenhauer told me at the time. Only then could it start building an effective fighting force instead of trying to revive the old Soviet one. "This military is not very good for anything at all."

It was good enough to bloody the nose of Georgia's brash young president, Mikheil Saakashvili, however. The New York–trained lawyer had transformed his impoverished country from a nearly failed state whose capital enjoyed only intermittent electricity into a promising emerging market. He also vowed to return South Ossetia and Abkhazia, another Moscow-supported separatist region, to Georgia. Both had broken away after a bloody civil conflict in 1992 that had been largely provoked by Georgia's nationalist former president Zviad Gamsakhurdia and halted with the introduction of Russian peacekeepers.

When I sat next to him at dinner earlier in 2008, Saakashvili spoke about his far-fetched promise—and his personal loathing of Putin—with such conviction that I was hardly surprised when the conflict broke out. The evidence suggests the Kremlin goaded him into attacking South Ossetia after many years of low-level violence and rhetorical brinkmanship. When Georgian troops stormed the South Ossetian capital, Tskhinvali, Russia launched a massive counterattack by troops who supposedly happened to be still massed on the country's southern border after taking part in military exercises there the previous month. Moscow had distributed passports to South Ossetians for years. Now it said it was acting to protect its own citizens from Georgian aggression.

Although it's easy enough to dismiss Russia's all but forgotten invasion as a comeuppance for Saakashvili, the Kremlin's intentions were far from clear at the time. Those who feared an attack on Tbilisi included a sober foreign policy scholar in Washington whom I telephoned days after the hostilities began. When she paused after I asked what she believed might happen, it took a few seconds for me to realize she was crying on the other end of the line. Regardless of Saakashvili's mistakes, the weeklong war marked Russia's decision to turn its back on the West if it had to by launching a military attack on a sovereign, democratizing US ally for the first time since the end of communism. And not just an attack. While politicians thumped their chests about Russia's international duty, state television news concocted alarmist propaganda about Georgian sabotage plots. It all sounded very Soviet-like and boded ill for the future of a country that appeared to see force as the surest means of getting its way in the world—in this case, force against a neighbor many Russians loved for its cuisine, charm and historically close ties.

Much finger-pointing followed in the ensuing weeks and months, including revisionist reports by the BBC and *The New York Times* that blamed Saakashvili for taking Moscow's bait—as if the conflict had been between equals. Unfortunately, there was less talk about Russia's longtime practice of fanning ethnic conflict for the sake of increasing its influence over the region. Or about how two decades of brainwashing South

Ossetians had perpetuated a frozen conflict that reduced their economically unviable region to an impoverished dependency on Moscow. Now the Kremlin was stationing thousands of troops there in defiance of a French-brokered cease-fire, in confidence that critics would do little about it.

After Gori, I traveled to the ruined South Ossetian capital Tskhinvali, the epicenter of the recent fighting. Traffic there mainly consisted of Russian personnel carriers and army trucks. Many buildings had been destroyed and trees blown apart. Disabled Georgian tanks stood in the middle of a road where locals praised the Russians as saviors.

Violence was still taking place: outside the town, a handful of ethnic Georgian villages were being systematically destroyed. Blazing in the darkness of night, houses burned in the forest. During the day, bulldozers emerged to eradicate neighborhoods in what could only be called small-scale ethnic cleansing. In Gori, I had met a group of Georgian refugees who fled the attacks by Russian troops and their South Ossetian allies. A gray-haired woman named Manana Giashvili wept as she described how she and thirty others had hidden in a field for several days. "We were told to get out of our houses or we'd be shot," she said. "Then they burned down the village, and now my husband is missing."

Western countries brushed the invasion under the carpet. NATO reestablished its council with Russia after a brief hiatus, the EU resumed talks on a special partnership agreement, and even Moscow's recognition of independence for South Ossetia and Abkhazia—essentially revenge for the West's recent recognition of Kosovo—passed with little controversy. Seeing compromise and accommodation as weakness, Moscow exulted in what it saw as a significant victory.

It also felt relief. Russia's invasion had been partly motivated by fear of the color revolutions in former Soviet republics. Georgia's Rose Revolution in 2003—which installed Saakashvili in place of longtime President Eduard Shevardnadze—was followed by Ukraine's Orange Revolution in 2004, prompting alarm in Moscow that popular discontent could also contaminate Russia. Accusations that the West meddled in both countries by helping remove their old regimes have since become a constant trope in Russian foreign policy. Never mind that the Kremlin spent millions of dollars campaigning for the pro-Moscow candidate Viktor Yanukovych during the Ukrainian presidential election, when outrage over his victory in rigged voting prompted tens of thousands to take to the streets.

When Gazprom cut off natural gas to Ukraine after a price dispute during a bitterly cold winter the following year, Moscow said it was simply implementing a long-delayed end to Soviet-era subsidies in favor of market rates. In fact, Russia broke a five-year contract to provide gas at a very cheap price, which it had urged Ukraine to accept in 2004 in order to boost Yanukovych's election chances.

Russian fears have since waned, at least temporarily. After Georgia's humiliation in 2008, Yanukovych repudiated the Orange Revolution by winning the next Ukrainian presidential election in 2010, setting Moscow further at ease about its dominion over the former Soviet republics Medvedev once called part of Russia's "special zone of influence." However, such nineteenth-century formulations will continue stoking tensions by reinforcing the belief that being feared means being respected, a Soviet foreign policy model the Kremlin has tried to emulate.

In the 1970s, my father occasionally met with the London representatives of Novosti, the Soviet news agency that dealt with foreign correspondents while providing flimsy cover for countless KGB officers and agents. During one meeting, he wondered aloud why Moscow kept refusing permission for a handful of Russian women who had married Englishmen to join their husbands abroad. British newspapers' periodic articles about such puzzling cruelty colored the perceptions, not at all brightly, of British people who otherwise cared very little about the Soviet Union. The answer of the Novosti men said something about Soviet bureaucracy. They said of course they knew what he was talking about, but "our bosses don't give a fig about British readers. They only care about trying to please *their* bosses, who also know nothing about the West."

Thirty-five years later, I'm often asked why Moscow savages its reputation by cutting off gas to Ukraine and threatening Europe with nuclear missiles. Rather than not caring about its image abroad, however, the Kremlin, I believe, sees bad publicity as valuable in its way. Treating Russia as an actor they see as rational—that is, led by people who make decisions based on their benefit to the country rather than to themselves—Western governments often seem to miss that about Russia. Many foreigners also fail to notice another key trait: Russians tend to believe the rest of the world functions as their country does. When American newspapers publish articles critical of

Putin, for example, Russians often perceive them to be ordered by the White House because that's how things are done, aren't they? When Medvedev sought to explain one of Putin's accusations that Washington wanted to overthrow his government, he suggested it was normal for the United States to seek to influence Russian domestic politics "because we also try to do that."

In Putin's conception, his government valiantly steered an exemplary economy through a global financial crisis that other countries foisted on Russia. Chief among them is the United States, a "parasite" on the global economy that lives beyond its means and threatens financial markets by destabilizing the dollar. Such pronouncements, usually intended for a domestic audience, catch foreigners by surprise because Russia isn't Yemen or North Korea. The world's biggest country in area and volume of energy resources, it has nuclear weapons, a sizable economy and seemingly every reason to engage constructively with an international community in which it still holds considerable influence. But Moscow, seeing conspiracies everywhere that reinforce its assumption that the rest of the world functions as it does, rarely responds to constructive engagement.

President Obama's recent "reset" policy toward Russia succeeded in changing such attitudes enough to boost cooperation, which brought benefits to both sides. In addition to his main achievement in relations with Russia, a nuclear arms reduction agreement called New START, the two countries signed a long-delayed deal to cooperate on civil nuclear power technology. Moscow allowed US troops and supplies to cross Russia en route to Afghanistan, albeit for almost extortionate payment. And the Kremlin, motivated partly by its own frustration with its ally Iran, agreed to new UN sanctions against Tehran in response to its nuclear ambitions. Russia got American help to finally enter the World Trade Organization after applying for almost two decades, while the White House tacitly agreed not to directly challenge Russia's interests in Ukraine, Belarus and other countries in what it considers its backyard.

That finally began to change in late 2012, when Hillary Clinton warned that Moscow was trying to re-create a new version of the Soviet Union under the guise of economic integration. "It's going to be called a customs union; it will be called Eurasian Union and all of that," she said at a news conference. "But let's make no mistake about it. We know what the goal is and we are trying to figure out effective ways to slow down or prevent it."

Putin's continued vilification of the United States nevertheless doesn't mean Russia wants to become a pariah state by seeking armed conflict or prolonged confrontation. Many of its positions, such as its criticism of the war in Iraq and independence for Kosovo, might be dismissed as bluster. Still, its obstructionism can pose serious problems in international affairs.

Richard Pipes believes Russia's geography makes it a major player in global politics. "She is not only the world's largest state with the world's longest frontier, but she dominates the Eurasian land mass, touching directly on three major regions: Europe, the Middle East and the Far East," he wrote. "This situation enables her to exploit to her advantage crises that occur in the most populous and strategic areas of the globe."[1]

Westerners are especially confused by the Kremlin's occasional switch to cooperative and conciliatory rhetoric. That often comes when Russia sees opportunities to use geostrategic leverage to drive hard bargains. Allowing NATO to fly supply planes over Russian territory made Moscow appear helpful. In fact, Russia has squeezed hundreds of millions of dollars from Washington, profiting handsomely by allowing the United States to tackle one of its own major security issues.

However, Moscow has other tools at its disposal. When the United States and thirteen other members of the UN Security Council voted for a resolution in 2012 calling on Syrian President Bashar al-Assad to step down after his government had killed thousands of civilians, Russia used its veto to derail the measure. China followed Moscow's lead, crippling the international ability to pressure Assad, who proceeded to launch military assaults that killed many tens of thousands more people in Syrian cities. Responding to Hillary Clinton's labeling of the Russian veto as "despicable," Russia's stern foreign minister, Sergei Lavrov, called her reaction "indecent" and "almost hysterical."

A staunch protector of failing dictatorships' national sovereignty—no doubt because he can easily picture his own country in the same position—Putin was dismayed by NATO's earlier bombing of Libya and blamed other countries for tricking Russia into supporting the UN resolution that opened the way for military action. Syria would be different. Moscow's last Cold War–era ally in the Middle East provided a port for Russia's naval ships and orders for its arms, and Damascus was even more important for the leverage it provided the Kremlin. Suddenly all diplomatic eyes were on Moscow because little could happen without its consent. Putin used the limelight to lash out at Western countries, accusing them of backing the Arab Spring to advance their commercial interests. "I can't understand that bellicose itch," he wrote in one of his election manifestos. Instead of promoting democracy, he said, the revolts in Tunisia, Egypt and Libya had given rise only to religious extremism.

Putin's moment of diplomatic glory came when he stymied a Western military response to the Syrian government's chemical weapons attack against civilians. Appealing to a U.S. administration loath to take action, the Kremlin proposed an unlikely plan to put Syrian chemical weapons under international control. After the White House agreed, Putin made it clear Russia would undermine any Security Council resolution that would back the scheme with force, and the Syrian war continued ravaging the country unabated.

Moscow also had broader geostrategic considerations concerning the Middle East's tortured politics. Syria's Shia leaders were backed by Russia's longtime ally Iran. Traditionally suspicious of Tehran's Sunni rival and Washington ally Saudi Arabia, Moscow had built a nuclear power reactor in Iran and pushed back against several American-led drives to impose sanctions in response to fears that Tehran was building nuclear weapons in secret. No doubt the Kremlin will continue to attempt to obstruct US policies in the Middle East, posing as a facilitator and peacemaker in order to punch above its weight in international relations. After its energy supplies to European countries, Moscow's veto power in the Security Council is its most powerful foreign policy tool.

Little wonder Russian officials are frequently compelled to restate Moscow's position that the UN is the sole appropriate forum for resolving international conflicts. During the standoff over Syria in 2012, Medvedev went so far as to warn that the principle of state sovereignty was at such risk that it threatened to destroy the world order through nuclear war. The same Medvedev also once stridently advocated a proposal for a new European security structure that was so vague few took it as anything more than an attempt to undermine NATO and other existing organizations Moscow sees as hostile.

The arrival in Russia of the former US intelligence contractor Edward Snowden in July of 2013 could have been seen as nothing less than a gift for Putin, who proceeded to play the fugitive American and US officials off against each other. The leader with the appalling human rights record seized the opportunity to take the moral high ground by portraying Russia as a supporter of Snowden's civil liberties and accusing the White House of hypocrisy. When human rights activists act "under the auspices of the United States and with their financial support, information and political backing, it is comfortable enough to do," he said, presumably about critics of the Kremlin. "But if someone is going to criticize the United States itself, it is, of course, much more complicated." Obama's decision to cancel a summit meeting with Putin appeared to signal the end of the reset.

Russia will no doubt remain less collected about American missile defense policy. Moscow has threatened to quit the New START pact if Washington continues its plans to deploy a missile shield over Russian objections. In late 2011, Dmitri Rogozin, the ambitious deputy prime minister in charge of the defense industry, repeated Putin's threat to target missiles at Europe, accusing Washington of seeking the capability of delivering a nuclear first strike against Russia and citing the missile shield's supposed ability to knock out Russia's submarine-based warheads as evidence.

No knowledgeable observer takes such claims seriously. Were the United States to attack Russia, an early warning radar system would give Moscow plenty of time to deploy its fifteen-hundred-odd nuclear warheads for a counterstrike, a deterrent no missile shield could affect. "It is as if Rogozin, Putin and many other top officials are living in the early 1980s, when the Kremlin truly believed the United States might deliver a 'decapitating' nuclear first strike, undermining the mutually assured destruction theory," wrote military expert Alexander Golts. "The irrationality of Rogozin's and Putin's arguments proves that Russia's hysteria over U.S. missile defense has no relationship whatsoever to the country's national security."[2]

When the White House decided in March 2013 to abandon the part of the missile shield against which Moscow had focused its ire—the installation of long-range interceptors in Poland and Romania, over which the Kremlin had all but threatened war—Russian officials responded with a barrel of cold water, saying the change was no concession to Russia. Rogozin appeared to throw in the towel soon after, however, by pouring scorn on Washington's plans. Moscow had "solved the issue of penetrating the missile shield," he announced. "We regret that the United States wastes their money on missile defense and compels us to do the same," he added. "The missile shield is nothing for us. It's a bluff. It poses no military threat but remains a political and economic problem."

Whether or not the matter is finally put to rest, however, officials have stuck to the view that the missile shield plans are evidence of America's drive to attain global military supremacy. Moscow continues to link the issue to Obama's goal of cutting both countries' nuclear arsenals beyond

New START, something Putin has further complicated by saying other nuclear powers should also be included. Columnist Yulia Latynina described Putin's "imaginary role as the point man in the geopolitical confrontation with Washington" as virtually impossible to pierce. "Every time Western leaders tried to avoid aggravating the bully by making concessions to the Kremlin," she wrote, "Moscow took that as a confirmation of its policy. But when the West refused to bow to Moscow's demands, the Kremlin perceived it as a personal insult, a sign that there is an exclusive club of chosen leaders that reaches agreements on how to rule the world."[3]

However, Cold War–style posturing may pale in comparison to the very real threat Russia may pose to international Internet security. The term *cyberwar* first drew public attention in 2007, when Internet sites in the Baltic Sea country of Estonia came under a series of attacks. They coincided with a bitter war of words between the former Soviet republic and a Kremlin furious over the relocation of a statue of a Red Army soldier from the center of the Estonian capital, Tallinn.

Seeing the bronze soldier as a symbol of Soviet occupation, most Estonians thought their government—now a member of the European Union and NATO—was well within its rights. Russia saw it differently and condemned the statue's removal as an affront to the memory of what it calls the Soviet liberation of Estonia from Nazi control in World War II. In Moscow, the pro-Kremlin youth group Nashi organized street protests against "Fascist" Estonia as the government cut off oil shipments. Then a flood of requests overwhelmed a number of Estonian Internet sites maintained by parliament, various ministries and banks, among other organizations.

Many of the so-called distributed denial-of-service (DDoS) attacks were executed by botnets, groups of infected computers carrying out instructions from a handful of hackers. Estonia's then-defense minister, Jaak Aaviksoo, was certain they were meant to "destabilize society and question the government's capabilities to maintain law and order in cyberspace." Although he told me there was little more than circumstantial evidence that the Russian government orchestrated the attacks, he nevertheless pointed to the Kremlin. "The nature of those attacks, the high level of coordination and focus," he explained, "means there were considerable material and human resources behind them."

Although the attacks were the most serious of their kind, they were far smaller and more disorganized than another wave that took place the following year in another former Soviet republic that had rubbed Moscow the wrong way.

During Russia's invasion of Georgia in August 2008, DDoS attacks against the presidential administration, various ministries and private companies disrupted communications and disabled twenty sites for more than a week.

Russia has denied any involvement in either of the attacks. However, Irakli Porchkhidze, President Saakashvili's deputy national security adviser at the time, told me the assault actually began a month before the conflict broke out and involved tens of thousands of botnets, mostly controlled by a St. Petersburg criminal group. Some of the attacks disseminated images of Saakashvili in Nazi uniform and other propaganda. The size, timing and complexity of the assault implicated the Kremlin, which Porchkhidze believes used the attacks as a weapon. "It was a new page in the history of cyberwarfare," he said.

More recently, the arrests on piracy charges of Greenpeace activists who attempted to hang a banner on a Gazprom Arctic oil rig reflect Moscow's hard-nose tactics in the emerging drive to stake claims to natural resources there.

Russia's various forms of opposition to Western policies fit a general pattern of thinking that what's good for its perceived rivals is bad for Moscow—and, conversely, what's good for Moscow is bad for its rivals. It will probably continue to act according to that zero-sum calculus as long as Putin or one of his circle remains in power. For Westerners in general and Americans in particular, that means Russia's perennial instability will almost certainly create problems far into the future because even more than in Western societies, its leaders' personal needs will continue determining the direction of foreign policy. Good things rarely come from the feelings of insecurity that go together with those of inferiority. In Russia's case, those feelings, present no matter how powerful the country's military establishment may be—and Russia's will long remain weak—often prompt defensive posturing and sometimes, as in the war with Georgia, dangerous aggressiveness.

Dealing with them will require the kind of tactical flexibility Obama displayed early in his presidency by attempting to integrate Russia into the international community where possible. But it will also require doing significantly more to draw lines in the sand on important issues—such as democracy in former Soviet republics—and calmly making clear that Western countries will stand up for their values. Ensuring the stability and security of Russia's neighbors will be crucial for encouraging Moscow to alter its current path. More important, developed democracies must do far more to support the opposition and the protesters who are trying to establish democracy in their own country. One matter is essential, however: for Russia policies to work, Western countries must have no illusions about what kind of country they are dealing with.

———

Living in Russia often seemed to me an ongoing lesson in precisely how not to conduct politics, business and almost every other human endeavor. But although Moscow's streets are generally dangerous in addition to being dirty and difficult to negotiate, the capital can't be faulted for being boring. The loud and often smelly megalopolis shares something with New York in that it serves as a magnet for strivers from far and wide. Restaurants, theaters and all sorts of other establishments are constantly opening and closing, and there's always something worthwhile to see or do—in short, the city is very much alive. I feel instantly at home arriving in Moscow because it's exciting in its way, seething with raw human emotion. That still often appeals to me more than the museum-like qualities of many Western cities, where superficial niceties and the dull veneer of normal life conceal their own inequities and injustices.

My friend Kolya Pavlov remains typically Russian in many ways. His youthful idealism having been worn down by Moscow's dog-eat-dog reality, much of his free time away from his work as a television producer—along with his disposable income—has gone toward respite in the form of shopping for clothes or consumer goods and visiting nightspots where prodigious amounts of vodka are downed. Although just hearing about the frenetic pace of his entertainment seeking often exhausts me, and although when I was living in Russia we sometimes didn't see each other for weeks or more, we still share an understanding that comes from observing no formalities or pretenses. No problem was or is too embarrassing or dull to stop one from burdening the other; no plan for journalistic projects or exotic vacations too unrealistic to discuss in detail—often while luxuriating at the *banya*. Our friendship opened an aspect of human experience, a dimension of unquestioned camaraderie and ability to utterly relax, that I've rarely found in the West and that continues to attract me to Russia.

Cultural differences are much harder to reconcile in marriages, however. They were largely responsible for my parents' divorce after twenty-five years together. My mother never lost the traits that enabled her to evade and buck communism's restrictions, particularly her delight in defying all conventions that stood in her way, nor did she doubt she would achieve even her most improbable goals. Whereas my father, much as he loved Russians' uninhibited natures and personal warmth, appreciated many Western practices she found superficial.

When they were still living in London in the 1970s, Serafima joined them by traveling there on a tourist visa, then applying to stay. The serious effort to obtain permission for her visit included an article George wrote for *Reader's Digest* that prompted one of the many human rights demonstrations in front of the Soviet embassy, near Hyde Park. I remember a photograph from the time of demonstrators carrying signs that read FREEDOM FOR SERAFIMA LEIMER! However, that kindest and gentlest of souls, who had never really recovered from Zhora's arrest, did not adapt to her life in the West.

Utterly dependent on her willful daughter and foreign husband, she endured regular admonitions about her overly cautious nature and various faux pas, such as dropping an occasional tissue during the walks my parents all but forced her to take for exercise. Having taken her unconditional love for granted, I'm haunted by a memory of her imploring me, when I was six years old or so, to climb down from a tree along a country road in Spain. Ignoring my order to leave, she refused to budge even after I proceeded to throw stones in her direction, stopping only after one hit the bridge of her nose. When my parents later asked why it was bleeding, she didn't dream of telling them.

After suffering a stroke in 1985, Serafima returned to spend her last days back in Moscow. Cared for by her cousin Olga Kiva—who had taken her and Tatyana in when they had nowhere to live after they returned from Siberia at the end of World War II—she was soon diagnosed with cancer and died. Her remains are interred in a wall of Moscow's famed Novodevichy Convent beside her beloved firstborn daughter, Natasha.

Novodevichy is on a pond in a district otherwise consisting of severe Stalin-era apartment houses. It's one of Moscow most beautiful sights, and its onion-dome cupolas seem to dispel the sense of passing time and daily worry. The cemetery's entertainingly ornate tombstones, with their reliefs and statuettes, read like a work of Russian history: Gogol and Chekhov are buried there, along with the composer Sergei Prokofiev, Andrei Tupolev—the airplane designer and mentor to Zhora Leimer—Khrushchev and Yeltsin. Visiting the site inevitably reminds me of my personal connection to Russia and its tragedies, reinforcing my conviction that Russians don't have a unique soul that must forever remain a mystery to outsiders and that their great country isn't irrevocably fated to repeat its history. Like my parents, I've always hoped, sometimes even trusted, that it will someday take its place among more civilized countries.

But as I've tried to show, Russia's fate can no longer be ascribed to bad luck, however much of it the country has endured. Its fundamental beliefs, attitudes and ways will almost certainly remain essentially the same as long as they form the foundation of its society's practical workings. As the Kremlin challenges almost every Western foreign policy initiative, from Darfur to South America, the importance of accepting that Russian political and social bodies work according to their own logic can't be stressed enough. That's *my* message, at least, although others may dismiss or deny it, insisting that Western logic is the only real logic.

The spectacular fizzle of the promise of 1991, when the Soviet Union collapsed, continues to fascinate me—I think less because I witnessed it than because it revealed just how deeply the traditional culture runs. Maybe the Russian character reflects my own in that it's buoyed by great plans and hopes so often diminished or destroyed by insecurity about the possibility of achieving them. The much-derided but inadvertently brilliant phrase of Yeltsin's longtime prime minister, Victor Chernomyrdin, keeps sounding in my ear: "We hoped for the best, but it turned out as it always does." Although he was speaking about economic reform, his words have become universal for Russians.

Despite its extravagant squalor, waste, greed and indifference, Russia remains full of life, inventiveness and beauty, qualities that will continue to challenge our ideas about the country. Although many or most Americans hope or trust that it's moving toward more openness and democracy because we tend to think such progress is ultimately inevitable—on top of it being far more exciting to hear about what we perceive as good news than that the bad old days are here to stay—Russians' own experiences, of course, continue to shape them and set their priorities. However, as long as they keep mining their society's deep ironies and paradoxes, they will sustain the possibility that its fundamental values may one day adapt to the postindustrial world despite the obstacles caused by all the deeply rooted factors that helped create their national character.

ACKNOWLEDGMENTS

This book grew out of a project first conceived by my father, George, many years ago. We had planned to write it together until it became apparent that our experiences in Russia were too personal to interweave coherently, partly because they took place at very different times. He has been central to the book, not only because it contains my version of his story but also because of his critical editing and support.

My mother, Tatyana, who patiently described the details of her own life, has been no less central. And my wife, Elizabeth—who's not only a careful reader but also spent most of my time in Russia with me—provided some of the best ideas.

I'd like to thank my agent, John Silbersack of Trident Media, who helped develop the project's concept and believed in its worth throughout.

Thanks to Cary Goldstein, who acquired the book for Twelve, for feeling there's still something important to say about Russia and for his editing. Thanks also to Sean Desmond for his incisive editing. Barbara Clark's graceful copyediting and thorough fact checking have been essential.

Although this book is largely journalistic reportage, I owe a great deal of my understanding of my experiences in Russia to my professors at Harvard, including Edward Keenan, Timothy Colton, Svetlana Boym, Richard Pipes and Vladimir Brovkin.

In Moscow, I relied on the help of Sergei Sotnikov and Boris Ryzhak. Thanks also to Jay Tolson at Radio Free Europe in Prague, who gave me plum assignments on top of time off to do some of the writing.

Ultimately this book is a product of the many relationships and conversations at the core of my experience of Russia, with people from Kolya

Pavlov—whose friendship has colored everything I know about the country—to Yuri Vaschenko, whose incisive theories about its paradoxes entertained as well as elevated my understanding, to countless others whose stories are part of the fascinating, maddening place.

NOTES

1. THE HIDDEN RUSSIA

1. In *The Russian Review* 45, no. 2 (1986), 119.

2. EXTRAVAGANCE

1. *Forbes* magazine Russian edition, April 19, 2012.
2. Michael Voslensky, *Nomenklatura: The Soviet Ruling Class* (New York: Doubleday and Company, Inc., 1984), 95.
3. Voslensky, 206.
4. Masha Charnay, "Marat Guelman: 'Things Can Work Differently,'" in *Russia beyond the Headlines*, May 17, 2012, http://rbth.ru/articles/2012/05/17/marat_guelman_things _can_work_differently_15657.html.
5. Interview in *Vedomosti*, February 20, 2013.
6. Thane Gustafson, *Wheel of Fortune: The Battle for Oil and Power in Russia* (Cambridge, Mass.: Belknap Press of Harvard University Press, 2012), 198–202.
7. Mikhail Khodorkovsky, "Conveyor Belt of Russian Justice Legalizes Abuse," *Nezavisimaya Gazeta*, March 3, 2010.
8. *Moskovskiie Novosti*, April 11, 2012.
9. *The Moscow Times*, January 18, 2012.
10. *Nezavisimaya Gazeta*, May 15, 2012.
11. Alexander Radishchev, *A Journey from St. Petersburg to Moscow*, trans. Leo Wiener (Cambridge, Mass.: Harvard University Press, 1958), 159.
12. *Financial Times*, November 1, 1997.
13. *Forbes* magazine Russian edition, March 23, 2013.
14. Michael McFaul and Kathryn Stoner-Weiss, "The Myth of the Authoritarian Model: How Putin's Crackdown Holds Russia Back," *Foreign Affairs* 87, no. 1 (January–February 2008), 69.
15. *The Independent*, July 16, 2009.

3. POVERTY

1. Tony Wood, "Collapse as Crucible," *New Left Review* 74 (March–April 2012), http:// newleftreview.org/?page=article&view=2952.
2. *The Guardian*, April 11, 2011.
3. From the US Department of State's Bureau of European and Eurasian Affairs, cited at www.state.gov/r/pa/ei/bgn/3183.htm.
4. My translation from Anna Akhmatova, *Works*, vol. 1 (Munich: Inter-Language Literary Associates, 1965), 360.

5. Moshe Lewin, *Russia/USSR/Russia: The Drive and Drift of a Superstate* (New York: The New Press, 1995), 139.
6. Anton Chekhov, "Peasants," in *The Portable Chekhov*, ed. Avrahm Yarmolinsky (New York: Penguin Books, 1947), 352.
7. Boris Kagarlitsky, "Opposition Needs to Reach Beyond Moscow," *The Moscow Times*, May 17, 2012.
8. Fyodor Dostoevsky, *Poor Folk*, trans. Robert Dessaix (Ann Arbor, Mich.: Ardis, 1982), 27–28.
9. *The Moscow Times*, May 16, 2012.
10. *The Washington Post*, March 29, 2013.
11. Anton Chekhov, from *Letters of Anton Chekhov to His Family and Friends*, trans. Constance Garnett (New York: Macmillan, 1920), 209.
12. Sergei Zakharov, "Kak vymeraiet Rossiia: Karta otpustevshykh gorodov," Slon.ru, March 19, 2013, http://slon.ru/economics/kak_vymiraet_rossiya_karta_opustevshikh _gorodov-920081.xhtml.

4. DRINKING

1. World Health Organization Global Alcohol Report for the Russian Federation, 2011, http://www.who.int/substance_abuse/publications/global_alcohol_report/profiles/ rus.pdf.
2. Richard Pipes, *Russia under the Old Regime* (New York: Collier Books, 1992), 157.
3. Edward L. Keenan, e-mail to the Johnson's Russia List forum, May 16, 2003, http:// www.cdi.org/russia/johnson/7184-1.cfm.
4. Nicholas Faith and Ian Wisniewski, *Classic Vodka* (London: Prion Books, 1997), 49.
5. Faith and Wisniewski, 36.
6. Faith and Wisniewski, 38.
7. William Pokhlebkin, *A History of Vodka*, trans. Renfrey Clarke (London: Verso, 1992), 138.
8. Pokhlebkin, 159.
9. Sergei Romanov, *Istoriia russkoi vodki* (Moscow: Veche, 1998), 222.
10. Pokhlebkin, 143.
11. David Nowak, "The Stench of Death and Alcohol in Pskov," *The Moscow Times*, November 7, 2006.
12. *The Moscow Times*, November 7, 2006.
13. John Sweeney, "Vodka's My Poison," on *This World*, BBC Two, March 14, 2007.
14. Tony Halpin, "Millions of Men Disappear as Demon Drink Takes Its Toll," *The Times* (London), March 29, 2011.
15. Reuters, "Russians Wrongly Think They're Healthy," April 27, 2011.
16. Vitaly Korotich, *Zhili-byli-eli-pili* (Kharkov, Ukraine: Folio, 2005), 53.
17. Venedikt Erofeev, *Moscow Stations*, trans. Stephen Mulrine (London: Faber and Faber, 1997), 1.
18. Erofeev, 20.
19. Korotich, 62.
20. Korotich, 63.
21. Martin McKee, "Alcohol in Russia," *Alcohol and Alcoholism* 34, no. 6 (1999), 827.
22. McKee, 828.
23. Sergei Roy, "The Vodka Mess," *The Moscow News*, May 12–18, 2004.
24. Mark Lawrence Schrad, "Moscow's Drinking Problem," *The New York Times*, April 16, 2011.
25. Korotich, 17.

26. McKee, 825.
27. Schrad.
28. Korotich, 36.
29. Schrad.
30. Fyodor Dostoevsky, *Crime and Punishment*, trans. Jessie Coulson (New York: W. W. Norton and Company, 1989), 8.
31. Dostoevsky, 18.
32. Vladimir Nikolaev, *Vodka v sudbe Rossii* (Moscow: Parad, 2004), 61.
33. McKee, 825.
34. Roy.
35. Roy.

5. INTIMATES

1. Edward L. Keenan, "An Approach to Russian History," in *Studying Russian and Soviet History*, ed. Abraham Ascher (Boulder, Colo.: Social Science Education Consortium, 1987), 4.
2. Keenan, 5.
3. Keenan, 5.
4. Maura Reynolds, "A Soviet Legend Dies Hard," *Los Angeles Times*, November 12, 2002.
5. Katerina Clark, *The Soviet Novel: History as Ritual* (Chicago: University of Chicago Press, 1981), 10.
6. Orlando Figes, *The Whisperers: Private Life in Stalin's Russia* (New York: Metropolitan Books, 2007), 15.
7. Abram Tertz (Andrei Sinyavski), *On Socialist Realism*, trans. George Dennis (New York: Pantheon Books, 1960), 40–41.
8. Svetlana Boym, *Common Places: Mythologies of Everyday Life in Russia* (Cambridge, Mass.: Harvard University Press, 1994), 7.
9. Nadezhda Mandelstam, *Hope Against Hope: A Memoir*, trans. Max Hayward (New York: Atheneum, 1970), 34–35.
10. Boym, 1.
11. Including "Soviet Children's Fear of Being Left Alone," *The Moscow Times*, June 5, 2012.
12. Vladimir Shlapentokh, *Public and Private Life of the Soviet People: Changing Values in Post-Stalin Russia* (New York: Oxford University Press, 1989), 156.
13. Shlapentokh, 159.
14. Boym, 115.
15. Alena Ledeneva, *How Russia Really Works: The Informal Practices That Shaped Post-Soviet Politics and Business* (Ithaca, N.Y.: Cornell University Press, 2006), 119.
16. Richard Lourie, "Zombie Russia," *The Moscow Times*, May 23, 2011.
17. Shlapentokh, 170.
18. United Nations Demographic Yearbook, http://unstats.un.org/unsd/demographic/products/dyb/dyb2008.htm.
19. Rb.ru, October 25, 2011, http://www.rb.ru/article/sredniy-klass-v-rossii-eto-nad-chertoy-bednosti/6805177.html.
20. Ellen Barry, "A Hunger for Tales of Life in the American Cul-de-Sac," *The New York Times*, December 10, 2012.

6. DOMESTIC ORDER

1. *The Times* (London), March 29, 2011.
2. Richard Pipes, *Russia under the Old Regime* (New York: Collier Books, 1992), 17.

3. Nicholas Riasanovsky, *A History of Russia*, 5th ed. (Oxford: Oxford University Press, 1993), 430.
4. *The Guardian*, June 16, 2006.

7. INDOLENCE AND INEFFICIENCY

1. See Simon Shuster's "Off with Their Heads," *Foreign Policy*, December 5, 2012, http://www.foreignpolicy.com/articles/2012/12/05/off_with_their_heads?page=0,2.
2. Edward L. Keenan, "Medieval and Early Modern Russia" (lecture, Harvard University [history 1353], Cambridge, Mass., fall 1997).
3. Keenan.
4. James H. Billington, *The Icon and the Axe: An Interpretive History of Russian Culture* (New York: Vintage Books, 1970), 78.
5. Alexander Gerschenkron, *Economic Backwardness in Historical Perspective* (Cambridge, Mass.: Belknap Press of Harvard University Press, 1962).
6. Martin Malia, *The Soviet Tragedy: A History of Socialism in Russia, 1917–1991* (New York: Free Press, 1994), 59.
7. Edward L. Keenan, "Muscovite Political Folkways," *The Russian Review* 45, no. 2 (1986), 165.
8. Malia, 66.
9. Ibid.
10. Keenan, 166.
11. Keenan, 167.
12. Keenan, 171.
13. Malia, 189.
14. Tony Wood, "Collapse as Crucible," *New Left Review* 74 (March–April 2012), http://newleftreview.org/?page=article&view=2952.
15. Malia, 201.
16. Malia, 203.
17. Astolphe, Marquis de Custine, *Journey for Our Time: The Russian Journals of the Marquis de Custine*, ed. and trans. Phyllis Penn Kohler (Washington, D.C.: Regnery Gateway, 1987), 66.
18. Custine, 58.
19. Custine, 63–64.
20. Ivan Goncharov, *Oblomov*, trans. Natalie Duddington (New York: E. P. Dutton and Co., Inc., 1960), 4.
21. Goncharov, 6.
22. Bloomberg, March 17, 2013.

8. THE AVANT-GARDE

1. David Burliuk, Alexander Kruchenykh, Vladimir Mayakovsky, and Victor Khlebnikov.
2. Olga Khvostunova, "Science for Others," Institute of Modern Russia, June 4, 2013, http://imrussia.org/en/society/484.
3. Ibid.
4. Nikolai Berdyaev, *The Russian Idea* (New York: Macmillan, 1948), 3.
5. Martha Gellhorn, *Travels with Myself and Another* (New York: Jeremy P. Tarcher/Putnam, 2001), 258–59.
6. Isaiah Berlin, "The Birth of the Russian Intelligentsia," in *Russian Thinkers* (New York: Penguin Books, 1979), 119.
7. Berlin, "Birth," 129.

8. Isaiah Berlin, "1848," in *Russian Thinkers* (New York: Penguin Books, 1979), 4.

9. Boris Groys, *The Total Art of Stalinism: Avante-Garde, Aesthetic Dictatorship, and Beyond*, trans. Charles Rougle (Princeton: Princeton University Press, 1991), 4–5.

10. Kazimir Malevich, "From Cubism to Suprematism: The New Painterly Realism," in *Russian Art of the Avant Garde: Theory and Criticism 1902–1934*, ed. John Bowlt (New York: Viking Press, 1976), 122.

11. Alexander Herzen, *Selected Philosophical Works*, trans. L. Nazorov (Moscow: Foreign Languages Publishing House, 1956), 362–63.

12. Benjamin Bidder, "Powerful Enemies: Kremlin Targets Russian Facebook Clone," *Spiegel Online*, May 2, 2013, http://www.spiegel.de/international/business/kremlin-targets-russian-facebook-clone-vkontakte-a-897487.html#spRedirectedFrom=www&referrrer=.

13. Grani.ru, February 4, 2013, http://grani.ru/Internet/m.211237.html.

9. COLD AND PUNISHMENT

1. Vissarion Belinsky, *Selected Philosophical Works* (Moscow: Foreign Languages Publishing House, 1956), 537.

2. Anne Applebaum, *Gulag: A History* (New York: Doubleday, 2003), 113.

3. Astolphe, Marquis de Custine, *Journey for Our Time: The Russian Journals of the Marquis de Custine*, ed. and trans. Phyllis Penn Kohler (Washington, D.C.: Regnery Gateway, 1987), 73.

4. George Feifer, "Russian Winter," *Harper's Magazine* (February 1982), 39.

5. Galina Stolyarova, "Not a Pretty Picture," *Transitions Online*, January 31, 2013, http://www.tol.org/client/article/23576-russia-prison-women.html.

6. Nicholas Riasanovsky, *A History of Russia*, 5th ed. (Oxford: Oxford University Press, 1993), 152.

7. Edward L. Keenan, "Muscovite Political Folkways," *The Russian Review* 45, no. 2 (1986), 147.

8. I've been unable to find out whether the verse is Zhora's own or whether he was quoting someone else. Scholars I've consulted told me it may be the work of a minor poet of the time.

9. Anton Chekhov, from *Letters of Anton Chekhov to His Family and Friends*, trans. Constance Garnett (New York: Macmillan, 1920), 218.

10. Chekhov, 134.

11. Quoted in Henri Troyat, *Chekhov*, trans. Michael Henry Heim (New York: E. P. Dutton and Co., Inc., 1986), 129.

12. Vassily Aksyonov, *The Burn*, trans. Michael Glenny (London: Abacus, 1985), 221.

13. Edward L. Keenan, "An Approach to Russian History," in *Studying Russian and Soviet History*, ed. Abraham Ascher (Boulder, Colo.: Social Science Education Consortium, 1987), 7.

14. Anton Makarenko, *A Book for Parents* (Moscow: Foreign Languages Publishing House, 1954), 268.

15. Aksyonov, 221.

16. Ivan Kireevsky, *Polnoe sobrannie sochinenii Ivana Vasilieicha Kirieevskago*, vol. 2 (Moscow: Tipografia P. Bakhmetova, 1861), 233–34.

17. Richard Pipes, *Russia under the Old Regime* (New York: Charles Scribner's Sons, 1974), 221–22.

18. James H. Billington, *The Icon and the Axe: An Interpretive History of Russian Culture* (New York: Vintage Books, 1970), 49.

19. Billington, 55.

10. CLAN RULES

1. *The Moscow Times,* June 25, 2009.
2. Harold Berman, *Justice in Russia* (Cambridge, Mass.: Harvard University Press, 1950), 154.
3. Edward L. Keenan, "Muscovite Political Folkways," *The Russian Review* 45, no. 2 (1986), 144.
4. Edward L. Keenan, "Medieval and Early Modern Russia" (lecture, Harvard University [history 1353], Cambridge, Mass., fall 1997).
5. Edward L. Keenan, "An Approach to Russian History," in *Studying Russian and Soviet History,* ed. Abraham Ascher (Boulder, Colo.: Social Science Education Consortium, 1987), 7.
6. Vladimir Pribylovsky of Moscow's Panorama Center provides some of the most incisive analyses of the clan rivalries that dominate Russian politics, including in "Clans Are Marching," openDemocracy, May 30, 2013, http://www.opendemocracy.net/od -russia/vladimir-pribylovsky/clans-are-marching.
7. Catherine Belton, "A Realm Fit for a Tsar," *Financial Times,* November 30, 2011.
8. *The Guardian,* July 30, 2009.
9. *Financial Times,* October 1, 2012.
10. Catherine Belton, "Suleiman Kerimov, the Secret Oligarch," *Financial Times Magazine,* February 10, 2012.
11. Gregory White, "Share Deals Open Window on Kremlin," *The Wall Street Journal Europe,* March 27, 2012.
12. Keenan, "Folkways," 142.
13. Jerome Horsey, "Travels of Sir Jerome Horsey," from *Russia at the Close of the Sixteenth Century,* ed. Edward A. Bond (London: Hakluyt Society, 1856), 163.
14. Keenan, "Approach," 3.
15. Yulia Latynina, "Ia ne narod," Gazeta.ru, December 12, 2011, http://www.gazeta .ru/column/latynina/3938086.shtml.
16. Mikhail Khodorkovsky, "Kak pomentiat' vlast' v Rossii: osnovnye zadachi oppositsii," Gazeta.ru, February 29, 2012, http://www.gazeta.ru/comments/2012/02/29_a _4016241.shtml.
17. Dmitri Travin, "Does Putin Need His Parliament?" openDemocracy, March 19, 2013, http://www.opendemocracy.net/od-russia/dmitri-travin/does-putin-need-his -parliament.
18. *The Moscow Times,* May 22, 2012.
19. *The Moscow Times,* Feburary 12, 2013.
20. Reuters, May 7, 2012.
21. Georgy Bovt, "Why Guriev Chose Paris Over Krasnokamensk," *The Moscow Times,* June 3, 2013.
22. Alexander J. Motyl, "Inside Track: Is Putin's Russia Fascist?" *The National Interest,* December 3, 2007, http://nationalinterest.org/commentary/inside-track-is-putins -russia-fascist-1888.

11. GRANDIOSITY AND BOMBAST

1. Alexander Pushkin, "The Bronze Horseman," in Wacław Lednicki, *Pushkin's Bronze Horseman: The Story of a Masterpiece,* University of California Publications: Slavic Studies, vol. 1 (Berkeley, Calif.: University of California Press, 1955), 142.
2. Astolphe, Marquis de Custine, *Journey for Our Time: The Russian Journals of the Marquis de Custine,* ed. and trans. Phyllis Penn Kohler (Wahington, D.C.: Regnery Gateway, 1987), 97.

3. Nikolai V. Gogol, "Peterburgskiie zapiski 1836 goda," in *Sobranie sochinenii v vos'mi tomakh* vol. 7 (Moscow: Izdatel'stvo Pravda, 1984), 168.

4. Joseph Brodsky, "Less Than One," in *Less Than One: Selected Essays* (New York: Farrar, Straus and Giroux, 1986), 5.

5. Alexander Dugin, "The World Needs to Understand Putin," *Financial Times*, March 12, 2013.

6. Richard Pipes, "Pride and Power," *The Wall Street Journal*, August 24, 2009.

7. Kathy Lally, "Russia Expects Olympics to Retool Its Image," *The Washington Post*, February 9, 2013.

8. *The New York Times*, January 12, 2013.

9. Ilya Ponomaryov, "Arrest People with High Fences on Rublyovka," *The Moscow Times*, March 1, 2013.

10. Alexei Malashenko, "The Dynamics of Russian Islam," Carnegie Endowment for International Peace, February 1, 2013, https://www.carnegieendowment.org/2013/02/01/dynamics-of-russian-islam/f88a.

11. James H. Billington, *The Icon and the Axe: An Interpretive History of Russian Culture* (New York: Vintage Books, 1970), 72.

12. Nicholas Riasanovsky, *A History of Russia* (Oxford: Oxford University Press, 1993), 395.

13. Shaun Walker, "Portrait of a Nationalist," RussiaProfile.org, April 21, 2009, http://www.russiaprofile.org/politics/a1240333330.html.

14. Charles Clover, "Russian 'Civilisation' Stirs Resentment," *Financial Times*, December 11, 2012.

15. Nikolai Berdyaev in *Vekhi*, ed. Boris Shragin and Albert Todd, trans. Marian Schwartz (New York: Karz Howard, 1977), 10.

16. Piotr Struve in *Vekhi*, 148.

17. Bogdan Kistiakovski in *Vekhi*, 115.

18. Yegor Gaidar, *Collapse of an Empire: Lessons for Modern Russia*, trans. Antonina Bouis (Washington, D.C.: Brookings Institution Press, 2007), 109.

19. *Financial Times*, March 22, 2012.

12. FUTURE DELAYED

1. Richard Pipes, "Pride and Power," *The Wall Street Journal*, August 24, 2009.

2. Alexander Golts, "Why Putin Is Mad at Me," *The Moscow Times*, January 23, 2012.

3. Yulia Latynina, "Putin Is Joining the Dictators' Club," *The Moscow Times*, June 6, 2012.

INDEX

Note: Page numbers in *italic* type refer to photographs.

ABOUT THE AUTHOR

Gregory Feifer is a former Moscow correspondent for National Public Radio who has reported from Russia for almost a decade. Educated at Harvard University, he is the author of *The Great Gamble*, a history of the Soviet war in Afghanistan, and has written for numerous outlets, including the *New Republic*, the *Washington Post* and *World Policy Journal*. He lives in Boston with his wife, Elizabeth, son, Sebastian, and daughter, Vanessa.

ABOUT TWELVE

TWELVE

TWELVE was established in August 2005 with the objective of publishing no more than twelve books each year. We strive to publish the singular book, by authors who have a unique perspective and compelling authority. Works that explain our culture; that illuminate, inspire, provoke, and entertain. We seek to establish communities of conversation surrounding our books. Talented authors deserve attention not only from publishers, but from readers as well. To sell the book is only the beginning of our mission. To build avid audiences of readers who are enriched by these works—that is our ultimate purpose.

For more information about forthcoming TWELVE books, please go to www.twelvebooks.com.